# 7 Different Plays

357 W 20th St., NY NY 10011
212 627-1055

7 Different Plays



First printing: September 1988

ISBN: 0-88145-051-0

Design by Marie Donovan

Set in Aster by L&F Technical Composition, Lakeland, FL

Printed on acid-free paper and bound by BookCrafters, Chelsea, MI

## Contents

*Editor's Note* by Mac Wellman . . . . . . . . . . . . . . . . . . . . *v*
*Apropos of 7 Different Plays* by Mike Steele . . . . . . . . . . . . . . . . *vii*
*No Mercy* by Constance Congdon . . . . . . . . . . . . . . . . . . . . . 1
*Kid Twist* by Len Jenkin . . . . . . . . . . . . . . . . . . . . . . . . 41
*Der Inka von Peru* by Jeffrey M. Jones . . . . . . . . . . . . . . . . . 103
*A Bright Room Called Day* by Tony Kushner . . . . . . . . . . . . . . 181
*In a Pig's Valise* by Eric Overmyer . . . . . . . . . . . . . . . . . . 261
*In His 80th Year* by Gillian Richards . . . . . . . . . . . . . . . . . 339
*The Bad Infinity* by Mac Wellman . . . . . . . . . . . . . . . . . . . 387
*Afterwords* . . . . . . . . . . . . . . . . . . . . . . . . . . . . . . 433

# Editor's Note

## Mac Wellman

Each of these plays, each in its own way, sets off in a new direction, explores fresh territory, employs a tactic of its own, in charting the ongoing disaster of current American social discourse. These plays are not made to order, nor racked on a classical bed of Procrustes. I chose them because each seemed unlike anything I had read or seen, and possessed a resolute integrity besides.

Because these—obviously—are all writers with a lot to say, as the saying goes, I asked them for statements of whatever kind: personal, practical, theoretical, pataphysical; these are gathered at the end of the volume.

Lastly, these plays are for the unlikely non-classicists who like new plays because they *are* new—sharp, unequivocating, disturbing, beautiful as only the new can be, unlikely and unalike.

# Apropos of 7 Different Plays

## Mike Steele

In an era of swirling visual imagery and high-tech vocabularies, the word gets lost. People don't read, we're told, and they don't listen. Theater tries to copy TV and people ignore it, choosing the real thing. It's a post-literate society.

The seven writers in this anthology, then, all highly literate and lingually gifted, might seem anachronistic, even quixotic, as they not only pursue language, but language for the live theater.

But I don't think they are. They're all very involved with the contemporary zeitgeist. They're conversant with technology; some have even worked with it intimately. They aren't last-stand conservatives fighting to keep some academic literary glimmer glowing. None of them are conventional writers and few use language conventionally.

I think they might be seers, writers with, ironically, splendid sight. While steady floods of visual images course through the backs of our brains, flooding the synapses and drowning the world view in a stream of seductiveness, these writers seem to see through the murk. Language remains our strongest tool for thinking, for defining ourselves and our world, communicating, arguing with the universe and explaining what it is we're watching. Sooner or later even the glossiest visual images are turned back into words in our brains so we can sort them out, understand, explain, and find meaning in them.

If there is such a thing as a purely visual theater of images, these writers are its counterpoint, a theater of images emerging through language. You don't always need a linear plot, a beginning-middle-end narrative or language that sounds just like plain people talking in everyday life. This is often language that soars, language that comes close to poetry or pure texture or music, language that is elusive and allusive and asks for the sensual and intellectual participation of audiences. It's language that carries immense rewards for those willing to embrace it and involve themselves in its life.

---

MIKE STEELE is Drama Critic for the *Minneapolis Star Tribune*.

Beyond that these writers are quite different from each other. One play uses "found" texts. Another uses poetic irony. Yet another revels in the high-energy language of pop culture and mythmaking. Some are funny, some somber, some personal, the occasional one metaphysical; one is musical.

The thing they all have in common is the freshness and sparkle of the writing. They believe in writing and use language with zealous force and committed integrity. Some of them may puzzle at first, but stay with them. Hear them. Sense their textures and color and music. Extraordinary insights emerge.

They're language-oriented, for sure, and splendid craftspeople. But they aren't throwbacks to the days of Inge and Odets. They're as here and now as the latest technological gadgetry, electric, unconventional, unexpected, and, just possibly, visionary.

Constance Congdon

# *No Mercy*

CONSTANCE CONGDON was born in Iowa and grew up in Kansas and Colorado. Her first play, *Gilgamesh*, was produced at St. Mary's College of Maryland in 1977. While earning her MFA at the University of Massachusetts, Amherst, Congdon wrote her next four plays: *Boarders, Fourteen Brilliant Colors, The Bride,* and *Native American. Boarders* was produced in New York City in 1980. *The Bride* won the 1981 American College Theatre Festival national playwright competition. In 1983 *Native American* received the $1,500 honorable mention Joseph Kesselring Award and had its professional premiere at the Portland Stage Company. It also has been optioned for London production. Congdon is co-author of *Phantomnation*, produced at the Bay Area Playwrights Festival in 1983. In addition to being named co-winner of the Actors Theatre of Louisville's 1985 Great American Play Contest, *No Mercy* was a finalist for the Susan Smith Blackburn prize. A member of New Dramatists, Congdon is literary manager and resident playwright at Hartford Stage Company. Her adaptation of Mark Twain and Charles Dudley Warner's *The Gilded Age*, commissioned by The Acting Company, opened at Hartford Stage in October 1986 and then became part of The Acting Company's touring repertory. Congdon is the recipient of a National Endowment of the Arts Playwright Fellowship for 1987.

*No Mercy* was presented at the Actors Theatre of Louisville on March 14–22, 1986 as part of the tenth annual Humana Festival of New American Plays. Jackson Phippin directed. Set and lighting were designed by Paul Owen, costumes by Ann Wallace, and sound by David Strang. The cast was as follows:

YOUNG ROY LAYTON .................... Robert Brock
GENE .................... Bruce Kuhn
ROBERT OPPENHEIMER .................... Jonathan Bolt
JANE .................... Melody Combs
ADAM .................... Jeffrey Hutchinson
ROY LAYTON .................... Bob Burrus
RAMONA LAYTON .................... Adale O'Brien
JUSTIN .................... Joshua Atkins
JACKIE .................... Beth Dixon

*No Mercy* was commissioned and first presented in workshop during February 1985 by the Hartford Stage Company as part of their "First Drafts," funded by a National Endowment for the Arts Special Projects grant.

*No Mercy* is for Sam Johnson.

For information regarding stock and amateur production rights, please contact: Peter Franklin, William Morris Agency, 1350 Avenue of the Americas, New York, NY 10019.

*Playwright's Note*: 1945 and 1985 exist simultaneously on an open and fluid stage. The play's various locations are minimally suggested: a recliner facing a TV set on a stand establishes ROY and RAMONA's living room; a swivel chair, JACKIE's TV studio; a double bed, ADAM and JANE's bedroom. Rooms, doors, windows, mirrors, other things referred to in stage directions to motivate actors' movements are not meant to be actually present on the set. A sense of space, of light and sky, must predominate.

When JACKIE is speaking on camera, the actor always speaks live, addressing the audience. When ROY and RAMONA's TV is tuned to JACKIE's program, her voice is also heard coming from their set.

OPPENHEIMER is lost in time. He does not appear gratuitously or wander aimlessly, but follows a purposeful path which leads him offstage and brings him on.

*Characters*

ROBERT OPPENHEIMER, age 40
ROY LAYTON (YOUNG ROY), age 20
GENE PROBST, age 20
ADAM NEWELL, age 25
JANE NEWELL, age 20
ROY LAYTON, age 60
RAMONA LAYTON, age 58
JUSTIN, age 6
JACKIE, age 35

*Time*: 1945 and 1985

*Place*: The West

(*Outside on the Trinity site in the Jornada del Muerto area of southwestern New Mexico. Before dawn, July 16, 1945. Total darkness.*)

YOUNG ROY: (*Singing*)
I saw the light, I saw the light,
No more darkness, no more night

(*Near him, someone starts to pee.* YOUNG ROY *continues, but louder.*)

YOUNG ROY:
Now I'm so happy, no sorrow in sight,
Praise the Lord, I saw the light.

Gene, don't be doing that while I'm singin. Don't you have any respect?

(*Half-light up on two young soldiers. Around them on the stage, barely visible, are: a gray-haired man sitting in a recliner and holding a guitar; a nicely dressed woman sitting in a plush executive chair, her back to the audience; two sleeping forms in a double bed upstage.*

GENE: (*Finishing and zipping up.*) I didn't think we were in church, Roy. Hey, but you're good. You really are.

YOUNG ROY: Well, I'm getting the guitar part down really good. Hey, wait a minute. There he is.

(*They look upstage. All that can be seen there is the red tip of a lit cigarette.* OPPENHEIMER *coughs several times, takes a drag of the cigarette, and then crosses quickly and exits into the offstage control shed. A bright light washes onstage briefly before he shuts the door behind him.*)

GENE: That the guy?

YOUNG ROY: (*In admiration, bordering on awe.*) Yeah.

GENE: Rolls his own?

YOUNG ROY: Oh yeah. In the dark.

GENE: Well, once you get used to doing it. (*He takes out a pack of Lucky Strikes and lights one.*)

YOUNG ROY: They had the thing on the dining-room table—in what used to be the ranchhouse? They were rolling it around with a stick,

---

looking for little holes, filling them with Kleenex. Then polishing it and polishing it.

GENE: Experts.

YOUNG ROY: Then they were putting the whole *gadget* together at the tower. That's what they call it—the gadget.

GENE: The gadget.

YOUNG ROY: And that's when the storm hit.

GENE: Didn't it get all wet?

YOUNG ROY: They pitched a tent around it. And then he made them so nervous they asked him to leave.

GENE: Kicked out, huh?

YOUNG ROY: And then the thing that held the thing wouldn't fit.

GENE: Army engineers.

YOUNG ROY: No, it was all machined perfect, but it all got too hot, see? So they had to leave it to cool down.

GENE: This thing gets hot?

YOUNG ROY: Oh yeah. You shoulda heard those Geiger-counter things—going like a bunch of rattlesnakes.

GENE: You mean to tell me that this thing—whatever they call it—

YOUNG ROY: The plug.

GENE: This plug gets hot by itself?

YOUNG ROY: Yeah.

GENE: Well, where did it come from?

YOUNG ROY: They made it.

GENE: Do you think these guys really know what they're doing?

YOUNG ROY: Gene, these guys are the smartest and the best in the whole goddam country—and a few other countries thrown in. We got Germans, we got an Italian, and that Russian guy that climbed the tower and held the flashlight so they could set the cameras—

GENE: They're taking a picture of it?

YOUNG ROY: I guess. I was getting the mattresses—to put under it all in case it fell, you know.

GENE: Well, I hope they had a lot of mattresses.

YOUNG ROY: Oh yeah. Sixty–seventy, at least.

GENE: And I hope they were from the officers' quarters.

YOUNG ROY: The lightning was the worst. He asked a guy to go up and, you know, babysit it.

GENE: It?

YOUNG ROY: Yeah, *it*, all put together in the tower.

GENE: What was he supposed to do if lightning had hit it?

YOUNG ROY: I don't know. Warn us all, I guess

(*The offstage door opens again, spilling light.* YOUNG ROY *and* GENE *snap to attention.*)

YOUNG ROY: General.

(*The light disappears. The soldiers relax again.*)

GENE: Hey, it's gotten lighter. What time is it?

YOUNG ROY: (*Looks at his watch.*) Not dawn yet.

GENE: Looks like it's clearing up.

YOUNG ROY: (*Suddenly noticing the sky.*) Look at that star! Boy, you can't get much brighter than that! I'm gonna tell 'em.

(*He runs toward the control-shed entrance, is met by* OPPENHEIMER, *who passes by him and enters the open area, looking at the sky.*)

YOUNG ROY: Are we going to go ahead now, Dr. Oppenheimer?

(*Suddenly* OPPENHEIMER *turns and exits quickly.*)

GENE: Boy, he really knows who you are. Are you sure you even met him?

YOUNG ROY: Last night. I was pulling in the first load of mattresses. I caught him in the light of my flashlight. He was just sort of standing around—worrying, I think. I *recognized* him. And then he *talked* to me. He told me how he named this project—it comes from two poems.

GENE: Two poems? It took two poems?

YOUNG ROY: I told him how we came out here on the train. I mean, he *listened* to me. And he shook my hand.

GENE: Well, I don't think you're gonna make it in his memoirs.

(*Sound of a far-off and scratchy radio playing* "The Star Spangled Banner.")

YOUNG ROY: What's that?

GENE: Somebody's got a radio somewhere, I guess.

YOUNG ROY: They playing that for us?

GENE: Can't be. This is all top secret.

YOUNG ROY: Well, I'm sure they would if they could.

(*They listen in silence.*)

GENE: Where were you last?

YOUNG ROY: Berlin.

GENE: I was sure I'd be in Japan by now.

(YOUNG ROY *takes out a bottle and begins to put the contents on his face.*)

GENE: What's that?

YOUNG ROY: Suntan oil.

GENE: Have you gone nuts?

YOUNG ROY: Dr. Teller gave it to me.

GENE: To wear at night?

YOUNG ROY: It's for the—explosion. It might burn.

(YOUNG ROY *offers* GENE *the bottle. He ignores it.*)

GENE: You and those longhairs.

("The Star Spangled Banner *ends.*)

RADIO VOICE I: Good morning. This is KCBA, your Voice of America station. We're opening this morning with Tchaikovsky's "*Serenade for Strings.*"

(*The* "Serenade" *begins. The soldiers put on their welder's goggles.*)

YOUNG ROY: Hey, soldier, you've got a crack in your goggles.

GENE: Huh? Oh, it don't matter.

YOUNG ROY: Here. You take mine. (*He switches goggles with* GENE.) You're the one who's gonna be back there with all the brass. You want to look good.

(*Over the P.A. system comes a long mechanical wail.*)

YOUNG ROY: That's it!

(GENE *and* YOUNG ROY *exit quickly in opposite directions. Silence for five seconds except for the sound of Tchaikovsky on the faint radio. A blinding flash. Blackout. Silence. A woman's voice.*)

JANE: Adam?

(ADAM *wakes up and kisses* JANE, *puts his head gently on her stomach. She is pregnant. His clock radio comes on.*)

RADIO VOICE I: —attributed to Shiite Muslims a spokesman said today.

(JANE *exits.*)

VOICE: This is KOMA, your sound of the Eighties. Hey, if you get a chance, check out the sunrise—it's absolutely beautiful. And now for our next half hour of uninterrupted mus—

(ADAM *shuts the radio off; gets up, naked; goes to the window, looks out. The sunrise is particularly beautiful. He opens the window to have a better look. The sunlight hits his face.*)

ADAM: (*Under his breath.*) My god.

JANE: (*Reentering*) Adam—

(JANE *comes to* ADAM *with a bathrobe, covering him. He exits. During the next scene,* JANE *makes the bed, and then sits down on the end of it, exhausted, staring at herself in the mirror.*)

(*Lights up on the living room of a small tract house. A gray-haired man, dressed up except for a coat and tie, sits in the recliner and sings, accompanying himself on the guitar, which he does not play well. He wears glasses with one dark lens. This is* ROY, *forty years later.*)

ROY: (*Singing*)
I saw the light, I saw the light.
No more darkness—

(*He has trouble with the chord change on the guitar, stops until he gets it, continues.*)

ROY:
—no more night.
Now I'm so happy, no sorrow in sight.
Praise the Lord, I saw the light.

(*Talking to himself*) I hope they got a piano player down there. (*To* RAMONA, *who is offstage.*) Baby?

RAMONA: (*Entering from the back of the house, carrying two ties.*) What tie are you gonna wear?

ROY: I hope they got a piano player down there.

RAMONA: (*About one of the ties, a striped one.*) I think this one is good.

ROY: They told me no stripes. It does something to the cameras. (*Taking the other tie, handing* RAMONA *the guitar.*) I wish you'd come down there with me.

RAMONA: (*Wiping off the guitar.*) You really gonna try to play this? It's been a helluva long time. These strings look rusty.

ROY: I know, but I gotta try.

RAMONA: Now what time will you be on?

ROY: I don't know. They run all day. I could be on any time.

RAMONA: You mean I have to watch this show all day long?

ROY: Baby, if they like me, I might could be on more than once even. Wouldn't that be something?

RAMONA: Roy, you're getting your hopes up.

ROY: Better comb my hair. I don't know about this tie.

(ROY *exits to the back part of the house.* RAMONA *is putting the guitar in its case, still shining it.*)

RAMONA: (*Thinking* ROY *is still there.*) I wish you wouldn't go. (*She goes off after* ROY.)

(OPPENHEIMER *reenters. He stares at* ROY *and* RAMONA'S *living room,* ADAM *and* JANE'S *bedroom, stops, thinks.*)

OPPENHEIMER: (*Shaking his head as he crosses.*) No. No no no no no. (*Laughs to himself, exits.*)

(ADAM *reenters, wearing slacks and a shirt—his tie is untied. He's finishing a bowl of cereal.* JANE *ties his tie for him as they talk.*)

ADAM: I have to go in a few minutes.

JANE: I know.

ADAM: We have to believe the doctors. They know what they're doing.

(*A six-year-old boy—*JUSTIN*—enters, carrying a Tinker-toy construction and a box of Ivory Snow. He runs to* ROY *and* RAMONA'S *house, goes straight to the TV, and turns it on. He stares at the TV and plays with his toy.*)

JANE: I'll be all right.

ADAM: You'll be all right. I wish it weren't my first day.

(JANE *finishes his tie.*)

ADAM: Hey, you're getting good at that.

(ADAM *exits to finish getting dressed.* JANE *sits down on the bed. Still in dim light,* JACKIE *swivels to face the TV camera and begins speaking in a pleasant, low-key, and sincere manner, almost chatty. Her voice comes from* ROY *and* RAMONA'S *TV.*)

JACKIE: He goes on to say that we can tell when we see all these signs that have been predicted, like the leaves appearing on the fig tree say what season it is to people in Israel. When we first see these signs, that's the tribulation, when they start to accelerate, He says that we will know that He is near, that He is right at the door, right at the door—

(*Although* JUSTIN *changes the channel,* JACKIE *continues her talk as lights come up on her area. She has the sophistication in manner and dress of a female executive. She occasionally swivels her chair to a different camera angle.*)

JACKIE: —ready to return. But the punch line comes next—

(JUSTIN *switches the channels very fast, finally decides on a violent car chase, and sits down in front of the TV, stares at it, still fiddling with his toy.*)

JACKIE: —verse 34. He says, "Truly I say,"—now when Jesus says, "Truly I say," He means to really pay attention, to stop, look and listen. He says, "Truly I say, this generation shall not pass away until *all* these things shall take place." Of course, the generation He is talking about is the generation that would see the signs begin to appear. Who would that be? Yes. Us.

(*As* JACKIE *speaks,* ADAM *is finishing dressing for work. He comes into full view, looks into the mirror, adjusting his Air Force uniform. He puts on his hat.*)

JACKIE: We—are—that—generation.

(ADAM *exits.*)

JACKIE: And what does He say would happen? He says, "The generation that sees all the signs come together will be the generation that sees them all fulfilled."

(*During the following,* JACKIE'S *speeches occasionally overlap* ROY *and* RAMONA'S *conversation.*)

RAMONA: (*Entering and seeing* JUSTIN.) Now what are you doing here?

JACKIE: Now, I am glad to be a part of that generation. Why?

RAMONA: Did you even knock?

JACKIE: Because I want to be part of all this famine and war and suffering?

RAMONA: You walked right in.

JACKIE: Because I want to see the world go through its worst tribulations?

RAMONA: I wish you'd talk to me sometime. Why won't you talk?

(JUSTIN *takes the Tinker-toy he's been working on and shows it to* RAMONA.)

JACKIE: Because I want to see the nations of the world begin what most certainly will be *the* Armageddon?

(ROY *enters the living room. He's wearing a Western string tie, and carrying his guitar in its case.*)

ROY: I decided on the bolo tie.

(JUSTIN *runs out of the house, leaving his toy and Ivory Snow box.*)

RAMONA: (*To* JUSTIN) Don't go!

ROY: Don't that little boy have a home?

JACKIE: No. I'm glad that I'm part of that generation Jesus talks about—the Last Generation—because I get to see the Lord in my lifetime.

RAMONA: (*About* JUSTIN) I wonder where he lives.

JACKIE: I will get to see the Lord face-to-face in that final moment.

(ROY *switches TV channels and finds* JACKIE.)

ROY: There she is.

(ROY *sits to watch* JACKIE. *Her voice now comes through the TV speaker again, as well as being heard from her own space.*)

JACKIE: The Greek word for "moment" is atomos—A-T-O-M-O-S, which is the word from which we get atom—A-T-O-M, which means "that which is indivisible."

ROY: Listen to that—she really knows all this stuff.

RAMONA: No oomph.

ROY: She doesn't need oomph—she's got brains.

JACKIE: Think about it—two thousand years of waiting and *we* are the ones who will see the prophecy fulfilled at that one indivisible moment when we will see Jesus. Praise God.

ROY: This woman's got two college degrees—two of 'em.

JACKIE: So no matter how bad it gets—and it gets pretty bad sometimes—it's just birth pangs.

RAMONA: What does she know about birth pangs.

ROY: Now, baby.

JACKIE: The birth pangs of a world that's about to begin.

(*Music comes out of the TV speaker.* JACKIE *holds and then turns upstage in her swivel chair, a segment of the show being over.* RAMONA *turns the TV off.*)

RAMONA: That music sounds like what you hear at the dentist's office.

ROY: Well, I guess they're trying to do something about that.

RAMONA: It's not the kind of preaching you or I was raised with.

ROY: I'm surprised you remember.

RAMONA: Roy, now don't start with me on that.

ROY: Everything she says is from the Bible. Not enough people preach the entire Bible—they just preach the parts they like.

RAMONA: Well, she doesn't sound like she likes any of it—she just drones on and on.

ROY: She's written a book, you know, about all this stuff. She knows Greek—*Greek*.

RAMONA: Roy, you always think everyone is smarter than you are.

ROY: I wish you'd come down there with me.

RAMONA: No . . .

ROY: We could walk around downtown.

RAMONA: No, it's too far.

ROY: You gonna leave the house today?

RAMONA: I've got too much to do.

ROY: Baby, I'm worried about you.

RAMONA: I'm worried about *you*. You can't play that guitar. You haven't sung in years. I don't know what you're doing.

ROY: It's been two months you haven't left this house.

RAMONA: That's not true.

ROY: By yourself? When was the last time you went to the grocery store by yourself?

RAMONA: I like it better when you drive me.

ROY: You hardly even go out on the lawn anymore.

RAMONA: I have trouble breathing when I get out there. I think I'm developing an allergy.

ROY: To what? What's out there? This neighborhood's beautiful—always has been.

RAMONA: It's been known to happen.

ROY: Well, I gotta go. Wish you'd change your mind. (*No answer. He kisses her.*) See you later, baby.

(ROY *crosses to exit with his guitar, stops to wave at* RAMONA. OPPENHEIMER *enters, sees* ROY, *and stops to stare at him, as if* ROY *sparked some memory.* RAMONA *waves back and* ROY *exits. Confused,* OPPENHEIMER *exits the way he came, crossing near but not seeing* ADAM, *who is entering with his briefcase.* RAMONA *settles down in her chair to read the Sunday papers.* JACKIE *swivels to the camera.*)

JACKIE: Paul tells us: "In the twinkling of an eye, we shall all be changed." Now how quick is that? (*Not moving*) 'Bout *that* quick. Want to see it again? (*She holds a smile, then swivels away from the camera, takes off her body mike, and looks through her notes.*)

(ADAM *enters his bedroom, with briefcase, ready to go.*)

ADAM: Did I tell you about my console?

JANE: Part of the best computer system in the world. Yes.

ADAM: Did I tell you about my chair?

JANE: Better than the President's.

(ADAM *kneels in front of* JANE *and massages her legs as she talks.*)

ADAM: There'll be pressure.

JANE: Well, being cooped up for twenty-four hours . . . and everything . . . else. Adam, how close are you to the ah—the ah—thing.

ADAM: I never see it. Not my job, really. Hey, it's a lot better than being cooped up for nine months.

JANE: More than nine months. Adam, I can't stop worrying.

ADAM: He must like it in there.

JANE: She.

ADAM: Once I'm sealed in. You can't talk to me.

JANE: I know.

ADAM: No communication with the outside world—except NORAD in Colorado.

JANE: If you can call that the outside world.

ADAM: One of the guys said it's built on giant springs, so if there's ever a direct hit, the whole complex sort of goes boing. It's kinda brilliant, really. When you think about it.

JANE: How long do you have to wait for the van?

ADAM: It's always early. Because you can never be late. It's nice down there.

JANE: You told me.

ADAM: Launch Control is one of the best assignments in the whole Air Force. We're very lucky. We're set for life now.

JANE: Yes.

ADAM: The doctors on this base are some of the best in the world. They're experts in their field.

JANE: Yes.

(ADAM *goes to the mirror. Horn honks.*)

JANE: You have to go. (*She holds on to him.*) You have to go.

(ADAM *removes her arms, turns, kisses her—she breaks it. He leaves, looking back for something from her. She doesn't respond.*)

JANE: (*To herself*) You have to go.

(JUSTIN *enters and runs to* RAMONA'S *living room. He stares at* RAMONA, *waiting for her to wake up.*)

RAMONA: (*Awake, to* JUSTIN.) Oh, you're back! (*Getting up.*) Do you want a cookie?

(JUSTIN *nods, reaches for the cookie. She moves it away from him.*)

RAMONA: Where do you live?

(JUSTIN *just stares at her, not speaking. She gives in, hands him the cookie, and takes him to the window.*)

RAMONA: Can you point the direction? I bet it's up there in the circle drives, right? Do you live on a street with a star name? An Indian name? Why won't you talk? Hey, show me.

(OPPENHEIMER *enters from the control shed.*)

OPPENHEIMER: It can't be New Mexico because I'm walking on grass. And there's a woman . . . and a child. . . . I—I can't see more . . . it's too blurry. Their movements are so slow.

(OPPENHEIMER *crosses upstage, looks one way, considers, then exits in another direction, again near* ADAM, *who doesn't see him.* ADAM *crosses to wait for the elevator into the silo. During* RAMONA'S *speech, we hear the elevator arrive.* ADAM *gets in; we hear it descend.*)

RAMONA: (*To* JUSTIN) Look at this street. I used to know who lived in every single house. Everybody. We used to play Scrabble and gin rummy with those people—they're gone. We used to have barbecues with this half of the street. Now I don't know a soul there or anywhere else, for that matter. I really wonder if anyone lives in any of these houses. I see lights on in the evenings, but it seems I never see anybody come and go. Trash cans appear in the early morning and somebody carries them away. Nobody beats rugs or shakes out dust mops, any of the things that got people outside. It's like the houses are the only things that are alive. Might as well be on Mars. Mars.

(ADAM *steps out of the elevator and exits.* ROY *enters and* JACKIE *stands when she sees him.*)

JACKIE: Oh—Roy Layton.

RAMONA: (*Puts* JUSTIN *down.*) Now, you stick around for a little while at least. Okay?

(RAMONA *and* JUSTIN *exit to the kitchen to get more cookies.*)

JACKIE: (*Coming to* ROY.) I heard you sing many, many years ago. It was at your church. My Aunt Dorothy introduced us.

ROY: My church?

JACKIE: Pillar of Fire. On Maple Street.

ROY: That's not my church, ma'am. I just used to sing there.

JACKIE: Oh. I'm so glad. They're exactly the opposite of what I'm trying to do here. This must be your guitar. May I . . . see it? (*She opens his case.*)

ROY: You don't have a piano player, do you?

JACKIE: (*Taking out the guitar, looking at it with awe.*) I was twelve or thirteen. You stood in front of the altar. You sang an old hymn I'd never heard before—about the ending of the day and then the dawn?

ROY: That was the song with all the B-flat chords. They're hard.

JACKIE: I was wearing a yellow pants suit—I was the only girl there in pants. Afterwards I asked you if I could strum your guitar. You talked to me quite a while.

ROY: Uh-huh.

JACKIE: You *do* remember.

ROY: No ma'am, I don't.

JACKIE: Well, it doesn't matter. Really. Do you need to tune this . . . or anything?

ROY: If you want me to. Ma'am, I'm pretty nervous.

JACKIE: Oh, here. (*She hands the guitar to him.*) Sorry. It was wonderful to see it again.

ROY: Ma'am—

JACKIE: I know—out of the clear blue I call you up. Well, I asked you here because—well, I've received some criticism that this program is rather . . . cold.

ROY: Uh-huh.

JACKIE: You *do* think it's cold.

ROY: No ma'am. I watch it every day.

JACKIE: Well, then you know what I'm trying to do here. They make me furious. And all those holy roller churches with their falling on the floor, laying on of hands are fooling around with something that is not in their domain.

(OPPENHEIMER *enters, very agitated, crosses behind* ROY *and* JACKIE *and exits. No one notices him.*)

JACKIE: Trying to bring down the power of God, attract the Holy Spirit like it's something that can come down a lightning rod if you wave it in a bad storm. A church should be built on the Word. The Word is the Church's domain. The Word. And it has to stop with that.

ROY: Really—I just used to sing there.

JACKIE: They did have the best music.

ROY: Yes ma'am.

JACKIE: What is this around your neck?

ROY: Bolo tie.

JACKIE: Oh, is this one of your hobbies—making these?

ROY: No ma'am. I bought this. New.

JACKIE: I'm sorry I got so vehement. The one thing I don't want to get is preachy.

ROY: No, I wanted to say it's been a while since I played . . . this guitar.

JACKIE: Well, we are on again in a couple of minutes. Now I'm using your song to end the program—kind of like the benediction. I'll introduce you and then I'll have to hurry around to the studio door—I'm going to stand and shake hands as the audience leaves. Now when the red light on that camera goes out, you're off. But just finish the song anyway, like you would normally. By the way, please sing something other than "I Saw the Light"—the new Hank Williams biography has really devalued him for Christians. You understand. Nothing personal.

ROY: Ma'am. I don't want to do this.

JACKIE: Why not?

ROY: I can't. I can't play this guitar anymore. Simple as that.

JACKIE: Oh. My. They wanted—specifically asked for a guitar. You know, to increase the . . . warmth factor.

(JANE *is sitting on the bed talking on the phone. She is upset.*)

JANE: Yes, that's who I mean. He's a new Launch Control Officer—

ROY: Well, I guess that does it. (*Puts his guitar back in the case.*)

JANE: Yes, L.C.O.—whatever. (*Pause*) His wife.

JACKIE: Wait. Wait. I'll think of something. Sit here. I'll come up with something.

(ROY *puts his guitar down and sits off-camera.* JACKIE *returns to her chair and waits for her camera cue.*)

JANE: I know his duty just started, but this is kind of an emergency. No, I'm not in labor—that's the problem. Yes, this is our first baby. Thank you. Are they sealed in the control room yet? I thought it took longer. No. I—I just need to talk to him. I understand. I understand.

JACKIE: I want to talk to you today about something that most preachers never speak about although it's found throughout the Bible.

JANE: I understand.

JACKIE: I'm talking about what will happen to each one of you on that day at that last moment.

JANE: I understand. (*She sits holding the telephone receiver for several beats, desolate, not knowing what to do.*)

(RAMONA, *looking at her watch, enters with* JUSTIN. *They have a plate of cookies.*)

RAMONA: Better turn the TV on—don't want to miss Roy.

(RAMONA *turns it on.* JACKIE *is heard through the TV.*)

JACKIE: Today we're looking at the Rapture, that moment when "we shall be changed, in the twinkling of an eye." Now the word *rapture* means—this is from Webster's Dictionary:

RAMONA: I wonder who does her hair? (*She sits down.*)

JACKIE: —"the state of being transported by lofty emotion; ecstasy or the transporting of a person from one place to another, especially to heaven." So plane, bus, train, or rapture—all forms of transportation.

RAMONA: (*Takes a small snapshot out of her pocket and shows it to* JUSTIN.) This is my boy.

JACKIE: What it is is the coming of Christ for the Church in which He instantly catches up all living believers to meet Him in the air and translates them into perfect and immortal bodies without them experiencing physical death.

(JUSTIN *gives snapshot back to* RAMONA.)

JACKIE: So you could be raptured, like that, and someone is standing there looking at a pair of your empty shoes.

(RAMONA *turns the volume down.*)

JACKIE: There are signs leading up to the Rapture, of course. And these I was describing earlier this morning. But they are all part of the Tribulation—Armageddon being the climax of many years of suffering, war, natural disasters, droughts, world famines. And can any of us deny that these signs are present and increasing? All we need to do is watch the news, read the paper. And any of us then might pray that we might be raptured before we have to witness any more suffering.

I, myself, many times think it should happen now because the world has had enough. When I see the faces of children who are starving because a drought has ravaged their country, or a war has ravaged their country, or I see bodies being removed from the site of an earthquake and people wandering, looking for a lost father or a daughter, I—planes with bombs over our heads right now! The leaders of the world . . . no one is doing anything, no one is listening. IT'S COMING. WHO'S READY? DEAR GOD.

(*Disoriented by this sudden burst of emotion,* JACKIE *finds herself on her feet. She looks briefly at* ROY, *confused, sits down and finds her place in her notes.* ROY *stares at her.*)

JACKIE: The word *rapture* comes from the Greek *harpazo,* which is translated as "caught up." That moment of rapture is prophesied by Matthew: "For as the lightning comes from the east, and flashes even unto the west; so shall the coming of the Son of Man be."

(ROY *experiences a sharp pain in his blind eye. He jerks off his glasses, and covers his eye.*)

JACKIE: And now the final word will be a benediction sung by an old friend of mine, Roy Layton. I've asked Roy to sing a cappella so that we can all carry just the words away with us. And I'll be at the studio door ready to shake hands with all those who worshipped here with us today. Roy? Roy—

(ROY *comes to and stands.* JACKIE *signals to the booth, and exits quickly.*)

RAMONA: That *is* Roy! But where are his glasses?

ROY: (*Singing*)
The sun is slowly sinking,
The day is almost gone,
Still darkness falls all around us

(OPPENHEIMER *crosses laterally, stops when he hears* ROY'S *singing, watches him.*)

ROY:
And we must journey on.
The darkest hour is just before dawn
The narrow way leads home.
Lay down your soul at Jesus' feet
The darkest hour is just before dawn.

(*During the song,* JANE *leaves her bedroom and walks straight across the stage to* ROY. *He doesn't see her until the end of his song, when she is right in front of him.*)

JANE: Help me.

ROY: What?

JANE: Please, I'm overdue. I'm scared.

ROY: Ma'am, I think I'm on television here.

(RAMONA *stands up in front of her TV.* ROY *looks up helplessly at the control booth, gets nothing.*)

ROY: Don't you need a doctor?

JANE: I have doctors at the base. But they won't help me. They won't even tell me anything. (*She takes* ROY'S *hands and puts them on her stomach.*) Please. Please. You can start now.

ROY: (*Taking his hands away.*) I'm not a faith healer, ma'am.

JANE: I have faith. (*Putting his hands back.*) Please. I know it will help.

ROY: I—I bless thee in the name of the Father, and the Son—

JANE: No! That's for when it's born. I need something for now. *Please.*

(JACKIE *enters.*)

ROY: (*Closing his eyes in panic.*) Dear Jesus.

JANE: I—I feel something!

ROY: Dear God.

JANE: I FEEL SOMETHING! I FEEL SOMETHING! I—

(JANE *collapses in* ROY's *arms and he lowers her to the ground.* JACKIE *runs to help. The TV program goes to static and* RAMONA *pounds the TV and switches channels, trying to get* ROY *back.*)

RAMONA: Damn TV! Dammit!!

(JUSTIN *picks up his toy and Ivory Snow box and is gone before* RAMONA *can stop him.* OPPENHEIMER *stares at* ROY.)

OPPENHEIMER: Something about him. Something about him.

(ROY *stands up.* JACKIE *stays with* JANE. OPPENHEIMER *moves to* JANE's *bed and sits on it, after testing it to make certain it's real. He remains very interested in what he can see in the TV studio.*)

(RAMONA *sits on the edge of her chair, staring at the empty television. After a moment she begins looking through the phone book. During the following action, she finds the number, dials, gets a busy signal, dials, until she finally gets through.*)

JANE: What happened?

JACKIE: You fainted.

JANE: No. No. It was wonderful. I felt something—I felt tingly and then just floated away. That's the first time anything like that has ever happened to me. (*To* JACKIE) Do you think the feelings I had went down to the baby?

JACKIE: I—I don't know. Do you feel all right?

JANE: (*Interrupting*) I'm not really, that religious—no offense. I was just so desperate—all I wanted was to just know I tried. So I could have a little peace. But this—(*She gets up*—JACKIE *helps her—and crosses to* ROY.) I just want to say. That you're a real preacher.

(JANE *takes* ROY's *hand and kisses it, then exits, ignoring* JACKIE's *efforts to help her.* JACKIE *signals to someone offstage to help* JANE.)

RAMONA: (*On the phone*) Hello? I'm looking for my husband. Roy Layton. The singer. Can you have him call his wife? His *wife*.

(OPPENHEIMER *begins to roll a cigarette, not taking his eyes off* ROY.)

JACKIE: (*To* ROY) What happened?

ROY: I don't know. We aren't still on, are we?

JACKIE: No, thank God. Did she just faint?

ROY: I don't know.

JACKIE: You don't know?

ROY: I never done it before in my life. Honestly. She took my hands, put them on her stomach. What could I do?

JACKIE: You could take you hands away!

ROY: How could I? She looked up at me and said "I have faith." When people have that much faith, what do you do? Don't you give them what they want?

JACKIE: You could just pray for her.

ROY: I did. That's what I did.

(*Phone rings at* RAMONA'S. *She answers it quickly*.)

JACKIE: And then she fainted. (*No answer from* ROY.) And then she fainted. Pregnant women faint.

RAMONA: Yes?

ROY: I guess so.

RAMONA: I was hoping you were someone else.

JACKIE: That's all it was then, wasn't it?

RAMONA: Can't you keep track of that little boy?

ROY: I'm just a singer. And not a very good one.

RAMONA: (*Still on the phone*.) Well, I understand that you're just the babysitter, but—. Yes, he usually drops in once a day. A couple of time today. Listen, I'm expecting an important phone call.

(JACKIE *crosses to* ROY, *takes both his hands and looks at them.* OPPENHEIMER *stands*.)

JACKIE: When I heard you sing that time you don't remember. I didn't tell you—you made me cry.

Roy: Baby doll, that was the song. It was the song.

(Jackie *exits.*)

Ramona: Uh-huh. Well, it's nice to finally know where he lives. No, I'll be here. I'm always here. Right. (*She hangs up the phone, crosses to the picture window, and stares out.*) This world. (*She turns the TV on.*) I dunno. I dunno.

(*Alone,* Roy *stares at his hands.*)

Roy: Like electricity coming down my arms.

(Ramona *sits in the recliner.*)

Ramona: Little boy. Little boy. (*She closes her eyes.*)

(Roy *senses the presence of someone.*)

Oppenheimer: Something about him.

Roy: (*Not seeing* Oppenheimer.) Who's there?

(Ramona *is asleep in her chair, the TV on but nothing on the screen except light. It is now late at night.* Justin *enters and goes to the kitchen cupboard, looking for cookies. Instead he finds a box of Ivory Snow and brings it back into the living room. He likes the picture on the box—it's a mother holding a baby. He curls up with it beneath the light of the TV screen.* Ramona *sleeps through the next scene.* Roy *exits, passing* Young Roy, *who enters pulling a large cart filled with Army-issue mattresses secured with ropes. He shines a flashlight in* Oppenheimer's *eyes.*)

Young Roy: Who's there?

(Oppenheimer *finds himself at Jornada del Muerto, the Trinity site, in the shadow of the tower that holds the gadget. It is the day preceding the test, just before dawn.*)

Oppenheimer: What?

Young Roy: Dr. Oppenheimer?

Oppenheimer: Yes, yes. Can—can you turn that light off?

Young Roy: (*Turns it off.*) Sorry, sir.

(Young Roy *approaches the tower base, walks under it cautiously, looks up at where the gadget is suspended, and rolls the cart to what he thinks is a spot directly under the gadget. With shaking hands,* Oppenheimer *starts to light a cigarette he rolled while watching the previous scene.*)

YOUNG ROY: (*About the proximity of the gadget to the match*) You gonna light that here? Sir?

(OPPENHEIMER *looks at* YOUNG ROY *for a beat, then at his own hand, as if he never saw it before.*)

OPPENHEIMER: I don't remember rolling this. (*He lights his cigarette. This brings on a bad coughing spell. When he's done, he looks at his watch.*)

YOUNG ROY: (*About the mattresses*) They're bringing some more. In a truck. From Base Camp.

(*Pause.* OPPENHEIMER *nods, distracted.*)

YOUNG ROY: They think ten to twelve feet. Will that do it?

OPPENHEIMER: Do what?

YOUNG ROY: Cushion the fall. Just in case.

OPPENHEIMER: Just in case?

YOUNG ROY: It falls.

OPPENHEIMER: It?

YOUNG ROY: The gadget. Are you all right, Dr. Oppenheimer?

OPPENHEIMER: I'm just kinda tired. I think I nodded off . . . I was in the control shed and then I wandered—no, this is the tower . . . I was up on the tower checking the . . .

YOUNG ROY: Gadget.

OPPENHEIMER: (*Snapping to*) The gadget? It's not going to fall. It's secure.

YOUNG ROY: Well, as they say, better safe than sorry, sir.

OPPENHEIMER: Who are you exactly?

YOUNG ROY: (*Coming to attention and saluting.*) Corporal Roy Layton, sir.

OPPENHEIMER: How do you do. (*Looking at watch again.*) Where is everybody?

YOUNG ROY: Getting the mattresses.

OPPENHEIMER: Oh. Right. That's good. I'm—I'm waiting . . . here. Here.

YOUNG ROY: (*Readjusting the cart, looking up at where the gadget would be.*) Excuse me, sir, but what do you think? Is this a good way to do it? Or should they be just laid on the ground? Maybe in a wide circle? Or just piled up every whichaway? What do you think? Sir?

Oppenheimer: What?

Young Roy: What do you think about this configuration of mattresses here?

Oppenheimer: That will probably be fine.

Young Roy: Yes, sir.

Oppenheimer: Where *is* everybody?

Young Roy: Any minute now. They only went ten miles.

Oppenheimer: What? Oh.

Young Roy: Everything going all right, sir?

Oppenheimer: I think I need to get to my next . . . stop.

Young Roy: All the vehicles are gone.

(Oppenheimer *crosses to* Roy's *guitar, left from the previous scene, and picks it up.*)

Young Roy: Oh, that's mine. (*He takes it and puts it upstage, near the mattresses.*)

Oppenheimer: I've just been so tired. We've been working so hard. It's been very hard, particularly these last few months. Hornig called in for the weather report yeaterday—fell asleep on the radio, waiting for the answer. I just now nodded off myself. Had a dream—classic—like running for a train, never catching it. I was in a place, a lot like here, but different. . . . There was a woman and a child. Strange. Even now, I feel groggy. In parallax, like a camera. You look up here at an image that's coming through down there backwards and upside down. You look familiar. I feel like what you say, you've said before. What we do is. . . . Even those goddam mattresses . . .

Young Roy: I'd be glad to drive you anywhere you want to go. Drove Dr. Teller the other day. He's a helluva guy. He's famous, isn't he? Not that you're not, sir.

Oppenheimer: That's all right. I'm not. Fermi is the famous one. *Fermi. Fermi.* Yes, I talked to him last night! (*He's relieved—a familiar name.*)

Young Roy: Everything is all right, isn't it, sir? I mean *it's*—(*Motioning to the gadget.*)—okay, isn't it?

OPPENHEIMER: (*Patting* YOUNG ROY's *shoulder and arm to establish that he's real.*) Everything's—going—as—scheduled. Yes, that's right. I'm certain of that. I had a bad night last night—coughing. That's why I'm so tired.

YOUNG ROY: I was there at the ranch house, you know. When they were putting the two halves together and polishing it.

OPPENHEIMER: So you are—somebody I work with . . .?

YOUNG ROY: I was there in one of the jeeps.

OPPENHEIMER: (*A memory comes*) With the motor running? With the motor running!

YOUNG ROY: We were ordered to do that, sir. So you all could make a quick getaway in case it blew.

OPPENHEIMER: (*Joyous*) In case it blew! Right!

YOUNG ROY: So that was a close call, huh? I wondered about that. I did. Boy, it was pretty scary, I can tell you now. Sitting out there, waiting, not knowing if the whole thing was gonna go blewey or not!

OPPENHEIMER: Go blewey?

YOUNG ROY: Blow up! Explode! And take alla us with it.

OPPENHEIMER: The plug would never blow up by itself.

YOUNG ROY: Right. What?

OPPENHEIMER: Would never happen. What do you think we've spent all this time on? I mean, we're worried sick that this goddam firing mechanism isn't going to work. *Yes.* YES!! That's it! That's what's next! Oh, thank God. WE'RE TESTING IT NEXT. THE FIRING MECHANISM!

(OPPENHEIMER *laughs with relief.* YOUNG ROY, *as excited as* OPPENHEIMER, *whoops in joy. Exhilarated, they scramble to the top of the mattress pile.*)

YOUNG ROY: Great. Great! I'm excited, too. I have to tell you, sir, ever since I got here—there's something about this place.

OPPENHEIMER: Do you really think so?

YOUNG ROY: There's something about it.

OPPENHEIMER: It is beautiful, particularly right now, for some reason. Some people find it barren.

YOUNG ROY: No place in this country is barren, sir.

OPPENHEIMER: They call this place the Jornada del Muerto, you know.

YOUNG ROY: What's that—Spanish?

OPPENHEIMER: The conquistadores. Cheerful bunch.

YOUNG ROY: What's it mean?

OPPENHEIMER: Journey of Death. I'm suddenly so happy. I don't know why.

YOUNG ROY: I thought this was called Trinity.

OPPENHEIMER: No. That's just the project and the buildings and all that.

YOUNG ROY: I just wondered what the name meant.

OPPENHEIMER: Well, the Trinity—

YOUNG ROY: I know what the Trinity is, sir. I was just wondering what all this has to do with the Father, the Son, and the Holy Ghost.

OPPENHEIMER: Nothing—I—I named it that. I never thought that it might offend anybody.

YOUNG ROY: No offense taken, sir.

OPPENHEIMER: Of course, I realize now how it might—

YOUNG ROY: Oh, it's a nice title, sir. Don't get me wrong. I just wondered, you know.

OPPENHEIMER: They called me in Berkeley for a name. And I had been reading a poem by John Donne—he was a *minister*, you know:
"As West and East in all Flatte Maps are One,
So Death doth touch the Resurrection."

YOUNG ROY: Uh-huh.

OPPENHEIMER: Death *touches* the Resurrection.

YOUNG ROY: Uh-huh.

OPPENHEIMER: And it's quite flat out here.

YOUNG ROY: Okay.

OPPENHEIMER: And I thought of my favorite poem by this same minister:
"Batter my heart, three-person'd God—

(*Skipping to the last two lines.*)
Unless you enthrall me, I never shall be free,
And ne'er be chaste unless you ravish me."

(YOUNG ROY *really doesn't get this one at all. He waits, instead of replying.*)

OPPENHEIMER: "Batter my heart, *three*-person'd God."

(YOUNG ROY *just continues to look at him.*)

OPPENHEIMER: We needed a name.

YOUNG ROY: Well, it's sure better than Journey of Death.

(*They laugh.*)

OPPENHEIMER: Last night Fermi was taking bets on whether the explosion would just suck all the oxygen out of New Mexico or out of the entire Northern Hemisphere. He looked up at the Oscuras—that mountain range—at sunset—they were never more beautiful. And all he could say is, "Ah, the earth on the eve of destruction." Just then, a tarantula sidled up next to him. He ran in *real* terror then. Oh shit. I shouldn't be telling you that.

YOUNG ROY: Oh, that's all right, sir. I'm not afraid of tarantulas. I'm really not afraid of anything out here. Two months ago, if I thought I'd be here in New Mexico, well, I would've laughed. I got my orders home in Berlin, and they told us we'd get a month off then go back to, you know, clean up. But when I reported for duty, they put us on this train and the next thing I know, we're heading west. A whole train full of soldiers heading west for no reason. Seemed like then. And we stopped in Nebraska—*Nebraska*—for three days and played baseball to kill time. And still we have no idea where we were going or why. And then, and then, back on the train and further west, and the ground starts to change. My buddy wakes me up and presses my face to the window. Lord! There's a herd of antelope galloping alongside the train and I look up and got my breath took away again! Mountains! Blue-green, almost black the pine is so thick. They are so still and big, they look painted on. Well, that's when I knew I was going somewhere important. Something about the speed of that train—I swear once we got close to here, we went faster and faster—I think those guys could've lost control like *that*. (*Snaps fingers.*) I mean, that prairie blurred into the desert and the day went *by*. And then, bang, we were stopped. 'Cause we were here. Stopped. Dead. And it was so quiet. The sky was full of stars. And I could feel that train moving inside me for the whole next day.

OPPENHEIMER: Then you've been away in the war quite a while.

YOUNG ROY: Yes sir.

OPPENHEIMER: Three years?

YOUNG ROY: Yes sir.

OPPENHEIMER: And they send you home for just thirty days and then out here?

YOUNG ROY: I'm not complaining. This is just about the most exciting thing that has ever happened, sir? I mean, I missed the invention of the motor car, I missed Christopher Columbus, I missed the time when Lord Jesus was walking around on earth, I missed the invention, no, *discovery* of electricity. I was beginning to think that absolutely nothing was ever gonna happen to me. You know?

When I think that the smartest men, why, in the whole world are here. And all the knowledge that's went into this, from way back there. When the first guy got an idea, like a little light bulb going on over his head, and, wham, he invents that light bulb. And then another guy makes it better. And another guy says, "We got a light bulb, we need a socket." And, wham, we got a socket. And then a lamp. And then, the next thing you know, the whole world is lit up. Lamps everywhere! No more darkness.

OPPENHEIMER: "If the radiance of a thousand suns,
Were to burst at once into the sky—"

YOUNG ROY: Was that from the Bible?

OPPENHEIMER: It's from something called "The Song of the Lord."

YOUNG ROY: Our Lord—Lord Jesus?

OPPENHEIMER: An ancient prince—that kind of lord. He's supposed to go into battle. All his enemies are assembled. But he won't go—he has doubts. But *his* god, Krishna, appears to him. Blazing and radiant with light and with many arms, all holding weapons. And then Krishna shouts, "I am become Death—"

(OPPENHEIMER *stops. Long pause.*)

YOUNG ROY: Is that how it ends?

OPPENHEIMER: No ... no ... Krishna shouts, "I am become death—the shatterer of worlds."

YOUNG ROY: And that does it, huh? That's all it takes, I bet.

OPPENHEIMER: He goes into battle. He goes and—

YOUNG ROY: Wins? Right? He wins. There's your happy ending. You see? You see, now that's what we call a good omen where I come from. Like when you open the Bible with your eyes closed and you read whatever verse your finger falls on? And that verse has meaning for you right then? You were meant to read it. Like now, you were meant to think of that poem.

OPPENHEIMER: I remember now. I remember this.

(*Horn honks offstage.*)

YOUNG ROY: Hey, they're here! With the mattresses! (*He jumps down off the mattresses.*) I'll be there tomorrow morning, sir. I get to be in one of the trenches. A kind of forward observer.

OPPENHEIMER: You haven't seen it. You haven't seen it yet.

YOUNG ROY: That's right! That's exactly it! 'Cause you can't even begin to imagine. 'Cause you just know it's gonna be incredible. Oh, sir, it's gonna go great. And then you'll be able to get some sleep, you'll see. Can I shake your hand? I want to tell my kids someday.

(OPPENHEIMER *leans down from the top of the mattresses and shakes* YOUNG ROY'S *hand.* OPPENHEIMER *tries to hold on to* YOUNG ROY *briefly, but he disappears into the darkness.* OPPENHEIMER *lies back on the mattresses, confused and desolate.*)

(*At* ROY'S *and* RAMONA'S *house it is now morning. The TV is still on.* JUSTIN *is gone.* RAMONA *wakes up suddenly in her chair.*)

RAMONA: Oh my God. (*She gets out of the chair.*) Oh my God. What time is it? (*She goes to the back bedroom.*) Roy? Roy! You let me *sleep* in my chair! Roy? Roy—(*She reenters the living room looking for him, then goes into the kitchen, growing more frantic.*) Roy? ROY! (*She stands bewildered at her front door.*) Maybe it's a binge. Maybe he just went out on a binge—

(YOUNG ROY *appears, inebriated, and trying despereately to cover it up. He is in uniform and carrying a duffel bag. One eye is covered with a bandage.*)

YOUNG ROY: Hi, baby. I had an accident. Didn't want to tell you when I called you from New Mexico. They sent me home on a plane! An airplane! (*Coming to her.*) I saw something incredible in New Mexico. Something incredible. But I can't talk about it. I can't talk—(*Kissing her gently.*) I'm sorry I'm late. I lost track of the time. Okay? Okay? I lost track of the time.

RAMONA: Roy—

(YOUNG ROY *passes* RAMONA *and crosses into the house. He stops and puts his hand on his bandaged eye—the pain stopping him.* ROY, *age 60, approaches the house.*)

ROY: (*Starting to talk the moment he sees* RAMONA.) It's like something you always knew, deep inside you. You *knew.*

(YOUNG ROY *exits into the back of the house.*)

ROY: And one day someone says it and *wham*! It all breaks loose! Of course. Of course, death *meets* the Resurrection.

RAMONA: Where have you been? Where are your glasses?

ROY: Now I know. There was some reason why I was there, some reason why this—(*Points to his blind eye.*)—happened to me. With this eye—(*His good eye*)—I see this world. And with my blinded eye, I got to see the next.

RAMONA: I remember—I remembered.

ROY: I been walking all around. Looking at everything. Just in case. Saying goodbye.

RAMONA: And you never talked about it again.

ROY: 'Cause it can happen any moment—"In the twinkling of an eye, we shall all be changed." Like that.

RAMONA: What happened, Roy?

ROY: Do you know how many neighborhoods there are around us? Islands of houses everywhere. And each house has people in it, and God watches over every single one of them. How does He keep track? How does He keep track?

RAMONA: Where's your guitar?

ROY: Oh, I don't need it anymore. I sing by myself. I make people *cry.*

RAMONA: Roy, honey, come in now. Come on in.

ROY: I hate to. I hate to. Come to me.

(RAMONA *comes to him. He puts his arm around her shoulder.*)

ROY: Look. (*He's still looking at the world.*) It's a shame, isn't it.

(*Blast of light and, this time, a rumble that grows until it simulates the real blast at the Trinity Site. When it stops,* ROY *and*

RAMONA *stand still and* OPPENHEIMER *stands on top of mattresses, looking at the mushroom cloud of the test. Cheers and shouts can be heard everywhere: "It worked! It worked! Oh my God, it worked!"* GENE *comes running in, his goggles around his neck. He sees* OPPENHEIMER, *but not* ROY *and* RAMONA. *He acts as if it's natural that* OPPENHEIMER *is on top of the mattresses. He's very excited.*)

GENE: It worked!! It worked!! Hey, Dr. Oppenheimer! The war is over for sure now, huh? Colonel Kisto—, Kistow—, the Russian guy? Says you owe him ten dollars.

OPPENHEIMER: (*Climbing down, looking in his billfold.*) I—I'll have to pay him tomorrow.

GENE: Tomorrow! Right! We got a million of 'em now the war is over! I have to admit, I never thought it would work.

(GENE *grabs* OPPENHEIMER'S *hand and shakes it.* OPPENHEIMER *sees* ROY *and* RAMONA *and runs after* GENE *as he exits.*)

OPPENHEIMER: Help me! (*He exits.*)

RAMONA: I can't breathe. I have to go in.

ROY: Stay. Stay with me. My whole life makes sense now. I see it all.

RAMONA: Roy, when our boy was killed, you did this. You stayed up for two days figuring it all out. Do you remember?

ROY: I even figured that out now. You see, Danny was conceived right before I went to work on the bomb. Maybe right at the time—when the die was cast, and I was going to be there. So he had to die, you see.

RAMONA: He did not have to die! You can't tell me he had to die! Roy, you've gone too far. People die all the time and none of it makes any sense!

ROY: (*With increasing agitation.*) His father conceived him and went immediately to a place called Journey of Death which was also called Trinity. You see? Father, Son, and Holy Ghost. And finally, the last piece is there. I healed somebody, Ramona. The Holy Ghost came down my arms and into this woman's body. I could feel it, Ramona, like electricity coming down my arms. It was real. And she could feel it, too. And she wasn't even religious. I know that's what the Holy Ghost is, then—electricity, coming down my arms. God's like lightning coming through us into the world.

RAMONA: (*Trying to bring him out of it.*) Roy, you're not part of the Trinity. Or some place called Journey of Death. Some person named those places, not God. You're my Roy—that's who you are.

ROY: But I'm trapped there, Ramona. I'm caught.

RAMONA: Roy, that was forty years ago!

ROY: Forty years ago I saw with my own eye what everybody's been waiting for since the world began!

RAMONA: What? What?

(OPPENHEIMER *enters, still chasing* GENE, *but finds himself back where he started. He stops when he sees* ROY *and* RAMONA.)

ROY: The end! I saw it! For real with one of my eyes! And then the power of God came down my arms. So it does all make sense!

RAMONA: No. No!

ROY: You see, Ramona, I was never really sure that God existed. I believed it, of course. But I didn't *think* it. But now I have proof. I have a fact. So that means—that means it's all true. The Bible, Revelations, Hell—it's really gonna happen. Trinity. Trinity. Baby, we're caught.

RAMONA: (*Running into the house.*) NO.

(ROY *stays outside.* OPPENHEIMER *watches him during the next scene.* RAMONA *notices something out the picture window. It is* JACKIE *coming up the walk. She is carrying* ROY'S *guitar in its case. She's dressed in the same clothes, looks disheveled. She looks through the window of the front door.* RAMONA *opens the door and looks at* JACKIE.)

JACKIE: Is Roy here?

RAMONA: He's at work.

JACKIE: I—I need to talk to him.

RAMONA: He's not here.

JACKIE: I have to tell him something.

RAMONA: Oh?

JACKIE: This is his guitar.

RAMONA: I see.

JACKIE: We were at the hospital all night, Mrs. Layton. That woman came down during the program yesterday and asked for the laying on of hands . . . I don't do that. I didn't want my church to be a carnival, accent on the carnal.

RAMONA: Well, that's a comfort.

JACKIE: And then her water broke, and the baby started to come. We made it to the hospital all right. (*She breaks down.*) I'm sorry. I've been up all night.

RAMONA: (*Taking the guitar.*) Why don't I take this now.

(JANE *enters her bedroom. She is in the dress she wore at the TV studio.*)

JACKIE: They called the base and her husband was on his way. He'd just gotten off duty—they couldn't get hold of him. She wouldn't stay, so I took her home.

(JANE *crawls onto the bed painfully and curls up on her side.*)

JACKIE: Roy doesn't know. The baby died.

(ROY *enters.*)

JACKIE: The baby died, Mrs. Layton. (*She and* ROY *see each other.*) You have to tell him.

(JACKIE *exits quickly.* RAMONA *turns and sees that* ROY *has heard. She tries to touch him, but he turns from her and crosses numbly to the door and goes outside. She exits into the back of the house.* ADAM *enters his bedroom, still in his uniform.*)

ADAM: NO!!!!!

(ADAM *crosses and looks at* JANE *in bed. She doesn't look at him.* OPPENHEIMER *crosses to* ROY *and speaks to him.*)

OPPENHEIMER: It was like a wheel that somebody started rolling a long time ago. As a discovery, it was beautiful, as all pure knowledge is. It's the same wheel that transported us this far, and into—

ROY: —rapture.

OPPENHEIMER: When you're at the door, don't you go through it? Particularly when you turn around and see there's a line forming behind you? You can't stop reaching for mystery.

(*During this,* ADAM *climbs into bed behind* JANE, *his uniform still on.*)

Roy: You can leave. You can put your hands in your pockets and just go home.

Oppenheimer: I know you now.

Roy: I carried the mattresses.

Oppenheimer: Yes. *Yes.* You helped me that day. You had such faith.

(Roy *looks at* Oppenheimer *for a beat, then crosses to his house and enters. He turn on the TV, keeping the volume low. The music for* Jackie's *program begins.* Roy *sits down.* Oppenheimer *lights a cigarette, turns and exits, coughing.* Jackie *enters the TV studio, carrying a Bible. She is in the same clothes. She motions for the booth to cut the music. She addresses the audience, not the camera, and doesn't sit in her chair.*)

Jackie: I'm unprepared. This won't be a lesson. For those of you who got out your world maps, I'm sorry—I don't want to talk about history tonight . . . or prophecy.

(*Jumping to something she knows, reading.*) *Matthew.* "And in the fourth watch of the night, Jesus went to them, walking on the sea. When the disciples saw Him walking on the sea, they were terrified, and said it is an apparition and cried out for fear. Thereupon Jesus spake to them, saying, 'Take courage, it is I. Be not afraid.' And Jesus called to Peter, saying, 'Come, Peter, come.' So Peter came down out of the ship, and walked on the water, to go to Jesus. But perceiving that the wind was strong, he began to sink, and cried out, saying 'Master, save me.' And Jesus immediately stretched forth His hand and took hold of him, saying, 'O ye of little faith, why didst thou distrust me?'"

I've been thinking a lot about Peter. Out in that boat.

I had to sit somewhere last night and wait. There was nothing else I could do. It seemed I had done everything I could do, and it wasn't enough. I'd never had a time quite like that. I guess I'm inexperienced.

I got into this because I was touched a long time ago by a human life, by the life of one man, Jesus. He was the first really friendly person I ever met in the Bible, and I felt I knew Him. I never really understood the mystery of His life, I never really figured out, even with all my study, how He could die for my sins. And, frankly, no one has ever really explained to me how that really works. But now, even talking about it in front of all of you—I feel very moved.

I think we're the brightest animal that God made. In fact, we're God's spoiled brat, sometimes. We're so smart, so bright, so intelligent that we don't *think* we believe in anything anymore. We *think* we don't have any faith. The one thing that most people do have faith in is how much faith they *don't* have.

So . . . where was I? Peter, yes. (*Reading from the Bible.*) "So Peter came down out of the ship, and walked on the water, to go to—" (*She stops for a second, looking hard at the page.*)

Peter "came down out of the ship" and he "walked on the water." Maybe it was only a couple of steps, but he "walked on the water." Peter walked. He was *walking* there . . .

(ROY *crosses to the TV.*)

JACKIE: So how much faith do we need?

(ROY *turns the TV off.*)

JACKIE: How much faith do we need?

(ROY *sits in the recliner.* JACKIE *exits. After a beat,* JUSTIN'S *toy is thrown up on top of the mattresses, then the Ivory Snow box.* JUSTIN *appears, climbing up. He arranges the Ivory Snow box so he can see the picture, then lies down on top of the mattresses and goes to sleep.* RAMONA *enters from the back of her house, talks to* ROY.)

RAMONA: I thought you were laying down.

ROY: Couldn't.

RAMONA: Grocery store's open late tonight. We could get a head start on the week.

(ROY *gets up numbly.*)

ROY: Okay.

RAMONA: Roy, please. It's like living with a dead person.

ROY: I'm sorry, baby.

RAMONA: Roy, we just had a bad time. Everybody has them, sometimes. (*She embraces him.*) Lookee here—bet you thought I forgot this one.

(RAMONA *sings and rocks* ROY. JANE *gets up out of bed and goes to the mirror, leaving* ADAM *asleep.*)

What a fellowship,
What a joy divine,
Leaning on the everlasting arms.
What a blessedness—

(ROY *stops* RAMONA.)

ROY: No more.

(*Phone rings.* RAMONA *answers it.* ROY *puts his glasses on.*)

RAMONA: Yes. No, not today. Oh no. Oh, don't. Don't Of course I will. Yes. (*She hangs up the phone.*) He's been lost before.

ROY: Who?

RAMONA: Little boy. Justin. But he always comes *here*.

ROY: Oh, that little boy.

RAMONA: Every day he comes to see me.

ROY: Oh baby, he'll be all right.

RAMONA: It's just so late, Roy. That was his mother on the phone—she's home for once. She was crying.

ROY: It is late. Well, they'll call the police.

RAMONA: She said the police are looking. They've been looking most of the day.

ROY: They'll find him. They're experts at it. Those guys know what they're doing.

RAMONA: Roy, you always say that.

ROY: I do? (*Pause*) I do.

RAMONA: Yes.

ROY: I'll get the flashlights. (*He exits to the back of the house.*)

RAMONA: (*Taking the afghan from the back of the recliner.*) I'll take this—just in case he's gotten wet. I'll leave the TV on for him.

(ROY *returns with the flashlights.*)

ROY: We'll have better luck if we split up.

RAMONA: Outside . . . by myself . . . in the dark?

ROY: I know, baby. What's his name again?

RAMONA: Justin.

(*They go outside.*)

RAMONA: It's so dark, Roy.

ROY: I know.

RAMONA: Well . . . you go that way. And I'll go this way.

(*They separate.*)

RAMONA: Oh Roy, tell me we're gonna find him.

ROY: We'll find him, baby.

RAMONA: Do you really believe that?

ROY: I have to.

(*They exit calling* "JUSTIN!" *Not moving from the mirror,* JANE *wakes* ADAM.)

JANE: Adam? Adam?

ADAM: What? Are you all right?

JANE: It's so cruel, Adam. My body doesn't know. Everything is working the way it should. It's just going on, as if everything was fine.

ADAM: Maybe you should've stayed at the hospital.

JANE: (*She crosses to the window.*) Hold me.

(*He comes to her, embraces her from behind. His hand touches one of her breasts.*)

JANE: It's so amazing, Adam. I have milk.

(*After a beat, they exit. The sound of birds just before dawn.* JUSTIN *wakes up on the mattresses. He climbs down. As he takes down his toy, it breaks. He hears someone coming and crosses away from the sound.* OPPENHEIMER *enters, crosses to him.*)

OPPENHEIMER: Are you lost, too?

(JUSTIN *turns, nods his head yes, and hands* OPPENHEIMER *his broken toy.* OPPENHEIMER *sees immediately what's wrong with the toy.*)

OPPENHEIMER: I see. (*He fixes it, hands it back to* JUSTIN.) How's that? (*The door of the control shed opens, spilling its light onto the stage.*) Oh thank *God*! (*He runs toward the door, stops, and looks back at* JUSTIN.) You'll be all right.

(OPPENHEIMER *exits into the control shed. The light is shut off with the closing of the door.* JUSTIN *looks after* OPPENHEIMER, *then lifts his toy into the air and flies it as he exits into the dark, making a flying noise with his breath.*)

JUSTIN: WHOOOOOOOOOOOOSHHHHHHHHHHH.

*END OF PLAY*

Len Jenkin

# *Kid Twist*

LEN JENKIN'S works for the theatre include *Limbo Tales, Dark Ride, My Uncle Sam, A Country Doctor,* and *American Notes*. Mr. Jenkin has received three OBIE awards, as well as grants from the National Endowment for the Arts, the Rockefeller Foundation, and the New York State Council on the Arts. His novel, *New Jerusalem,* was recently published. Mr. Jenkin also has written for television and film.

*Kid Twist* was first presented by the Mark Taper Forum theatre in Los Angeles at the Las Palmas Theatre in 1979. The cast included Todd Susman, Vincent Schiavelli, John A. Neris, Martin Azarow, Jeff Chandler, Kim Miyori, Jenny O'Hara, Tony Abatemarco, Michael Tucci, Regina Baff, Herb Voland, and Raymond Singer, David Schweizer directed the production.

*Characters*

SARGE
PUGGY
BIG SID
JAKE THE PAINTER
KID TWIST
BABYFACE
GOLDIE
THE JOKER
BABE RUTH
CAPTAIN PRUSS
THE RABBI
THE REPORTER
THE D. A.
FINKLE
PITTSBURGH PHIL
SHIRLEY RELES
EXTERMINATOR
THE WARDEN
LAE-LIN
MAN in Santa Claus suit

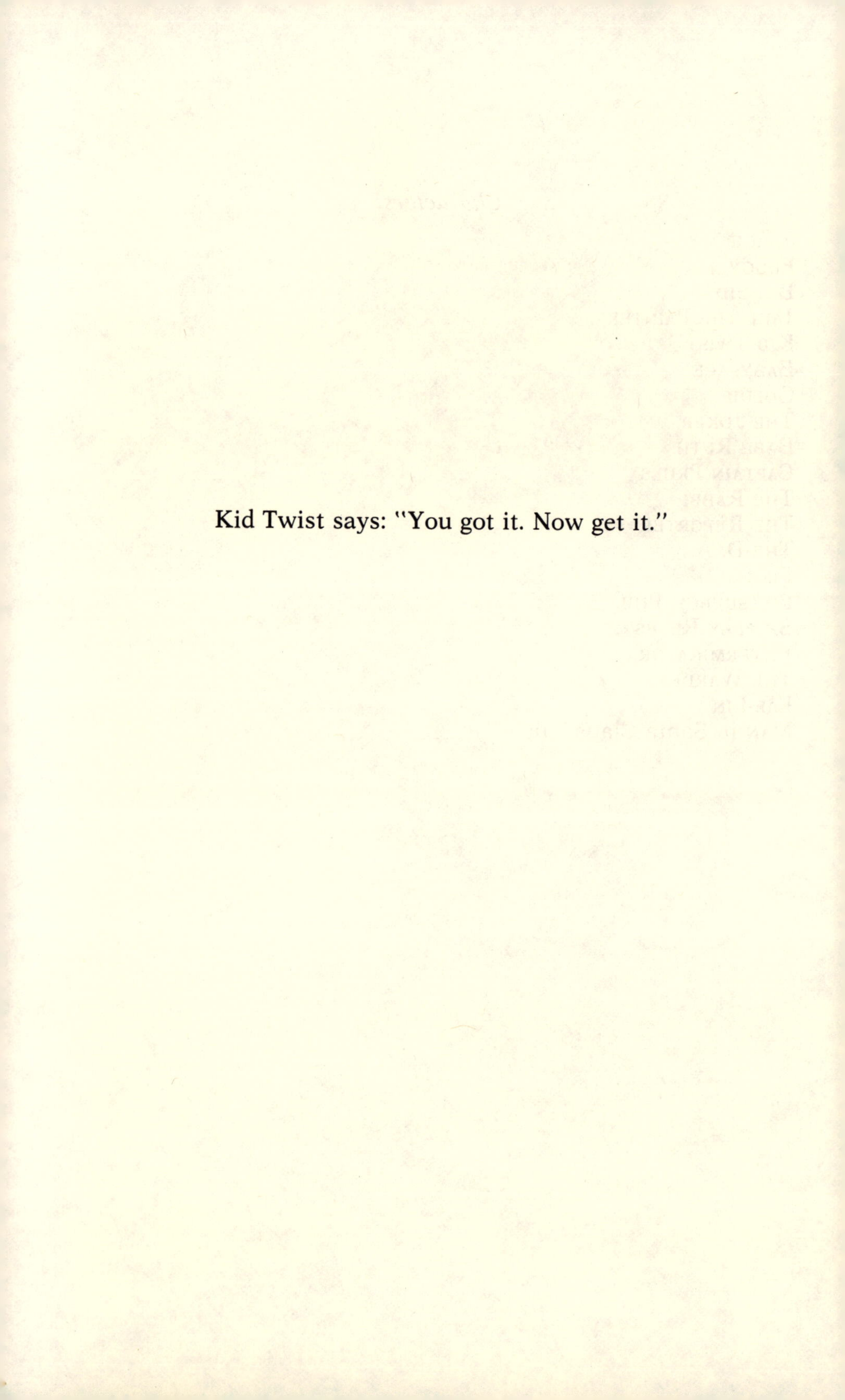

Kid Twist says: "You got it. Now get it."

# Testimony

(*To be heard over speakers in the theatre before the house lights go down. . . .*)

Q: Mr. Reles, did you kill a labor delegate named Seligman?

A: Yes. In 1933 or '34, I think.

Q: And can you tell the jury the circumstances here?

A: It was an easy pop. I follow the guy into the movies. The picture is *Each Dawn I Die.* Dorothy Lamour. The guy takes a seat in the last row. I grab the fire-ax off the wall and sink it in the guy's head in the dark. He makes a big noise. Everyone starts to run outta the theatre. I just run with them. It was a natural.

Q: Did you kill a man called John DeStefano on Columbia Street?

A: John the Polack. I was a party in it. There were two of us pulled triggers.

Q: And how did this take place?

A: We were looking for John the Polack. We got this shotgun which me and Phil take out to the lots in Canarsie, by the Gowanus Canal, and try it. Both barrels work real good. We wait in a car down the block from his house, and the bum comes walking up from the subway. Phil steps out with the shotgun. I pick up my pistol from the seat next to me with my right hand, and steer with my left. I'm moving and I'm shooting at him through the car window. Then Phil comes up behind him and blasts away at the top of his head. It sounds like a car backfiring. The bum drops. There is an old lady sitting on the stoop of a house. No doubt, she sees what happens. She let out a yell.

Q: Did the defendant have blood on him?

A: I didn't see any.

Q: Harry Straus, who you call Pittsburgh Phil, the defendant, was with you in the car?

A: Yeah.

Q: Did you notice blood on his clothes?

---

A: How could I drive the car at eighty miles per and notice Phil's clothes at the same time? I told you. He was there.

Q: Are you acquainted, Mr. Reles, with a place called the Frolics Club?

A: Yes.

Q: And with the owner of that club?

A: Yeah. It's Moey Dimples joint.

Q: Do you know a man named Rudnick who was killed in that same Frolics Club?

A: George Rudnick. In a card game. He was playing cards in the back room where I took him. I shot him. And we drag him out to the car.

Q: Tell the jury, please, who was with you at the time.

A: The Dasher Abbadando, and Dukey Maffetorre, and Phil.

Q: Was there any difficulty putting Rudnick's body in the car?

A: He's too long. Dasher crumples him up, you know, makes the guy shorter, and the guy gives a little cough. And Phil says "This goddamn bum ain't dead yet." Phil begins punching the guy with the ice pick. The blood comes out. Then Dasher and me shove him down so you couldn't see him from the window when the car is moving.

Q: What kind of car was it?

A: A black Buick.

Q: And who prompted you to murder Mr. Rudnick?

A: Lep.

Q: Who is Lep?

A: His name is Lepke. We were doing Lep a favor.

Q: This is Louis Buchalter?

A: Yes.

Q: You are part of his operations?

Q: We got connections. Where they count. We work with Bugsy Seigel in California, with the Purple Mob out of Detroit, and with Lepke and the troops he's got.

Q: Troops?

A: Yeah, like the Boy Scouts, only different. We are with Charley Lucky, with the Jersey troop too, and with Cleveland. All over.

Q: Who else in New York are you connected with?

A: Pittsburgh Phil and me go out, social, we meet guys—Shimmy Salles, Charlie the Bug, Mendy. Joey A., too. Adonis. He's with Anastasia in Brooklyn. The time the war is on with Waxey Gordon's mob, me and Phil were bodyguards for Joey A.

Q: When Rocco Morganti was killed, you killed him, didn't you?

A: I helped. I was part of it.

Q: And this was in your apartment?

A: Yes.

Q: Tell the jury what went on in that living room.

A: Once we got him in there, I put the radio on a little louder, 'cause the bum is making noise. I go for the rope, I got back over to the couch with it, and Phil is laying over him so he shouldn't move. Bugsy is hitting him to make him quiet, pounding him. Bugsy holds the head up so me and Phil can get the rope under. We twist it around good, and then we tie him up in a little ball. I know we gotta burn the bum so nobody will know him, so I tell Bugsy to go get some gas. He comes back with the can, and we go down along Flatlands Avenue to the garbage dumps. Bugsy throws the body on the lot. He pours the can of gas on the stiff. Then he puts a match on it. Nobody know the difference if you put a match on him there. The dumps are always burning.

Q: Mr. Reles, in any of your associations, did you ever hear the term Murder Incorporated?

A: Are you kidding? That's a name to sell papers.

Q: Tell me, Mr. Reles. You're a human being. How did you conceivably justify your participation in so many hideous crimes?

A: I wanted to eat steak and drink champagne and go to Florida.

Q: Did you realize, when you were committing these murders, that when you did so you were facing the electric chair?

A: If I was caught, I was.

## Act One

(*Darkness. Suddenly a white curtain, very brightly lit. On the curtain are lines for height measurement. The voice of* SARGE *come out of the air.*)

SARGE: (*Voice*) You are here. Grand. Most people don't show. Every minute of every day they're robbed, raped, and murdered and they don't show up to help their local lawmen locate the one who makes it happen, the one we're all here to identify: the guilty man.

(SARGE *appears. He is a New York City policeman, but is not in uniform. He is heavyset, fifties, white hair, beat-up suit, small gold badge. He wears a gun in a shoulder holster under his suit jacket. He is off to one side, facing the stage, out of the bright light.*)

SARGE: (*Continuing*) We got 'em. We got a lot of 'em here in the holding pens. We got 'em in cages right down below the floor.

(SARGE *stamps loudly on the floor. A sound like the growling of hundreds of apes rises in response.*)

SARGE: (*Continuing*) But if we don't discover what they're guilty *of*, we can't hold 'em. Away they fly, over the roofs of your houses, over the Canarsie flatlands, out over Sheepshead Bay. Then they wheel around over the ocean and come back to me, some of 'em feet first. (*Pause*) Let's start the parade. Wake up. Open your eyes. Look 'em over. (*Calling offstage*) First man.

(*A fat man in a rumpled suit and tie, unshaven, comes blinking out into the light, stands against the curtain. As* SARGE *gives directions for movement, he follows them.*)

SARGE: (*Continuing*) Herman Feinstein. They call him Puggy. The light won't hurt you, Puggy boy. Shoulders back, head level. Suck in your gut. Look straight front. Is that him? Is he the one? Puggy's been here so often he thinks he's the captain. So long, Puggy. He won't work and we ain't found an excuse to fry him, yet. Next man.

(PUGGY *exits, and another man comes into the light. He is taller, and somewhat better dressed, though his suit is also dirty and rumpled.*)

Sarge: (*Continuing*) *Mister* Rosensweig. Stand up straight, you bastard. This ain't the street corner. These are Brooklyn punks, ladies and gentlemen, a bunch of live wires from nowhere. Looks like you been doing good for yourself, Sid. Picked you up for taking money from the girlies again. Turn around, Sid. Good. Just wanted to see the back of your head, so when they turn you over some day, I'll know who you are. Even if your face is gone. Next man.

(Big Sid *exits, and another man comes into the light, older and better dressed than the other two.*)

Sarge: (*Continuing*) Jacob Greenblatt. They call him Jake the Painter 'cause he worked once. He's a dope dealer and a boss of killers. He's been here before. Look him over. Jake needs a doctor, or a shot. Look at those eyes. He oughtta have a bullet between 'em. So long, Jake, Next man.

(Jake the Painter *exits, and* Kid Twist *enters. He wears a grey suit, dirty white shirt, no tie. He has dark hair, is of medium height, and is about thirty-five years old.*)

Sarge: (*Continuing*) This is him. Abe Reles. Kid Twist. Nice to see ya, Kid. How ya been? He's a killer. He's a singer. Look him over. He invented the tire iron, the baseball bat, and the freeze frame. He's clever, ain't you, Kid? Turn around, slow.

(Kid Twist *does not move in response to these orders.* Sarge *does not react to this but continues as if they were being obeyed.*)

Sarge: (*Continuing*) Chin up. Let 'em see your face, Kid. Your beautiful face. Let 'em see your eyes. What's your business these days?

Kid: I'm a luncheonette proprietor.

Sarge: Coming up in the world. Last time you was in here you were a soda jerk.

Kid: Don't fuck with me.

Sarge: That'll be all. Nice to see you, Kid, real nice. Next man.

(Kid Twist *does not move from stage center.*)

Sarge: (*Continuing*) Look 'em over. Next man. See the man who robbed you? See the man who murdered you? See anything you like? See anything you remember?

(*The white curtain behind* KID TWIST *disappears, revealing a sixth-floor room in the Half Moon Hotel, Coney Island, New York, late Autumn 1941. The hotel is on the boardwalk, and overlooks the beach, amusement rides, and the green sea. The room has no walls. Its window is at a height created in the space, like a windy tower or crow's nest. It is clearly defined, though not a physical "window." When someone on stage looks out this "window," he is facing the audience. The room has in it an unmade bed, a framed picture of a sailing ship, a radio, a small table, chairs, a hatrack. Each object is distinct and separate.*)

(*MUSIC NOTE: There is a radio in the room. The music is 1940s jazz, not big band stuff, but "hot," played by five men in tuxedos (probably piano, drums, bass, trumpet, and clarinet). They could be a live band with an old-fashioned microphone in front of them, or the music could be on tape. There can be more or less music in the play, depending on the production, but it can be thought of as adding texture or counterpoint in certain scenes, and as before and after sound. There could also be music in whatever (if any) intermission(s) the production discovers.*)

(*In the hotel room is the police officer called* BABYFACE, *half-asleep in a chair. He is big, young, and blond. He is in civilian clothes, small silver badge on his suit jacket, tie loosened about his neck. He carries a gun in a shoulder holster. The room is dimly lit. Perhaps the radio is playing softly.* KID TWIST *still stands facing the audience stage center.* SARGE *continues to speak.*)

SARGE: (*Continuing*) Relax, Kid, relax. Sleepytime. Sweet dreams.

(SARGE'S *voice fades to very soft as the* KID *turns and walks to the bed, lies down, and sleeps.*)

SARGE: (*Continuing*) Look 'em over . . . look 'em over . . . next man . . .

(KID TWIST *is asleep.* SARGE *enters the room.* BABYFACE *looks up at him. Dawn.*)

SARGE: How's he been?

BABYFACE: Nothing new.

SARGE: Any trouble?

BABYFACE: No trouble.

SARGE: He ain't crying in his sleep, is he?

BABYFACE: Naw. He likes sleeping.

SARGE: So do I, when I get the chance. It's been three years since I closed my eyes at night.

BABYFACE: If I was him, I couldn't sleep. I'd be afraid of the dreaming.

SARGE: You ain't him.

(*A nightclub singer appears in another area of the stage. This is* GOLDIE. *She is accompanied by the* JOKER, *playing a toy piano. The* JOKER *is as he appears in Batman comics: white face, green hair, purple suit and gloves.*)

GOLDIE: (*Sings*)
Wake up and live, what are you afraid of
Just follow through, show what you're made of
You got to get up and give
Give yourself a shake-up and you'll wake up and live.
Wake up and live—hey fella,
Find your place in the sun.
Wake up and live, say fella,
Just be a go-getting son of a gun
Wake up and live (etc.) . . .

(GOLDIE *and the* JOKER *exit.*)

(SARGE *goes over to the* KID *and begins to shake him.*)

SARGE: Wake up, Kid. Rise and shine.

KID: Get your hands off me. (*He sits up, then gets up, begin to comb his hair, straighten his clothes.*) Hello, boys. Have a nice night? Keep that one eye open so's I don't fly the coop in my sleep? (*Pause*) What's today?

SARGE: Thursday.

KID: Three more days in the beautiful Half Moon Hotel. (*Pause*) You ever rent a room here, Babyface?

BABYFACE: What I make, nothing's left to rent nothing. I'm a cop, remember?

KID: I remember. Listen, you kill enough people, Babyface, the Brooklyn D.A.'ll let you stay here for free. With two big strong protectors to make sure nobody hurts you. (*Pause*) Three more days of your fuckin' protection. Then I'm gone. It's gonna be Sunday. You can go to church instead of watching me. A Jewboy like me getting outta here on Sunday . . . whattaya think of that, Babyface?

SARGE: Kid, lay off. It's early.

KID: I'm going out of town. Nobody knows me, and nobody finds me. Ever. Whattaya think of that, hah? Talk, both of you. Make me happy. You ain't deaf.

SARGE: Keep it up, Kid, and you're gonna turn simple. I mean it. You ain't got far to go.

KID: I'm hungry. Where's Finkle?

SARGE: He'll be here. You know, Kid, I hear you look real peaceful sleeping. Like a baby, or a dead man—a dead millionaire, left his money to a home for stray cats, and died thinking about all those furry little bodies loving him for years and years.

BABYFACE: At least you don't sleepwalk. You ever see that? My little sister's a sleepwalker. I'd wake up hearing some noise, and think there's a burglar in the apartment, and I'd grab my gun off the nighttable and move real quiet to the door and she'd be standing there by the bathroom, her eyes wide open, dreaming. It was like having a ghost in the place. Her husband must be going nuts.

KID: That's real interesting. (*Pause*) Don't you guys ever watch each other sleeping? I ain't that beautiful.

SARGE: We don't sleep on the job. Every man sleeps on his own time. We're on your time, Kid.

KID: Not for long. I give this last testimony, and it's all over. Every drop of blood—I told 'em where it fell, and who was watching it fall. I told everything I ever done. I told it to the D.A. I told it to the papers. I told it to Phil's jury, I'm gonna tell the rest of it to Lepke's Grand Jury, and then I'm gonna go away where none of you bastards is ever gonna find me. You're gonna miss me, and then you're gonna forget me.

SARGE: Them guys you're giving speeches about, they remember. They get paid to remember.

KID: What the fuck am I supposed to do? Die?

SARGE: Some people would think so, yessir. (*Pause*) I like you, Kid, but outside this room your chances ain't good. You're a lot dumber than you look, ain't you?

Kid: Do I hafta tell you again why I'm simple enough to spill my guts all over New York? I woke up one morning and it occurred to me that my mouth needed exercise. I started talking and I'm still talking and now I'm almost done. I made up my mind.

Sarge: You're a funny guy. You do your talking, and Pittsburgh Phil takes a trip upstate. They burned him, Kid.

Babyface: Wasn't he your pal?

Kid: Yeah, he was my pal. (*Pause*) Now I wanna tell the two of you something important. I woke up a little horny, see. Whattaya say I slip each of you a fin and you get me a broad up here? You go down on Surf Avenue, and you say, "I got this friend up in the room at the Half Moon, see, and he's sick, so's he can't go out, but he's not too sick, you know what I mean. Nothing contagious." (*Pause*) Whattaya say?

Sarge: No.

Kid: Whattaya think? You think I'm Jack the Ripper gonna spill the whore's guts out over the floor?

Sarge: No.

Kid: I never come up on anyone if I didn't get paid. That's the truth and I been telling it. . . . I'll make it ten apiece.

Sarge: We don't take. Lotta guys like to get in here and say hello to you while you're sleeping. If we were taking, Kid, you'd be dead.

Kid: How much you make? How much you make for sitting on your asses here with me for fifteen months? You squares are a laugh. You get something extra, I get a piece of ass, and who gets hurt? You got kids at home. Don't you wanna bring your kids a little present, Babyface? A big bunny rabbit. Don't you wanna take a chance?

Sarge: You got funny ideas about chances.

Kid: You know, I like having you guys around to protect me, getting paid to see nothing happens to me. Keeping me happy. If I change my mind about going before this jury the D.A. is gonna hang the two of you up by your balls in a back room and forget you.

Sarge: We're not that easy to push. The D.A. ain't so big in this town.

KID: Yeah? With the press I'm getting him, who's bigger?

BABYFACE: La Guardia's bigger.

KID: That little guinea. That D.A. is a young guy. He's smart and he's square. If he keeps his nose open and keeps telling stories I can prove, he's gonna be mayor.

SARGE: Maybe. Did you dream another one of those funny dreams last night?

KID: Yeah.

SARGE: How was it?

KID: Funny. Some friends of mine were on the Hindenburg. They never been near a blimp. I musta read about it in the papers.

(*The figure of* BABE RUTH, *the* JOKER, *and* CAPTAIN PRUSS *of the Hindenburg appear, but in prison uniforms, with bars in front of them. The* JOKER *pushes* KID TWIST *violently at this group of "cellmates." He lands in the midst of them. The cops fade into shadow. A* RABBI, *bearded, wearing a prayer shawl and holding a large book, is off to one side.*)

PRUSS: Ah! The accused!

RABBI: At last. At long last. The Hesed. Number four.

PRUSS: (*To* RABBI) Quiet in court! We proceed. Babe, speak the words to him.

BABE: You got the nerve. You got the goddamn nerve, busting into a private little home like you just did.

PRUSS: A breach of good conduct. Where is your sense of the proprieties?

KID: Hey, I. . . .

PRUSS: Hay is for horses. This is not a barn. This is a cell. You've just been apprehended breaking into it. Babe has apprehended you.

BABE: Also, Mr. What's-your-name, it ain't friendly.

KID: I remember you guys . . . all of you. So quit kidding me, hah. I didn't pick this cell. And I'm gonna be out of it before I get usta your stink.

JOKER: You're making a grievous error, my good henchman. You seem to think we are joking. We are not joking. You have been apprehended, and you will be tried.

KID: Ain't it enough I'm in the fucking big house, you punks gotta mess with. . . .

PRUSS: Silence, please. Have respect . . .

BABE: Or we'll hang you up by your balls.

JOKER: Mein Kapitan, the charge.

PRUSS: Breaking and entering.

JOKER: Breaking and entering what?

PRUSS: Breaking and entering our happy home, Judge.

JOKER: How do you plead?

KID: The bulls threw me in here. "Row B for you, Kid" one bastard yells. I'm. . . .

PRUSS: Not guilty is the plea.

BABE: Not guilty?

(*The* JOKER *laughs.*)

PRUSS: First witness.

BABE: I saw him do it.

PRUSS: What did you see?

BABE: What he did.

JOKER: The decision of the court is that the prisoner, Abraham Reles, is guilty as charged. He is hereby sentenced to turn all his worldly goods over to the court, for distribution as the court sees fit. Babe, convert him.

(BABE *turns* KID *upside down, holding him in the air by his feet. Loose change falls out of his pockets onto the floor.* PRUSS *and the* JOKER *scramble about collecting it.*)

PRUSS: That will teach you not to break into jail again . . . at least without knocking. By the way, what are you in for?

KID: I don't know yet.

JOKER: Let's see what the grapevine says. . . .

(*A grapevine twists out onto stage, wraps itself around* JOKER. *He listens.*)

JOKER: It says you'll be with us for quite a while. It says you're a freshman, Kid, and graduation's a long way from here. But you can always drop out, Kid. Shhhhh. Remember, happy henchmen tell no tales.

BABE: Wanna hear what we're in for?

KID: Lemme think, willya.

BABE: I'm in for batting an eye. (*He laughs wildly.*)

PRUSS: I'm in for killing ninety-seven people, burning them, burning them to death with inflammable gas. . . .

RABBI: (*In his book*) The book of Splendour tells us that there was a great drought, and Rabbi Levi the Invisible ordered a public fast. The people starved, and still no rain came. Rabbi Levi said to God: "Master of the Universe, you sit alone on high, and you have no compassion for your children." Then the rain came, but Rabbi Levi became lame for the rest of his life. (*He turns to* KID TWIST.) I'm guilty of letting human souls slip out of God's hands. Help me. They'll set us free if you tell them, Abie. . . .

(*The* JOKER *interrupts the* RABBI *with laughter. . . .*)

JOKER: I'm in for dreaming, dreaming about Gangland. Ever been to Gangland, Kid? It's like Dreamland, but only for us. We'll go there together, Kid. Everything you want is there, in spades. Steaks, champagne, trips to Florida. The chorus line from the Frolics Club, Kid, all of them, crazy for you. All the Milky Ways you can eat . . . and nobody fucks with you, Kid—ever. They got nothing on you. Just *shhhhh,* and you're back on the golden streets, this time with the Joker. Remember the time I stole the Parachute Jump, Kid? Eclipsed the moon? Be my henchman, Kid. We'll have it all. Stick with the Joker. You wanna go to the Palace Chophouse for dinner, Kid? You wanna ride the Wonder Wheel?

RABBI: The Black Butterfly! Abie. . . .

(*Everyone but* KID TWIST *is gone.* KID *stands by the bars.*)

(*A phone booth glides onstage. In it, the* REPORTER, *suit and tie, pad and pencil. In his hatband there is a card which reads "PRESS." The* KID *does not react to his presence. He talks into the phone.*)

REPORTER: Morning Sun? Copy desk, and make it snappy. Copy? This Lulu? Hiya, honey. Lulu, take this for the early-bird, will ya. PRESIDENT WARNS NATION IS FACING WAR. Got it? Here we go. "Dateline, Washington. President Roosevelt declared today that our country may soon be forced, by the Nazi peril, into another war. (*Poetic*) Standing bareheaded on a windswept hill in Tennessee, near the Tomb of the Unknown Soldier, the President told a nationwide radio audience that the people of America believe liberty to be worth fighting for. And of liberty he said: 'This is the duty we owe, not to ourselves alone, but to the many dead who died.'"—Sure—I'm an American boy, sweetheart. My rifle's always ready.—All right, here's the rest of it. (*Takes a breath.*) "Speaking to prospective war mothers in the shadow of the Capitol dome, Roosevelt declared that the U.S.A. may once more have to pour blood, sweat, and tears into the trenches of Europe, till they're full right up to the tippy-top, an irrigation project causing European vegetables to grow in strange shapes through the following half-century." (*Pause*) Got it? You're damn right he did. Whaddaya think, I make this stuff up? I'm a *reporter*, honey. How about you and me for a little drinkypoo after your day in the salt mines? You got it. So long, honey, and see the chief gets that, will ya? . . . I know. I'll be there.

(*The* REPORTER *hangs up the phone. The phone booth glides offstage as the* REPORTER *rushes out of it and exits.* KID TWIST *grabs the bars of his cell.*)

KID: (*Shouting*) I wanna see someone! I wanna see a man about a dog! (*Pause*) I know what I'm gonna do. Hell ain't for Jews. You wanna know what I'm in for? (*Yelling through the bars again.*) I'm sick! I got cramps! These creeps are molesting me! Come on, dammit!

(*The* D.A. *appears. The bars are gone.*)

D.A.: Oooowee! You and me, Kid. We are gonna hang Lepke and his Park Avenue lawyers higher than a kite's ass. I'm gonna stick it right to him, and all his filthy flunkies. You know something, Kid? This city is gonna be clean again. It is gonna be clean. Decent people gonna have a chance for a decent life. Everything's gonna be coming up roses. (*Sings*) Zipadee doo dah, zipadee ay, my o my. . . . We gotta take care of you, Kid. You are a big witness. You are the biggest witness. This ain't no page thirty-two rape case. And I want you to notice, Kid, you ain't in jail. The prosecution on your case is pending. You hear that, Kid? Pending. That means it ain't yet. You are a free man, Kid. But you gotta be protected. We are gonna put you in a safe hotel with cops right in the goddamn room with you, twenty-four hours a day, make sure none of these bastards get any fancy ideas about my motherfucking witness. What a world, witnesses getting shot out from under me, crying shame the way these people flout the laws of God and man. Crying shame. Sworn to protect, that's me. Don't give a shit where the hammer falls. Let 'em all take their chance before God and the judge, I say. Let the innocent man have no fear, and let the guilty cringe and lick the boots of the prosecuting attorney. (*Pause*) Kid, you're all right. Tell me something. Why'd you call for me, the Brooklyn assistant D.A., and not the police, or the mayor?

KID: I hear you ain't interested in favors. I hear you don't owe nobody.

D.A.: You heard right. I'm honest, and I'm one of a goddamn few, let me tell you. You wouldn't believe the amount of graft that comes through this office. It's a river, a godalmighty ever-flowing stream of blood money. And there are people in this very building who are swimming in it like drunken fish.

KID: Put me in a safe place. Some people are upset with me.

D.A.: All right. I'm gonna get you three squares a day. I'm gonna get you twenty-four hour protection. You got a hotel you like, Kid?

KID: Put me in the Half Moon, out in Coney Island. I can look at the water.

D.A.: Room with a view, hah? All right. You ain't gonna be able to get around much till these trials come up, a few weeks, a month. The law grinds slow sometimes. We gotta get this thing up before a judge who doesn't owe the bookies anything, doesn't play with the girlies . . . and then we'll think about you, Kid. You got a bad record, Kid, but we'll see what we can do. (*He starts to leave, then turns back toward* KID TWIST.) Reles?

KID: Yeah.

D.A.: I'm sticking my neck out pretty far on this. If I don't get convictions, I am up shit's creek without paddle number one.

KID: You'll get 'em. I'm the best witness you ever had. Anybody ever had. I seen it all. I seen it all, ever since I was born. You'll be all right, pal. I'm turning all the cards face up.

(*The* D.A. *exits. The two cops are back in the light.*)

KID: (*Looking up from the newspaper.*) There's been nothing about me for days. You guys hushing it up so all the fireworks go off at once, right up somebody's ass? Nothin' in here but LaGuardia's face, and the news about the goddamn war we ain't even in.

(*Sounds of knocking, from offstage.*)

FINKLE: (*O.S.*) Room service.

SARGE: It's Finkle. Let him in.

(BABYFACE *exits and returns with* FINKLE, *an elderly waiter. He is in uniform, a shabby waiter's jacket, striped pants. He carries a loaded tray.*)

KID: You got anything right this time?

FINKLE: I got everything right. One steak, medium-rare, two poached eggs on top, bagel with a schmear, three cups black coffee. It's all here.

KID: You boys take good care of me. I think about it when I'm eating. Finkle, send the bill over to the precinct with my compliments.

FINKLE: You're feeling good today, Kid. Got a good feeling about anything sepcial?

KID: Finkle, you owe me. Money. From yesterday.

FINKLE: Money? I don't got none of your money. Are you calling me a thief? Don't say it. Even if you think it, don't say it.

KID: Yesterday, remember. I took a horse with you, and I said "Gimme a slip" and you said, "It's you and me, Kid, both Jews. We don't need no slips."

FINKLE: I don't like to tell you, Kid, but you're losing your grip cooped up in here. I always give a slip. You think I can remember all the action I book every day? You don't got a slip, I don't got your money.

SARGE: Pay him, Finkle. We saw it.

FINKLE: You saw it. You saw it. You think I didn't see it? You think I'm blind? You think I don't remember a bet Mr. Reles makes with me? You think I wanna ruin my reputation around here? I gotta living to make. I'm just kidding him along is all. I figure he needs a little cheering up. Kid, here's your money. (*He hands* KID *a stack of bills.*) The losers pay for the winners, and the winners pay for the losers. I got a system. But no more races for you, Kid. You're too smart for the horses. You're a man got good feelings about more things than horses, and what you got, I can take it. I book 'em here in the Half Moon Hotel, on the boardwalk, along Surf Avenue, on Mermaid Avenue by the Gulf station, and down by the sea. (*Sings*) "By the sea, by the sea, by the beautiful sea. You and me, you and me, oh how happy we'll be. . . ." How do you like the Yankees today? You got a good feeling about Joe D.?

KID: It's almost winter. The baseball season's over. Besides, I'm from Brooklyn.

FINKLE: That don't mean anything. Lots of guys from Brooklyn.

KID: I'm a Dodger fan. I told you.

FINKLE: All right. Nobody comes to me looking for an honest wager and gets turned away. Not even you, Kid.

BABYFACE: Sarge, you gonna let this guy make book in here?

SARGE: Yeah. I'm gonna let this guy make book in here. The Kid ain't got that much to do.

FINKLE: Old Sarge puts something in with me a time or two I can remember. He don't hock the family jewels, but he puts something in.

BABYFACE: You know, Finkle, you shouldn't make book. Why don't you just work the room service, and take the money home to the old lady, hah?

FINKLE: Are you kidding, Mister? I got expenses. I got expenses you don't know nothing about.

KID: He's chasing chorus girls.

BABYFACE: I think, waiter, it's about time you disappeared. Come back lunchtime, hah?

FINKLE: You gonna arrest me? You start arresting people for taking chances, there ain't gonna be nobody left. Just dead meat. In the old days I deal them higher than a cat's back, and you can believe it or die. I'm still fast and solid. Kid, you read the papers, don't you?

KID: I read 'em. So what?

FINKLE: You think we're gonna go to war with the Nazis and the Japs?

KID: Yeah. I think so. I think we're gonna do that little thing.

FINKLE: Tomorrow?

KID: No.

FINKLE: Why not tomorrow?

KID: It ain't gonna be tomorrow.

FINKLE: What's with you? You think you can tell the future? You some kinda prophet like Moses? You want I should get you a booth down on the boardwalk?

KID: Get outta here, Finkle. I had enough with you.

FINKLE: I can tell the future. I got a system. Do you mind? You wanna play? I give you fifteen to one and I take us to call the Japs tomorrow.

KID: It would be stealing your money.

FINKLE: That's my business. You want the action or do I take it out on the street?

KID: Okay. Twenty bucks worth.

FINKLE: You got it. Lunch is the usual?

KID: Yeah. Wait a minute. I wanna slip.

FINKLE: A slip? Between you and me? Kid, I trust you. So long, coppers. (*He exits.*)

BABYFACE: It's just like robbing a crazy man. . . .

(*The cops move back into shadow as two men tumble onstage, fighting furiously with each other. They are* PUGGY FEINSTEIN, *whom we saw in the lineup, and* PITTSBURGH PHIL. PHIL *is big, and about 30. He's a sharp dresser. As they roll in, beating on each other,* KID TWIST *joins the pile, helping* PHIL *beat* PUGGY *down to the ground.*)

KID: Down! Down, you bastard. You wanna get somebody killed? Whatcha trying to do? Philly? Philly, you got the gun?

PUGGY: Gun? What the hell you need a gun for? I'm down here, ain't I? What the hell is this about?

PHIL: It's about nothing. We was just taking a walk, and saw you passing by.

PUGGY: Is this a fuckin' stickup? If this is a fuckin' stickup why the fuck don't you say, "This is a stickup?"

KID: Are you telling us what to say, Mister? That ain't friendly. Phil, where's the gun?

PHIL: In your pocket, stupid.

KID: It ain't in my pocket. You got it.

PHIL: Oh. (*Takes out a large gun, a .45.*)

KID: You brought that cannon. That cannon gonna make a big boom boom around here.

PHIL: We could say our car backfired.

KID: We could say we was hunting pigeons.

PHIL: American boys having a little target practice. Getting ready for the Nips.

KID: We can't shoot that thing in this neighborhood. Put it away, ape-face. We need something else to do the job.

PUGGY: Do the job! I'll do the job on you, you cocksuckers!

KID: Why don't you be quiet, friend. You ain't got a whole lotta time.

PUGGY: I got a request. I'd like to do one thing before you pop me.

PHIL: What's that?

PUGGY: Fuck your mother.

(PHIL *kicks* PUGGY *in the face and belly.* PUGGY *screams, then quiets.*)

PHIL: Ruined my goddamn shine.

KID: Shaddap, stupid. How we gonna croak this fuck?

(*From the shadows behind* PHIL, PUGGY, *and the* KID *steps* BABE RUTH. *He wears his 1927 New York Yankees uniform, and has a baseball bat over his shoulder.*)

BABE: Hiya boys. Maybe I can help you out.

KID: It's the Babe! Hiya, Babe! I thought you retired.

BABE: Naw, Kid. I'm still around when you need me. Here. Take this.

(BABE *holds his bat out to* KID TWIST, *who takes it.*)

KID: Gee, thank, Babe. You know I was always a fan of yours, even though I root for the Dodgers.

BABE: I'm just glad to help, Kid.

KID: God that was a great game, Babe, when you smacked those four homers.

BABE: That's the same bat I used against the Athletics in that ball game, Kid. It's yours for keeps.

KID: Jesus piss. Thanks, Babe. I don't know what to say.

(KID *takes a few practice swings, then suddenly turns and smashes the bat down into* PUGGY'S *head. It comes up bloody. He smashes it down again.* PUGGY *screams.*)

PHIL: It's going, going, gone! A grand slam over the center field fence!

(PUGGY *is dead.* PHIL, *the* KID, *and* BABE *stand over the corpse. The* JOKER *appears, circling around them, grinning. He and the* BABE *are gone.*)

PHIL: Puggy makes a nice stiff, don't he.

KID: It ain't so funny.

PHIL: All right. It ain't funny. Let's you and me get some Chinks, hah?

KID: Every time we make a hit you wanna eat chow mein.

PHIL: So? So I wanna eat chow mein. So what?

KID: I don't know what. It's funny, that's all.

PHIL: Let's go.

(PHIL *exits.* PUGGY'S *body is gone. The* REPORTER *enters with his phone booth.*)

REPORTER: Hello, Copy? Sharpen your pencil, Peaches, 'cause I got the word, and I'm gonna put it in your pretty pink ear. Umm. . . . Don't remind me, sweetheart. . . . Here it is, and they can have it with their roll and coffee. (*Pause*) FEINSTEIN FOUND DEAD, SUSPECT GANGLAND SLAYING. Dateline, Brooklyn. The body of Herman "Puggy" Feinstein was found near Cropsey Avenue under the IRT Elevated Line early this morning. The rosy fingers of the sun had just glinted their first glint off the tracks, when . . . (*Pause, for interruption.*) I know, Peaches. I ain't thrilled either. It's the third one this week. Hey, it sells papers. (*Pauses, then continues.*) . . . when the local milkman discovered the body, which had multiple stab wounds in the chest. Officers of the fourteenth precinct suspect foul play. Mr. Feinstein was an unemployed construction worker. Services will be held tomorrow at Synagogue Beth Shalom on Eastern Parkway in Brooklyn. Got it? (*Pauses, then continues.*) You get used to it is all . . . There's more innaresting things than that I'd show you, if you'd gimme the chance. Love it! Oh yeah. Honey, better take this too. It's about a three-liner.

(*The* REPORTER *appears to be making up the following news item as he goes along.*)

REPORTER: "HINDENBURG TO ARRIVE SHORTLY. Dateline, Lakehurst, New Jersey. The arrival of the Graf Zeppelin Hindenberg is awaited eagerly here by hundreds of well-wishers gathered in the Happy Landings Canteen. Presently over Brooklyn and halted by strong headwinds, the Hindenburg is due to dock sometime within the next three days." Finito. And if that seems a little brief, honey, it's 'cause I never made it out to Jersey. Tell the chief I'll be there when the damn thing touches down. (*Pause*) Don't worry your beautiful little head about it. That's why they call me Seymour Scoop. See ya later, Kiddo. Don't take any wooden nickels.

(*The* REPORTER *exits.* SARGE *comes forward.* BABYFACE *brings in coffee. He and* SARGE *pick up newspapers.* KID TWIST *moves to the window.*)

KID: How the hell they ever build that boardwalk? Miles of fence to keep us outta the sea. (*Pause*) It's wood. I got a splinter in my heel to prove it. (*Pause*) Lookit them old people down there, sitting. They think the sun can burn away the years. Hey, lady! You can't get a tan in your wrinkles. When they smooth you out at the funeral parlor you gonna look like a Jewish zebra! (*Pause*) I can see the sun, and the afternoon moon, and the sea. All the light in the world is always coming up outta the sea in a grey glow. That sea holds the fish in its belly. If it wasn't for the sea the fish would jump over the world in big leaps, light shining outta their sides like they been simonized. OCEAN! That's nuts. I'm nuts. Ocean! . . . Don't you wanna be friends? You big blind bastard. I wanna give you something. I wanna give you my shirt. (*He takes off his shirt, and crumples it into a ball, ready to throw.*) I can't throw that far. If you want it, come and get it. There's gonna have to be a flood to get you on up here to the sixth floor . . . a great flood. That's gonna make the old mommas jump, sitting down there in the sun with their eyes closed. When the salt water hits their feet those old eyes are gonna open to see that wave rising thirty stories over them and they're gonna call out for their dead husbands to come up out of graveyards in Queens and carry them over the flood. Look at 'em. They ain't got a dime, and no one wants to touch them, and they're hoping that nobody can take the sun, like they took everything else. . . . (*He turns away from the window, to cops.*) I don't know how to swim. Nobody showed me.

BABYFACE: Lots of people can't swim. If you don't learn when you're little, you never do.

SARGE: Bullshit, Officer. What I do, Kid, is be in the water just like the jellyfish. They don't need to know how to swim. They just ride in the waves.

KID: Sarge, I just remembered the dream I had last night, looking at Babyface here. I had a dream about your wife, Babyface.

BABYFACE: You fuck, you don't even know my wife.

KID: In the dream she had a sign on her, said "Babyface's wife." She was standing on the corner in front of Rose's candy store, and me and some of the guys are reading the papers. I'm drinking an egg cream and Phil is looking at the comic books. Rosie yells, "Hands off the funny books if you're not gonna buy." "We're good Jewish boys" we say to Rosie. "We'll show you. You see that shiksa out there, the one with the big boobs waiting for the bus to get her outta this neighborhood? We're gonna show how polite we are." Out we go and ask your wife to come inside. She gets a big smile on her face like she knows what's gonna happen. We take her into Rosies's back room in the middle of all the old newspapers. It's black dark in there once we close the door, and the guys are all around your wife, Babyface, and Phil is tearing at the front of her dress, digging out one of those big tits. Then I hear Phil scream and I grab for the lightstring and when I pull it I see that it ain't your wife in there with us at all, but a lobster, a real big one, all red and snapping her claws around. We are scared shitless and manage to get out, locking in the lobster. Rosie is yelling, "Where's that girl who went in with you?" That giant lobster is making a lot of noise back there, trying to get out so she can eat Brooklyn, but Rosie don't seem to hear it, and asks her question again. "Where's that girl who went in with you?"

BABYFACE: You're lucky that dream wasn't about my wife. You don't even know my wife.

KID: I ain't lucky. You gonna kill the state's number one witness for telling a dream? That dream was the truth. I dreamed it. The truth is all I'm telling these days. Listen to it, Baby-face. Ain't your wife the loud-mouthed blonde bitch who keeps yelling, "Why dontcha come home at night? These kids are driving me nuts. You're always down at the Blarney Stone drinking beer with fat Sarge and those other bums. If they wasn't police officers they'd be two-bit killers like Kid Twist."

BABYFACE: You scum. I'd like to bust your teeth in with my stick. I'd. . . .

SARGE: Quiet down yourself, officer. (*Pause*) Listen, Kid. Do you like me?

KID: I like you all right.

SARGE: Good. I want you to like me. We're pals. How do you like "Babyface" here?

KID: I don't know. I can't feel nothing about Babyface.

SARGE: You hear that, officer? Better do better. Better do better. We got a job here. A helluva job. We got to take care of this man. Officer, get yourself some coffee. You're falling asleep.

BABYFACE: I'm wide awake, Sarge.

SARGE: You call that awake? I call it sleeping, and it don't matter what you call it, 'cause you're talking in your sleep. Right, Kid?

KID: Sergeant, you never made lootenant 'cause you're fucking nuts.

SARGE: You know, Kid, I am gonna make lootenant one of these days. And even though I ain't a lootenant now, I know something. What I know is, we have to take care of you.

(SARGE, KID, *and* BABYFACE *in shadow.* GOLDIE *enters with* BIG SID. *She is in her early 20s, costumed as a nightclub dancer under her coat.*)

GOLDIE: Here's my little apartment, Sid, and thanks for taking me home. It's so rough at that place where I dance. A real gentleman like you, you can't imagine what those people say to me.

SID: I got an idea, honey. I got a spot in a club of mine. It's a nice place. No bums. Any guy gets fresh with the help I throw him out personal. The girl I got in there now ain't got your talent. You'd start at a hundred a week.

GOLDIE: Sid, honey, that would be wonderful. I could even send some money home to Mom.

SID: You like Big Sid, Goldie?

GOLDIE: Sure I like you, Sid. I like you a lot.

SID: C'mere.

(*They embrace. Kisses and rude fondling by* BIG SID. *He whispers something in her ear. She breaks away.*)

GOLDIE: You know a girl needs rules for herself in the big city, Sid. I've got three of them. No-nos. No questions. No favors. No credit. Maybe after I start dancing at that club of yours . . .

(*He grabs her again and she pulls away.*)

GOLDIE: Sid, please! Why don't you sit down and make yourself a drink. Lemme change, honey. I wanna get outta this costume, okay? I'll be back in a minute. (*She exits.*)

SID: Okay, honey. Make it quick is all.

KID: (*Moving into the light.*) Got your pecker up, Sid?

PHIL: (*Appearing behind* KID.) You got the itch, Sid?

SID: What the hell you doing here, you nickel hoods. You wanna see me, you see me downtown.

KID: (*Takes out gun.*) Shut up, Sid. Shut the fuck up. You understand English? Or you want I should say it in Yiddish?

SID: Kid, it don't gotta happen like this. We can change it. We can. . . .

KID: Enough, Sid. You said enough. I'm gonna shoot your prick off for you. I'm gonna shoot it off and serve it to you on a fuckin' plate. Or maybe I'll feed it to your mother. You got a mother, don't you, Sid? Or do I hafta go out onna street and get you one?

(SID *starts to respond.*)

PHIL: We heard your sweet talk, Sid. Not bad. (*Mimics*) Do you like Big Sid, honey?

KID: What were you gonna tell her so you could stick her, Sid? Were you gonna pay her two hundred a week?

(GOLDIE *returns. She has not changed clothes.*)

GOLDIE: Abe! Abe, you said you'd take him out of here.

KID: Shut up.

(PHIL *moves around behind* SID, *takes an ice pick out of his pocket, wraps one arm around* SID'S *neck, and with the other drives the ice pick into his back.* SID *struggles. Blood. The* JOKER *appears in the room. He grins.*)

PHIL: He's kicking me, damnit!

GOLDIE: You bastards. Not in here! He's bleeding. The pig's bleeding on the rug. You fuckers. I'm getting out of here.

(*She runs for the door. The* KID *grabs her.*)

KID: No you don't. Philly, let him go.

(PHIL *lets* SID *drop to the ground. He looks up at the* KID.)

SID: Kid, lemme off, hah. Anything you want. . . .

KID: You're still thinking you won't have to pay. Who'd hire me, Sid, if you don't wake up dead tomorrow? So long, Sidney. You shoulda been a tailor, or a grocery guy. . . . (*He kills* BIG SID *with two quick shots.*) Philly, get him in the car.

(PHIL *exits, dragging* SIDS *corpse.*)

KID: Goldie, get your coat. We're going out on the town after we drop this stiff. Come on, honey. You don't gotta ride with Sid. You can ride in the front. Phil don't mind dead company.

(GOLDIE *exits. The* JOKER *smiles in approval, and he's gone.* KID TWIST *remains, but moves into shadow. The phone booth glides onstage. As it does, the* REPORTER *rushes after it, and into it. He picks up the receiver and talks. He does not need to dial.*)

REPORTER: Daily Mirror? Copy desk, honey, and try to stick your plug in the right place. I always do. Hello? Mary Lou? That's right, and don't crack wise with me. I got it red hot and I want you to take it before it cools. Ready? "SIDNEY ROSENSWEIG FOUND DEAD. Suspect Underworld Slaying. The body of Sidney Rosensweig, president of local 62 of the Amalgamated Pants Pressers, was found early this morning in a sitting position on the doorstep of his fashionable home in Greenpoint, Brooklyn. He had been shot once through the right temple with a thirty-eight caliber revolver. Mr. Rosensweig was a universally admired and respected labor leader and a noted contributor to charitable causes. Mr. Rosensweig is survived by his wife, Stella, and two daughters." Finito. (*Pause*) Okay. Now I got another, Mary Lou baby, a real backpager.

(*The* REPORTER *appears to be making up the following news item as he goes along.*)

REPORTER: (*Continuing*) "HINDENBURG DUE TOMORROW. Dateline, Camden, New Jersey. Officials at the Happy Landings Canteen are preparing a welcoming dinner for the captain and crew of the mighty airship on its arrival. Skies are overcast, however, and the wind is from the . . . blah blah blah." Got it, baby? If the old man needs anymore, tell him to make it up himself. What? Radio play-by-play of the big gasbag coming down? OK, OK. I'll be live from Jersey tomorrow while it's happening. Tune me in, sugar. Nate Newshound, here and gone.

(*The* REPORTER *rushes out of the booth and exits as the booth itself glides off. The zeppelin Hindenburg enters. On board are Captain Pruss, the* JOKER, *wearing a flight officer's hat,* BABE RUTH, *the* RABBI, MRS. SHIRLEY RELES *(*KID'S *wife), and* GOLDIE. MRS. RELES *is a good-looking, plainly dressed woman of thirty. The* CAPTAIN *and the* JOKER *are toward the rear.* KID TWIST *looks up.*)

CAPTAIN: Right rudder, three degrees.

JOKER: Jawohl, Kapitan.

CAPTAIN: Check ascendancy.

JOKER: Asendancy rate zero, Kapitan. We are level!

CAPTAIN: Thank you. You can go to the lounge. Mingle. I'll handle this watch myself.

JOKER: Thank you, sir. (*He moves to the rear of the Hindenburg.*)

CAPTAIN: Ah, a glorious day. My ship sways gently, like God's pillow, in the fine air of the new world. America! The simple farmers look up, the laborers of the cities look up, and all fall to their knees as the great silver shoe glides above them. "Momma, what is that?" says an awe-struck child of Brooklyn. The mother answers: "It's Captain Pruss, child, guiding his ship through the day, and the night, and again into the sun." The swastikas on our underbelly wiggle waggle over America. (*He wets one finger in his mouth, holds it up.*) The wind is from the east. A light breeze as yet, but soon the hurricane, sweeping all before it into everlasting night!

(*He laughs manically, then gathers himself together as* BABE RUTH *enters the forward section of the zeppelin.*)

BABE: Captain, did I feel a shiver? A shake? I know I must sound nuts to you, but I've been wetting my pants all across the Atlantic.

CAPTAIN: My dear Mr. Ruth, the Hindenburg is the safest mode of travel known to modern man. In a few years, the air will be full of zeppelins, and they'll meet, a joyous congress in the sky, like stuffed animals in a child's bed. Why don't you go into the lounge, join the other passengers. We're over New York. I believe that's the Brooklyn coastline below. Look out the observation windows. A view of your homeland will calm your fears. We'll be coming in quite low, and perhaps the face of a friend will look up in welcome, a smiling blob of pink. Go. Remember, no smoking, except in the lounge.

(BABE *joins the others toward the rear of the zeppelin, the "lounge" where the* JOKER *is serving.*)

JOKER: Sir, there are five thousand cubic feet of highly explosive hydrogen just above your head. Intriguing, isn't it?

BABE: Whaddaya mean?

JOKER: (*To various passengers*) Mint? Cognac? Zigarette?

BABE: What would happen if this blimp caught on fire?

GOLDIE: Kaboom, sweetheart, Kaboom!

JOKER: Ah! Look below. The skyline of Brooklyn beckons!

BABE: Hey, there's Ebbets Field . . . naw, it's the little league park off Surf Avenue. Hey! The boardwalk! The parachute jump! There's the Wonder Wheel!

SHIRLEY: Lookit that ferris wheel go round. It's moving so slow. Now it's stopped. I'll bet there's two people stuck at the top, getting dizzy, wondering if the man running the wheel went to get coffee and they're gonna be hanging there an hour, scared to look down.

GOLDIE: He went to take a piss and he had a heart attack in the bathroom. He slumps down over the terlit and they're left hanging up there forever and ever, with nothing but each other, the sky, and the wheel.

SHIRLEY: Is that what you'd think if you were stuck on top of a ferris wheel?

GOLDIE: Maybe.

RABBI: (*Reading from his book.*) In the Book of Splendour we find that a Christian lady asked Rabbi Honi the circle maker, "In how many days did God create the world?" The Rabbi said, "In six days." She replied, "What has he been doing since?" The Rabbi answered, "The Holy One, blessed be He, is sitting and making ladders, so that some can go up, and some can go down."

SHIRLEY: There! There! That big pink building right on the boardwalk. That's the Half Moon Hotel!

ALL:(*In the lounge, pushing to the rail.*) The Half Moon Hotel!

CAPTAIN: (*Rushing back and pushing to the rail.*) The Half Moon Hotel!

SHIRLEY: That's where my husband's living while I'm away. Maybe he's looking up at us.

GOLDIE: What's your husband's name, honey?

SHIRLEY: Abe. Abe Reles.

GOLDIE: Kid Twist.

SHIRLEY: You know him?

GOLDIE: Everybody knows him. He's in the papers. I'm gonna wave to him. Hiya, Kid! And hello Brooklyn!

RABBI: Abie, be a good boy. I'm watching you from up here in the clouds. I'm saying prayers in the dark middle of the night for you. Keep singing, Abie. Keep on. . . .

BABE: Hey Kid! Kid! It's me! The Babe! Way up here in the sky! Kid, can you see me? Can you hear me? Hey, Kid, it's me!

(*The zeppelin Hindenburg exits. The cops come forward.*)

BABYFACE: Everytime I look at the paper I think I'm going nuts. Nothing but wars and murders. Or maybe the world's going nuts. I don't understand why all these countries don't just . . .

KID: It's a cinch.

BABYFACE: What's a cinch?

KID: It's a cinch. There's a new guy, this Hitler, who wants to take over, and push some people around. And some other guys are running the show, and they got some artillery to prove it. And the guys running the show scream bloody murder that the new guy is a fuckin' gangster. And then all of them go at it, and there's a few million schmucks caught in between, eating their shit as they go along. The schmucks don't have a chance.

SARGE: You think it's funny, don't you?

KID: Yeah. It's funny. A schmuck on the corner, works in a fucking button factory ten hours a day, and then goes out and gets his ass blown off by some other dumb schmuck he don't even know, and the pay is lousy.

SARGE: They all fall, Kid, sooner or later. Even the wiseguys. Lepke ain't a schmuck, is he Kid? He figured it all out, nobody could touch him. Now he's sitting up in Sing-Sing, scared to take a crap, along with all the other nickel hoods.

KID: Lep ain't no nickel hood. I ain't no nickel hood. I'm a businessman. Me and Phil and Dukey and Tannenbaum. We were in business. Like Meyer with the Italians, like Lep in the garment center, we sell a service. . . .

SARGE: You forget sometimes. You get noisy and forget—that all we gotta do to quiet you is look the other way. (*He moves to the window.*) Just watch the sand turning over in the wind. Just look at a place where two walls come together. (*He does so.*) Looking for spiders. (*He turns back quickly to* KID TWIST.) I'm still watching you, Kid. I'm watching you and I'm watching the door. But I'm feeling sleepy. I don't get no rest nights, even if I close my eyes. Insomniac, my wife calls me. Is that a nice name to call a person, Kid? I haven't been sleeping nights for years. Maybe that sleep will catch up with me. You know what happens if we fall asleep?

KID: You guys ain't getting yours to look away. You ain't like that. Besides, everyone knows it's you sitting here . . . so quit pushing me.

SARGE: What happens is that Little Moey or Izzy Cohen or one of the eye-talian guys comes through the door with a peashooter and says, "Here's a little something from Lepke, with his best regards." Some of them guys like to be funny. Do you like to be funny, Kid?

KID: You wouldn't tip me.

SARGE: Or maybe one of those cops who's doing ten for being on the take'll send a friend . . . or some judge who's scared you might say something about his trips to Florida. . . . Everybody out there loves you, Kid.

KID: You wouldn't tip me. You got your job to think about. You got families. I got a family. I got two kids. I'm going away. Soon, nobody hears me no more.

SARGE: Relax, dummy. We ain't gonna set you up. I'm just tickling you. To see if you laugh. Besides, I liked seeing Phil burn. I wanta see Lepke burn. He's gonna feel bad when they light up his ass like a neon sign.

KID: You two shits ain't supposed to be up here to fuckin' threaten me.

SARGE: Kid, you're taking chances. The officer here is sensitive. Don't get us upset, or some night we're all gonna fall asleep together like the three bears, and baby bear is gonna have a visitor.

KID: Bullshit. That ain't gonna happen.

SARGE: Poor Kid. He's talking big 'cause he's still scared we're gonna look the other way. Which way's the other way, Kid?

(*Cops move back into shadow as* MRS. SHIRLEY RELES *enters, along with a formica-top table, two chairs. Breakfast and a newspaper are on the table. She is in a bathrobe.*)

SHIRLEY: It's ready.

(KID TWIST *joins her at the table. They eat.*)

SHIRLEY: Abe? How come you always eat so fast? Look at you. I haven't even started. Don't you wanna taste anything?

KID: I taste everything. It's fine.

SHIRLEY: You always eat like you think someone is gonna sneak up behind you and rip the plate away.

KID: Maybe somebody is.

SHIRLEY: That's dumb. You're not a wolf. Why don't you eat like a human being. You think I like sitting here watching you?

KID: Do you? Do you like sitting there watching me?

SHIRLEY: No. I don't like it. It's like feeding time in Prospect Park. I want you to eat like a human.

KID: Shirley, you're making a lot of talk. I'm trying to be nice, but I get trouble eating when you're talking like this in my ear. (*Pause*) Did you see today where Phil got his name in the paper? They took him down for questioning, about some guy in the Bronx had an accident. Phil never been to the Bronx in his life.

SHIRLEY: Too bad the cops is always bothering you and Phil.

KID: I don't pay no attention to them. They don't like to see a Jew making good is all. If there was an earthquake they'd come find me. Pretty soon you'll see the papers: Abe Reles from Brooklyn starts World War Two. They know I got that luncheonette, they know I do good business. I gotta hang around there.

SHIRLEY: You gotta hang around there. Fine. Pretty soon your kids'll forget you're their father. You're never home. I'm sitting here at night listening to the dumb radio while you're out somewhere playing handball or something. I'd like to get out too, you know.

KID: You went to the movies with Helen just a few days ago. You told me all about the picture.

SHIRLEY: Three days ago you came home with Phil and *sent* me to the movies with Helen. You think that's how I wanna go out?

KID: We had business here. Important business. We hadda meet with a guy.

SHIRLEY: You hadda meet with a guy so I couldn't even stay in the next room, my own bedroom in my own apartment, 'cause you hadda meet with a guy. What do you think I am? (*Sound of knocking on the door, offstage.*) God. That must be some of your friends, Phil or Murray or somebody.

KID: Murray's dead.

SHIRLEY: You're funny, Abe. Murray sent you a letter yesterday. I saw it.

KID: Murray is doing twenty upstate. If that ain't dead, it's close.

SHIRLEY: What? You never said . . . (*Knocking again*)

KID: Will you see who it is, Shirley? And don't open if you don't know, even if they say it's for me.

SHIRLEY: All right.

(SHIRLEY *goes off to door.* KID *is nervous, picks up newspaper, reads. Sounds of voices, door closing.* SHIRLEY *returns, followed by the* EXTERMINATOR. *He wears a baseball cap, glasses, carries an exterminator's tools, and has his pants tucked inside his white socks.*)

SHIRLEY: It's the exterminator. I saw some roaches yesterday. He's only here once a month. I want him to spray.

KID: (*Still looking down at his paper.*) Send him away. He can come tomorrow, when I'm not here. I don't want some bastard in here squirting bug stuff all around where I'm eating.

EXTERMINATOR: Hey, buddy, you wanna have bugs in your food? I'm just doing my job.

SHIRLEY: He don't come back for a month.

KID: Then let him come back in a month, willya.

SHIRLEY: I want him in here now.

KID: Shut up. (*He turns and looks at the* EXTERMINATOR *for the first time.*) How come you got your pants tucked in your socks?

EXTERMINATOR: Ya see, before they die, the roaches get up a little extra energy, see, and they start crawling fast. Last little spasms. The bastards can go right up your pants leg. You know what I mean. They ain't so dumb.

KID: Get the hell outta here! Killing helpless little roaches. You murdering fuck! Get outta here!

(KID TWIST *gets up and pushes and pummels the confused* EXTERMINATOR *offstage. Noise of door slamming.* KID *returns.*)

KID: (*Continuing*) You shoulda seen him. He took off down the hall like a rabbit.

SHIRLEY: That was a mean thing to do.

KID: It was funny.

SHIRLEY: I don't think it was funny.

KID: Whatsa matter? You like the guy? You been making it with the exterminator? Once a month? First he kills the roaches, and then you can't think of a better way to thank him than by spreading your legs.

SHIRLEY: I'm not talking to you. I just can't talk to you no more. That's all.

SHIRLEY: Shirley, I'm sorry I said that. I'm in a funny mood. I ain't got time to keep talking to you right now. I gotta go. I'll see you later. (KID *picks up his hat and coat. There is another knock at the door.*)

KID: Shit. (*Calling to whoever is knocking.*) I'm coming out! Just a goddamn minute.

(KID *goes off, sound of door opening. The two cops,* SARGE *and* BABYFACE, *enter, pushing* KID TWIST *back into the room.*)

BABYFACE: Abe Reles?

KID: Yeah?

BABYFACE: You're under arrest.

KID: Under arrest? What the hell for? You guys come shoving in here, upsetting my wife, busting up my house. What the hell you doing here? What's the charge?

SARGE: You left your car in front of a fire hydrant. You know Mr. Reles, that's a serious offense. You're gonna hafta come downtown with us.

SHIRLEY: What are you saying? What *is* this?

SARGE: Let's go, Kid.

(*The two cops leave, dragging* KID *with them.* SHIRLEY *cleans up dishes, begins to sing a bit to herself. Then she, table, and chairs are gone. The* KID *and the two cops emerge from shadow.* FINKLE *enters, carrying a tray.*)

FINKLE: Lunchtime! Cheese blintzes, applesauce, sour cream, a tuna on rye, butter and no lettuce, black coffee, and a pack of Philip Morris. Perfect. Perfect.

KID: Finkle, save the speeches and just put it down.

FINKLE: I'm saying things you wanna hear. I owe you money. You took me big yesterday, Kid. I thought Roosevelt would be over there in Berlin by now, playing on his trumpet. No guts. The people in this country is chicken to fight. They got it too good is all. Well, you dope something wrong, you gotta pay. (*He pays* KID.) Listen, Kid, you're leaving after tomorrow. I'm gonna miss your action, so I got something good for you today. You wanna piece of a five hundred-to-one shot? Long shots are my specialty.

KID: No thanks, Finkle.

FINKLE: Whatsa matter? You think my prices are off? You wanna deal with Willie the Worrier or the Pig from Bensonhurst? Those guys don't make book. They just know how to rob people. I make long range . . . long-range bets. It's a long time sometime before I collect. Years. How's the ocean look to you today, Kid. Look powerful. Strong, like Babyface, here? Look. Look. Take a look.

(KID *looks out the window.*)

FINKLE: The tide, is it high or low?

KID: I can't tell.

Finkle: I can tell. I live here all my life. I know the Coney tide better than the moon. You know what's gonna happen? There's gonna be a high tide. A real high tide. My figures don't lie. I know this ocean. Gonna be a record high tide here on Coney's island. Think so, Kid?

Kid: I don't know.

Finkle: That tide's gonna sweep up under the boardwalk, carrying seaweed, and the wrecks of ships, and shrimps and whales, and it's gonna wash the sidewalk in front of this hotel. Then it's gonna slide into the lobby, kinda green, wetting the feet of the bellboys. That tide is gonna float fresh seafood right into those banquet rooms! It's gonna be another Titanic in here. Wanna bet?

Babyface: Sarge, don't you think we oughtta do something about this? I mean the old guy's gonna lose everything he's making on this job.

Sarge: The waiter can take care of himself without your help, Officer.

Finkle: Right, Sergeant. I do good, you better believe it. A man with a system has one up. All right, Kid. You think that ocean's gonna stay in its bed, don't you? You're scared to make a little wager, ain't you? I'll give you even money on the Red Sea opens up into the Half Moon Hotel today. You wanna go twenty, I'll put you down.

Kid: All right. It's your funeral.

Finkle: Don't say it, even in a joke. I'll be seeing you. Have my money ready tomorrow. Right now I got things to take care of. So long, coppers. Eat your lunch, Kid. It's not bad. The chef, he's into me for a few hundred. He fixes everything for you special.

(Kid Twist *turns to the window, looks out toward the audience. The two cops pick up newspapers, read.*)

Kid: Deep and dark out there. You could drown in it from here, take the waves in through your eyes. Glub glub. Hey—some kinda light, blinking. Don't want ships hitting rocks out there so they put a light on the sea. (*Pause*) Looks like it's moving. It's coming in to shore. Hey! Hey you, you come in here, you light, the ships won't see you. All you'll be good for is to warn sea monsters away from the land. We didn't put you out there to help sea monsters. You're a servant of commerce, Franklin D. Roosevelt, and Kid Twist. Stay out there.

(*A light grows brighter on the* KID'S *face as he looks out.*)

KID: (*Continuing*) Hey, that light ain't on the water. It's up above it. I know what that's gotta be. A flying saucer, and I'm seeing it. I bet it's from Mars. Hiya doing, boys. Long ways from home, hah? I been to Mars. It's another world, like this one, only there's red light on everything all the time and the people are kinda spidery and don't talk much. They make Mars candy bars up there, and then they ship 'em to earth. I'd steal them. I'd go into a candy store with Phil who'd start to mess up the comic books, and while Old Man Schneider was yelling, "Strauss, this ain't your library, straighten up them funny books the way you found 'em," I'd pocket the Milky Way. We'd go out onto the street and Phil is laughing and I got that ice-blue feeling in the center of my back. I'm walking slow and that feeling is turning the skinny white nerve that runs up my spine into ice, and I'm numb and light and we turn the corner and I unwrap the bar and bite into it while the red ball of mars still floats inside my skull. . . . Whoa . . . it's getting closer.

(*Light grows brighter on* KID'S *face.*)

KID: (*Continuing*) Them spider men is gonna take me away. Hey, what's my wife gonna think if I ain't here no more, hah? You can't take me. I got business. There's people waiting to hear me. I got things to do here on the green ball. Find another sucker.

(*Light grows very bright on* KID'S *face.*)

KID: (*Continuing*) It's close, like looking into somebody's apartment from the fire escape. Jesus. If my fucking Rabbi could see this, the old man would piss in his black drawers. Look at them in there! God Almighty, wouldn't you know—it's been heaven all along—

(*The* JOKER *appears suddenly, his face alone lit, as if floating in the darkness. Three distinct lights:* KID TWIST, SARGE *and* BABYFACE, *the* JOKER. *The* JOKER *laughs.*)

*End of Act One*

## Act Two

(*The* RABBI *appears. He wears a flat black hat, long black clothes. He is pale and bearded. He holds a lighted candle and a large book.*)

RABBI: Abraham Reles is again in the Half Moon Hotel. The wheel of his dreams spins about this center. As it spins it turns us round and through, back to the center and the dark eye in the center of the center. Does Kid Twist believe that if he confesses completely to us all, he will be healed in a way he cannot yet imagine? Does he want his revelations to transform his actions into tales, harmless stories that, with time, will become untrue? Why is he singing this song no one wishes to hear? Is Kid Twist the Black Butterfly? I must consult the Book of Splendour. Between the hairs of the beard of Macroprosopus, as always, lies the truth, and the truth of the truth. (*He searches through his book, then reads.*) Ah! Rabbi Hanan the Hidden has said: Whosoever destroys a single soul has destroyed a complete world. Whoever heals a single soul heals a complete world: stone and flowering tree, bliss and sorrow, water and blood. That man makes new the dung in the fields, and the blue blue moon. Hmmmm.

(The WARDEN *and* PITTSBURGH PHIL *enter.* PHIL *is in a prison uniform, the* WARDEN *in a suit and tie, with a flower in his lapel.* PHIL'S *last mile. The* REPORTER *and the* RABBI *are waiting along his route to the electric chair. The* JOKER *is working on the chair's wiring.*)

WARDEN: Last guy I took this walk with was a nigger. He didn't even know how to die. He sticks some other shine in a fight uptown, you understand. When he sees the chair he dances up to it, the old soft shoe, whistling and humming, calling to the chair, saying it's his "sweet chariot that's gonna carry me over Jordan." Then he sits right down in it, starts buckling the straps on himself, and yells, "Mr. Edison's rocking chair, fly me home." No dignity. Embarrassing. The press was present, you understand.

PHIL: (*To* REPORTER) You from the papers?

REPORTER: Yeah.

PHIL: Tell 'em. . . .

REPORTER: Yeah?

PHIL: Write I didn't cry or nothing.—Write it.

WARDEN: We understood you were of the Hebrew persuasion. A priest of your faith is on hand if you'd welcome any final consolation.

PHIL: Naw. It's too late now. So long, Rabbi, and thanks for coming anyway. Say hello to God for me.

JOKER: Step right this way!

(*The electric chair glides toward them. Behind it is the* JOKER*: electrician-executioner. The chair is old wood and rusted metal, straps and buckles, and a thick cable leading to an immense on-off lever which floats in the air above it.* PHIL *resists violently. He is grabbed and strapped in by the* JOKER *and the* WARDEN. KID TWIST, *the* RABBI, *and the* REPORTER *watch. The two cops emerge as well and observe. The* JOKER *throws the lever. Electric flashes, sizzling sound, sparks.* PHIL *is terrified. The chair seems to fizzle out, leaving* PHIL *dazed but alive. The* JOKER *shrugs his shoulders, begins to check and repair the chair's wiring.*)

PHIL: See, Kid, it don't work. They can't get the juice through my thick ass. Kid, it's gonna be all right. They wanna fry me, and they can't do it. Somebody must love me, eh Kid? I don't mind. I don't mind a bit. When they're done trying to juice me, let's go down to Chinatown and get some of that chow mein . . . whaddaya say?

(*Repairs completed, the* JOKER *throws the switch again. Much more violent sizzling sounds, sparks,* PHIL *twitching and jumping in agony.*)

PHIL: Kid! The sun's inside my head. Can you see it shining! Can you see it, Kid? See it! Here it comes!

(PHIL *slumps over.* PHIL, *dead in his electric chair, the* JOKER, *the* WARDEN, *the* RABBI, *and the two cops are gone.* KID TWIST *is present but barely visible. The* REPORTER *enters his brightly lit phone booth. He is already talking.*)

REPORTER: *Evening Star*? Yeah, gimme the copy desk. Hello? Sue Ann? She's on vacation this week? Well, who are you? Okay, Cheryl honey—I'm out here in Jersey, looking up. Yeah, for the big Nazi balloon. I'm patched in for the radio play-by-play? OK, I'll tell you when to switch me on. Meanwhile, sweetheart, another baddy bit the dust. Take this while it's hot, willya? PITTS-BURGH PHIL DIES IN CHAIR. "Dateline Oswego, N.Y. Harry Straus, alias Pittsburgh Phil met his death in the electric chair in Sing Sing prison today. He was a gangland enforcer who was put behind bars by the testimony of Abe 'Kid Twist' Reles, another notorious killer. Mr. Straus was calm and resigned throughout, and received the final consolation of his faith. The warden stated: 'I was sorry to lose him. Kind of death we like to see. Jews ain't all bad. Good pinochle player.' No relatives or friends of the deceased have as yet come forward to claim the body." (*Slight pause*) Howdja like to come on over to my place later? I got a fifth of Four Roses that needs emptying. (*He looks up as the Hindenburg enters.*) Switch me to live broadcast, honeybun, the damn thing's in sight. Am I on? (*Into his microphone*) Seymour Scoop, live from Lakewood, ladies and gentlemen, and here it comes. The mighty airship Hindenburg. And what a sight it is! Passengers are delightedly looking out the windows, waving and smiling. Captain Pruss is giving his crew final mooring instructions. (*Pause*) It's coming down out of the sky pointed toward us, the mighty propellers biting into the air. No wonder this great floating palace can travel at such marvelous speeds. The sun is striking the windows of the observation deck on the eastward side, and sparkling like glittering jewels on a background of black velvet. . . .

(*The* REPORTER *is gone. Aboard the Hindenburg are* CAPTAIN PRUSS, GOLDIE, SHIRLEY RELES, BABE RUTH, *the* JOKER *wearing his flight officer's hat, and the* RABBI, *who is with* PITTSBURGH PHIL. PHIL *sits dead in his electric chair.* KID TWIST *looks up. The cops are in shadow..*)

(*A landing party is in progress onboard. Drinks, streamers.* CAPTAIN PRUSS *is at the controls, singing* "Deutschland Uber Alles.")

(*The passengers begin to sing Spike Jones's* "Der Fuhrer's Face.")

PASSENGERS:
Ven de Fuhrer says, ve is der Master Race
Ve heil, heil, right in der Fuhrer's face
Ven Here Goering says, ve is a super race,
Ve heil, heil, right in Herr Goering's face!

BABE: Helluva landing party! Famous people on board. Me, for instance. And that's Pittsburgh Phil in the chair over there. He invented the ice pick.

GOLDIE: Phil ain't famous. He's a schmuck. Lookit that creep he goes around with now that he's dead.

RABBI: (*Holding large old book.*) The Book of Splendour tells us that the pious Rabbi Zelig of Pinsk set out for Hell to see what they were doing there. He came to a large gate, a demon opened it wide, and he entered and saw all the unimaginable torments of the damned. He turned to go, but the demon had locked the gate. Rabbi Zelig protested, saying he was a holy man, and had come only to observe God's justice. "I'm sorry," said the demon, "but I cannot let you out again—ever." Suddenly a great wind rose in Hell. Beelzebub, Prince of the Air, arrived, riding on the storm, to go out upon the Earth. The burning corpses shook and trembled like leaves. In the roaring of the wind of hell, Beelzebub opened the gate, and the Rabbi slipped out after him, and suddenly he was back in his study in Pinsk. The next day Rabbi Zelig noticed he had a cough in his chest. He had swallowed a little piece of the wind of hell. Day after day the coughing grew worse, until one day Rabbi Zelig's chest was torn apart by his coughing, and he died."

GOLDIE: You see, he's an old wise-ass.

SHIRLEY: I'd rather look at the sky and the ocean. It's more interesting than some people's smart remarks.

JOKER: I agree with you, Mrs. Reles. Potentially a very entertaining planet.

GOLDIE: The hell with all of you. We'll be coming in sooner or later. I better fix my face.

RABBI: Abie, look up . . . before the zeppelin eats the sun. Look up, into the light. . . . You're a good boy, Abie. Hesed. You can save us both. Sing! From the beginning, the *word*. . . .

ALL: (*Except* PRUSS *sing.*) Ven der Fuhrer says, ve is the master race . . . etc.

PRUSS: (*Sings*) Deutschland, deutschland, uber alles . . . etc.

(*The Hindenburg is gone. The* KID *stares after it. The cops come back into the light. A knock at the door.* BABYFACE *goes off to respond, gun drawn as usual. He returns.*)

BABYFACE: Kid, it's your wife.

(MRS. SHIRLEY RELES *enters.*)

BABYFACE: How are you, Mrs. Reles?

SARGE: How's tricks, Mrs. Reles?

SHIRLEY: All right, Sergeant. How's Abe?

Sarge: You should ask him, Mrs. Reles. He's right here with us.

Shirley: Hello, Abe, I brought some news. It's not so nice.

Kid: What is it?

Shirley: Your uncle. Your uncle Jacob with the place up in South Fallsburg where we usta go all the time . . .

Kid: Yeah.

Shirley: He died. Your uncle's dead, Abe.

Kid: That's too bad. That is really too bad. I liked him. We usta play pinochle. You know, he's the one who taught me how to play pinochle when I was little.

Shirley: Somebody shot him through the head. He was an old man. They went up there looking for you, Abe, and they found him.

Kid: Okay. Okay. I can't do nothing. Here I am. What am I supposed to do? You want me to kill some people when I get outta here, Shirley?

Shirley: I'm just telling you.

Kid: I'm leaving here, after tomorrow.

Shirley: I heard. It's in the papers.

Kid: Are you doing okay? You look tired.

Shirley: I'm all right. The D.A. calls me up. He says the same things you say. "How are you, Mrs. Reles? You okay?" You look lousy, Abe. You been sick?

Babyface: He's sick all right.

Shirley: Be quiet, you slob. Sergeant, can't he keep his mouth shut? Please have him shut it, or I'll put my shoe in it.

Kid: I'm coming home.

Shirley: What home? Did you think about me and the kids when you decided to get your name in the papers? What do you think you're coming back to, Abe? You think cause you gotta play hide and seek for the rest of your life, we're gonna play? We didn't do nothing, Abe. The kids didn't do nothing.

Kid: I'm coming home. You hear me. Then we're going away. I wanna sleep with you. I wanna sleep without dreaming. (*Pause*) Shirley, say something. I'm waiting. Talk to me. I'm gonna come home. You understand that. And you are gonna be there.

SHIRLEY: You're not gonna gorilla me, Abie. You're not gonna push me. (*She begins to cry.*) You always make me crazy. I'm not even unhappy. I feel so stupid.

KID: Stop it, damnit. If you don't stop that crying I'm gonna rip those eyes out. How you gonna cry then? How you gonna cry then?

(KID TWIST *suddenly grabs his wife, begins to shake her. The cops pull him off and hold him.*)

SHIRLEY: It's all right. It's all right. I came to tell you something else, Abe. The apartment's gone. I moved out. Some other people live there now. People you don't even know.

KID: Who are they?

SHIRLEY: It doesn't matter who they are.

KID: Who are they? What are their names?

SHIRLEY: Forget them, Abe. They didn't do anything. I did. I'm living at Esther's with the kids, and I don't want to see you.

KID: No. We're going away. I can't stay around here. We're going away.

SHIRLEY: You are, Abe. Without me.

KID: What is this? You're my wife, right? You know what I'm doing. You gotta know, I'd breathe in and the air would mix with me, and I'd breathe out, and you'd breathe it in. That's how we slept. Everyday. Day after day. You saw me.

SHIRLEY: I don't know, Abe. I don't know what's happening to you. You never told me. You never gave me a chance, and now I don't care. Let the world listen. I don't want to hear you.

KID: What do you want? You want a divorce?

SHIRLEY: I don't know what I want.

KID: Why the hell did you come here?

SHIRLEY: To tell you. I came to tell you.

KID: You told me. You told me, all right. Now get out. This is my hotel room. Get out.

SHIRLEY: Abe, I want. . . .

KID: I don't wanna hear it. (*He puts his hands over his ears.*) GET OUT. GET OUT. GET OUT!

(SHIRLEY RELES *exits.*)

KID: You see that? Did you see that?

SARGE: Yeah, we saw that.

KID: Can you believe these goddamn women? Can you believe it? She has two kids. Mine.

BABYFACE: You are lower than shit, Reles. That woman's more than you'll ever deserve.

SARGE: That's enough, Officer. It's a rough break, that's all.

KID: You don't know nothing about it. Nothing.

(SARGE *and* BABYFACE *pick up their newspapers, sit.*)

KID: You guys always read the papers while I'm awake. Whaddaya do when I'm sleeping? Whack off?

SARGE: We read your press clippings, Kid, and then we take turns watching you dream. (*Pause*) Kid, we're waiting. Let's hear last night's. Let's hear your next to last dream in the Half Moon Hotel.

KID: Last night in my dreams I was walking. I was walking down Pitkin Avenue looking to buy a suit, but I didn't care if I found one or not. It was something to do. It's a sunny day, see, and I'm looking in the windows and there's glare. My reflection is full of lights like little lightnings and I shade my eyes looking in this one window of a tailor shop, but once my head is over my eyes I can see very deep, like inside that window was under the sea, and I'm staring through the glass, and through my reflection, and through the tailor's dummy in the window, and at the very back of the shop in the dark is the tailor, sitting crosslegged on a low bench, and a piece of thread is in his mouth. He's wetting it to thread a needle, and a piece of work covers his knees like a blanket. He looks up at me and then somehow I see through his glasses and through his eyes to someplace very peaceful. Then he looks away. A little bell rings, and I'm awake. Whaddaya think about that?

SARGE: I hear it, Kid, but I don't think about it at all.

BABYFACE: (*To* SARGE) I wanna ask him a question.

SARGE: Sure. Ask him anything you want. He's a good answerer.

BABYFACE: You killed a lot of guys, hah?

KID: You read the papers.

BABYFACE: You said you didn't feel a thing. How can you kill people and feel nothing? You don't even hate them, and you blow their guts all over their clothes.

KID: I don't think about it.

BABYFACE: Don't the blood make you feel anything?

KID: You ever get laid?

BABYFACE: What?

KID: You ever get laid?

BABYFACE: Sure, but. . . .

KID: How was it the first time? Were you nervous? Scared?

BABYFACE: Yeah. Sure.

KID: How is it now? I'll bet you just go in there and fuck yourself silly. How come you ain't scared no more?

BABYFACE: I got used to it is all.

KID: So did I. Even though it's a new mark every time, I got used to it. I felt something sometimes, but I got used to that too. I remember one guy I shot in the belly with a thirty-two. It's just slow enough so's he can still stand up. He gets his hands over the holes and he holds on. He looks down, sees the blood on his nice grey suit, coming out between his fingers. He looks up and says, "Lemme alone, Kid, lemme alone. You shot me." He's kneeling down now. "Please," he says. I come up close and give him the rest of it. The back of his head blows away, and he falls over.

(*Cops and* KID *move into shadow, as a bathtub enters. In it is* JAKE THE PAINTER, *who we saw in the opening line-up in a tuxedo. The bathtub is ornate, luxurious. On a small table alongside it are a bowl of fruit, whiskey bottles, and a brass box.* JAKE *is talking to a very beautiful Chinese woman, who sits by him on the edge of the tub, working an adding machine. This is* LAE-LIN. *She wears a cheong-sam, slit to the thigh. She is blind.*)

JAKE: That does it for this week. Doing all right, hah? (*Looks at adding machine totals.*) Yeah. We're doing okay. A little too much still gets taken off the top for my taste. We still gotta grease a lot of people. A lot of fuckin' overhead in this business. One of these days I'm gonna open a goddamn candy store. What the hell, hah. We're doing okay. Whatsa matter, beautiful? You ain't talkin'. Are you getting snotty on me again?

LAE-LIN: (*Slight oriental accent*) Sorry. I am talking now. Forget, please . . .

JAKE: I think I better forget, or you'll be on your back again at Uncle Wong's, beautiful, getting banged by every guinea who gets off the boat. I'm gonna forget, but you better remember. Set up the layout, will ya.

(LAE-LIN *feels for, finds, and opens the brass box. She takes out a pipe, an alcohol lamp, a long needle, and a little tin of opium.*)

JAKE: Fix me a good one. Is that the new stuff?

LAE-LIN: Yes. Very good. I can smell it.

(*She cooks the opium on the needle, then loads the pipe, holds it out to* JAKE. *He takes it and smokes.*)

JAKE: Lemme have an orange. Oranges go real good with hop.

(*She feels for an orange, finds one, holds it out. He takes it, begins to eat it. He caresses her. She does not respond. A bell rings.*)

JAKE: See who it is, beautiful, and send 'em away. I don't wanna see nobody.

(LAE-LIN *goes off and returns.*)

LAE-LIN: I tell him to go away. He say, "No." It is one man. He say to tell you, "Kid Twist is here."

JAKE: Yeah . . . yeah . . . I sent for him tonight. I got a little job for him. Somebody needs a long vacation. Let him in.

(*She exits, returns with* KID TWIST.)

KID: You wanted to see me.

JAKE: Yeah, that's right. Take the Kid's coat, hah, and hang it up somewhere. Sit down, Kid. You want some hop?

KID: I ain't a hophead.

JAKE: The black smoke makes you feel good, Kid. Nice and easy. Uncle Wong's best. Sit down.

KID: I never tried that stuff.

JAKE: You never had no hop before?

KID: Never.

JAKE: I ain't gonna give nobody his first pipe. That's a responsibility. Bad luck. (*To* LAE-LIN) Come back to the tub, baby. Over here.

(*She comes to the tub.*)

JAKE: (*Continuing*) Hand the pipe to the Kid, hah.

(LAE-LIN *takes the pipe from* JAKE.)

LAE-LIN: Could you speak again, please, so I know where you are.

KID: I'm right here in front of you, lady.

LAE-LIN: Thank you.

(*She holds out pipe to* KID. *He takes it.*)

KID: She's blind.

JAKE: Yeah. What of it?

KID: Nothing. I'm just asking. You can't tell by looking at her.

JAKE: Yeah. She knows her way around here perfect.

KID: Don't she ever go out?

JAKE: Naw, she stays here and listens to the radio. Take a puff, Kid, and draw the smoke down to your toes.

(KID *puffs.*)

JAKE: There's this guy, see, who got unlucky. He made a couple bad bets. He's into a friend of mine for a few grand, and I told this friend I'd collect for him, a little favor. The guy don't wanna play. I see him on the street, he calls me names. He talks about the cops allatime. So I'm thinking it would be convenient for me, and good for my reputation, if this guy took a little vacation. . . .

KID: We can arrange it. He could go up to Saratoga for the races, and buy a farm up there, and never come back. . . .

JAKE: You feel the hop? Kid, you feel it?

KID: Yeah. I feel something funny. (*To* LAE-LIN) You wanna get me a glassa water.

LAE-LIN: Yes. I go into the kitchen, please.

(*She exits.* JAKE *calls after her.*)

JAKE: Get me one too, willya. . . . (*To* KID) Water goes good with hop.

(KID TWIST *stands up.* LAE-LIN *comes back in, with a glass of water in each hand, and stands motionless upstage throughout what follows. The* JOKER *watches from over her shoulder.* KID *takes out a knife and stabs* JAKE.)

Jake: No, Kid, no! You're makin' a mistake. It's me! Jake! It's me! Me!

(Jake *dies. The water in tub turns blood red.* Kid *puts away his knife. He takes a glass of water out of* Lae-Lin's *hand.*)

Kid: Put the water down. Jake ain't gonna want it.

(*She puts the other glass down.*)

Lae-Lin: Where is he? I can't hear his heart.

Kid: In the tub.

(Lae-Lin *moves toward the tub as lights fade. She caresses* Jake's *body. Her hands are wet with blood, but she can't see it. She and* Jake's *corpse and the tub are gone. So is the* Joker. Kid Twist *moves into shadow. The phone booth glides onstage. The* Reporter *is in it, talking.*)

Reporter: *Daily World*? Copy desk, and make it snappy. Hello, Peaches? I'll bet you do, and I know where. Business first, baby. Another tragedy in the Big Town. My heart's bleeding. Ready? "JACOB GREENBLATT FOUND DEAD. Jacob Greenblatt, 52, died early this morning when his business office, in which he had been working late, was invaded by persons unknown. In attempting to defend his premises Mr. Greenblatt, a public accountant, was shot to death by the intruders. Mr. Greenblatt's secretary, Gloria Chow, described the killers as masked negroes in Good Humor man uniforms, who ran downstairs into a BMT station and disappeared in the crowd. Police spokesman stated: 'We don't got a fart's worth of evidence in this one.' Unquote. I writes 'em as I hears 'em, sugar. (*Pause*) Yeah. The kraut blimp's still up there. The wind's funny or something, but it should land any minute. When it starts the final approach, I'll cue you, and we'll send it through America's radios. Hey. . . . There's a little place near here, the Honeymoon Auto Court. Maybe you could—Solid! Soon as the zeppelin docks and I can get the hell out of here.

(*The* Reporter *is gone. The Hotel Room, the two cops and the* Kid. *A knock.* Babyface *checks, opens the door.* Finkle *enters.*)

Finkle: Dinner is soived! A nice piece Roumanian tenderloin, stuffed cabbage, mashed potatoes with onions the chef fixes it special. I taste all your food on the way up, Kid. Tiny bites. Look. Could you see I tasted? No. You get protection, and you don't even know. You never get poisoned if I'm the waiter, I'm telling you. And a bottle seltzer. That seltzer's cold. Brr! It freezes me just to look at it. I got it in ice like champagne. Tonight's your last night here, Kid, so I'm making nice. Tomorrow, like a bird!

KID: Just put it down.

FINKLE: It seems you win a big bet from me yesterday. Whaddaya know, the tide don't come up into the hotel, and the night clerk's feet are still dry, even though he sleeps at the desk. You're a winner. (*He tosses* KID *a big wad of money.*) But you gotta give me a chance at it, Kid. You know what I figure? I think the world's gonna end, Kid. Tonight. Before morning.

KID: You think it's gonna be all over, hah? How come you think that?

SARGE: He's got a system, Kid.

BABYFACE: He can't tell you how his system works, Kid. It's top secret.

FINKLE: Don't make fun with something you don't know what it's about. The world will end before dawn, and considering it's you, Kid, I'm gonna make a special price. I figure you'll figure the world ain't gonna end, 'cause that's what your system says. I'm gonna make you a price that nobody ever got yet on something like this. (*He sniffs the air.*) Uh oh. Somebody knows something. The odds are changing. I'm giving you even money. You try and get a price somewhere's else. They'll figure if they win they won't be around to collect, so it's a dumb proposition. Collecting is the least of my worries. I'll find you. I know you ain't gonna welch on me, even if the world is over. If you do, Kid, I'm gonna hire *you* to bump *you*. That's a good one. I can feel it in my funny bone.

KID: Finkle, you got too much mouth. I want the bet. I'm gonna take it. How much you go for?

BABYFACE: This is crazy. Finkle ain't that stupid.

SARGE: You go ahead, Kid. You're your own man. You know what you're doing.

KID: I wanna get on.

FINKLE: I'm sorry, Kid. I got a limit on this bet. I ain't Mr. Moneybags. One buck.

Kid: One buck!

Finkle: One buck. Take it or leave it.

Kid: I'll take it.

Finkle: You're on. Believe me, win or lose, you got something good. Sergeant, Officer, goodnight, goodnight.

(*As* Finkle *exits,* Goldie *bursts into the room. She rushes toward* Kid. Babyface *grabs her.*)

Goldie: Hey Kid, I hadda see you. Lemme go, damnit. Kid, tell 'em to let me go.

Sarge: Let her go. How's business, Goldie?

Babyface: Hey, Kid, you got some nice-lookin' friends.

Goldie: Listen, Kid, you gotta help me out. I'm in a little trouble. Some people don't seem to like me no matter how nice I am to them. They're mad at me. It's crazy. Can you stake me, honey. I wanna leave town. I'll pay it back soon as I get settled. My brother'll put me up for a while 'til I find a job. He's got a farm. Can you believe that? You could come down there and stay with me whenever you wanted to. You could milk cows. Kid Twist, sitting on a stool in overalls, both hands fulla cowtit. No joke. I really need it, Kid. I gotta have a couple hundred.

Kid: Goldie, get off my back, willya. I won't carry anybody anymore. Why don't you be a good girl and get outta here.

Goldie: We done everything together, Kid. We had some real good times.

Kid: They're holding my money. The Sergeant's got it. He's not gonna let me give you nothing.

Goldie: If you ask him he will.

Sarge: You know, Goldie, you been acting kinda funny for the past three years or so. You gonna end up on the street, you don't be careful.

Kid: She ain't no whore.

Babyface: How can you tell?

Kid: She ain't no whore 'cause I didn't give her no money.

GOLDIE: Kid, I'll tell you the truth. I'm sick. I'm gonna be sick. I been hanging around with some wrong guys since you went in. They musta got on me 'cause you were tipping in pals of theirs. Uncle Wong can take care of me. One or two pipes, and a little to carry me, and I'll be going out of town. I'll take the bus. You don't want Goldie to be sick, do ya? Kid, you left me nothing. You left me out there with nothing. What was I supposed to do?

KID: You think I'm gonna know what you was supposed to do? Find a sucker, that's all, a take-it-easy John with a nice roll and a sick wife and let him keep you in yen shee and bathrobes.

GOLDIE: Nobody means nothing to you, do they? You're in here kissing your own ass. Well, I ain't gonna kiss it, that's for sure.

KID: Goldie! You wanna end up like Uncle Wong, a glazed-over corpse? That's all I'm gonna say.

GOLDIE: Will you look who the fuck is talking. You think this is a Sunday school where you gonna put me on your knee and tickle my ass? This is the Half Moon Hotel, sweetheart, it ain't Sunday school. I'm gonna do whatever I feel like. I'm gonna cash it in if I feel like. I don't know what you're doing here. Why don't we go to the farm and pick raspberries? (*She sings, as she approaches, first* SARGE, *then* BABYFACE, *and then* KID TWIST.)

Wake up and live, don't mind the rainy patter
Up on your toes, it's mind over matter.
You got to get up and give.
Give yourself a shake-up and you'll wake up and live.
Come out of your shell, Hey fella, find your place in the sun
Come out of your shell, say fella
Just be a go-gettin' son of a gun . . .
You son of a bitch!

(GOLDIE *pulls a small knife from her purse, rushes at the* KID. *She is trying to kill him. The cops grab her, pull her away.*)

KID: What'd you do that for, hah?

GOLDIE: For love.

SARGE: Who sent you, Goldie? Who said they'd buy you junk if you just. . . .

GOLDIE: Nobody paid me, Sergeant. Killing that bastard was my own idea.

SARGE: Have them take her downtown.

Goldie: You can't arrest me. It's not like I tried to cut a human being. That's Kid Twist.

Kid: Get her out of here.

Goldie: So long, Kid. It was nice knowing you.

(Babyface *takes* Goldie *outside.* Sarge *drifts back into shadow. The* Joker *enters.*)

Joker: Mr. Twist, I presume. You can't know how exactly you correspond to my picture of you. (*Pointing to his own head.*) My pho-tos. Taken from a height. Aerial.

Kid: Joker! You slay me. You escaped! You're back in business! How come you got no henchmen with ya?

Joker: Bunglers! Cheap hoods who can't even wear their hats at the right angle. Torpedoes that fail to detonate. I've eliminated them. I want you to be my henchman, Kid. We'd make quite the team. You can still have it all back, Kid, and more. Steak, champagne, trips to Florida—Your wife, your girlfriend, your pals, even Pittsburgh Phil. Go along with the Joker.

Kid: If I work for you I'll have to worry about. . . .

Joker: My dear henchman, Batman was a sight gag of mine to increase public interest in my exploits. He has been eliminated. Batman never existed and now he's gone. Once I conceived the Big Plan he wasn't needed.

Kid: I'll bite. What's the plan this time?

Joker: All the while I was behind bars I dreamed of humiliating the world in a specially humorous way.

Kid: Joker, you are totally bananas, you know that?

Joker: It's my most charming trait. With your help, Kid, I plan to strip this planet clean. To loot and pillage the earth of its treasures! The two of us load the plunder aboard my rocket. We embark for Mars. To foil pursuit, we simply blow this planet up behind us. My last jest. BOOM! It's a cinch.

Kid: Joker, I'm a businessman. I work at it. I'm ready for a good thing, but this plan of yours is a little whack-o.

Joker: Whack-o? Who are you, a peanut-grifter, to decide what is and what is not "whack-o?" Kid, with your brains, you'll be back robbing candy stores tomorrow. Luckily, I happen to have room, on this final project of mine, for just you. The big boys are moving. Wars are starting. BOOM! Accidents will happen. Stick with the Joker. Leave the courtrooms behind. *Shhhh.* Plenty in it for you, Kid. Plenty. We can't miss.

(*Sounds of gunfire, dogs, voices offstage. A rocket ship, a two-seater, the kind you'd find on a kiddie ride in an amusement park, appears. It is loaded with the treasures of the world, which are rather gaudy. The sound of baying hounds grows louder.*)

JOKER: All aboard! It's time to leave the hounds to choke in our dust.

(JOKER *gets in front, the* KID *in back. Loud sound of take-off. They are pressed back in their seats by acceleration. Sounds of pursuit fade. They are in space. Planets, stars. Mounted on the rocket is a big red button.*)

JOKER: (*Manically cackling*) We've got the swag, and on that blue-green ball below are the suckers, preparing their posse. This red button ignites the launch apparatus of a little missile of mine with a three-megaton warhead, its guidance system prepared to direct it to the center of Moscow. The lettering on its sides is lovely: U.S.A., in red, white and blue. Wake it up, Kid. Tickle it. That's what I pay you for. Your finger. (*He wiggles his own finger in the air.*) Trigger finger.

(KID *hesitates, then pushes the red button. Silence. Both look down.*)

KID: There it goes. It looks like a black handball, burning.

JOKER: Easy come, easy go. The remaining citizens of planet Earth are busy trying to put each other out. We're safe as mice. Safe as swans.

KID: Yeah.

JOKER: (*Drawing gun.*) You must know the moral of our little story, Kid. Crime Does Not Pay. Did you ever really think I was going to divide my ill-gotten gains with you? Did you ever believe I'd share all *this* with a small-time hood from Brooklyn?

KID: No.

JOKER: (*Stands up in the rocket.*) What? You don't expect me to believe you foresaw this last twist?

KID: (*Stands up as well.*) I don't expect anything. I been covering my ass for too long. Your gun ain't loaded.

Joker: We can easily test that statement, on your head. (*He fires at the* Kid's *head; the gun clicks, empty.*) I believe you're right. Kid, your comic sense is keen. A triumph. One more turn of the wheel than I'd bargained for. (*Pause*) If you kill me, Kid, there'll be no one else left to die. You'll be the last man alive. Without my guidance you'll reach Mars in three years or so, if all goes well. When you arrive I doubt you'll be too steady, skullwise.

Kid: That'll be my trouble. (*He draws his gun.*) Thanks for the ride, Joker, but I made up my mind. I want to pay. I don't need any dreams. I remember me.

(Kid *fires one shot into* Joker, *who slumps over, dead.* Kid Twist *steps out of the kiddie rocket. It moves off, carrying the loot and the* Joker's *corpse. The cops come into the light.* Kid Twist *moves to the window, and looks out. Below him an old man enters in a red bathing suit, wearing a Santa Claus beard and a Santa Claus hat. He is followed by the* Reporter, *who is taking pictures of him. The old man makes swimming motions for the camera, flexes his muscles.*)

(*The* Kid *speaks as he watches this from the window.*)

Kid: It's the Polar Bear Club. Crazy old fuckers. They do this every winter out at Coney Island. They get one of 'em dressed up as Santa and he runs into the ocean. Gets his picture on the front page of the *Daily News.*

(Santa *runs to the ocean, followed by the* Reporter.)

Kid: (*Continuing*) There he goes. Yahoo! Go on, Santa! It's cold out there. He's wading in. Shit, he's in that freezing ocean up to his neck, smiling and waving. People are cheering, flashbulbs popping. He's still waving. Uh oh, a wave just took off that red hat of his. There it goes. Santa's got as much hair as a cueball. Hey, he's struggling out there. The tide's got him. His beard is caught in the waves. Come on, Santa! Come on! Swim, you fucker! You gotta swim! (*Pause*) Where is he? Where are you? There! Santa's going under . . . he's gone. (*Pause*) The waves didn't even notice him. Coral bed below. Look down there, fish swim by your eyes.

Sarge: You OK, Kid? Wanna fly away? Wanna disappear? Changing your mind about singing the rest of your song? I wouldn't blame you. You chose the hard road, Kid. Stony road. (*Pause*) But you're all right, Kid. You should be. After all, you're getting yours. Even though you did all those nasty things, you're gonna walk away.

BABYFACE: You been bought, Kid, just like everyone else.

KID: Bullshit. I'm getting me, that's what I'm getting. Everytime I tell the truth, I say good-bye, and soon I'll be leaving. There's something I learned and I goddamn taught it to myself. The sound of my voice chases them away. All those crazy people I became are waving good-bye. That, in case you wanna know, is what I been doing here in the Half Moon Hotel. Saying good-bye. When I walk out of here on Sunday, I'll be clean. Abraham Reles, one day old.

(KID TWIST *does a little dance of joy.* SARGE *and* BABYFACE *stare at him, wait till he's done.*)

SARGE: We can't have you cracking up, Kid. Not right before your release. You're gonna need all the cards you got left in your deck when you hit the street.

KID: I ain't cracking up.

SARGE: We can't have you cracking up, and we can't have you escaping, right before your release. That would be special embarrassing. So we gotta take special precautions.

KID: I'm gettin' outta here tomorrow. Why in the hell would I wanna escape?

SARGE: I don't know, Kid. The motives of a prisoner are sometimes difficult to evaluate, even for a trained officer of the law. Just so we don't take no chances I'm gonna lock the door to this room . . . (*He takes a key out of his pocket, locks door.*) . . . and I'm gonna swallow the key. (*He swallows the key.*) Don't worry. I'll shit it out in the morning. Well, here we are, a cozy threesome. One thing I've learned about jails—the jailer's always there, along with the prisoner.

BABYFACE: Hey, Kid, you wanna cigarette?

KID: Yeah. I'll take one. That's real generous of you.

BABYFACE: Sarge?

SARGE: Sure.

(*All three light cigarettes.*)

BABYFACE: I know we're not supposed to do this, but 'cause it's your last night . . . You wanna drink?

SARGE: Make it three.

(BABYFACE *brings out a whiskey bottle and three shot glasses. He pours.* KID TWIST *drinks.* BABYFACE *and* SARGE *set their glasses down, untouched.*)

SARGE: Say, Kid, you got any letters you want mailed? Our pal here is pretty good with a needle. You want your socks sewed up or something?

KID: I don't want any more favors.

SARGE: Just making sure. I hadda feeling and I was just making sure.

BABYFACE: Kid, you want a rubdown? I give a pretty good one.

SARGE: Maybe you'd like a little entertainment. The Officer here and me, we do a little skit where we apprehend a criminal. A take-off on the force. It's the annual highlight of the Policeman's Ball. . . .

(SARGE *and* BABE *throw arms around each other, dance across the stage. They begin their pantomime skit.*)

KID: I'd like it to be quiet.

(SARGE *and* BABYFACE *stop their performance.* SARGE *sits on the bed alongside* KID TWIST.)

SARGE: Kid, there's something I wanna tell you, this being your last night and all. I got a garden. A garden behind my house. It's real beautiful in the summer. Then I pull up the vegetables, the petals drop off the flowers, a cold wind blows, and it's just dirt. Makes me sad every time.

(BABYFACE *sits on the other side of the* KID. *All three are now in a row.*)

BABYFACE: You know, my wife had a baby. A month ago. That's number three. A girl. We named her Catherine. I guess we'll end up calling her Cathy. Those maternity bills are hell. I'm gonna be owing that hospital for months.

SARGE: I got a kid in college. Good kid. He says he's gonna be a lawyer. Gonna go to law school.

BABYFACE: I just wanna do my job, but sometimes it don't make sense.

SARGE: The world's turning one way, and if you run the other way, you never get there. Up the down escalator, Kid. Never stop.

BABYFACE: Kid, eat your dinner. It's been sitting there awhile already. Getting cold. It's like ice.

(BABYFACE *brings* KID TWIST *his dinner, sets it on his lap.* KID TWIST *looks groggy, out of focus. The drugged liquor is taking effect.* SARGE *reaches over and smashes his tray of food onto the floor.*)

KID: Hey, whadya do that for?

SARGE: Kid, this town is burning up. You put the heat on, and everybody's cooking. They don't know which way to run, Kid. Their asses are on fire.

BABYFACE: A little bird like you starts to sing, and a lot of grown men start to shit green.

SARGE: A lot of people are pissing in their pants, Kid. They can feel the piss running down their legs while they're on their way to the office. Big bills at the cleaners. They wake up, and it's dark. Clock says four a.m. Been dreaming of you, Kid. The heat's strong. Everybody sweats.

(KID TWIST, *struggling to keep himself upright, slips to the floor. He's conscious, moaning, but can barely move. He crawls feebly toward the door.* SARGE *and* BABYFACE *strip the bed, begin tying the sheets together.*)

BABYFACE: You know, I look in my pay envelope this week, and there ain't even enough in there to get my kid a piggy bank for the pennies he finds in the street. I'm teaching my kid to walk with his head down, looking at the sidewalk. He might find a few nickels that way. (*Pause*) Bill collectors sitting on my stoop. I need a break, today. Yesterday would've been good.

SARGE: I figure, Kid, there's always gonna be some hard times in this world. You can't change it, and you can't stop it. (*Pause*) Take it as it comes, that's all. Kiss it as it flies. You go popping off all by yourself, trying to make it fly right, who knows? Nobody plays a lone hand, Kid. Then the cops think you're a robber, and robbers think you're a cop. In the middle. Nobody should be in the middle, Kid. It's gotta be empty or the wheel won't turn. Didn't they teach you that in school?

(BABYFACE *ties one end of the line of sheets to the bed.*)

SARGE: (*Sings*) "Oh, the deacon went down, to the cellar to pray, he met Mae West, and he stayed all day, I ain't gonna grieve, my

Lord no more." That's an old Irish fiddle tune, Jewboy. It's full of happiness. . . .

Babyface: Say something, Kid. Say something that would make us like you. I wanna like you.

Sarge: We gotta live. Your song's too loud, Kid. It's making me deaf to hear it. Lepke don't want to hear it. The Judge don't want to hear it. Nobody wants to hear it. You got pointed in the wrong direction, Kid, and there's no other way to turn you around.

(Sarge *tosses one end of the line of sheets out the "window," so it hangs down.* Babyface *grabs the half-conscious* Kid, *and hauls him over to the window.*)

Sarge: There's your line, Kid. There you go, trying to escape. Can you see you? It's windy out there. All your sleep is waving in the breeze. You wanna fly, don't you, Kid? That's why you been mouthing off in those courtrooms. You're gonna flap over those Brooklyn roofs like a fat black bird. Your dark shadow's gonna burn into the sand, Kid, and even the tide won't wash it away.

(*They grab* Kid Twist, *ready to push him out the window. They freeze. The zeppelin Hindenburg enters, tilted at a crazy angle, shaking, billowing in and out. The* Reporter *enters below with a radio microphone, and looks up. On the Hindenburg are* Captain Pruss, Babe Ruth, *the* Joker, *the* Rabbi, Phil *in his electric chair,* Goldie, *and* Shirley Reles. *They are yelling, panicking, running back and forth.*)

(*Sound of an enormous explosion. Flashing light. The Hindenburg bursts into flames. Panic.*)

Reporter: My God! It's in flames, it's flashing, it's flashing terrible! . . . It's burning, bursting into flames, falling on the mooring mast! This is one of the worst catastrophes in the world! . . . Oh, it's into the sky! Oh, the humanity, and all the passengers!

Rabbi: (*Reading from his book, oblivious to the events around him.*) When Rabbi Isaac the Sinner was wandering in the wilderness, he came on a beautiful castle, all in flames. The castle was burning, and no one was trying to stop the fire. Rabbi Isaac said, "This castle must be without a master." Then the Lord God, blessed be He, looked out at him from a high window, through the flames, and said, "I am the Master of this Castle."

Goldie: Shut up, you old fart. We're gonna crash!

Joker: He did it. (*Pointing to* Kid Twist.) Abe Reles. Kid Twist. He blew up the world. He blew *us* up.

BABE: Yeah, it was him all right. He got us into this.

SHIRLEY: Abe, you didn't. . . . You wouldn't kill us all just like. . . .

CAPTAIN: You madman. We're finished!

KID: Don't fuck with me!

GOLDIE: Shut him up! Shut him up! I can't stand listening to him anymore.

RABBI: The Black Butterfly! Hesed!

PHIL: Kid! The sun's inside my head. Can you see it shining? Can you see it! Here it comes!

(*The Hindenburg falls flaming offstage. The voices of those on it fade. There is* no *sound of a crash.*)

REPORTER: (*Moving offstage under the Hindenburg.*) President Roosevelt, fishing for tarpon from his yacht in the Mexican gulf, sent a message of condolence on the loss of the great airship to Chancellor Hitler. . . .

(*The* REPORTER *exits.* KID TWIST *is pushed out the window by* SARGE *and* BABYFACE. *He falls. His right ankle tangles in the sheet. He hangs from the window, upside down, like the Hanged Man in the Tarot pack. A police siren begins softly, and grows louder through the following speech.*)

KID: No way to kill me. Kid Twist is dead already. Can't kill a dead man. The dead can say anything, and no one minds. (*Pause*) Momma, momma. I don't wanna go down. Keep me up . . . keep me floating. . . . Up into the *light*. . . . (*Pause*) Can you hear me out there? Can you still hear me?

(*From offstage, a ragged chorus chants the Mourner's Kaddish, in Hebrew . . .*)

CHORUS:
Yis-ga-dal vi'yis-ka-dash sh'may ra-bo
B'ol-mo dee-v'ro chir-u-say, v'yam-leech mal-chu-say,
B'cha-yaychon uv'yo-may-chon, uv-cha-yay d'chol bays yisroayl
Ba a-go-lo u'viz'man ko'reev, v'im-ru Omayn.

(*Siren wail full.* KID TWIST *still hangs upside down. The white curtain with measuring lines for height that began the play appears behind the inverted form of* KID TWIST. *Very bright light.*)

Sarge: Ladies and gentlemen, this here's Kid Twist. Look him over. Look him over. Look him over.

(*Darkness.*)

*End of play*

Jeffrey M. Jones

# *Der Inka von Peru*

JEFFREY M. JONES is a playwright whose works include *The Fortress of Solitude* (1972); *Nightcoil* (1978); *70 Scenes of Halloween* (1980); *The Confessions of a Dopefiend* (1982); and the historical quotation series, *A History of Western Philosophy by W.T. Jones*, which consists of Vol. I, *Der Inka von Peru* (1984); Vol II, *Tomorrowland* (1985); Vol. III, *Wipeout* (1987). Mr. Jones was an NEA Playwriting Fellow in 1982, and won Honorable Mention for *Der Inka* ... from Victory Gardens Theatre in the 1984 FDG/CBS New Play Program. He has been a member of New Dramatists since 1980, and associated with Creation Production Company in New York since 1978.

*Der Inka von Peru* was originally produced by Creation Production Company at The Performing Garage in New York City, April 30–May 23, 1984, with the following cast:

SHANNON MALLESON, Hospital Administrator.... Karla Barker
SELDON CLARK, a detail man.................. Keith Druhl
CAROL MALLESON, R.N................... Zivia Flomenhaft
JASON WILFRED M.D., Chief of Surgery....... Zach Grenier
CLIFF SINCLAIR M.D.,.................. Patrick O'Connell
DIVINA............................ Barbara Somerville

Direction and Design were by the author; Daniel Moses Schreier composed the score; Quina Fonseca designed the costumes; and James L. Schoenfelder was stage manager.

The author would like to thank Mac Wellman for including him in this anthology; Kip Gould for publishing it and Tom Saunders for figuring out how; Liz LeCompte for use of the Performing Garage; Matthew Maguire for his continued support; and Page Burkholder for giving him hope.

(*Preset: Sound: The* "Exotic Loop"*—a continuous loop of the first few bars of* "Autumn Leaves" *(*The Three Suns.)

(*The performance space is divided into three areas. The forestage runs the full width of the theatre, and from the front row of the audience twelve feet upstage to the wall. Three gray wood chairs are placed SL, center, and SR on the forestage, eighteen inches downstage of the wall.*)

(*The wall runs from floor to ceiling and stops three-and-a-half feet from either theatre wall, creating SL and SR entrances to the forestage. The wall is painted off-white.*)

(*In the center of the wall is a window, an aperture ten feet wide, running from three-and-a-half to six-and-a-half feet high. Through the window, the audience can see into the room.*)

(*The room is sixteen feet wide and seven feet deep, defined by three off-white walls which form an inverted "U" shape. There are downstage entrances into the room SR and SL which are masked by the downstage window wall.*)

(*In the center of the back wall of the room is a smaller aperture, four-and-a-half feet wide and running from four-and-a-half to six-and-a-half feet high, known as the peephole. Three feet upstage of the peephole is a masking wall, painted hospital green.*)

(*Fade out preset lights.*)

(*Prolog: Sound: Crossfade to* "Terry's Theme" *(Billy Vaughn).*)

(*Lights up.*)

(*Forestage:* SELDEN *sitting in SL chair. He wears brown trousers and a shortsleeved white shirt.* JASON *sitting in center chair. He wears a lab coat over a dark, three-piece suit.* CAROL *in SR chair, wearing a lab coat over a green nurse's uniform.*)

(*Forestage:* SHANNON *enters SR. She is wearing a lab coat over an office dress. She crosses center and addresses the audience.*)

SHANNON: Ummmm,
The reason I've asked you all here today is to tell you
I'll be taking my father's place as administrator of the hospital.
I know it's going to be very difficult for me,

---

But seeing you all here like this is very reassuring,
And I'm confident I can count on your continuing support.

(*Forestage:* CAROL *takes an apple out of her pocket and attracts* JASON *and* SELDEN'S *attention by the way she eats it.*)

SHANNON: Now, we desperately need another surgeon,
And it's essential that I find someone to replace my father as soon as possible.
When I do, I'll let you know all the details;
Until then, we'll continue to send out emergency cases to the public hospital.
Well—I guess that's all for now.
I can't think of anything else to say at the moment.
Thank you all for coming,
And keep up the good work.

(*Forestage:* SHANNON *exits SR to polite applause from the others. Then* CAROL *exits SL, followed by* SELDEN. JASON *follows* SHANNON *off SR.*)

(*Room:* SHANNON *enters SR and crosses SL, then* JASON *enters SR.*)

(*Fade forestage lights down to pools.*)

JASON: A little brief, but very much to the point.
Well done.

(*ROMEO 1*)

(*Room:* SHANNON *is writing on clipboard.*)

SHANNON: I drew up the contracts today for Cliff Sinclair.
It's too bad we're in such a hurry for a surgeon.

(*Room:* JASON *crosses to* SHANNON.)

JASON: Weren't you satisfied with his references, Shannon?

SHANNON: His references were fine.
It's just that we don't know anything about him:
His family situation, his background, that sort of thing.
Why would he want to work for us, I wonder?

JASON: Is it the man or the surgeon that you're hiring?

SHANNON: Well, a surgeon is a man first, isn't he, Jason?

(*Room:* JASON *crosses away from* SHANNON.)

JASON: You seem very distant.

SHANNON: What?

JASON: Sometimes you feel so far away, so withdrawn,
I can't help wondering what you're thinking about.

(*Sound:* "Terry's Theme" *plays out; segués* to "The Way We Were" *(Richard Hayman and his Orchestra.)*

SHANNON: I'm sorry, Jason, it's just that . . .
Well, it's just that I've been kind of busy, that's all.
Ever since Father died there's been so much to deal with,
And Carol's been driving me crazy!
But things will be better soon.
Just be patient, all right?

(*FAITHLESS 1*)

(*Room:* SHANNON *crosses to* JASON.)

SHANNON: I'm thinking of having a party at my house next week.
We spend so much time working here at the hospital,
We tend to forget there's a great big world out there.
We'll have a buffet supper outside,
Brightly colored paper lanterns,
And music, so we can dance . . .
Like the idea?

JASON: I'd like it a whole lot better if we could announce our engagement at the party, Shannon.

(*Room:* SHANNON *breaks free of* JASON.)

SHANNON: Not now, Jason. Please don't ask me now.
It wouldn't be kind to the memory of my father.

JASON: People die, Shannon, but the world doesn't—
Your father said so himself.

SHANNON: And you said you'd be patient and wait.

JASON: Please, Shannon—say yes, just say yes.
You know I'll make you happy.
In the spring, you'll be Mrs. Jason Wilfred—
Then I'll show them what it means to be a Clark from Clarksville.
The hospital is dying,

But the hospital can be brought back to life!
Don't you see, Shannon—we can do it, you and I!
Say yes, please—I promise you'll never regret it.
Do I have to get down on my knees?

(*Room:* JASON *kneels.*)

SHANNON: All right then . . . I'll marry you.

(*Sound: Crossfade to* "Ricercare Concertate" *(Matelart).*)

SHANNON: I just ask one thing.

(*Room:* JASON *crosses to embrace* SHANNON.)

JASON: Anything.

SHANNON: That we keep this a secret
Until everything returns to normal.

(*PRESCOTT 1*)

(*Forestage:* DIVINA *enters SR with book and stands by wall. She is wearing pearls, a black cocktail dress, and heels. She crosses to a pool of light and addresses the audience.*)

(*Room:* SHANNON *stands in SL corner of window;* JASON, *behind her, is stroking her hair.*)

DIVINA: It is not easy at this time
To comprehend the impulse given to Europe
by the discovery of America.
It was a world of romance that was thrown open.
For whatever the luck of the Spanish adventurer,
Gold was ever floating before his distempered
vision.

(*Forestage:* DIVINA *crosses SL.*)

DIVINA: Under the pressure of this spirit of enterprise,
The whole of the mighty continent,
From Labrador to Tierra del Fuego,
Was explored in less than thirty years after its
discovery.
But while the eastern coast had been explored,
The veil was not yet raised that hung over the
golden shores of the Pacific,
And floating rumors of a mighty nation at the south,

(*Room:* CAROL *enters SR, unobserved, and watches* JASON *and* SHANNON *from back wall.*)

DIVINA: Teaming with the metal they so much coveted,
Were continually reaching the ears
And kindling the dreamy imaginations of
The colonists. . . .

(*FAITHLESS 2*)

(*Forestage:* DIVINA *turns upstage, one foot on the SL chair, and watches the room.*)

JASON: You know how I feel about you, Shannon.

SHANNON: Jason, please, you're messing my hair.

CAROL: Why—Dr. Jason Wilfred—what an unexpected surprise!

(*Room:* SHANNON *guiltily breaks free of* JASON.)

CAROL: I thought you said you were working late at the hospital tonight.

JASON: I'm afraid you must have misunderstood, Carol.

CAROL: Obviously.
Maybe you don't understand how this looks to
other people, Dr. Wilfred,
Human nature being what it is.

(*Room:* JASON *crosses upstage to* CAROL.)

JASON: Well, what would you like me to do about it?

CAROL: Why don't you give me a call, Jason—
After you're done here.

JASON: Oh, I think it can wait until morning, Carol,
Don't you?

(*Room:* JASON *turns back to* SHANNON, *who confronts him.*)

SHANNON: What's going on around here, anyway?

JASON: Oh, nothing, darling.
It's just kind of hard to explain, that's all.

CAROL: I know.
I've tried explaining it to myself.

SHANNON: It really isn't necessary to explain, Jason.
In fact, it's kind of embarassing.
You two play whatever games you want—I'm leaving!

(*Room:* SHANNON *exits SL;* CAROL *follows after her, then turns to* JASON *and smiles.*)

CAROL: "Play games with him? . . ."
Who would want to?

(*Room:* CAROL *exits SL;* JASON *turns away, crosses to the window down center.*)

(*Sound: Superimpose opening chords of third movement of Mahler's* "Ninth Symphony".)

(*PRESCOTT 2*)

(*Forestage:* DIVINA *crosses SR.*)

DIVINA: Such was the state of feeling in the little community of Panama. . . .

(*Room:* SELDEN *enters SR along upstage wall.*)

DIVINA: And in 1524, three men were found
In whom the spirit of adventure triumphed over every consideration of danger.
One of them was selected,
As fitted by his character,
To conduct it to a successful issue.
That man was Francisco Pizarro.

(*CAMPAIGN 1*)

(*Forestage:* DIVINA *crosses and exits SL. Room: From window,* JASON *follows her with his gaze.*)

JASON: For I am come home again,
But there is nobody to kill the calf or to play the music.

SELDEN: Yes, sir.

(*Sound: Fade out* "Ricercare Concertate".)

JASON: For I have adventured myself in the name of the Lord
And He hath marked me for His own.

SELDEN: That's right.

JASON: For the word of God is like a sword on my side,
No matter what other weapon, a stick or a straw.

SELDEN: Yes, sir.

JASON: For in my nature I quested for beauty,
But God, God hath sent me to sea for pearls.

SELDEN: That's right.
You had a job to do and you did it.

JASON: That's right.

SELDEN: What choice did you have?

(*Room:* JASON *turns SL away from window and begins to pace around the room counter-clockwise, against the walls.* SELDEN *stays standing at attention, SR upstage.*)

JASON: Well, the point is,
Do you ever have any choice . . .
That is the point.

SELDEN: That's right, sir.

JASON: So, what you really come to is,
What do you do?

SELDEN: Right, right. . . .

(*Room:* JASON *wheels on* SELDEN.)

JASON: Yeah, well—any ideas on that?

SELDEN: Well, sir, we . . .
We need more money.

(*Room:* JASON *crosses to window down center and resumes pacing.*)

JASON: Hell, I know that—
That's the thing I kept raising with you,
When you said: We need 20,000 or 100,000 or something—
I said: Yeah, that's what we need today,
But what do we need tomorrow,
Or next year,
Or five years from now. . . .

SELDEN: That's right.

JASON: You know what I mean?

SELDEN: Yes, sir.

JASON: I'm talking about the big picture.

SELDEN: Right, sir.

(*Room:* JASON *wheels on* SELDEN.)

JASON: So how much money do you think we need?

SELDEN: I would say a million dollars over the next two years.

JASON: A million dollars?

JASON: Oh, over the next two years.

SELDEN: That's right.

(*Room:* JASON *crosses to window down center.*)

JASON: All right, look—now, let me tell you something:
On the money, we can get the money—we can get that.
There is no problem in that.
It isn't going to be easy, but it can be done—
We'll get the money. No problem.
But let me say this. . . .

(*Room:* SELDEN *follows* JASON *to window.*)

SELDEN: Yes, sir?

JASON: Let Peter rejoice with the Moonfish,
Who keeps up the life in the waters by night.
Let Jude bless with the Bream,
Who is of melancholy from his depth and serenity.
Let Andrew rejoice with the Whale,
Who is arrayed in beauteous blue and is a combination of bulk and activity. . . .

SELDEN: Yes, sir. . . .

(*Sound: Fade in a continuous "tone".*)

JASON: This is a war.

SELDEN: Right, sir.

JASON: We take a few shots and it'll be over.

SELDEN: That's right.

JASON: We give 'em a few shots and it'll be over.

SELDEN: Yes, sir.

JASON: So let's send somebody else to take them on.

SELDEN: Right, right. . . .

JASON: And not some big clown, you know what I mean?

SELDEN: Yes, sir.

JASON: And get some pros to help him.

SELDEN: We'll get some pros.

JASON: That's right.

SELDEN: What an exciting prospect.

(*TOXIN 1*)

(*Forestage:* DIVINA, *concealed in a shawl, enters SR carrying a box, and crosses furtively to SR corner of window. She opens the box and green light plays on her face.*)

DIVINA: Scorpions?

(*Sound: Superimpose opening chords of third movement of Mahler's* "Ninth Symphony".)

(*Room:* JASON *and* SELDEN *turn to* DIVINA.)

JASON: That's right.
And we'll pay a good price for them, too.

(*Room:* JASON *walks up SL, away from window.*)

DIVINA: But why do you want them?

SELDEN: Uhhh—we're teachers in a missionary school;
We want to teach the children how to recognize them.

DIVINA: Don't you realize these insects are dangerous?
They could kill you.

JASON: Yeah, we know, how much do you want for them?

DIVINA: I would say a million dollars over the next two years.

(*Room:* SELDEN *crosses up to* JASON *to confer.*)

JASON: What did she say?
A million dollars?

SELDEN: Over the next two years.

JASON: That's ridiculous.

(*Room:* SELDEN *returns to SR edge of window.*)

SELDEN: That's ridiculous.
We'll give you fifty bucks a pair.

DIVINA: All right, then.
I know when I'm beaten.
But the Lord will reward me for being so generous.
The little ones are deadly;
The big ones can make you sick, but they won't kill you.
Be sure and remember this.
Your lives will depend upon it.

(*Forestage:* DIVINA *hands box to* SELDEN *in room.*)

(*Room:* JASON *is already starting to exit SL.*)

SELDEN: We'll try and keep it in mind. . . .

(*Sound: Fade out "tone"; fade in* "Exotic Loop".)

JASON: (*Off*) Right. . . .

(*PRESCOTT 6*)

(*Room:* SELDEN *has followed* JASON *off SL.*)

(*Forestage:* DIVINA *throws shawl off her head. She moves SR chair from wall to center of light pool directly downstage, midway to audience. Fade out room lights; fade up peephole lights.*)

DIVINA: However,
Before accompanying the march of Pizarro and his followers into the country of the Incas,
It is necessary to make the reader acquainted
With the critical situation in the kingdom at that time.

The Prince of Quito, Atahuallpa,
Best-beloved of the Inca's children,
Had beaten his enemies, taken their capital, set foot on the neck of his rival,
And won for himself the ancient scepter of the Children of the Sun.
His triumph was complete.
But Atahuallpa had not read the handwriting of the heavens.

Comets were seen flaming athwart the skies.
Earthquakes shook the land.

(*Sound: Slow crossfade to* "Nocturne in E Flat, Op. 9, #2" *(Chopin).*)

DIVINA: The moon was girdled with rings of fire, and an eagle,
Chased by several hawks,
Was seen screaming in the air above the great square of Cuzco,
Pierced by the talons of his tormentors. . . .

(*ROMEO 4*)

(*Peephole:* CLIFF *enters from SR, facing SL in profile, and remains in SR corner.*)

(*Forestage:* DIVINA *crosses SR to wall as* SHANNON *enters SL and slowly crosses to SR chair. She is wearing an evening gown and walks as if dreaming.*)

CLIFF: Excuse me . . .

SHANNON: (By night on my bed,
I sought him whom my soul loveth.)

CLIFF: I'm looking for Dr. Malleson.

SHANNON: (I sought him but I found him not.)

CLIFF: Excuse me . . .

SHANNON: (I will rise now, and go about the city in the streets;
And in the broad ways,
I will seek him whom my soul loveth.)

CLIFF: I'm looking for Dr. Malleson.

SHANNON: (I sought him but I found him not.)

(*Peephole:* CLIFF *crosses SL in profile.*)

CLIFF: Excuse me . . .

(*Forestage:* SHANNON *suddenly looks out at audience.*)

SHANNON: Yes?

CLIFF: I'm looking for Dr. Malleson.

(*Peephole:* CLIFF *exits SL.*)

SHANNON: I'm Dr. Malleson.

(*Room:* CAROL *enters SL and crosses SR in window. She wears a kimono over a slip and is hobbling as if one leg were longer than another.*)

CAROL: I don't suppose you're all dressed up on my account.

(*Room:* CAROL *exits SR.*)

(*Forestage:* SHANNON *turns up to room.*)

SHANNON: What?

(*Room:* CAROL *enters SR and remains in SR corner of window. She is holding one red high-heeled shoe.*)

CAROL: I said: Do you want a drink?

SHANNON: Oh.
Just some mango juice, please.

CAROL: I don't suppose you're all dressed up on my account.

SHANNON: No. . . . I won't be having dinner here this evening.

CAROL: Are you going out with Jason Wilfred?

SHANNON: Yes, I am.
We have some important matters to discuss.

CAROL: Business?

SHANNON: Yes. Business.

(*Sound: Fade "wave sounds" under Chopin.*)

(*Room:* CAROL *walks to SL edge of window, turns.*)

CAROL: You don't want to admit you're dating, do you?

(*Room:* CAROL *exits SL.*)

SHANNON: (The watchmen that go about the city found me,
To whom I said:
Saw ye him whom my soul loveth?
It was but a little that I passed from them,
But I found him whom my soul loveth . . .)

(*Peephole:* CLIFF *enters SL, facing SR in profile, and crosses SR.*)

CLIFF: Excuse me . . .

SHANNON: (I held him and would not let him go.)

CLIFF: I'm looking for Dr. Malleson.

(*Room:* CAROL *enters SL, crosses to SL edge of peephole against back wall.* CLIFF *is at SR corner.*)

CAROL: I talked with Jason this afternoon, you know.

SHANNON: What is your name?

CAROL: I suppose you're just dying to know what we
talked about.

(*Peephole:* CLIFF *at SR corner turns to face out.*)

CLIFF: Call me Ishmael.

(*Room:* CAROL *crosses down center to window and leans across sill.*)

CAROL: I said: I talked with Ja . . .

SHANNON: Where did you see him?

Cliff: Excuse me. . . .

Carol: Didn't he tell you?

Cliff: I'm looking for Dr. Malleson.

Shannon: We didn't get much chance to talk all day.

Cliff: Call me Ishmael.

Shannon: We were both too busy.

Carol: I suppose you're just dying to know what we
talked about.

Shannon: Not really.

Cliff: How old are you?

Shannon: Twenty-nine.

(*Sound: Fade out "wave sounds" under Chopin.*)

Cliff: A very good age to be married at.

Carol: Oh, yes you are.

Cliff: And you've never been married?

Shannon: Never been married.

Cliff: Never been married?

Shannon: Never been married.

Carol: I can tell by the look in your eyes.

Shannon: I thought you were French,
But from you voice, you sound as if you might
be American.

Carol: Well, you don't have to worry.
The good Dr. Wilfred just isn't my type.

(*Peephole:* Cliff, *facing forward, starts moving sideways SL.*)

Cliff: You don't have to worry.

Carol: And I'm obviously not his.

Cliff: The good Dr. Wilfred just isn't my type.

(*Forestage:* Shannon *crosses back up SL to* Carol *in window.*)

Shannon: Carol, what are you trying to prove?

(*Peephole:* Cliff *exits SL.*)

CLIFF: And I'm obviously not his.

SHANNON: Or are you just making trouble for the fun of it?

(*FAITHLESS 3*)

(*Room:* CAROL *exits from window SL, as* JASON *enters SL on forestage. Fade up forestage strip lights; fade out peephole.*)

(*Sound: Fade out Chopin.*)

JASON: Well, well . . .
Alone at last, I see.

(*Forestage:* SHANNON *wheels on* JASON.)

SHANNON: Carol tells me she spoke with you today.

JASON: Ah . . .
Did she . . . tell you what we talked about?

SHANNON: No—was it important?

(*Forestage:* SHANNON *turns away and crosses SR.*)

JASON: Of course not, just business.

(*Forestage:* JASON *crosses to* SHANNON, *SR by chair.*)

JASON: You know I really like you with your hair like this.

(*Room:* CAROL *enters window SL; sees him embrace her.*)

SHANNON: What on earth's come over you?

JASON: I'm just getting the party going, that's all.
You know, it's really amazing:
For sisters, you're such completely different people.

CAROL: We're stepsisters.

(*Room:* CAROL *crosses to center of window.*)

CAROL: And there's not much love lost between us, either.

(*Forestage:* SHANNON *guiltily breaks free of* JASON.)

SHANNON: Jason, please, Carol's watching.

JASON: Carol loves it, don't you Carol?
Don't you want to see some more?

(*Forestage:* JASON *crosses up center to* CAROL.)

CAROL: Carol's had far too much wine.
Any minute now she's going to lose control and make a spectacle of herself.

JASON: Then I suggest you take yourself home right away, Carol.
This is, if you want to remember what you did tonight.

(*Room:* CAROL *reaches over sill and puts her arms around* JASON, *who is on the other side of the wall in the center of the window.*)

CAROL: Would you like to escort me to my bedroom, Doctor?
At the risk of making my step sister insanely jealous,
I just want you to know
I'd be absolutely delighted if you undressed me and put me to bed.

JASON: Get out!

(*Forestage:* JASON *pushes* CAROL *away and turns to* SHANNON.)

CAROL: Oh, yes!
They flee from me that sometime did me seek with naked foot stalking in my chamber. . . .

Of course, I'm very vain about my feet.
Jason always said I had such pretty feet.
But that's not as good as having a hospital,
Is it, Jason? . . . .

(*Forestage:* SHANNON *crosses up center to* JASON.)

JASON: It's been over a long time, Shannon.
I told her we were finished months ago.

CAROL: Oh, you told me lots of things!
You told me you were through with her for good!
Only then her father died and she inherited the hospital and then things were different, weren't they?
Weren't they?

(*Forestage:* JASON *crosses SL in front of* SHANNON.)

JASON: We don't have to listen to this.

(*Sound:* "Emperor Waltz" *(J. Strauss).*)

CAROL: That's right—you don't want her to hear that, do you?
How her father hated you?
How he threatened to throw you out of the hospital if you didn't stay away from her.
But it's not that easy, Jason—
Even if old men that get in your way do die when you want them to.

SHANNON: Stop it, stop it!

(*Forestage:* SHANNON *slaps* CAROL, *who steps back.*)

(*Sound: Cut music.*)

CAROL: You'll pay for that, Shannon.
Maybe not now, maybe not for a long time,
But you'll pay for that, I swear it!

(*Room:* CAROL *exits SL.*)

(*Forestage:* JASON *crosses towards* SHANNON, *who backs away.*)

JASON: Listen to me, she was drunk and she was lying.
She was talking nonsense and you know it.
If anything, you should feel contempt and pity for her.

SHANNON: It's true, isn't it?

JASON: What are you talking about?

SHANNON: Everything she said—it's true—all of it!

JASON: You're confused, Shannon.
Mixed-up.
You're not thinking clearly.

(*Sound: Fade in* "Neptune" *from* "The Planets" *(Holst).*)

JASON: Your father's death has evidently been too great a strain;
I'm concerned about your mental health.

(*Forestage:* JASON *tries to grab* SHANNON.)

SHANNON: Let go of me!

(*Forestage:* SHANNON *runs past* JASON *and exits SR.* JASON *follows after her and calls to her, off.*)

JASON: But you need help.
You need rest.
You need professional care.

(*TOXIN 2*)

(*Forestage:* CAROL *enters SL. Fade forestage lights down to pools.*)

(*Room:* SELDEN *enters SL and crosses SR reading from the little book. The box is under his arm.*)

SELDEN: Order Scorpionida/Morphology:
Scorpions (fig. 258) are elongated terrestrial arachnids/
large claws/stout pedipalps/anterior/posterior/caudal/
stinger/discharge of venom . . . Paragraph Two:
Its habits.

(*Forestage:* JASON *crosses slowly SL to* CAROL.)

SELDEN: There is a story common in the areas where scorpions are found that when surrounded by a ring of fire a scorpion will sting itself to death.

(*Forestage:* JASON *grabs* CAROL *in an embrace.*)

SELDEN: This story is based on an misconception.

(*Room:* SELDEN *exits SR.*)

JASON: I owe you an explanation.

CAROL: Oh, God, Jason—don't say anything.

JASON: You know how I feel about you, Carol.

CAROL: I thought you did. Once.

(*Room: As before,* SELDEN *enters SR and crosses SL reading from the little book.*)

SELDEN: Pathogenesis. . . .

JASON: I have a favor to ask of you.

SELDEN: Symptoms resemble strychnine poisoning:
Itching/twitching/nausea/vomiting/perspiration/paresthesia/
Numbness/convulsions and death.
Treatment. . . .

(*Offstage:* SHANNON *screams.*)

(*Peephole:* SHANNON *runs across, SR to SL.*)

(*Room:* SELDEN *stops, looks up and smiles; resumes.*)

SHANNON: (*Off*) Don't go in the bedroom.

JASON: Why not?

SHANNON: (*Off*) There's another big scorpion in there.

SELDEN: . . . . injection.

(*Room:* SELDEN *exits SL.*)

SHANNON: (*Off*) I don't know how it could have gotten in.

JASON: Why didn't you kill it, Shannon?

SHANNON: (*Off*) I was afraid to.
It's as big as my hand, and it really moves fast.

(*Room: As before,* SELDEN *enters SL and crosses SR, reading from the little book.*)

SELDEN: Prophylaxis: precautions . . .

CAROL: Have a nice evening, Shannon. . . .

(*Forestage:* CAROL *crosses SR.*)

SELDEN: . . . against contact with scorpions
Constitute the most practical means of prevention.
Attempts to reduce the scorpion population . . .

(*Forestage:* JASON *catches up with* CAROL *and turns her around.*)

JASON: Well . . . do you like my idea?

SELDEN: . . . have not proved particularly effective.

CAROL: More than I can tell you.

(*PRESCOTT 3*)

(*Forestage:* CAROL *exits SR, followed by* JASON. DIVINA *steps away from the wall and crosses SL to SR edge of window.*)

(*Room:* CAROL *enters SR and crosses SL, followed by* JASON. SELDEN *gapes at* CAROL'S *slip;* JASON *turns his face around SR as* CAROL *exits SL.*)

DIVINA: No time was now lost in preparing for the voyage.
The three associates had little difficulty in obtaining the consent of the governor,

(*Room:* JASON *and* SELDEN *are conferring up SR.*)

DIVINA: And fortified with funds,
Agreed that Pizarro should take command.
There was more difficulty in obtaining the necessary complement of hands.
Still, there were many idle hangers-on in the colony,
Who had come out to mend their fortunes,
And were willing to take their chances on doing so, however desperate. . . .

(*ROMEO 2*)

(*Forestage:* DIVINA *sits in SR chair, flings her hair back.*)

(*Sound: Crossfade to* "Eventide" *(Count Basie).*)

(*Forestage:* CLIFF *enters SR. He is wearing khaki trousers and a pink shirt, with a checked, cream-colored sport coat over his shoulder. He crosses to the SR chair and stands behind* DIVINA.)

CLIFF: Nel mezzo del cammin di nostra vita,
Mi ritrovai per una selva oscura
Che la diritta via era smarrita.
Ah, quanto a dir qual era e cosa dura, esta selva selvaggia e aspra e forte,
Che nel pensier rinnova la paura!
Tant'e amara che poco e piu morte;
Ma per trattar del ben ch'io vi trovai,
Diro dell'altre cose ch'i'vh'ho scorte.

DIVINA: I know the sad condition you are reduced to by your separation from your prince.
You have found the true and only way.
You see, sir—it is not so difficult.

CLIFF: Well, said the fifth boy,
Had he not been so kind and so beautiful,
Such good fortune had never come to his lot.

But, tell me . . .

DIVINA: Okay.

CLIFF: But, tell me . . .

(*Sound: Fade "wave sounds" in under* "Eventide")

DIVINA: Okay.

CLIFF: Whatever became of the Inka?

(*Forestage:* DIVINA *stands.*)

DIVINA: Indeed, I know not.

(*Forestage:* DIVINA *turns and exits SR.* CLIFF *follows her with his gaze.*)

(*Sound: Fade out* "Eventide", *leaving "wave sounds".*)

CLIFF: Why then, said the fifth boy,
Who can tell me something about him? . . . .

(*CAMPAIGN 2*)

(*Forestage:* CLIFF *sits in SR chair.*)

(*Room:* JASON *and* SELDEN *cross down to center at window and watch* CLIFF.)

JASON: So, that's the fish?

SELDEN: That's the fish.

JASON: The big fish . . .

SELDEN: Yeah. . . .
He's someone that I, over the years, have grown to have enough faith in that could
Really show us how to put this thing together.

JASON: Well, he is obviously flailing around like a wild man at the present time.

SELDEN: No—no, he's not, really . . .
I think he was earlier. He was frantic.
But he's a good man,
And he's a man, incidentally, that could . . .

(*Room:* DIVINA *enters SL, crosses upstage of them, rubbing her hair with shawl as if drying it.*)

DIVINA: He's a strange man.

(*Room:* DIVINA *exits SR.*)

JASON: Strange? . . .
Strange or strong—what did she say?

SELDEN: Strange *and* strong.
He's tough—he's really tough.
He's a good man,
And he's a man, incidentally, that could . . .

JASON: Okay, how do we get to him?

SELDEN: Oh, I would think an appeal directly to . . .

JASON: Why don't we do that tonight?

SELDEN: I would think that's easy enough.

JASON: Good.
So, it's in the mill!
We've finally started something.

For the nets come down from the eyes of the Lord
To fish up men to their salvation. . . .

(*Room:* JASON *exits SL,* SELDEN *following.*)

SELDEN: What an exciting prospect!

JASON: (*Off*) I wouldn't want to be on the other side right now,
Would you?

(*Fade up forestage striplight; fade out room.*)

(*ROMEO 3*)

(*Offstage:* SHANNON *is heard whistling* "The Way We Were".)

(*Forestage:* SHANNON *enters SR, crossing SL behind* CLIFF. *She is wearing a lab coat over her office dress and writes on the clipboard.*)

CLIFF: Excuse me . . .

(*Forestage:* SHANNON *stops center, turns to* CLIFF.)

SHANNON: Yes?

CLIFF: I'm looking for Dr. Malleson.

SHANNON: I'm Dr. Malleson.

(*Forestage:* CLIFF *stands.*)

CLIFF: Oh, I'm sorry, I . . . didn't realize . . .

(*Sound: Fade out "wave sounds".*)

SHANNON: That I was a woman?
Yes, my name confuses people sometimes.
You must be Dr. Sinclair.

(*Forestage:* SHANNON *crosses to* CLIFF *and shakes hands.*)

CLIFF: Please—call me Cliff.

SHANNON: All right, Cliff.

CLIFF: Do you mind if I ask you a personal question?

SHANNON: Of course not.

CLIFF: How old are you?

SHANNON: Twenty-nine.

CLIFF: Twenty-nine. . . .
A very good age to be married at.

And you've never been married?

(*Forestage:* SHANNON *turns away and crosses SL,* CLIFF *following.*)

SHANNON: Never been married.

CLIFF: Never been married?

SHANNON: Never been married.

CLIFF: Never been married?

SHANNON: Never been married. . . .

(*Forestage:* SHANNON *turns to face* CLIFF.)

SHANNON: I thought you were French,
But from the sound of your voice,
You might be American?

CLIFF: I am.

(*Sound: Fade in adagio from* "Sleeping Beauty" *(Tchaikovsky).*)

SHANNON: Would it be prying if I asked you
What made you give up your work in Paris to come here?

(*Forestage:* CLIFF *turns away from her.*)

SHANNON: What doom is pursuing you—what violent fate casts you on this shore?

CLIFF: Well, we have to go back a long way for that. . . .

(*Forestage:* CLIFF *crosses SR.*)

CLIFF: Some years ago . . .
(Having little or no money)
My sponsors in baptism . . .
(Having little or no money)
Wherein I was made . . .
(Having nothing on shore)
A member of Christ, the child of God . . .
(Nothing particular,
Nothing to interest me—an inheritor of the kingdom of Heaven) . . .

(*Forestage:* SHANNON *crosses to* CLIFF *in time to the music.*)

CLIFF: I thought I would sail,
Thought I would sail about a little,
Thought I would see the water, the watery part—
I thought I would see!

I sought him, but I found him not. . . .

SHANNON: I hope you're not having second thoughts about coming to join us?

CLIFF: Not at all;
In fact, I'm liking it more and more.

(*Forestage:* SHANNON *turns to go off SL, then turns back to* CLIFF.)

SHANNON: I'm having a party at my house tonight—
Buffet supper, music so we can dance. . . .

I hope you can come.

CLIFF: I'll be there.

(*CAMPAIGN 3*)

(*Forestage:* SHANNON *exits SL.* CLIFF *crosses SL to center, stops.*)

CLIFF: But I must go down to the seas again,
To the lonely sea and the sky.
And all I ask is a tall ship and a star to steer her by.
And the wheel's kick,
And the wind's song,
And the white sails shaking;
And a gray mist on the sea's face,
And a gray dawn breaking. . . .

(*Peephole:* JASON *enters at SL corner.*)

JASON: You can join us in our quest for new horizons.

(*Sound: Crossfade to* "Sirens" *from* "Nocturnes" *(Debussy).*)

JASON: But you must have the vision to see things
Not as they are, but as they could be.

(*Peephole:* JASON *exits SL.*)

(*Room:* SELDEN *enters at SR corner of window.*)

(*Forestage:* CLIFF *crosses to* SELDEN.)

SELDEN: Imagine. . . .

As the eastern sky slowly brightens,
A distant chorus of peepers cheerfully announces spring.
In this delicious valley,
The Incas built the most beautiful of their palaces.
Here, when wearied of the dust and toil of the city,
They loved to retreat with their favorite concubines,
Wandering amidst groves and airy gardens that shed around their soft, intoxicating odors,
And lulled the senses to voluptuous repose.

(*Room:* JASON *enters SL, a lab coat over his shoulder. He crosses to the center of window and sits on the sill.*)

SELDEN: Here, too,
They loved to indulge in the luxury of their baths
Replenished by streams of crystal water,
Conducted through silver channels
Into basins of gold,
While by their sides were plants and flowers skillfully imitated in gold and silver,

Among them, Indian corn—
The golden ear amid the leaves of silver, and the light tassel floating gracefully from the top. . . .

JASON: If the above scene is familiar to you,

SELDEN: Or you wish it were,

(*Forestage:* JASON *swings over the wall beside* CLIFF.)

JASON: Come along right now and join us—
We few, we happy few, we band of brothers.
For he today that sheds his blood with me shall be my brother.

SELDEN: I, too, have gone through much;
Like you, have been roughly handled by fortune. . . .

(*Forestage:* JASON *throws the lab coat over* CLIFF'S *shoulder and leads him by the arm down center.*)

(*Room:* SELDEN *exits SR.*)

JASON: Your fellow chapter-members are the kind you've always wanted to meet—
Sincere, dedicated outdoorsmen.
We'll give you the in-depth training it takes to compete and make big money!

(*Forestage:* SELDEN *enters SR.*)

SELDEN: You risk nothing! So don't delay!

(*Forestage:* JASON *leads* CLIFF *SR, indicating that "Peru" is SL.*)

JASON: Then, drawing his sword,
He traced a line with it in the sand.
"Friends and comrades,
On that side are toil, hunger, nakedness, the drenching storm, desertion and death.
On this side, ease and pleasure.
There lies Peru and its riches—
Here, Panama and its poverty.
Choose . . .

SELDEN: Choose . . .

JASON: Choose each man what best becomes a brave Castilian!"

(*Sound: Fade in Sun Chorus from* "Gurrelieder" *(Schoenberg).*)

(*Forestage:* JASON *steps back from* CLIFF *SR as* CLIFF *runs SL to center.*)

JASON: So saying, he stepped over the line.

(*Forestage:* DIVINA *enters SR.*)

CLIFF: And yes I said yes I will yes!
I must go down to the seas again,
To the vagrant gypsy life,
To the gull's way and the whale's way, where the wind's like a whetted knife.
And all I ask is a merry yarn
From a laughing fellow-rover,
And a quiet sleep, and a sweet dream,
When the long trick's over. . . .

(*Forestage:* SELDEN *crosses SL to* CLIFF.)

CLIFF: A thousand hearts are great within my bosom!

(*Forestage:* JASON *crosses SL toward exit.*)

JASON: So, we will go with him all together!

(*Forestage:* JASON *exits SL as* CLIFF *and* SELDEN *follow.*)

CLIFF: You know, I'm really looking forward to this little trip. It'll be just what the doctor ordered.

SELDEN: My true friend—
I will not desert you to my life's end!

(*PRESCOTT 5*)

(*Forestage:* CLIFF *and* SELDEN *exit SL as* DIVINA *crosses to SL chair. Fade forestage lights down to pools.* DIVINA *moves SL chair from wall to center of light pool directly downstage, midway to audience. Peephole:* SELDEN *and* CLIFF *enter SL, in profile, as* CAROL *enters SR, in profile. They have glasses in their hands. Throughout this scene and the next, the characters in the peephole improvise cocktail-party conversation by having one performer speak one of the lines from Prescott's* Conquest of Peru *(see below), and another respond: "Yes, that's. . . . I've been told that many times. . . ."*)

*Party Dialog*:
Another legend speaks of certain white and bearded men advancing along the shores of Lake Titicaca.
The noble roads were lined with people who swept away the stones and stubble, strewing them with flowers.

No wonder that the government should have dealt with sloth as a crime.

The Peruvian mountains teemed with gold.

The magazines of grain, in particular, would have sufficed for several years.

Many of these stones were of vast size, some being fully thirty-eight feet long and six feet thick, so tightly joined that it was impossible to introduce even the blade of a knife between them.

After the lapse of centuries, they still retained their individuality as a people.

The body of the deceased Inca was skillfully embalmed and removed to the great temple of the Sun at Cuzco.

They went through their labors with the same joyous spirit, regulating their movements by the measure of the chant, of which the word *hailli* was usually the burden.

The flocks of llamas were appropriated exclusively to the Sun and to the Inca.

Even the proudest of the Inca nobility could not venture into the royal presence unless barefoot.

(*Peephole: The dialog and response continues as* DIVINA *addresses the audience from SL chair on the forestage.*)

DIVINA: Having thus solemnly invoked the blessing of Heaven on the enterprise,
Pizarro and his followers sallied forth for the conquest of Peru.

(*Room:* JASON, *no longer wearing a lab coat, enters SR and paces back and forth.*)

DIVINA: Yet the force at his command seemed but a small one for the conquest of an empire.

(*Sound: Crossfade* "Gurrelieder" *out, fading in* "Terry's Theme" *(Billy Vaughn).*)

DIVINA: The whole number did not exceed one hundred eighty men,
With twenty-seven horses for the cavalry.
With this, the intrepid chief proposed to commence operations.

(*CAMPAIGN 4*)

(*Peephole:* SHANNON *makes an "entrance", SR.*)

(*Forestage:* DIVINA *sits in SL chair, watching* JASON *in the room.*)

(*Room:* JASON *paces back and forth, practicing his speech. Party dialog continues in peephole.*)

JASON: My friends . . .
For some months past, I have been considering, working, calculating . . .
(Considering and calculating? . . .
*Working* and calculating. . . .")
My friends,
For some months past I have been working and calculating, for I am not without authority in my blah, blah, blah. . . .
. . . so on and so forth . . .
. . . Nineteenth Century . . .
For the Host is in the West,
The Lord make us thankful!
For while we gaze upon the radiant array of the heroic army of the dead, with all their something something . . .

(*Room: Green sidelight hits* JASON *from SL. He freezes, staring out; his voice changes.*)

JASON: (. . . *and Jechonias begat Salathiel begat* . . .)

(*Room: Green sidelight fades out;* JASON *appears momentarily dazed, then recovers.*)

JASON: For while we gaze upon the. . . .
Luminous array?
"For while we gaze upon the luminous array . . ."
"For while we gaze upon the *radiant* array . . ."

(*Room: Green sidelight again from SL.* JASON *freezes as before and his voice changes.*)

JASON: (. . . *and Jechonias begat Salathiel begat Eliud begat Eliazar.* . . .

(*Room: Fade out green sidelight as before.*)

JASON: . . . from every battlefield from the Ohio to the ocean,

(*Peephole:* SHANNON *exits SR.*)

JASON: It was indeed the cross,
The fiery cross,

The only sign of man's salvation by which generations
yet unborn were to be rescued from eternal perdidtion!
But it was still the cross!

(*Peephole:* CLIFF *crosses SR and exits.*)

(*Room: Green light as before.*)

JASON: (. . . *and Aram begat Asa, and Asa begat Josephat, and Josephat begat Joram, and Joram begat Ozias, and Jacob begat Joseph the husband of Mary of whom was born Jesus who is called Christ*!)

(*Forestage:* DIVINA *stands, crosses to SL side of window, then crosses SR to wall of theatre.*)

(*Peephole:* CAROL *exits SR as on forestage* SHANNON *enters SL and crosses to SL chair.*)

(*Peephole:* SELDEN *exits SR.*)

(*Room: Fade out green sidelight as before.*)

JASON: Oh, friends and comrades.
Is there among you one,
Who has not dreamed,
Or at least heard,
Of Peru. . . .

(*ROMEO 5*)

(*Room:* CAROL *enters SR with a glass, crosses to* JASON *center and kisses him. They exit SL, as* CLIFF *enters SR on forestage and crosses to SR chair.*)

(*Sound:* "Terry's Theme" *has played out.*)

SHANNON: Admiring the view?

CLIFF: I was just thinking how easy it would be to
get addicted to this country. . . .
So immense is the scale on which nature works in
these regions that it is only when viewed from
a great distance that the spectator can comprehend
the relation of the several parts to the
Stupendous whole.

SHANNON: Mmmmm—I know what you mean.
Sometime I'd like to show you the desert.

CLIFF: I'd like that.

(*Forestage:* SHANNON *crosses SR to* CLIFF.)

SHANNON: See that patch of green over there?
That's the garden where we had breakfast this morning.
Over there—next to the tower—see it?

CLIFF: No—where?

SHANNON: See the tower?

CLIFF: Now I see it.

(*Forestage:* SHANNON *suddenly turns away from* CLIFF *and murmurs.*)

SHANNON: (And there. . . .
A little speck on the verge of the horizon
That was to spread wider and wider
Till it burst in thunder on the devoted nation. . . .)

CLIFF: I'd rather look at you.

SHANNON: Maybe we'd better go now.

(*Forestage:* SHANNON *crosses up SL.*)

CLIFF: You're so beautiful, Peggy.

(*Forestage:* SHANNON *stops, her back to* CLIFF.)

SHANNON: No, Cliff. Please, don't.

(*Forestage:* CLIFF *crosses up SR.*)

CLIFF: But what's the matter, Ann?
Why don't you tell me what's wrong?

(*Forestage:* SHANNON *turns to* CLIFF.)

SHANNON: All that I know distresses me.
All that I see afflicts me.
The sky and the sea oppress me.
My life has become such a burden.

It is Lameir that so oppresses me.
Lameir is what distresses me.
Lameir that pains me so.

(*Sound: Fade in* "Don Juan" *(R. Strauss), first introduction of theme.*)

CLIFF: Sweet, lovely woman—so it is with me:
Lameir and you are what distress me.
My dearest lady,
You and you alone and the passion you inspire
in me have turned my wits and robbed me of
my reason. . . .

(*Forestage:* SHANNON *crosses down to SL chair.*)

SHANNON: (He said)

CLIFF: I have gone astray so utterly
That I shall never find my way again.

SHANNON: (He said)

CLIFF: All that I see irks and oppresses me.
It all grows trite and meaningless.
Nothing in the wide world is so dear to my heart
but you.

SHANNON: (He said he said)

(*Forestage:* CLIFF *crosses to* SHANNON *by DSL chair.*)

CLIFF: Enter Romeo.

SHANNON: (He said he said)

CLIFF: He jests at scars that never felt a wound.

SHANNON: (I said: Enter Juliet above at a window;
He said he said he said)

(*Forestage:* SHANNON *crosses SL to theatre wall.*)

CLIFF: But soft, what light through yonder coo coo-coo?
It is the East, and Juliet coo coo-coo!

SHANNON: (I said: Aye, me!
He said he said)

CLIFF: She speaks! Oh, coo coo-coo coo-coo!

(*Forestage:* SHANNON *turns to face* CLIFF.)

SHANNON: (I said: Oh Romeo, Romeo, wherefore art thou, Romeo?
He said)

CLIFF: Aside: Shall I hear more or shall I speak at this?

(*Forestage:* SHANNON *crosses SR, upstage of* CLIFF.)

SHANNON: I said: 'Tis but thy coo that is my coo coo-coo,
Coo-coo coo-coo coo-coo coo-coo coo-coo.
What's Montague?

(*Room:* SELDEN *enters SL, notices* SHANNON *and* CLIFF.)

SHANNON: It is nor hand nor foot
Nor arm nor face nor any other coo
Coo-coo coo-coo coo-coo coo-coo coo-coo
Coo-coo coo-coo coo-coo coo-coo a rose
By any other name would smell as sweet.
(He said)

(*Room:* SELDEN *exits SL, as* CLIFF *crosses SR to* SHANNON *on forestage.*)

CLIFF: Call me but love, and I'll be new baptized.

SHANNON: I said: O, gentle Romeo,
If thou do'st love, pronounce it faithfully.

(*Room:* JASON *and* SELDEN *enter SL and watch* CLIFF *and* SHANNON.)

CLIFF: Cecily,
Ever since I first looked upon your wonderful and incomparable beauty, I have dared to love you wildly, passionately, devotedly, hopelessly.

SHANNON: My own Ernest!

CLIFF: And you really love me, Gwendolyn?

SHANNON: Wildly, passionately, devotedly, hopelessly.

(*Room:* JASON *and* SELDEN *exit SL.*)

CLIFF: Darling, you don't know how happy you've made me.

(*Forestage:* CLIFF *and* SHANNON *kiss as* JASON *and* SELDEN *enter SL.*)

JASON: Shannon!
There is something I must talk to you about.

(*Forestage:* SHANNON *guiltily breaks free of* CLIFF.)

SHANNON: You can speak in front of Cliff.
There are no secrets here.

JASON: Privately.
I insist.

SELDEN: It's the Inka.
He's had a relapse.

SHANNON: Okay. Let's go to the conference room.
I'll be right back.

(*Forestage:* SHANNON *exits SL followed by* JASON.)

SELDEN: So, how do you like your new colleagues?

CLIFF: I think I'll do very good work here.
Dr. Wilfred seems to be very open and expansive on every subject, and Shannon. . . .

SELDEN: You're on a first-name basis already?

CLIFF: Her name suits her, doesn't it?
A beautiful name for a beautiful woman.
She's unusually lovely—or hadn't you noticed?

SELDEN: Of course I have.

(*Forestage:* CLIFF *crosses SR.*)

CLIFF: Oh, she doth teach the torches to burn bright.
It seems she hangs upon the cheek of night
Like a rich jewel in an Ethiope's ear.

(*Sound:* "Gurrelieder" *fades out; fade in "tone"* .)

CLIFF: And yet—there's something kind of secretive about her.
Whenever you mention the past, she becomes vague—
Evasive—
Almost as if she had something to hide.

Do you think there's anything between them?

SELDEN: She hasn't told you, then?

CLIFF: Told me what?

SELDEN: Told you they're engaged to be married.

(*FAITHLESS 4*)

(*Forestage:* CLIFF *brushes past* SELDEN *and exits SL, followed by* SELDEN, *as* SHANNON *enters room SL and crosses up SR, as* JASON *enters SL.*)

JASON: I won't let you do that.

SHANNON: Why not?
Because you'd lose the hospital?
Well, there is nothing you can do to stop me!

(*Room:* JASON *crosses up SR to* SHANNON.)

JASON: You don't understand.
I've waited for that hospital too long!
For the sin against the Holy Ghost is Ingratitude.
You'll be my wife and you'll stay my wife.

For the angel Gratitude is my wife—God bring
me to her or her to me.

(*Room:* SHANNON *breaks free of* JASON, *crosses down to SR corner of window.*)

SHANNON: All right, then—take me back!
But I won't stay with you—I won't!

JASON: I never thought you would.
You've been under a great strain since your father died, Shannon.
You're sick.
That's why you need to be put away.

SHANNON: You can't put me away—you can't!
Everybody knows I'm sane.

(*Sound: Fade in* "Ave Maria" *(Ockeghem) under "tone"* .)

JASON: Do they? . . .
I wonder. . . .

(*Room:* JASON *crosses down SR to* SHANNON.)

SHANNON: No—you won't lock me up!
Let me go!

(*Room:* JASON *grabs* SHANNON *in SR corner of window and kisses her fiercely. She struggles, as:*)

(*PRESCOTT 4*)

(*Forestage:* DIVINA *crosses SL from SR theatre wall to SR corner of window.*)

DIVINA: There is something striking, isn't there,
In the spectacle of a few brave souls thus consecrating themselves to a daring enterprise.
A handful of men,
Without food,
Without clothing,
Carrying on a crusade against a powerful empire.
This was the crisis of Pizarro's fate.

(*Forestage:* DIVINA *crosses center.*)

Had Pizarro faltered now, his name would have been buried with his fortunes.
For there are moments in the lives of men which, as they are seized or neglected,
Decide their future destiny.

(*Forestage:* DIVINA *crosses SL, as in room,* JASON *steps back from* SHANNON.)

DIVINA: But his constancy was equal to the occasion.
And his conduct here inspired others with a confidence in him which was the best
Assurance of success.

(*TOXIN 3*)

(*Forestage:* DIVINA *crosses SL to theatre wall, as* CLIFF *enters SL in room, sees* SHANNON *and* JASON.)

(*Room:* SHANNON *runs out SL, followed by* CLIFF.)

(*Forestage:* SHANNON *enters SL, followed by* CLIFF, *as* JASON *exits SR from room.*)

(*Sound: Fade in* "Prelude" *Op. 28 #4 (Chopin); fade out* "tone" *and* "Ave Maria" *as on forestage,* SHANNON *crosses to center chair and sits.*)

CLIFF: So . . .
What was wrong with the Inka?

SHANNON: The Inka? . . .
Oh, we're not sure—the tetany tests were negative.
But there is one thing that bothers me.

Apparently the Inka and my father had the same kind of convulsions.
He kept screaming: Don't touch my feet!

(*Forestage:* CLIFF *crosses to* SHANNON.)

CLIFF: I thought your father died of a scorpion sting.

SHANNON: Well, yes—at the time, that's what we all thought.
But—

CLIFF: But?

SHANNON: Oh, it all sounds so crazy!
It's just—it seems to me several years ago there was one case I remember that. . . .
Well, it was a murder case.
He died of strychnine poisoning!

I'm sorry, Cliff—I have to go.

(*Forestage:* SHANNON *stands, starts to exit SR.*)

CLIFF: Why are you holding out on me, Shannon?

(*ROMEO 6*)

(*Forestage:* SHANNON *stops, her back to* CLIFF.)

SHANNON: I've had to change my plans very suddenly.

(*Forestage:* CLIFF *crosses SR to* SHANNON.)

CLIFF: Are you afraid people might talk?

SHANNON: What do you mean?

CLIFF: I was thinking of Jason, actually.
You're engaged, aren't you?

(*Forestage:* SHANNON *turns to* CLIFF *but notices* DIVINA *against SL house wall.* SHANNON *slowly begins to cross SL to her, walking past* CLIFF.)

CLIFF: Have I offended you?

SHANNON: (Every avenue to escape was closed . . .)

CLIFF: Are you okay?

SHANNON: (. . . waved a white scarf in the air,
The appointed signal . . .)

CLIFF: Are you angry?

SHANNON: (Then every Spaniard in the city,
Each in his dark column,
Rushing from the avenues in which they were concealed
Poured into the plaza. . . .)

(*Forestage:* CLIFF *crosses down to SR chair.*)

CLIFF: I thought . . .
I thought you really cared for me . . .
That you wanted . . .
But you don't.

SHANNON: (All were trampled under the fierce charge . . .)

CLIFF: You really aren't free, are you?

SHANNON: (The entrance to the square was choked with bodies . . .)

CLIFF: Do you always keep your promises?

SHANNON: (They made no resistance.
They had no weapons with which to make it.
And what wonder was it, says an ancient Inca to
a Spaniard who repeats it,

What wonder that our countrymen lost their wits,
Seeing blood run like water . . .)

CLIFF: Do you love him?

SHANNON: (And the Inca,
Whose person we all of us adore,
Seized and carried off by a handful of men.)

(*Forestage:* CLIFF *crosses SL to* SHANNON. *Their dialog overlaps.*)

CLIFF: I want you to know something . . .

SHANNON: (Yet though the massacre was incessant . . .)

CLIFF: Then I'll never say another word, I promise you.

SHANNON: (The whole time consumed by it—the twilight
of the tropics—)

CLIFF: I knew a woman once, and she died.

SHANNON: (Did not exceed half an hour. . . .)

CLIFF: She died in my arms.
I haven't cared for a woman since.
But you made me feel things I thought I would
never feel again,
And for this, I will always be grateful.

(*Forestage:* CLIFF *crosses up SL toward exit.*)

CLIFF: I love you, Shannon.

Good-bye. . . .

(*ROMEO 7*)

(*Sound: Fade in "tone" under* "Prelude".)

DIVINA: (*Whispers*) Let be ta'en.

SHANNON: Wilt thou be gone?

DIVINA: (*Whispers*) Let me be put to death.

(*Forestage:* CLIFF *stops up SL, his back to* SHANNON.)

CLIFF: I must be gone.

DIVINA: (*Whispers*) Let me be ta'en.

(*Forestage:* CLIFF *turns to face* SHANNON.)

CLIFF: Don't worry—you'll be in a lot of pain for
a while,
But in a few days you'll be back to normal.

DIVINA: (*Whispers*) Let me be put to death.

SHANNON: But there's already been a scorpion in the house.

DIVINA: (*Whispers*) Come, death, and welcome.

(*Forestage:* SHANNON *crosses to* CLIFF.)

SHANNON: Wilt thou be gone? It is not yet near day.
Therefore, stay yet—thou need'st not to be gone.

(*Sound:* "Prelude" *has played out.*)

CLIFF: I must be gone.
I must go down to the sea again,
For the call of the running tide
Is a wild call and a clear call
That may not be denied.
And all I ask is a tall ship
With its white sails flying,
And the flung spray and the blown spume,
And the seagulls crying.
Come, death, and welcome!

(*Room:* JASON *enters SR, forearms raised, wearing surgical scrubs, and stands up SR.* CAROL *enters SR behind him wearing scrubs, gown, hairnet, mask, and surgical gloves. She puts a surgical cap on* JASON *from behind.*)

SHANNON: So we'll go no more a'roving,
So late into the night,
Though the heart be still as loving,
And the moon be still as bright?

DIVINA: (*Whispers*) Come, death, and welcome.

(*Room:* CAROL *exits SR and returns with surgical gown, which she puts on* JASON.)

CLIFF: Though the heart was made for loving,
And the day returns too soon,
Yet we'll go no more a'roving by the
light of the moon.

SHANNON: Yond light is not daylight,
I know it, I.
Therefore, stay yet—thou need'st not to be gone.

(*Forestage:* CLIFF *steps away from* SHANNON.)

(*Room:* CAROL *ties a surgical mask around* JASON'S *mouth.*)

CLIFF: Though the heart was made for loving,
And the day returns too soon,
Yet we'll go no more a'roving by the
light of the moon. . . .

(*Forestage:* CLIFF *turns up SL.*)

(*Sound: Fade out "tone"; fade in* "Theme and Variations for Two Guitars," *Second Variation (Spohr).*)

CLIFF: Away.
I'm bound away.
'Cross the wide Missouri.

(*CAMPAIGN 8*)

(*Forestage:* CLIFF *exits SL, followed by* SHANNON.)

(*Room:* CAROL *exits SR and returns with glove, which she holds for* JASON.)

(*Forestage:* DIVINA *exits SL, lights dim to pools, as in room,* SELDEN, *in scrubs and cap, enters SL, forearms raised.* CAROL *exits SR and returns with second glove.*)

SELDEN: Well, as I see it,
The only problems we may have are the human problems,
And I will keep a close watch on that.

JASON: Union?

SELDEN: Human.
Human frailties.
His head is full of old recollections—
His past is always present to him—
And we must understand him.

(*Room:* JASON *crosses SL to* SELDEN.)

JASON: I pray you, tell me what they deserve that do
conspire my death?

SELDEN: . . . Sir? . . .

JASON: I said:
I pray you tell me what they deserve that do
conspire my death with devilish plots and have
prevailed against my body with their hellish
charms?

SELDEN: . . . Well, if. . . .

JASON: *If?*
Repeat that insolence and I will knock your
teeth down your throat!

(*Room:* CAROL *exits SR.*)

SELDEN: You can't do this, Dr. Wilfred—you can't!

JASON: I've done it!

(*Room:* JASON *crosses down to SR corner of window as* CAROL *enters SR with gown and crosses SL to* SELDEN, *dressing him in it.*)

SELDEN: And if someone should challenge you?

JASON: Who'd do that?
Don't try to bluff me, Selden.

SELDEN: And don't you try to bully me!

JASON: Then will you help me kill a friend?

SELDEN: I'd rather help you kill two enemies.

(*Room:* CAROL *exits SR.*)

JASON: Why, there thou hast it—
Two deep enemies—
Foes to my rest and my sweet sleep's disturbers.

(*Room:* CAROL *enters SR with glove; she holds it out.* SELDEN *crosses SR to her and puts it on.*)

JASON: They didn't have to do it.
Oh, no—they were doing this quite deliberately.
And they are asking for it.
And they are going to get it. . . .

(*PRESCOTT 7*)

(*Room:* DIVINA *enters SL and stands in down SL corner of window.* CAROL *exits SR and returns with second glove, which she holds for* SELDEN.)

DIVINA: Pizarro now saw that it was not politic to
stay in his present quarters, where disaffection
would soon creep into his followers unless
their spirits were stimulated by incessant action.
Yet he felt deeply anxious to obtain more particulars
of the actual conditions of the Empire;
Of the monarch who ruled over it,
And of his present situation. . . .

(*CAMPAIGN 4*)

(*Sound: Fade out* "Variation #2".)

(*Room:* JASON *crosses up SL and begins to pace back and forth against back wall.*)

JASON: It is now twenty minutes past ten.
At twenty-seven minutes past ten, Murchison
will launch the electric spark.
Thus, we still have seven minutes. . . .

(*Room:* CLIFF *enters SL, forearms raised, wearing scrubs and cap.* CAROL *exits SR.*)

CLIFF: A few instants alone separate us from
an eventful moment.

JASON: Yes, let us prepare.
For the more the light is defective, the
more the powers of darkness prevail. . . .

(*Room:* CAROL *enters SR with gown and crosses to* CLIFF, *dressing him.*)

SELDEN: One clasp of the hands, my friends!

(I have but one fear,
Which is that the wall might melt.)

CLIFF: Calm yourself, my worthy friend.

SELDEN: I feared it.

(*Room:* CAROL *exits SR and returns with glove, which she holds for* CLIFF, *who crosses SR to her.*)

CLIFF: Dear friend,
Hold close to me now and you will feel no fear of death.
If your heart is fearful, throw away fear.

(*Room:* CAROL *exits SR and returns with second glove, which she holds for* CLIFF.)

CLIFF: When two go together,
Each will protect himself and shield his
companion.

(*Sound: fade in* "Dead Waters" *(Schreier).*)

CLIFF: And if they fall,
They leave an enduring name.

Selden: Oh, my Lord—you may go on if you choose into
this land, but I will go back to the city!

(*Room:* Jason *crosses down to the window center.* Cliff *crosses to window SR of* Jason, Selden *crosses to window SR of* Cliff, Carol *crosses to window SR of* Selden*;* Cliff *and* Selden, *raise their surgical masks:*)

Jason: Enough!
Let it be no longer a question of returning.
We have already entertained it too long.
We must now decide how we can best place
ourselves to resist the shock.

(*Room:* Divina, Jason, Cliff, Selden, *and* Carol *(SL to SR) stand in a line at the window. Beat.*)

(*Peephole:* Shannon *enters SR and slowly crosses SL.*)

Shannon: That's my body they're looking for—
Those people,
The boats,
The cannon—
The body of Shannon Malleson.
No—Shannon Malleson Wilfred!
They're looking for the body of Mrs. Jason Wilfred.

(*Peephole:* Shannon *exits SL. Beat.*)

Jason: Well? . . .
Are we moving?
Are we really moving?

(*Room:* Carol *exits SR and returns, wheeling a cart, which she positions up SR.*)

Cliff: Yes.
Yes, we are moving—we are launched!

(*Room:* Jason *crosses up SR to cart, followed by* Cliff, *followed by* Selden.)

Jason: The road is open.
The will of heaven be done!

(*Room:* Jason *holds out his hand,* Carol *slaps a scalpel in his palm.*)

Jason: Ah, what voluptuousness to float amid this radiant
ether. . . .

(*Room:* JASON *raises the scalpel in the air.*)

JASON: We inhabit a new world, peopled by ourselves.

(*Room:* JASON *makes the first incision.*)

JASON: The empire is ours!

(*Room:* JASON *tosses scalpel into a bowl, crossing down SL to center and pulling down his mask.* CLIFF *turns to him from cart.*)

CLIFF: I do not think so, Captain.

(*Sound: Fade in "tone" under* 'Dead Waters".)

CLIFF: Beyond us, around us, human nature is at an end.
We are the only population of this microcosm.
We are lost. May God preserve us.

(*Room:* DIVINA *points out at audience as a large green floodlight comes on over the cart.*)

DIVINA: The sun!

(*Room:* DIVINA *exits quickly SL as the others turn to look out at the audience.*)

SELDEN: The sun . . .

CLIFF: The sun . . .

JASON: Yes, I expected it.

(*Room:* JASON *crosses SL, following* DIVINA.)

JASON: You and your companions will not have so much to complain of in the chance which bound you to my fate.
You are going to visit the land of marvels.

(*PRESCOTT 8*)

(*Room:* JASON *exits SL;* CLIFF *and* SELDEN *turn back to the cart and, with* CAROL, *mime an operation.*)

(*Forestage:* DIVINA *enters SL and crosses center to chair.*)

DIVINA: But while Pizarro had decided to march into the interior,
It is doubtful whether he had formed any more definite plan of action.
Unfortunately, he could not write,
And he has left no record to enlighten us as to his motive.

(*Forestage:* DIVINA *moves center chair from wall to center of light pool directly downstage, midway to audience.*)

DIVINA: The march of the troops was severe and
painful in the extreme.
The glare was intense,
And the rays of the vertical sun beat fiercely
on the iron mail until the troops almost
suffocated with the heat.
Nothing could be more dreary and disheartening
than the aspect of the country,
Where exhalations from the surface of the ground
poisoned the air,
And silence reigned unbroken.

(*Sound:* "Dead Waters" *has played out; fade out "tone" as fade in* "Cloches" *from* "Images" *(Debussy).*)

(*Forestage:* DIVINA *crosses SR.*)

DIVINA: The soldiers of Pizarro now cursed the hour in which
they had enlisted under his standard.

Pizarro, however, did not lose heart.

(*CAMPAIGN 6*)

(*Forestage:* DIVINA *exits SR, as in room,* CAROL *exits SL.*)

SELDEN: What are you daydreaming about?

CLIFF: Oh, nothing, nothing. . . .

Somehow, in the back of my mind, that
"Don't touch my feet" rings a bell. . . .

(*Room:* CAROL *enters SL with towel.* CLIFF *crosses to her center, pulls off gloves, wipes his hands.*)

CLIFF: Have you read Rousseau?

SELDEN: Jean-Jacques Rousseau?
The well-known French philospher and
author of *The Noble Savage*?

CLIFF: Yes.

Do you remember the part where he asks the
reader what he would do if he could become
rich by killing an ancient mandarin in China
by the sole act of his will?

SELDEN: Aren't you feeling well?

(*Room:* CAROL *crosses up SR to cart.* CLIFF *pulls down his mask and crosses down to window, center.*)

CLIFF: I am bothered by troublesome thoughts.
My heart is disquieted within me.
And then I said: O, that I had wings like a dove!
For then I would get me away far off and
remain in the wilderness.
For I have spied unrighteousness and strife
in the city.

SELDEN: You know that thoughts can be cured.

CLIFF: How?

SELDEN: By giving in to them.

(*Offstage:* JASON *is heard, speaking into a tin can to simulate the sound of a radio transmission.*)

JASON: (*Off*) Friendship 7—Guaymas—if, uh,
You have a chance,
Could you give us a blood pressure check, over?

(*Room:* CLIFF *crosses SL to corner of window. From behind the wall, he pulls out a turquoise telephone receiver on a long turquoise cord and begins talking on it as* SELDEN *continues to "operate".*)

CLIFF: Uh, roger—Friendship 7—we'll give blood
pressure check, over.

(*Forestage:* DIVINA *enters SL and crosses slowly SR.*)

CLIFF: I still have some of these particles that
I cannot identify coming around the capsule
occasionally, over . . .

JASON: (*Off*) Uh, roger—how big are these particles, over?

CLIFF: Uh, very small. . . .
I would indicate they are of the order of
a sixteenth of an inch or smaller, uh . . .

(*Room:* CAROL *exits SL.*)

CLIFF: They drift by the window and, uh,
Just as the,

(*Sound: Fade out* "Cloches" *as fade in* "Agon", Double Pas de Quatre *(Stravinsky).*)

CLIFF: Just at sunrise,
There were literally thousands of them,
It looked like just a myriad of stars,
Over.

(*FAITHLESS 5*)

(*Forestage:* DIVINA *exits SR.*)

(*Peephole:* CAROL *enters SL, crossing to SR corner of peephole.* SHANNON *enters SL.*)

SHANNON: You must help me.

CAROL: What do you mean, help you?
Just what did you have in mind?

SHANNON: I want to go into town.
I need you drive me.

CAROL: Jason know about this?

SHANNON: No, and he doesn't have to.
I know he doesn't like me going out at night, but I promised some friends I'd drop by.

I won't stay long.

JASON: (*Off*) Friendship 7, uh,
We'll remind you to start predockside, uh, checklist as soon as you lose contact with us.

CLIFF: Uh, this is Friendship 7, do read.

CAROL: Look, I don't want to get mixed up in this.

SHANNON: But you told me you hated him.

CAROL: Of course I hate him—so what?
I haven't got too much love for you, either.

SHANNON: But he's a murderer!
You and I both know that.

CAROL: That's the man you wanted—that's the man you got.

SHANNON: That's not what I wanted—you know that.

CAROL: You're wasting your breath.

JASON: (*Off*) Roger, Friend 7—
We'll give you the countdown, uh, for the retrosequence time, John, you're looking good.

CLIFF: Roger.

SHANNON: Listen, Carol!
Either take me into town or I'm going alone!

(*Peephole:* CAROL *turns SL to* SHANNON.)

CAROL: Oh, all right—my God, Shannon!
You'd think it was a matter of life and death!

SHANNON: Well, maybe it is . . .

JASON: (*Off*) Mark, Five . . .

SHANNON: Come on, let's go!

JASON: (*Off*) . . . Four . . .

(*Peephole:* CAROL *turns back, facing downstage.*)

CAROL: We can't.

JASON: (*Off*) . . . Three . . .

SHANNON: Why not?

JASON: (*Off*) . . . Two . . .

(*Peephole:* CAROL *holds up her hands.*)

CAROL: I'm waiting for my nails to dry.

JASON: (*Off*) . . . One . . .
Fire!

CLIFF: Roger. . . .
Retros are firing. . . .

CAROL: In about half an hour, say?

SHANNON: All right. Half an hour.
But you better be ready.

CLIFF: Oh, roger, ba-by—are they ever!
Feels like I'm going back to Hawaii!

(*Peephole:* CAROL *turns head in profile SL.*)

CAROL: You're a mess, honey.
You ought to lay off of those candy bars.

JASON: (*Off*) Don't do that.
You want to go to the East Coast.

SHANNON: Half an hour.

(*Peephole:* SHANNON *exits SL,* CAROL *crossing to SL.*)

CLIFF: Roger. . . .

(*Peephole:* JASON *enters SR;* CAROL *turns back to him.*)

CAROL: You know what that was all about?

(*FAITHLESS 6*)

JASON: I was just going to tell you how ravishing you look.

CAROL: "Ravishing" . . .
Now, there's an interesting word, Jason.

(*Peephole:* CAROL *tries to pass* JASON, *who stops her.*)

CLIFF: Uh, this is Friendship 7,
I think the pack just let go. . . .

JASON: You know I nearly blew it that night of the party.
Every time I kissed Shannon, I wanted you.
And you just stood there and watched!
We're two of a kind, baby—
For my angel is always ready at a pinch,
To help me out and to keep me up.

(*Peephole:* JASON *kisses* CAROL'S *neck.*)

CLIFF: Friendship 7—real fireball outside. . . .

CAROL: Why, Doctor—what's come over you?

JASON: You know you want this as much as I do.
You little minx—you know I wanted you.
I just couldn't afford to upset all my plans.

CAROL: Plans?
What do you mean, "plans"?

JASON: Do you think I've been staying in this backwater sweating my guts out because I'm a great humanitarian?
No. . . .

(*Peephole:* CAROL *sinks down on her knees in front of* JASON, *out of sightlines.*)

CLIFF: Hello, Cape—Friendship 7—over?

JASON: I've stayed and pretended to be in love with Shannon so I could marry her and get control of the hospital.
And, I'd have a beautiful wife . . .

(*Peephole:* JASON *winces, looks down.*)

JASON: Shannon isn't bad to look at, but she's cold.
Not like you, baby. . . .

(*Sound:* "Agon" *has played out; fade in "wave sounds".*)

(*Peephole:* CAROL'S *arms raise up into the peephole and entwine themselves around* JASON, *pulling him down.*)

CLIFF: Hello, Cape—Friendship 7—over?

JASON: (*Off*) Not like you at all. . . .

CLIFF: Hello, Cape—Friendship 7—do you receive—over?

(*Room:* CLIFF *tries to get a response from the receiver, then sets it on window sill and exits SL.*)

(*PRESCOTT 9*)

(*Forestage:* DIVINA *enters SL and crosses SR. Fade out all light in room except green floodlight.*)

DIVINA: Before him now rose the stupendous Andes,
Rock piled upon rock,
Presenting altogether such a wild chaos of magnificence and beauty as no other mountains in the world can show.
The path was steep;
In many places, tremendous fissures yawned open,
And the traveller was compelled to wind along the narrow ledge where a misstep would plunge him hundreds—nay, thousands of feet into the dreadful abyss.

SELDEN: Oh, shit!

(*Room:* SELDEN *starts pumping up and down on cart.*)

DIVINA: Still deeper in,
The climate changed,
And as they rose still higher, the men and horses suffered severely from the cold,
With only the loathesome condor sailing high above the clouds,

(*Sound: Fade in Sun Chorus from* "Gurrelieder" *(Schoenberg) and build volume.*)

DIVINA: Following with doleful cries in the track of the army,
As if guided by instinct
In the path of blood and carnage. . . .

(*CAMPAIGN 7*)

(*Room:* CAROL *enters SL and picks up the phone receiver.*)

CLIFF: But, tell me . . .

(*Forestage:* DIVINA *crosses SR to exit.*)

DIVINA: Okay.

CLIFF: But, tell me . . .

DIVINA: Okay.

CLIFF: Of what nature is the movement of the mind?

(*Forestage:* DIVINA *exits SR, as* SELDEN *crosses room down to* CLIFF, *who is on the phone in SL corner of window.*)

SELDEN: You're going around the bend, Captain!
You can't fool me—I've been watching you!
Up until now, you've had it pretty easy,
But luck has a funny way of changing, Captain!

(*Forestage:* DIVINA *enters SL and crosses quickly SR.*)

(*Room:* SELDEN *crosses up SR to cart, pulling a stethoscope from underneath and putting it on to listen to the "patient" on the cart.*)

DIVINA: Do you see yonder cloud that's almost in shape of a camel?

CLIFF: I do.

SELDEN: (Not a cloud on the horizon . . .)

(*Forestage:* DIVINA *crosses back SL, downstage.*)

DIVINA: Methinks it is like a weasel.

CLIFF: Or like a whale?

DIVINA: Very like a whale!

(*Forestage:* DIVINA *crosses back SR, upstage, as* SELDEN, *in room, is now listening to various places on the walls, etc.*)

CLIFF: But, tell me . . .

DIVINA: Okay.

CLIFF: But, tell me . . .

DIVINA: Okay.

CLIFF: Of what nature is the movement of the mind?

(*Forestage:* DIVINA *exits SR, as* SELDEN, *in room, tosses stethoscope through peephole and crosses down to* CLIFF, *who is on the phone in SL corner of the window.*)

SELDEN: I saw that—you're coming apart at the seams!
Why cucumber sandwiches?
Why such reckless extravagance in one so young?
Maybe you bought a one-way ticket, Captain.
But I'm bailing out before the end of the line!

(*Forestage:* DIVINA *enters SL and crosses quickly SR.*)

(*Room:* SELDEN *crosses up SR to cart and, kneeling SL of it, begins pulling objects from underneath it and tossing them over his shoulder against SL wall of room. First, surgical dressings, etc.*)

DIVINA: Then surely you remember our saying
That the motion which is in one place
Must move about a center
Like globes on a lathe?

CLIFF: I do.

(*Room:* SELDEN *is now tossing cotton balls.*)

(*Forestage:* DIVINA *crosses back SL, downstage.*)

DIVINA: Methinks it is like a weasel.

CLIFF: Or like a whale?

DIVINA: Very like a whale.

(*Forestage:* DIVINA *crosses back SR, upstage, as* SELDEN, *in room, begins tossing kitchen spoons.*)

DIVINA: So, you filet your fish, and then you bone it, and you put mixed salt and sugar and pepper on top, and then you put that on the meat side . . .

CLIFF: Not the skin side . . .

DIVINA: Not the skin side . . .

(*Forestage:* DIVINA *has begun circling center chair, as* SELDEN, *in room, has pulled a tangled mess of tubing from under the cart. In struggling with it, he gets his arms, head, etc. caught in it.*)

DIVINA: So then you put it on the meat side, and you chop a lot of dill on top, and then of these two kinds of motion,

That which moves about a center
Like globes on a lathe
Is most entirely similar to the motions of the mind.

CLIFF: Or like a whale?

DIVINA: Very like a whale.

(*Forestage:* DIVINA *exits SR, as* SELDEN, *in room, crosses to SR corner of peephole. He looks through it upstage, pointing off SL.*)

SELDEN: Look!
It's a giant monster!
That thing must be over sixty feet tall!
It's a living nightmare!

(*Offstage:* DIVINA *is heard screaming.*)

SELDEN: What's that matter, Captain?
You beginning to feel the strain?
You're starting to bust wide open!
You're not going to make it, Captain!

(*Room:* CLIFF *crosses up to SL corner of peephole, then looks through it upstage. He still holds the phone receiver in his hand.*)

CLIFF: Maybe not, Sargeant—but it's too late to worry about it.

SELDEN: That's right—it's too late for all of us!
Because you didn't have what it takes!

(*Room:* SELDEN *wipes his forehead with a handkerchief and throws it away. He wipes his forehead with another handkerchief and throws it away, etc.*)

SELDEN: That giant monster's growing bigger every minute!

(*Room:* DIVINA *enters SL and crosses SR in window.*)

SELDEN: Oh, no!
The giant monster's headed right at us!

(*Room:* CLIFF *drops phone receiver to floor as* SELDEN *repeats handkerchief action several times.*)

CLIFF: And yet, I look at you now, Utnapishtim, and your appearance is no different from mine.

SELDEN: Oh no—the giant monster crushed a battleship!

DIVINA: Okay.

CLIFF: And there is nothing strange in your features.

SELDEN: Oh no—the giant monster just crushed another battleship!

(*Room:* SELDEN *reaches underneath cart and produces a handsaw. He begins sawing on a block of wood attached to the cart out of sightlines.*)

DIVINA: Okay.

(*Room:* CLIFF *crosses down SR to* DIVINA *in window.*)

CLIFF: And I thought I should find you like a hero prepared
for battle, but you lie here taking your ease, on
your back, like a weasel.

DIVINA: Okay.
Or like a whale?

CLIFF: Very like a whale.

DIVINA: Okay.

(*Room:* DIVINA *steps on a step concealed behind the wall, up into the window, leaning through it, her arms outstretched. Simultaneously,* SELDEN *begins pounding on the top of the cart with a closed fist.*)

(*Sound:* "Gurrelieder" *swells.*)

SELDEN: Look! Look! Look!
The giant monster just destroyed the entire air force!

CLIFF: So tell me truly,
How was it that you came to enter the company of gods
And to possess everlasting life?

DIVINA: I was the world in which I walked;
And what I saw, or heard, or felt
Came not but from myself.

And there I found myself more truly and more strange.

(*Room:* SELDEN *crosses down center to window, between* DIVINA *SR and* CLIFF *SL.*)

SELDEN: The tanks couldn't stop it!
The bombs couldn't stop it!
We gotta get out of here!

DIVINA: Look!

(*Room:* DIVINA *turns and points at* SELDEN, *who is sucked up SR and disappears out of sightlines on the floor, as if dragged down by an unseen hand.* CLIFF *steps back to SL corner of window.*)

DIVINA: That giant monster just grabbed Sargeant Nelson!

(*Room:* DIVINA *hops down from window as* SELDEN, *on his knees, reappears up SR, waving his arms in the air.*)

SELDEN: Aaaaaaaaaaaaaaaargh! Captain! Help!
The giant monster got me!

(*Room:* SELDEN *again disappears out of sight.*)

DIVINA: Blow it up, Captain—now!

(*Room:* DIVINA *exits, SR.*)

CLIFF: And blow up Sargeant Nelson?
No, there's gotta be another way. . . .
But what?

(*Room:* SELDEN *reappears next to* CLIFF, *clawing at him.*)

SELDEN: Is this what you wanted, Captain?
Are you taking everybody with you to the end of the line?

(*Room:* SELDEN *again disappears out of sight.*)

CLIFF: (The men are all staring at me. . . .
Maybe the Sargeant was right. . . .
Snap out of it, Saunders! You gotta do something—
Anything!. . . .)

(*Sound: Fade in* "Marine Hymn" *(from the movie* 'Rocky'*) over* "Gurrelieder", *which fades out.*)

(*Room:* CLIFF *crosses down center in window.*)

CLIFF: Okay boys—looks like they wanna play rough!
So let's really let 'em have it!

(*Offstage:* DIVINA *and* SELDEN *alternate battle sounds.*)

| CLIFF: | |
|---|---|
| My dear Algy. I don't know whether you will be able to understand my real motives; you are hardly serious enough. But when one is placed in the position of a guardian, | DIVINA: Buddabudda buddabudda! SELDEN: Bratatatta bratatatta! DIVINA: Buddabudda buddabudda! SELDEN: Bratatatta bratatatta! |

one has to adopt a high
moral tone on all subjects.
We hold these truths to
be self-evident; that all
men are endowed by their
creator with certain
unalienable rights; that
among these are life, liberty,
and the pursuit of happiness.

However,
As a high moral tone can
hardly be said to conduce
very much to either one's
health or one's happiness—
*keep on pourin' it at 'em*
*till ya run outta ammo*!

DIVINA:
Buddabudda buddabudda!
SELDEN:
Bratatatta bratatatta!
DIVINA:
Buddabudda buddabudda!
SELDEN:
Bratatatta bratatatta!

DIVINA:
Buddabudda buddabudda!
SELDEN:
Bratatatta bratatatta!
DIVINA:
Buddabudda buddabudda!
SELDEN:
Bratatatta bratatatta!
DIVINA:
Whroom! Whroosh! Krunncchh!

(*Sound: Fade out* "Marine Hymn".)

(*Room:* CLIFF *crosses up SR to cart; presently* SELDEN *enters SL. Fade green flood and restore room.*)

SELDEN: I just want to tell you, Captain,
I did a lot of thinking at the end of the line:
Guess I was wrong about a lot of things.
Guess I was wrong about you—sir!

(*Room:* SELDEN *crosses up SR to* CLIFF *and shakes his hand.*)

SELDEN: That, my dear Algy, is the whole truth pure and simple.

(*Room:* DIVINA *enters SR as* CLIFF *crosses down center to window, followed by* SELDEN.)

CLIFF: The truth, my dear Algy, is rarely pure and never simple.
Modern life would be very tedious if it were either,
And modern literature a complete impossibility.

DIVINA: But in saying that the mind and the motion which is
in one place are like globes on a lathe,
We invented a fair image,
Which does no discredit to our imagination,
My dear Algy. . . .

(*Room:* DIVINA *turns and exits SR.*)

CLIFF: It does us great credit.

(*Room:* CLIFF *turns and exits SR.*)

CLIFF: But, tell me . . .

DIVINA: (*Off*) Okay.

CLIFF: But, tell me . . .

DIVINA: (*Off*) Okay.

CLIFF: (*Off*) What then is love? . . .

(*PRESCOTT 10*)

(*Room:* JASON *enters SL and crosses up to SL corner of peephole. He is wearing slacks, white shirt, and tie.* CAROL *enters SL and crosses SR to cart, which she drapes with a sheet and wheels off SR. She is dressed in her green nurse's unifrom.* JASON *and* SELDEN *watch, as* CLIFF, *on forestage, enters SR and slowly crosses SL.*)

JASON: But it was too late.
Below the adventurers, with its white houses gleaming in the sun, lay the little city of Cajamarca,
Like a sparkling gem on the dark skirts of the sierra.
And along the hills,
A white cloud of pavilions as thick as snowflakes for the space of several miles.

Behold the Indian. . . .

(*Forestage:* CLIFF *exits SL.*)

(*Room:* SELDEN *crosses up SL to* JASON.)

SELDEN: And what were the feelings of the Peruvian monarch when he gazed upon the martial cavalcade as, with banners streaming in the evening sun, it emerged from the dark depths of the sierrra over the fair domain which, until this period, had never been trodden by any other foot than that of the red man?. . . .

(*Sound: Fade in* "Exotic Loop".)

JASON: We are not informed.

(*PRESCOTT 11*)

(*Peephole:* DIVINA *enters SR and watches as* JASON, *in room, whispers in* SELDEN'S *ear.*)

DIVINA: Pizarro secretly rejoiced that he had brought matters to the issue for which he had so long panted.

(*Room:* JASON *and* SELDEN *exit SL.*)

DIVINA: He then summoned a council of his officers to propose to them the extraordinary plan on which he had decided:
This was to lay an ambuscade for the Inca,
And take him prisoner in the face of his whole army.
It was a project full of peril—
But the circumstances were desperate.

Sleep must have come late to those that were aware of the plan. . . .

(*ROMEO 8*)

(*Forestage:* SHANNON *enters SR and stands by SR corner of wall, reading a letter. She is wearing an overcoat over her dress.*)

(*Peephole:* DIVINA *watches* SHANNON *as she crosses SL and exits.*)

(*Sound: Fade in* "Violin Doodle" *(Schreier) as fade out* "Exotic Loop".)

SHANNON: July 17.
Dearest Cliff.
I've almost gone completely insane because I'm so worried about you.
I love you very much,
And more than anything, I want you to know that.
I'm just so lonesome for you and half out of my mind with worry.
I don't know about anything any more, or what's going to happen.

(*Sound: Fade in* "Neptune" *from* "The Planets" *(Holst).*)

SHANNON: Things are bad here,
And that only makes me not care,
But—

(*FAITHLESS 7*)

(*Forestage:* SHANNON *stops as she hears a sound offstage, then crumples up the letter and hides it as* CAROL *enters SL.* CAROL *is wearing a lab coat over her nurses's uniform.*)

SHANNON: Well? . . .

CAROL: Keep your voice down.

(*Forestage:* CAROL *crosses center, upstage by window.*)

CAROL: I'm afraid you won't be able to leave the hospital grounds, Shannon.

SHANNON: What?

CAROL: Nobody will.

(*Forestage:* CAROL *sets out on the window sill a syringe, alcohol prep, and a bottle of serum.*)

CAROL: There's been an emergency.
The Inka died around three o'clock this morning.

SHANNON: Surely that's not serious enough to—

CAROL: I haven't had a chance to tell you this,
But the Inka is the second person in two days to get sick in exactly the same way.
Last night one of my patients came down with the symptoms.

SHANNON: You think there's any connection between the cases? . . .
An epidemic? . . .

(*Forestage:* SHANNON *crosses SL to* CAROL, *who fills the syringe.*)

(*Peephole:* DIVINA *rises up from center and watches.*)

CAROL: Keep your voice down.
Listen—there must be many things with those symptoms.
But certain precautions have to go into effect anyway.
We'll have to inject the whole staff.
We have enough serum to start injections right away.

You want to go first?

(*Forestage:* SHANNON *takes off her coat and puts it on the window sill SR.*)

SHANNON: Sure—that's fine, I'm—trying to collect my thoughts.
We'll have to notify the public health authorities. . . .
And we must find the family and get them vaccinated. . . .

CAROL: Hold still. . . .

(*Forestage:* CAROL *injects* SHANNON *and pockets syringe.*)

CAROL: There. . . .

(*Peephole:* DIVINA *drops down out of sight, spinning around, her eyes closed.*)

SHANNON: Carol?

CAROL: Yes, dear?

SHANNON: What's the disease?

(*Forestage:* CAROL *crosses down to SR chair.*)

CAROL: Gee—I don't know. I've never seen anything like it.
Jason says the symptoms resemble strychnine poisoning:

(*Forestage:* CAROL *crosses up to* SHANNON.)

CAROL: You know—itching, twitching, nausea, vomiting, convulsions and death!

(*Forestage:* CAROL *crosses SL as* SHANNON *begins to feel weak.*)

CAROL: He was all stiff and funny, too—it was awful the way he kept screaming: Don't touch my feet!

SHANNON: But . . .
Dad was just like that when he died, too.

CAROL: I know.

(*Sound: Fade in second* "Neptune" *under first.*)

CAROL: Do you understand it at last?

(*Forestage:* SHANNON *crosses SL toward* CAROL, *bracing herself on window sill.*)

SHANNON: Do I understand it?
My head is splitting with it.
It is written in letters of fire!

CAROL: You have come to trouble our existence

SHANNON: Unintentionally.

(*Forestage:* SHANNON *lunges SL toward* CAROL, *who lets her drop on the floor, up SL.*)

(*Lights: Fade forestage to one pool on* SHANNON, *room out, peephole bright.*)

CAROL: You understand we have the right to treat you as enemies.
For the devil himself may be just in accusation and punishment.
I wish there were time for feelings, but there isn't.
And now I think I should leave you for a good, long sleep.

(*Sound: Fade in* "Angels' Loop" *from* "Neptune" *under other tracks.*)

CAROL: Goodbye, Shannon.
Goodbye forever.

(*TOXIN 4*)

(*Forestage:* CAROL *exits SL;* SHANNON *lies motionless.* DIVINA *enters SR and crosses very slowly SL to* SHANNON. *She wears the black shawl over her head and upper body, concealing her face.*)

SHANNON: She stood by the seashore
Watching a small boy, who seemed to be hers, wading into the water.
This he did until the water covered him and she could only see his head bobbing up and down.
The scene then changed to the crowded hall of a hotel.
Her husband left her,
And she entered into conversation with a stranger.

(*Forestage:* SHANNON *sits UP.*)

SHANNON: Mother—
I dreamed a second dream:
In the streets of strong-walled Uruk lay an axe.
The shape of it was strange and people thronged round.
I saw it and was glad.
I bent down, deeply drawn to it.
I loved it like a woman,
And wore it by my side.

Please!—Don't touch my feet, don't touch my feet, don't touch my feet!

Father? Don't you notice that I'm burning?

Go quick—get Cliff—
Tell him I've been stung by a scorpion!
Look—the scorpion is over there!

(*Peephole:* JASON *and* CAROL *rise up, center, and watch* SHANNON.)

SHANNON:
And there were, in the same country, shepherds abiding in the field, keeping watch over their flock by night.
And lo!

CAROL:
(She's delirious.)

JASON:
(I know. But everything is going to be all right, don't worry.)

(*Forestage:* DIVINA, *standing over* SHANNON, *pulls the shawl off her head and reaches to touch* SHANNON.)

SHANNON:
The angel of the Lord came upon them,

CAROL:
(It's not the normal reaction at all.

And the glory of the
Lord shone round about
them,
And they were sore
afraid

JASON:
(I know. But everything is
going to be all right,
don't worry.)

(*Lights: sudden blackout as* DIVINA *drapes* SHANNON *with shawl.* CAROL *and* JASON *are heard in darkness.*)

CAROL: (She's going to need another shot.)

JASON: (I know.
But everything is going to be all right, don't worry.)

(*ROMEO 9*)

(*Lights: Forestage up, revealing* CLIFF *standing by SR corner of window, holding* SHANNON'S *coat.* SHANNON, DIVINA, JASON, *and* CAROL *have disappeared. Room is dim; peephole is dim.*)

CLIFF: Going on,
Always on and on,
Alive, but parted from you—
Gone ten thousand miles or more with nothing sure about meeting again—
The thought of going home seems inconceivable.

Loving you, I become old.
Suddenly the time is late.
Enough—
I have nothing more to say.

Try to stay well . . .

(*PRESCOTT 12*)

(*Forestage:* DIVINA *enters SL around wall and beckons to* CLIFF, *who crosses slowly SL to her. The beckoning gesture continues as he does so.*)

DIVINA: The eyes of the Indian monarch flashed with fire,
And his dark brow grew darker as he replied:
I will be no man's tributary!
I am greater than any prince upon earth!
Your own God, as you say, was put to death by the very men he created.
But mine still lives in the heavens
And looks down on his children.

(*Room:* SELDEN *enters SR, pushing cart, followed by* JASON *with box.* SELDEN *positions the cart center.* JASON *sets the box on top of it, then kneels before the cart and opens the box. A green light plays on his face.*)

DIVINA: The friar, greatly scandalized, pointed to the book
which he held as his authority.

(*Forestage:* DIVINA, *stepping back, points off into the SL exit.*)

DIVINA: Do you not see that while we stand here wasting
our breath in talking with this dog
The fields are filling with Indians?

(*Sound: Fade* "Ava Maria" *(Ockeghem) under* "Neptune".)

DIVINA: Set on at once!
I absolve you!

(*Forestage:* CLIFF *exits SL.*)

DIVINA: Pizarro then saw that the hour had come.

(*CAMPAIGN 9*)

(*Forestage:* DIVINA *exits SL.*)

(*Room:* JASON *is now praying over the box.*)

JASON: Rejoice in God, O ye tongues:
Give glory to the Lord and the Lamb.
Let man and beast appear before him and
magnify his name together.

(*Room:* CLIFF *enters SL.*)

CLIFF: Captain?

JASON: Let Achsah rejoice with the pigeon,
Who is an antidote to malignity and will carry a letter;
For I bless God for the Postmaster General and all
conveyancers of letters under his care,
Especially Allen and Shelvock.

CLIFF: Captain, I must speak to you on a matter that
admits of no delay!

JASON: Let Hillel rejoice with Ammodytes, whose color—

CLIFF: Captain!

(*Room:* JASON *slams down lid of box.*)

JASON: What do you want?
I am busy, I am working.

CLIFF: Where's Shannon?

JASON: She is with the Inka now, Sinclair.

CLIFF: Where?

JASON: Room 101.

(*Room:* JASON *stands as* CLIFF *tries to cross SR.*)

JASON: Where do you think you're going?

SELDEN: I'm sorry, sir—no visitors allowed.

CLIFF: What's this all about?

JASON: We've got trouble.
Somebody's been filching scorpions from the dispensary in large quantities.

CLIFF: What?

JASON: Yes.
Now we have to find out who that somebody is.

CLIFF: But we don't carry large orders of scorpions.

JASON: That's just it, Sinclair.
Somebody's been putting orders through in your name.
Here—look at these.

(*Room:* SELDEN, *standing SR, reaches behind window wall and produces slips of paper which he holds up in his left hand.*)

JASON: What else did you find?

SELDEN: This instrument—

(*Room:* SELDEN *reaches behind window wall and produces a small object (glass nasal douche) which he holds up in his right hand.*)

SELDEN: The use of which I can only guess.

JASON: How do you account for that?

CLIFF: What the devil are you trying to say?

JASON: Shannon is dead!

(*Room:* CLIFF *crosses center to* JASON.)

CLIFF: Dead?. . . .

JASON: And the Inka had enough strychnine in him to kill four people.

(*Room:* JASON *crosses SL behind* CLIFF, *who turns to keep watching him.*)

CLIFF: He what?

JASON: Now the only way you can die of strychnine is during a convulsion—which means that somebody gave the Inka a second dose.
In the hospital.

CLIFF: Are you trying to say that Shannon and the Inka might have been poisoned?

JASON: Well, I don't see how it could have been an accident.

CLIFF: All right then—who could have done it?

JASON: A lot of people.

CLIFF: For instance?

JASON: For instance—you.

CLIFF: Is that your idea, Doctor?

JASON: I don't know, Doctor—there are so many confusing facts.
For instance,
You told me it wasn't tetany,
Yet that's what was put on the death certificate.
Why?

CLIFF: Because that's what *you* were treating the patient for.

JASON: And because strychnine would produce the same symptoms?

(*Room:* SELDEN, *standing SR, has surreptitiously prepared a handkerchief with chloroform.* CLIFF *is center, facing* JASON, *SL by corner of window.*)

CLIFF: Let me ask you one question, Dr. Wilfred!

JASON: None, sir—

(*Room:* SELDEN *grabs* CLIFF *from behind, placing the handkerchief over his mouth.* CLIFF *struggles but to no avail.*)

(*Sound: Switch the continuous "tone" on under* "Neptune".)

JASON: I have nothing more to say to you.
When I found out about the problem in the supply room,
I knew there could be only one person responsible.
You must be confined until I think fit to release you.

CLIFF: (*Muffled*) . . . You . . .

JASON: I advise you not to judge me, sir.
I am the law and I am the judge.

CLIFF: (*Muffled*) . . . Savages . . .

JASON: Savages?
So, you are astonished, Professor, at having set foot on a strange land and finding savages?
"Savages"—where are there not any?
Besides, are they worse than others, those whom you call savages?
You are right.
I am not what you call a civilized man.

(*Room:* CLIFF *falls unconscious and sags.*)

JASON: Behold, I am the dweller in terrors.
I am the crocodile.
I am strong!
I come to hew into pieces!
I make slaughter upon the earth!
And behold you this god, this mighty one of slaughters, shall wash himself clean in your blood and he shall bathe in your gore and you shall be destroyed.

(*Room:* SELDEN *lets* CLIFF *drop to the floor.*)

(*Sound: Switch out* "Ava Maria" *and* "Neptune"; *tone continues.*)

JASON: He will be dead in two hours.

(*Room:* JASON *crosses up SR to cart and gets box.*)

SELDEN: But I'm scared, Jason. What if someone finds out?

JASON: It's too late to change your mind now.
You brought him here.
Remember that.

(*CODA 1*)

(*Room:* JASON *exits SR with box as* CAROL *enters SL.*)

(*Forestage:* DIVINA, *veiled and reading in a low monotone from the little book, enters SL and crosses SR to center, then down to center chair. She sits, as* SHANNON, *wearing a hospital gown, enters SL and crosses to SL corner of window, where she stands and watches room.*)

(*Room:* CAROL *and* SELDEN *wheel the cart up center beneath peephole, then pick* CLIFF *up off floor. They take off his lab coat and sit him on the cart, then exit SR.*)

DIVINA: Given the right triangle ABC,
Two hours after sunset,
With the sides AB, BC and AC,
Inscribe the Spanish soldiery CD
Assembled by torchlight in the plaza
Perpendicular to AB from the point C
To witness the execution of the sentence.

(*Forestage:* SHANNON *reaches out with her right hand and speaks in a soft voice.*)

SHANNON: Doady?

DIVINA: It was the 29th of August.

SHANNON: I want to see Agnes.

CLIFF: I lay on my bed.

SHANNON: Doady, take me on your arm.

CLIFF: A gentleman known to me came in.

SHANNON: I want to speak to Agnes.

CLIFF: I wanted to turn on the light.

SHANNON: I want to speak to Agnes by herself.

CLIFF: But I could not.

SHANNON: I want to speak to Agnes quite alone.

CLIFF: I attempted to do so repeatedly.

SHANNON: Very much I want to see her.

CLIFF: But in vain.

SHANNON: Don't cry.
Oh, how my poor boy cries.

(*Forestage:* SHANNON *turns away and crosses down to SL chair, then sits, facing audience.*)

DIVINA: Now the side AB is proportional to the side AC
As the side AC is proportional to the line AD.
And Atahuallpa was led out, chained hand and foot,
Father Valverde at his side,

Striving to administer consolation and, if possible,
To persuade him at this last hour to abjure his superstition
And embrace the religion of his conquerors.

(*Beat*)

CLIFF: Thereupon my wife got out of bed in order to help me,
But she too was unable to manage it,
And being ashamed of her negligee in the presence of the gentleman,
She finally gave it up and went back to bed.

(*Beat*)

SHANNON: Only give Agnes my dear love,
And tell her that I want very much to see her,
And that I have nothing left to wish for.

DIVINA: Therefore the product AB and AD
Is equal to the square
Of the side AC.

CLIFF: I am poured out like water and all my bones are out of joint.

DIVINA: Now the side AB . . .

CLIFF: My heart is like wax . . .

DIVINA: Is also proportional . . .

CLIFF: It is melted in the midst of my bowels.

DIVINA: To the side BC . . .

CLIFF: They pierced my hands and feet . . .

DIVINA: As the side BC . . .

CLIFF: They part my garments among them . . .

DIVINA: Is proportional . . .

CLIFF: And cast lots on my vesture.

DIVINA: To the line BD.

Then Atahuallpa was bound to the stake . . .

SHANNON: I am going to speak to you, Doady.

DIVINA: And with the sticks . . .

SHANNON: I am going to say something I have often thought of saying lately . . .

Divina: That were to kindle his funeral pile . . .

Shannon: You won't mind?

Divina: Lying about him . . .

Shannon: Because . . .

Divina: Valverde . . .

Shannon: I don't know what you will think . . .

Divina: Holding up the cross . . .

Shannon: I don't know . . .

Divina: Besought him one last time . . .

Shannon: Perhaps . . .

Divina: To embrace it and be baptized . . .

Shannon: It is much better as it is.

Divina: Promising that, as AB is to BC as BC is to BD,
By so doing . . .

Shannon: Oh, Doady, I was too young and foolish!

Divina: The painful death to which he had been sentenced . . .

Shannon: I know I was too young and foolish.

Divina: Should be commuted . . .

Shannon: It is much better as it is . . .

Divina: To the milder form of the garotte . . .

Shannon: I said that it was better as it is.

(*Forestage:* Shannon *rises and exits SL.*)

Divina: A mode of punishment by strangulation
Used for criminals in Spain.

(*Beat*)

(*Sound: Fade in* "Ava Maria" *over tone.*)

Cliff: My God! My God! Why hast thou forsaken me?

Divina: Therefore,
The product of AB and BD
Is equal to the square of the side BC.

(*Room:* JASON *enters SL and stands facing upstage. He is wearing his dark, three-piece suit.*)

(*Forestage:* CAROL *enters SR and crosses to SR chair, then sits. She is wearing an orange dress suit and hat.*)

DIVINA: Now the unhappy monarch asked if this were really so,
And on its being confirmed by Pizarro,
He consented to abjure his own religion and receive baptism.

CLIFF: All this was so comical that I had to laugh terribly.

JASON: And there was a man named Nicodemus . . .

CLIFF: My wife said: What are you laughing at?

JASON: A ruler of the Jews . . .

CLIFF: What are you laughing at?

JASON: The same came to Jesus by night and said unto him:
How can a man be born when he is old?

CLIFF: But I continued to laugh . . .

JASON: Can he enter a second time into his mother's womb . . .

CLIFF: Until I awoke . . .

JASON: And be born?

CLIFF: And Jesus answered:
That which is born of the flesh is flesh,
And that which is born of the spirit is spirit.

DIVINA: Therefore,
The sum of the squares of the sides AC and BC
Is equal to the product of the side AB
Times the sum of AD and BD.

And the ceremony was performed by Father Valverde;
And the new convert received the name of Juan de Atahuallpa,
The name Juan being conferred in honor of Juan Baptista,
John the Baptist,
On whose day the event took place.

(*Peephole:* SELDEN *enters SR and watches as* CLIFF, *in room, rises and crosses down center to window where he kneels and prays on the sill.*)

CLIFF: Almighty and immortal God,
The aid of all who need,
The helper of all who flee for succor and resurrector of the dead . . .

SELDEN: (The moment had arrived—the moment I dreaded.
But I had to appear at ease,
Though my mind was numb.)

JASON: Dost thou renounce the Devil and all his works,
The vain pomp and glory of the world,
With all covetous desires of the same and sinful desires of the flesh,
So that thou wilt not follow nor be led by them?

CLIFF: I renounce them all,
And by God's help will endeavour not to follow nor be led by them.

SELDEN: (I'd rehearsed this scene a thousand times in my mind,
But now that it was a reality,
The idea of taking the life of a human being seemed like a hideous nightmare!)

JASON: Dost thou believe in Jesus the Chirst,
The son of the living God?

CLIFF: I do.

JASON: Dost thou accept him
And desire to follow him as thy saviour and Lord?

CLIFF: I do.

JASON: Wilt thou be baptized in this faith?

CLIFF: That is my desire.

(*Room:* JASON *turns and exits SL. Noticing he is gone,* CLIFF *rises, crosses up center to cart and sits.*)

DIVINA: Then turning to Pizarro as a last request,
He implored him to take compassion on his young children
And receive them under his protection.

(*Peephole:* SELDEN, *standing slightly SL of* CLIFF, *raises his right hand, holding a gun, slightly SR of* CLIFF's *head.*)

SELDEN: (My hand wouldn't move.
It were as if it belonged to someone else.
What if I didn't have the nerve to go through with it?)

(*Forestage:* JASON *enters SL, crosses to SL chair and sits.*)

JASON: But the sum of AD and BD is AB.

CLIFF: Then recovering his stoical bearing,
Which for a moment had been shaken,
He submitted himself calmly to his fate,
While the Spaniards, gathering round,
Muttered their credos for the salvation of his soul.

SELDEN: (I knew it had to be done tonight.
But I had to stall for time—
Time to get up my courage. . . .)

(*Peephole:* SELDEN *exits SL.*)

DIVINA: Therefore,
The sum of the squares of the sides AC and BC
Is equal to the square
Of the side AB.

(*Sound: Cut music and "tone".*)

(*Room:* SELDEN *enters SL, the gun in his right hand, a white lab coat in his left hand.*)

SELDEN: Sir?

CLIFF: What is it?

SELDEN: We are going to fly.

CLIFF: When?

SELDEN: Tonight.
And our first attempt must succeed;
If it fails, we shall never find another.

CLIFF: What country is it?

SELDEN: I do not know,
But whatever it is, we will take refuge there.
But if I am discovered,
I will force them to kill me.

CLIFF: Then we will die together, friend.

SELDEN: Yes. We know how to die.

(*Room:* SELDEN *tosses the coat to* CLIFF.)

SELDEN: You will be ready?

CLIFF: I will follow you.

(*Room: Hearing a noise,* CLIFF *rises.*)

CLIFF: Where did that sound come from?

SELDEN: Let us go! Let us go!
Run, sir, run!
Run, sir, run!

(*Room: After a moment's hesitation,* CLIFF *runs out SL, followed by* SELDEN.)

(*Beat*)

(*Offstage: The sound of a gunshot.*)

(*Forestage:* CAROL, DIVINA, *and* JASON *all rise.* DIVINA *turns her chair around to face upstage.*)

JASON: Thus, by the death of a vile malefactor,
Perished the last of the Incas.

(*Forestage:* DIVINA *steps down center and raises her veil as* CAROL *and* JASON *both carry their chairs to either side of the center chair, also facing upstage, then sit.*)

(*Sound: Fade in* "Exotic Loop".)

DIVINA: Therefore,
In any right triangle,
The square of the hypotenuse is equal to the sum of the squares of the other two sides.

(*CODA 2*)

(*Forestage:* DIVINA *exits SR.* JASON *and* CAROL *sitting in SL and SR chairs, respectively, facing upstage, watching the bright peephole through the darkened room.*)

(*Beat*)

JASON: I knew him, dear.
A fellow of infinite jest, of most excellent fancy.

CAROL: What time is the funeral tomorrow?

JASON: Three o'clock.

You know—the sleeping and the dead—
How alike they are, honey.
They are like a painted death.
For it is only the nymph of the dragonfly that sheds her larva and sees the sun in its glory.
There is no permanence, babe.

(*Peephole:* DIVINA *enters SR, with an embroidered shawl over her hair, looking at SL entrance to room.*)

DIVINA: But who is this who walks up the shore?
And why are your cheeks so starved and your face so drawn?
Why is despair in your heart and your face like the face of one who has made a long journey?
Yes—why do you come here,
Wandering over the wilderness in search of the wind?

(*Room:* SELDEN *enters SR, runs to the cart and falls to his knees, his arms outstretched to* DIVINA.)

SELDEN: My friend—
My friend who was very dear to me and who endured dangers beside me,
My brother whom I loved,
The end of mortality has overtaken him
And his fate lies heavy upon me. . . .

(*Room:* SELDEN *begins sobbing in a mechanical manner. This continues to end of play.*)

CAROL: So what shall we do tonight?
Go to the theatre?

JASON: No, I hate listening.

CAROL: Well, shall we go to a club?

JASON: No, I hate listening.

CAROL: Well, we could trot around to the Empire at ten.

JASON: No, I hate listening.

CAROL: Well, what shall we do then?

JASON: Nothing.

It isn't very easy, doing nothing—
But I'm willing to try, aren't you?

CAROL: No!

(*Forestage:* CAROL *rises and faces* JASON.)

CAROL: I don't want to call it an evening this early!
For once in my life, I'm having a good time in this god-forsaken place, and I certainly don't intend to stop now.

Come on—it's only nine o'clock.

(*Forestage:* CAROL *sits on* JASON'S *lap.*)

(*Lights: Fade out forestage.*)

CAROL: Let's go visit the pyramids.
I've heard they're absolutely fabulous at night!

DIVINA: Come to Peru.
Find out.
Find out from . . . your travel agent.

*Blackout*

*End of Play*

Tony Kushner

# *A Bright Room Called Day*

TONY KUSHNER is a playwright, director, and the Artistic Director of Heat & Light Co., Inc., a political theatre company. His plays include *The Age of Assassins, La Fin de la Baleine, The Heavenly Theatre: Hymns for Martyred Actors,* and *Hydriotaphia,* which was performed in 1987 at the Home for Contemporary Theatre and Art. He is the recipient of a NYSCA playwrighting commission for Redwing Performing Group, a NYFA Playwrights Fellowship, a NEA Directing Fellowship, and a Princess Grace Theatre Fellowship. Currently he is working on a play for Eureka Theatre—*Angels in America*—commissioned by the NEA and the Gerbode Foundation.

*A Bright Room Called Day* was first presented by Heat & Light Co. in a workshop production at Theatre 22 in New York City in April, 1985. Tony Kushner directed the following cast:

AGNES EGGLING . . . . . . . . . . . . . . . . . . . . Priscilla Stampa
BAZ . . . . . . . . . . . . . . . . . . . . . . . . . . . . Stephen Spinella
PAULINKA ERDNUSS . . . . . . . . . . . . . . . Alexandra Rambusch
ANNABELLA GOTCHLING . . . . . . . . . . . . . . . . . . . . Maria Makis
VEALTNINC HUSZ . . . . . . . . . . . . . . . . . . . . Peter Guttmacher
ROSA MALEK . . . . . . . . . . . . . . . . . . . . . . . . Kimberly Flynn
EMIL TRAUM . . . . . . . . . . . . . . . . . . . . . Jonathan Rosenberg
ZILLAH . . . . . . . . . . . . . . . . . . . . . . . . . . . . Roberta Levine
ZACHARY* . . . . . . . . . . . . . . . . . . . . . . . . . . . Michael Mayer
DIE ALTE . . . . . . . . . . . . . . . . . . . . . . . . . . Theresa Reeves
AH . . . . . . . . . . . . . . . . . . . . . . . . . . . . . . . . . . Tracy Martin
GOTTFRIED SWETTS . . . . . . . . . . . . . . . . . . . David Warshofsky

Steven Rosen and Tony Kushner designed the production.

The play premiered in San Francisco at the Eureka Theatre in October, 1987. Oskar Eustis directed the following cast:

AGNES EGGLING . . . . . . . . . . . . . . . . . . . . Sigrid Wurschmidt
BAZ . . . . . . . . . . . . . . . . . . . . . . . . . . . . . . . . . . . Jeff King
PAULINKA ERDNUSS . . . . . . . . . . . . . . . . . . . Carmalita Fuentes
ANNABELLA GOTCHLING . . . . . . . . . . . . . . . . . Abigail Van Alyn
VEALTNINC HUSZ . . . . . . . . . . . . . . . . . . . . . Michael McShane
ROSA MALEK . . . . . . . . . . . . . . . . . . . . . . . . . . . . . Ann Houle
EMIL TRAUM . . . . . . . . . . . . . . . . . . . . . . . David Warshofsky
ZILLAH . . . . . . . . . . . . . . . . . . . . . . . . . . . . . . . . . Lorri Holt
DIE ALTE . . . . . . . . . . . . . . . . . . . . . . . . . . . . . . . Ann Houle
AH . . . . . . . . . . . . . . . . . . . . . . . . . . . . . . . . . Jaimie Sempre
GOTTFRIED SWETTS . . . . . . . . . . . . . . . . . . . David Warshofsky

"Memories Of You" by Eubie Blake and Andy Razaff, © Shapiro, Bernstein and Co.
*Character died in the rewrites. RIP.

*A Bright Room Called Day* benefitted immeasurably from the editing and dramaturgical advice provided by Kimberly Flynn, Carl Weber, and Oskar Eustis. Through frequent discussion with Oskar Eustis the shape of the play has changed substantially since its first incarnation; this version incorporates many of his structural ideas and suggestions.

I also would like to thank Mark Bronnenberg for his keen eye and loving support.

*A Bright Room Called Day* is for Carl Weber, teacher, mentor and friend; for Kimberly Flynn, a true and triumphant heroine in the face of great adversity; and is dedicated to the memory of Florence Kushner: Zeicher tzadikah livrachah.

*Characters*

AGNES EGGLING—Mid- to late-thirties; heavyset. Bit player/character actress in the German film industry.

GREGOR BAZWALD (BAZ)—Early- to mid-thirties. Homosexual who works for the Berlin Institute for Human Sexuality.

PAULINKA ERDNUSS—Mid-thirties, but looks a little younger. Actress in the German film industry; a featured player on her way to becoming a minor star.

ANNABELLA GOTCHLING—Mid-forties. Communist artist and graphic designer.

VEALTNINC HUSZ—Mid-forties. Cinematographer. Hungarian exile. Missing an eye, he wears spectacles with one lens blackened.

ROSA MALEK—Mid- to late-twenties. Minor functionary of the KPD (Kommunistische Partei Deutschlands).

EMIL TRAUM—Mid-thirties. Slightly higher-ranking functionary of the KPD.

DIE ALTE—A woman, very old but hard to tell how old—somewhere between seventy and dead-for-twenty years. White face and rotten teeth. Dressed in a nightgown, once white but now soiled and food-stained.

GOTTFRIED SWETTS—Ageless; when he looks good he could be thirty, when he looks bad he could be fifty (or more). Distinguished, handsome, blond, Aryan.

ZILLAH KATZ—Contemporary American Jewish woman. Thirties. BoHo/East Village New Wave with Anarcho-Punk tendencies (of a mild sort).

AH—A very young child; blond, beautiful, dressed in a Hitlerjugend outfit minus the insigniae.

*A Bright Room Called Day* is set entirely in AGNES EGGLING'S apartment, a small flat in a large nineteenth-century apartment building in a low-rent district in Berlin. The apartment has probably no more than three rooms. Only the main room is visible. It is cluttered, cozy, and has large windows.

The set shouldn't be excessively literal; like the play, it should have one foot in the historical reality of Berlin in the early thirties and one foot somewhere else.

*A note about* ZILLAH: It has become increasingly clear to me that ZILLAH'S monologues are going to require constant updating, changing either slightly or drastically to keep an immediate political edge. Since I believe that Ronald Reagan's administration is of historic significance, I do not think it will be necessary to alter the fundamental comparison; the next president is likely to be no more than ordinarily awful, and I believe Reagan will continue to tower above other chief executives as uniquely atrocious and frightening. But I write this in 1988; times change; and ZILLAH undoubtedly will want to keep her panic as current as possible.

You know, upon our German stages,
Each man puts on just what he may;
So spare me not upon this day . . .
So in this narrow house of boarded space
Creation's fullest circle go to pace
And walk, with leisured speed, your spell
Past Heaven, through the Earth, to Hell.

*Faust*
(from the Prologue in the Theater)
[Walter Arndt, trans.—Norton]

The Republic had too much in common with its enemy; the spirit of revenge for Versailles, the fear of communism . . . But above all, the Republic was aware of its own tediousness. The people wanted theater.

*Heinrich Mann*
(Quoted in *The Brothers Mann*
by Nigel Hamilton)

"You'd be surprised how much being a good actor pays off."

Ronald Reagan
May 1, 1984

## Part One

### Prologue: Evening Meal in a Windstorm

(*Slides of crowds, drifting from the present to Germany in the thirties. Lights up on* ZILLAH *at her table, reading. Repeated slides of a huge crowd rallying in support of Hitler, everyone giving the fascist salute. With each slide the crowd draws nearer, til finally fixing on a single figure in the crowd, a woman who isn't saluting.* ZILLAH *looks up. Lights up on* AGNES' *apartment in Berlin.* [*Slide:* JANUARY 1, 1932.] *Seated around the table:* AGNES, HUSZ, BAZ, PAULINKA, *and* GOTCHLING. *It's night; the scene is lit by candlelight. Everyone has been drinking.*)

GOTCHLING: Capitalism is a system of . . . of . . .

PAULINKA: Digestion! A digestive system!

HUSZ: We've drunk too much.

GOTCHLING: Again.

HUSZ: (*To* GOTCHLING) You hold your liquor. I admire that. Did you know . . .

GOTCHLING: What?

HUSZ: Did you know that candlelight aids the digestive processes?

GOTCHLING: Yes. I knew that. And the fennel in grapeskins helps you see in the dark, but wine makes your gums shrivel prematurely.

PAULINKA: Ah! The advantages of opium.

BAZ: I think I'm going to vomit . . .

AGNES: Midnight. (*Beat*) HAPPY NEW YEAR!

(*General exultation*)

AGNES: Oh . . . (*Laughs*)

GOTCHLING: What?

AGNES: Oh my . . . (*Laughs*)

BAZ: What? What?

---

AGNES: All of you. Look at your faces. When we're together, and happy . . . a circle. It's a kind of perfect thing, like a circle, a round perfection.

GOTCHLING: Cheap sentiment. Cheap geometry. Time for coffee.

AGNES: No! I feel . . . what? Baz, what do I feel? I feel . . .

BAZ: Do you feel warm, Agnes?

AGNES: Yes.

BAZ: And . . . complete, Agnes?

AGNES: Complete? Mostly.

BAZ: Safe?

AGNES: Well . . .

BAZ: Relatively safe?

AGNES: We live in Berlin. (*Beat*) It's 1932. (*Beat*) I feel relatively safe.

HUSZ: Sufficient for the times. (*He stands up.*) Now I would like to propose a toast.

GOTCHLING: Excellent idea! A man of ideas! Propose, Husz.

HUSZ: To Agnes!

GOTCHLING: To Agnes! Good-hearted and brave!

HUSZ: Occupant prima of our affections, immovable tenant of this small, solid room: health, happiness and relative safety on this fierce and splendid night and for many years to come, dear heart.

EVERYONE: To Agnes.

(*Silence*)

PAULINKA: And in the silence, an angel passed over.

BAZ: Now what to do to begin the new year properly?

GOTCHLING: You were going to vomit.

BAZ: Yes, but now I have a better idea. Let's make up a story.

HUSZ: What kind of a story?

BAZ: One we compose together. A story about . . . something.

GOTCHLING: About a cold night.

Paulinka: A story about a cold night. Good. I begin.

Baz: Please! This is Agnes' party. Agnes' apartment. Agnes should begin. Begin, Agnes.

Agnes: Oh, let's see . . . Ha! (*Beat*) There was a winter once in Berlin when a terrible wind, cold as death, chased people through the streets at night and blew ice into their bones and killed them. Well there was one man who had to walk to work late every evening . . .

Gotchling: He was a night watchman, a working man. And he said to himself, "This wind is murder." And he decided to spend his last hard-earned penny on a thick woolen coat and an extra-long scarf and then the night wind could blow all it liked, he'd be warm and safe, "Our humanity", he said to himself, "is defined through our struggle to overcome nature." So he did buy those things, and . . .

Paulinka: And he wore them at night on his way to work, and the wind saw what he was up to, and it grew very angry and sharp, and it blew all the harder, and in seconds flat the man felt so cold he might as well have been naked. Score one for nature.

Gotchling: Score one for nature.

Baz: And he knew his plan had failed, and the wind was killing him, so with blue and frozen lips he prayed to God to save him from the wind, but of course God didn't, and he caught a severe influenza.

Husz: And as he lay on his deathbed, he thought he heard the wind whistle, "just you wait." His new coat and scarf hung from a peg on the wall. He could feel his life slipping away. He said to himself, "I wonder what's next?" and as he died he heard the wind calling . . .

(Gotchling *blows out the candles.*)

Agnes: "Just you wait."

(*In the darkness, everyone laughs. End of scene.*)

**Scene One: Die Alte (The Old One)**

([*Slide:* JANUARY 2, 1932. *AN HOUR AFTER MIDNIGHT.*] *The apartment is very dark. A figure is seated at the table, grinding something gritty in a large pewter mortar. A dim light grows on* Die Alte, *who looks at the audience and begins to speak.*)

DIE ALTE:
I remember the day; a sky
So bright that beneath it
Memory
Is stripped of every tint
Save innocence.
Summer, but the sun's
A chill apricot light
High up,
A dense, brilliant haze,
And we're expectant.
Yes.
Our hearts are in our throats,
Rising and falling:
Oh what a thing!
To wake up hungry
And smell the morning!
We had stopped for breakfast
At a little country railway station;
It was there that we learned
That war was declared.
I can't remember now
Which war it was, but
Then it seemed
Portentous, celestial;
We knew, we all knew
That a moment of History
Had come and gone, and touched by that,
By Destiny,
We continued to make our way to the North Sea,
Though it was too cold for swimming.
Towards evening, as I recall,
The weather changed abruptly . . .

(*Blackout. End of scene.*)

([*Slide:* APRIL 10, 1932. PRESIDENTIAL ELECTION. HINDENBURG DEFEATS HITLER.])

**Scene Two: Love Scene with Lemon**

([*Slide:* MAY 30, 1932.]) AGNES *and* HUSZ *together.* HUSZ *is taking off his coat,* AGNES *is turning on the radio: jazz music.*)

AGNES: I got a film.

HUSZ: How much?

AGNES: The rent, at least. Another nostalgia film. Swanboats and parasols. I play a wise old lady-in-waiting for the Kaiserin. Jolly twinkles. Want to see a jolly twinkle? (*She twinkles.*)

HUSZ: Terrifying. (*Beat*) Today on the set they were all complaining about the lack of good ideas for new films. So I suggested we make one about men from Mars: They live off the pus produced by bodily infections. They're covered with enormous boils, they have runny noses and eyes. The director says no, Germans don't want to see films about disgusting creatures like that, they want to see films about Germans. I said, "Herr Director, you simply do not understand the principle of metaphor."

AGNES: You'd better stop teasing them. Germans are sensitive.

HUSZ: Not sensitive; psychotic.

AGNES: Marx was a German.

HUSZ: Marx was a Jew. With a London address. And the soul of a Hungarian! I should never have left Hungary.

AGNES: You had to; they threw you out.

HUSZ: I should never have left Russia.

AGNES: If you wanted to stay in Russia you shouldn't have read Trotsky.

HUSZ: *Read* Trotsky, hell. I *knew* Trotsky. Goddamned Trotsky. In Russia we were making great films.

AGNES: But if you stayed there you'd never have met me, and you'd have to forego the pleasure of my company. (*Beat*) Let's have sex.

HUSZ: Ah, that reminds me. A present. (*He pulls a lemon from his pocket, hands it to her.*)

AGNES: Oh, a lemon! God, I haven't had a lemon in months! You shouldn't have, Husz, they're so expensive . . .

HUSZ: I stole it from the set. I pretended to be fiddling with the fruitbowl arrangement and I slipped it in my pocket.

AGNES: Let's have sex.

HUSZ: Not tonight.

AGNES: But I'm anxious tonight and I need to.

HUSZ: But I'm anxious too and I don't want to.

AGNES: Can I have a kiss?

HUSZ: Of course.

(*They kiss.*)

AGNES: Thanks for the lemon.

HUSZ: Small pleasures in bad times.

(*End of scene*)

**Scene Three: All Day in the Rain**

([*Slide:* MAY 29, 1932. OLDENBURG REGIONAL PARLIAMENTARY ELECTIONS. NAZI PARTY CANDIDATES WIN TWICE THE NUMBER OF VOTES AS THE SOCIAL-DEMOCRAT AND COMMUNIST PARTY CANDIDATES COMBINED] *Lights up on* AGNES *and* PAULINKA.)

PAULINKA: His name is Dr. Bloom. He's a Jew with a big belly and bushy eyebrows. He has a red leather couch and a little picture of Freud framed in gold. I lie back and pretend I'm in Vienna.

AGNES: Sounds romantic.

PAULINKA: Romantic? It's unspeakably erotic. He's so . . . hairy.

AGNES: How did you get the Studio to pay for psychoanalysis? I can't get tram fare out of them.

PAULINKA: I told them I was on the verge of a nervous breakdown.

AGNES: Are you?

PAULINKA: Perpetually.

AGNES: I still don't see why you have to back out of the skit.

PAULINKA: The demonstration's at the same time as my Wednesday appointment.

AGNES: Reschedule the appointment.

PAULINKA: Reschedule the demonstration.

AGNES: This is important.

PAULINKA: No. This is not important. This is a great opportunity for you to make a fool of yourself in front of a lot of . . . transport workers. Really, the idea of you joining the KPD. You aren't a communist.

AGNES: I am so.

PAULINKA: Since when?

AGNES: For . . . some time now. I just don't talk about it because I knew I wouldn't be taken seriously. But I am serious. I'm reading *Kapital.*

PAULINKA: Good luck. How far have you gotten?

AGNES: Well, not far, just the first . . .

PAULINKA: . . . paragraph? Oh, Agnes, there are more former communists in Germany than there are beer gardens and alchoholics. Even I was a communist once.

AGNES: Impossible.

PAULINKA: Oh yes. Full party membership. Really! It lasted about two weeks. The communists make the best films, so I thought I'd sign up and then after the revolution I'd get all the good parts.

AGNES: And what if the Nazis made the best films?

PAULINKA: The Nazis? Their films are all about mountain-climbing.

AGNES: Paulinka, this is serious! These are serious times!

PAULINKA: So they keep telling me.

AGNES: And what are you going to do about it?

PAULINKA: Smoke opium. And bring my dreams four times a week to Dr. Bloom.

AGNES: That doesn't sound very political to me.

PAULINKA: Oh, but it is. War reports from the battlefront within. Not much, I know, nothing compared to the Martyrdom of Red Agnes, Thespian for the Revolution, but from each according to her abilities . . .

AGNES: Stop, Paulinka. I need your help. Are you going to help, or not?

PAULINKA: Not. Sorry, my dear. Not. (*Beat*) When I get to be terribly famous, I'm going to write my autobiography. I'm thinking of calling it "The Decline Of The West."

(*Slight pause*)

AGNES: Last night I went to a big meeting. A man was giving a speech. I don't know who he was but he said things. That here is where capitalism will take its final stand. Here, in Germany. Not in twenty years, or forty, but soon. Today. If we go red the whole world will follow us. Everything bad and dangerous swept away.

PAULINKA: Imagine that.

AGNES: How can I stand back from that, Paulinka?

PAULINKA: I can't imagine.

AGNES: Paulinka, these are the most exciting days of my life.

(*End of scene*)

**1980–1988 #1**
**The Small Voice (Letter to the President)**

(*Lights up on* ZILLAH.)

ZILLAH: Dear Mr. President,
I know you will never read this letter. I'm fully aware of the fact that letters to you don't even make it to the White House, that they're brought to an office building in Maryland where a bunch of civil-servant types are paid to answer the sane ones. Crazy, hostile letters—like mine—the ones written in crayon on butcher paper, the ones made up of letters cut out of magazines—these get sent to the FBI, analyzed, xeroxed and burned. But I send them anyway, once a day, and do you know why? Because the loathing I pour into these pages is so ripe, so full-to-bursting, that it is my firm belief that anyone touching them will absorb into their hands some of the toxic energy contained therein. This toxin will be passed upwards—it is the nature of bureaucracies to pass things vertically—til eventually, through a network of handshakes, the Under-Secretary of Outrageous Falsehoods will shake hands with the Secretary of Pernicious Behavior Under The Cloak Of Night, who will, on a weekly basis in Cabinet meetings, shake hands with you before you nod off to sleep. In this way, through osmosis, little droplets of contagion are being rubbed into your leathery flesh every day—especially since, in this great country of ours, there must be thousands of people who are sending you poison post. We wait for the day when all the grams and drams and dollops of detestation will destroy you. We attack from below. Our day will come.

You can try to stop me. You can raise the price of stamps again. I'll continue to write. I'm saving up for a word processor. For me and my cause, money is no object.

Love,
Zillah

(ZILLAH *puts letter in envelope, licks and seals it, smiles. End of interruption.*)

**Scene Three A: Late Night Struggles on Towards Dawn**

([*Slide:* MAY 30, 1932. LATE NIGHT.] AGNES *is alone, working on the skit. She has: pencil, paper, various materials including the Red Baby—a doll—and a little Hitler doll, to which she is affixing the moustache. She stops to write.*)

AGNES: (*Writes, then reads out loud.*) Red Workers! Red Berlin! Arise! The world is perched on the brink of doom! (*She scratches out "doom" and writes, then reads:*) The world is perched on the brink of a catastrophe! (*She scratches out "catastrophe" and writes, then reads:*) The world. Is perched on the brink of a choice. The brink of a choice? Stupid, stupid. Perched on the brink of . . . shit. (*She goes to the radio, turns it on: jazz music. She goes back to the table, picks up the little Hitler doll.*) Hello. I'm Adolf Hitler. Thank you for inviting me here today on this lovely May morning. I love jazz. I love to tango. I love the dance music of dark-skinned peoples. Jewish wedding music. I love that! Dance with me. (*The doll dances a bit.*) Da-da-da . . . Dance with me! Vote for me! Kiss my ass! Watch me fly in my aeroplane! Look up! Here I am! (AGNES *makes propeller noises and flies the little doll about the room. Then she crashes it with great relish. She laughs to herself.*) RED WORKERS! RED BERLIN! ARISE! THE WORLD IS PERCHED ON THE BRINK OF . . . SOMETHING . . . CHOOSE! COMMUNISM OR FASCISM! THE REVOLUTION OR DEATH! STRIKE! NOW! REVOLUTION! NOW!

HUSZ: (*From off in the bedroom*) Who are you screaming at?

AGNES: I'm working on the skit.

HUSZ: Work more quietly. I'm trying to sleep.

AGNES: Perched on the brink of . . . (*She goes to the bedroom door and opens it.*) Husz, what are we perched on the brink of?

HUSZ: Come to bed.

AGNES: Perched on the brink of . . .

HUSZ: Fascism. Old age. Heart disease. Senility. Sleep.

AGNES: (*Closing the door, returns to table.*) Thanks. (*She picks up a lemon, cuts it open, sucks on it.*) Mmmm. Sour fruit.

(*End of scene*)

([*Slide:* JUNE 1, 1932. PRESIDENT HINDENBURG APPOINTS THE ARISTOCRATIC AND REACTIONARY VON PAPEN CHANCELLOR OF THE REPUBLIC. ONE OF VON PAPEN'S FIRST ACTS IS TO LIFT THE GOVERNMENT BAN ON THE SA AND THE SS.])

### Scene Four: Cold and Brutal but Exact and True

([*Slide:* JUNE 2, 1932.] AGNES *is alone with a glass of wine, struggling with the opening pages of* Kapital. BAZ *enters without knocking, followed by* GOTCHLING.)

BAZ: Guess where we've been.

AGNES: Where?

GOTCHLING: At a Nazi rally.

AGNES: You didn't.

BAZ: In Wedding. "Red" Wedding, I think you people call it. Now it looks more like Nazi Wedding. (*He produces a swastika pennant which he waves about.*)

AGNES: You went inside?

BAZ: We stayed for practically the entire event! You must have an intimate knowledge of the enemy.

GOTCHLING: He's apparently done this before. He thought I should see it happening first-hand.

AGNES: See what happening?

BAZ: The floodgates breaking open. The sewers backing up. Tell her what you saw.

GOTCHLING: A year ago I designed a series of posters for the Party office in Wedding.

BAZ: Which the Nazis blew up last month.

AGNES: It's being rebuilt.

BAZ: They'll blow it up again.

GOTCHLING: Tonight I recognized at least ten "comrades" whose faces used to decorate KPD functions. Devout communists. Now they're wearing swastikas.

BAZ: Right. Like bugs to a gaslamp. The Nazis make more noise, so bzzzzz. They attract the most insects. Fine specimens of Germanity, looking high and low—well, low, mostly, for any release for their desperately trapped sexual energies.

GOTCHLING: Oh not this crap again . . .

BAZ: Well they won't find it in the Communist Party. Membership requires a doctorate in hypocrisy. Let's see, which leg are we going to stand on this week, the left or the right? Can't decide? Call Stalin!

GOTCHLING: This is my poor friend Baz. Once he was a socialist. Then he discovered his penis, got distracted and became an anarchist. After which he got a job with the Institute for Human Depravity . . .

BAZ: Sexuality. Human Sexuality.

GOTCHLING: Where they taught him that Hitler is a manifestation of our collective retarded adolescence and the revolution will succeed when we get people to feel happy about masturbating.

BAZ: Glib reductionist.

GOTCHLING: Sex maniac. You open your mouth and out comes the same old sloppy nonsense, time after time. Half of those people at that rally tonight think that the Nazis are socialists. Half of the Nazis *are* socialists! This is no party, no ideology, just a shabby collection of borrowings from all over—a bad collage. When Hitler reveals himself as just another flunky for German capital, the working class will abandon him.

AGNES: They'll destroy him.

GOTCHLING: Absolutely!

BAZ: Economic analysis! So antiseptic! So sterile! The fascists don't try to make sense. They abandon morality, money, justice —Hitler simply offers a lot of very confused and terrified and constipated people precisely what they want, a means of release. These people are far beyond caring whether Hitler is a socialist or not. They're in love with the shine on his boots, they want a fatherly boot heel to lick, they want him to say "Daddy loves his children, now go and kill for me." They're completely deaf to your hair-splitting psuedoscience and jolly-comrade good will. They want bloody things.

GOTCHLING: Baz, you're a slob, an intellectual slob.

BAZ: Ouch. And I thought I was being marvellously eloquent, penetrating to the very heart of the Mystery of the Decade.

GOTCHLING: You're walllowing around in coffee-klatch bullshit. Without economics it all turns to drivel. You're never going to make a coherent political theory based on orgasms. The capitalist system is disintegrating. Inflation, devaluation, murderous unemployment, collapse. These people are frightened because the capitalists can't tell them how to save themselves and they haven't heard us yet. They will. The preconditions for revolution are in the making.

BAZ: Why do I detect a note of uncertainty?

GOTCHLING: You don't. I know it will look bad til then. People will make a lot of mistakes. A drowning man clutches at twigs.

BAZ: Yes. But this particular twig may very well save them.

AGNES: Hitler? How?!

BAZ: Once he's Chancellor he'll build an army and start looking for a war. Guns make jobs, right, comrade? It won't be hard convincing Hindenburg or the German people. Germans love guns, more than jobs. And before . . .

AGNES: Not true! The system can't recover from the Crash.

BAZ: Says who?

AGNES: Everyone. It hasn't yet. Its decline is Historically Inevitable. And for another thing, the German proletariat doesn't want war.

BAZ: I submit, Agnes, that you are a middle-class actress who knows very little about the German proletariat.

AGNES: I know enough. And I submit, Baz, that you are a condescending snob whose homosexuality alienates him from the proletariat.

BAZ: Indeed? (*To* GOTCHLING) Is she learning this from you?

AGNES: And your theories, by the way, of sexual repression as the root of all evil are half-baked.

BAZ: Half-baked. This from a Marxist who's never read Marx!

AGNES: I have so!

BAZ: *The Communist Manifesto* doesn't count. Everyone's read that! And my being a homosexual brings me into contact with more proletarians than you can imagine.

AGNES: So does working at the Studio.

BAZ: Right. They paint your face and clean up after you've finished acting. I have sex with them.

GOTCHLING: And they tell you they're voting for Hitler?

BAZ: Some do.

GOTCHLING: Do you still sleep with them?

BAZ: I'll never tell.

AGNES: Baz!

BAZ: What?

AGNES: You'd sleep with a Nazi?

BAZ: I didn't say that. You sleep with a Trotskyite.

AGNES: That's different.

BAZ: Not to Stalin it isn't.

AGNES: Evasion.

BAZ: I have to get to work.

AGNES: More evasion.

BAZ: No, but I do. The Institute is doing a big poster campaign. Abortion on demand. Free condoms. Great big posters. The Nazis will adore them. In the face of an erupting volcano we struggle hopelessly, hopelessly . . .

AGNES: Not hopelessly.

BAZ: Who can say? Prophecy is sorcery, sorcery is a sin.

GOTCHLING: More slop, Baz. You are the victim of a mental illness that deflects admirable energy into bad romantic posturing. It'll be money in the end, you wait—capital for the Fascists and the workers for themselves. Bad time to be wasting time. Join the Party.

BAZ: I can't.

GOTCHLING: Why not?

BAZ: They won't let me wear mascara. Good night. (*He exits.*)

AGNES: (*To* GOTCHLING) Do you think he sleeps with Nazis?

(*End of scene*)

([*Slide:* JULY 20, 1932. WITH MINIMAL OPPOSITION CHANCELLOR VON PAPEN DISSOLVES THE SOCIAL-DEMOCRATIC PRUSSIAN GOVERNMENT. HE DECLARES HIMSELF "STATE COMMISSIONER".])

**Scene Five: Fingerspitzengefuhl (Finger-tip feeling)**

([*Slide:* JULY 21, 1932. NATIONAL REICHSTAG ELECTION RESULTS: THE NAZI PARTY WINS 230 SEATS, THE SOCIAL DEMOCRATS 133, THE COMMUNISTS 89, AND THE RIGHT-WING NATIONAL PARTIES 37. THE NAZIS RECEIVE 37.7% OF THE NATIONAL VOTE. THE SOCIAL-DEMOCRATIC COALITION, KNOWN AS THE WEIMAR COALITION, IS DEFEATED.] AGNES *and* PAULINKA *sit over toast and coffee at the kitchen table.*)

PAULINKA: You know that in Munich he developed an incestuous infatuation for his cousin; she was fifteen. He forced her to live with him and a whole lot more besides. She killed herself. She was seventeen. And at the studio I heard from someone who has a brother high up in the Party that every woman that sleeps with him, who winds up in his bed, either kills herself or has an accident or is found murdered later.

AGNES: Oh, that's nonsense.

PAULINKA: You don't believe it? I do.

AGNES: It's all a lot of crap. Who wants to know about his perversions?

PAULINKA: They say he's a copraphilic.

AGNES: A what?

PAULINKA: Shit.

AGNES: Paulinka, please, that's disgusting.

PAULINKA: I didn't make it up. This woman told me that she actually knows a high-priced prostitute who spent the night with him. Now she's in terror for her life. She won't talk about what happened or what's got her so scared, but she rarely leaves her flat these days and she always feels cold.

AGNES: I don't want to hear any more.

PAULINKA: Agnes, do you believe in Evil?

AGNES: It's not something you believe in. There are evil men, of course.

PAULINKA: Evil as in diabolical? Diabolical evil?

AGNES: What are you asking me?

PAULINKA: Do you believe in the Devil, Agnes? That's what I'm asking you. Do you believe in the Devil?

AGNES: At my age?

PAULINKA: Because I do.

**Scene Five A: It Takes Three Invitations**

(*There is a sudden change of lighting. The room grows dim, and a brilliant spotlight hits* PAULINKA, *who warms to it immediately and begins to address the audience.*)

PAULINKA: I've seen Him. Well, not Him, exactly, or . . . When I had just started acting I did two seasons at the Municipal Theatre of Karlsruhe. Ever been to Karlsruhe? (*She smiles. It is a telling smile.*) We were giving Faust, Part One, a play I've always detested, and I was playing Gretchen, a part I've always detested, and I was not happy, not happy at all. There were nights I thought I'd be stuck in the provinces forever, never see Berlin, never see the inside of a film studio, die, go to Hell, and it'd be a place exactly like Karlsruhe. Black nights, you could imagine your whole life gone . . . You know the scene in the play where the black poodle turns into the Devil and offers Faust the world? All that demurring, endless, always seemed so coy to me. I'd say yes, in a minute. Wouldn't you? But so one night I was walking home after a performance and a very strange thing happened. I found myself going down a narrow street, an alley, really, one I'd never been down before, and suddenly BANG! There was this little black poodle, sitting on a doorstep. Waiting for me. Staring at me with those wet, black eyes. You know, those wet, dark, dog eyes. Staring. And I thought to myself, "It's Him! He's come to talk to me!" I felt dizzy, I almost fainted. I expected Him to stand up on His hind-legs and say "Paulinka! Fame, films and unsurpassable genius as an actress in exchange for your immortal soul." And that's when I knew it, and my dears I wish I didn't know: I'd never resist. I couldn't. I am constitutionally incapable of resisting anything. A good actress, a good liar, but not in truth a very good person. Just give me Berlin, sixty years of success,

and then haul me off to the Lake of Fire. Do business with the Devil.
But so anyway the poodle had other things in mind. I guess I must have startled it when I asked it if it wanted to make me an offer. It leaped up at me, barking and snarling and obviously out for blood. Chased me for blocks. I escaped by ducking into a bar, where I drank and drank and drank . . .
Probably just somebody's nasty black poodle. But I've always wondered . . . what if it really was Him, and He decided I wasn't worth it?

(*End of scene*)

([*Slide:* AUGUST 30, 1932. HERMANN GOERING ELECTED PRESIDENT OF REICHSTAG BY A COALITION OF NAZIS, NATIONALISTS, AND THE CATHOLIC CENTER PARTY, WHICH HAD PREVIOUSLY BEEN OPPOSED TO THE NAZIS.]

### Scene Six: Demonology

([*Slide:* SEPTEMBER 12, 1932. CHANCELLOR VON PAPEN, FINDING THE NAZIS LESS COMPLIANT THAN HAD BEEN EXPECTED, DISSOLVES THE REICHSTAG AND CALLS FOR NEW ELECTIONS.] AGNES *alone, sitting with* Kapital, *flipping the pages distractedly. There is a loud knock. She goes to answer it.*)

MALEK: (*Entering*) Comrade Eggling, we come as specially designated representatives of the Party's Central Committee. We've been sent to convey congratulations to you and your comrade collaborators for a highly successful agitprop performance.

AGNES: Oh well thank you that's very . . .

TRAUM: (*Entering behind* MALEK.) Long live the Revolution! Long live Germany!

AGNES: YES! Yes. Can I get you some . . . tea or . . .

MALEK: We hope you'll continue to contribute your efforts to the struggle.

AGNES: Oh absolutely. I mean, I intend to. I don't usually but . . . well, as much as I can. Absolutely. I . . .

TRAUM: Good. (*Beat*) Now there is one other matter and then we can be going. There are certain Left-deviationist tendencies in your play that must be corrected before it's performed again. Which hopefully will be very soon.

AGNES: Left-deviationist tendencies?

MALEK: Small problems, really.

TRAUM: Well, not so small . . .

MALEK: Fairly small.

TRAUM: Actually fairly large.

MALEK: Fairly small. (*Tiny, uneasy pause. To* AGNES:) It would be more appropriate, in keeping with current Party policy . . .

TRAUM: Look. This is the play about the Red Baby?

AGNES: Right. The Red Baby Play.

TRAUM: Highly amusing. The Red Baby . . . what is the Red Baby, comrade?

AGNES: It's . . . well, it's a symbol . . . a symbol of . . . of . . .

MALEK: A symbol of nascent communism in Germany.

AGNES: Right!

MALEK: Of the new-born proletarian revolution.

AGNES: Exactly.

TRAUM: Exactly.

AGNES: What?

TRAUM: Exactly. Exactly the problem. Look, comrade, as you probably already know the Comintern Executive has . . . (AGNES *isn't understanding a word.*) How to say this.

MALEK: Comrade Eggling, the focus of your play is very clearly the proletarian revolution in Germany, that it's going to happen very soon.

AGNES: Yes.

| MALEK: | TRAUM: |
|---|---|
| Well the difficulty is . . . | Exactly. And that is no longer an accurate reflection of the policy of the Comintern, nor of the KPD. |

AGNES: It isn't?

TRAUM: No. It is Left-deviationist adventurist opportunism. (AGNES *doesn't get it.*) You're rushing things.

AGNES: You mean there isn't going to be a proletarian revolution?

| MALEK: | TRAUM: |
| --- | --- |
| Well of course there has been one in Russia. In Germany . . . eventually, yes. But not necessarily the next step. | Oh, well, eventually, yes, but . . . |

AGNES: What's the next step?

TRAUM: Defense of Soviet Russia.

AGNES: But in Germany? Here?

MALEK: Well, a United Front Against Fascism . . .

TRAUM: But *not* with the Social Democrats.

MALEK: No. No. Not with the Social Democrats.

(*Again a tiny, uneasy pause.*)

| MALEK: | TRAUM: |
| --- | --- |
| Well, what we mean by that is . . . | Well, with the Social Democrat workers but not the leaders. The SPD leadership must be exposed as Social Fascist and hence indistinguishable from the Nazis. |

MALEK: Well, *not* indistinguishable.

TRAUM: Oh yes.

MALEK: No.

TRAUM: Yes! The Comintern's position on this . . .

MALEK: You're wrong! Not even the Comintern is stupid enough to say that.

TRAUM: Oh yes they are!

MALEK: You're wrong, comrade.

TRAUM: (*Pulling rank*) NO! YOU are!

(*There is a very uneasy pause.*)

TRAUM: We feel certain that in time the workers loyal to the SPD will come over to us.

AGNES: It looks like more of them are going over to the Nazis.

MALEK: True.

TRAUM: No! Not true! I mean it looks that way but . . .

AGNES: If there's not going to be a United Front with the Social Democrats then who are you going to be united with?

TRAUM: Look. It's not all our fault. They don't want us either.

AGNES: Maybe you should stop calling them fascists.

TRAUM: But they are fascists.

AGNES: No they're not.

TRAUM: Yes they are.

MALEK: No they're not!

TRAUM: MALEK!

MALEK: Well you know the same as I do. They aren't.

TRAUM: As comrade Malek knows perfectly well, holding a firm line against bourgeois parliamentary dictatorships is essential to the defense of the revolution.

AGNES: But there isn't going to be a revolution!

MALEK: Oh yes there is!

AGNES: He said there wasn't.

MALEK: Well, he's wrong.

TRAUM: NO, YOU ARE!

MALEK: *NO, YOU ARE!*

(*Silence*)

AGNES: Just tell me what to do with the Red Baby.

MALEK: We're not artists, comrade. You work it out. Try to de-emphasize the importance—the immediate importance—of revolution. The workers aren't ready yet.

AGNES: Do *you* believe this, comrade . . .

MALEK: Malek. Rosa Malek. No. But I believe in Party discipline.

TRAUM: I noticed. (*Pause*) We would also suggest that the Red Baby not be identified as proletarian. We're trying to sell the new concept of the KPD as a party for everyone, not just the workers. "Class struggle" seems to scare the petty-bourgeois right into the arms of the Nazis.

AGNES: I'll do what I can.

MALEK: Thank you, comrade. We appreciate it.

TRAUM: It's extremely important.

AGNES: It's just a skit.

TRAUM: No. Every effort from every corner brings us closer to victory.

(*Tiny uncomfortable pause.* TRAUM *leaves.*)

MALEK: You know, comrade, your play gave me nightmares.

AGNES: It did?

MALEK: The Red baby. The doll you used. I think it reminded me of a doll I once had. It wasn't red, of course—that's what did it. I don't mean this as a criticism but it's awful when you think about it, a *red* baby. Imagine a real red baby. Wouldn't that be horrible, like someone had painted it or boiled it or something.

AGNES: What was the dream about?

MALEK: I can't remember. There were several. It smiled a lot, maybe it grew. I don't remember. But I woke up all tangled in the sheets.

(*End of scene*)

**Scene Seven: Scenes from the Life: First Act**

([*Slide:* NOVEMBER 6, 1932. SECOND NATIONAL REICHSTAG ELECTION RESULTS: THE NAZIS LOSE 34 SEATS, THE COMMUNISTS GAIN 12. NAZIS STILL HOLD A MAJORITY BUT A REVERSAL IN THEIR POPULARITY IS WIDELY PREDICTED.] AGNES *is listening to the radio for news.* GOTCHLING *enters with her portfolio.*)

AGNES: Twelve new seats! We got twelve!

GOTCHLING: I heard.

AGNES: And they lost thirty-four! Thirty-four fascists out the door! Millions of votes! They're losing!

GOTCHLING: (*Taking materials out of portfolio.*) I have so much work to do. You have to help.

AGNES: God, I feel six years younger! WE WON! We're going to win. Up and up. And I feel like I helped, like I actually moved in time, the lump moved!

GOTCHLING: Help me cut this up. Along the blackened edges. And be careful.

AGNES: Gotchling! You MUST be happy tonight! Even you!

(*Small pause*)

GOTCHLING: My father had a little speech, we'd get it every night after he'd read the papers. "People are pigs. Pigs and lice. Human history isn't the story of the good man, not of the saint, but of the louse who shot, stabbed or bludgeoned the saint to death. Fond of mud, full of shit. Pigs. In my many years on earth, this is what I've learned." Every night, word for word. I think onions give me bellyache because he used to eat them all the time. He worked very hard and he was poor but he wouldn't join the Party because he couldn't let go of it—that contempt or despair or whatever the hell it was. "People are pigs." And last week when we thought the Nazis were going to *add* thirty-four seats I found myself saying "people are pigs" like a chant. But then they surprise you. The People. Five million come out of their rooms and they vote communist. Which is not easy for them to do. Five million people.

(HUSZ *enters without knocking.*)

GOTCHLING: (*At the top of her lungs, suddenly*) FIVE MILLION PEOPLE, HUSZ!

(HUSZ *pulls two enormous bottles of vodka from inside his coat.*)

HUSZ: Tonight, we swallow our differences. (*Pause*) Fire, Annabella. In the street, in our throats, in the sky. Red fire. The ground is shaking. I have felt this before. The masses are on the move.

(*End of scene*)

**Scene Seven: Scenes from the Life: Second Act**

([*Slide:* NOVEMBER 6, 1932. LATER THE SAME NIGHT.] HUSZ, AGNES *and* GOTCHLING, *who is working on the collage, cutting and pasting. It is late at night. No one is drunk, but everyone's been drinking.*)

HUSZ: Scenes from the life of Vealtninc Husz, one-eyed cameraman: Russian Episodes. One: I make Trotsky weep. (*Pause*) Interior shot, overhead pan of huge crowd milling, the Red Artists Congress in Leningrad, 1921. (*He starts to hum a soft* Internationale *under this.*)

HUSZ: Dolly in to big knot of people surrounding comrade Trotsky, mingling; track along behind him till he reaches the great Dziga-Vertov. Close-up on hand shake. Trotsky notices among DV's entourage a young Hungarian with an eye patch, asks Dziga-Vertov, "This Hungarian, what happened to his eye?" DV replies, "His name is Husz, he lost it in the revolution in Budapest, comrade Trotsky." Close-up on Husz, his black eye patch; jump to close-up of eye of Trotsky, behind its thick, magnifying lens. Looking at Husz. With a big, wet tear in his eye. (*Pause; he gets up to get drink.*) Music!

GOTCHLING: (*Singing*)
Arise, ye prisoners of starvation,
Arise, ye wretched of the earth.
For Justice thunders condemnation;
A better world's in birth.

HUSZ: Two: (*Pause*) Huge close-ups, the mouth of Dziga-Vertov, thin-lipped, and the ear of Vealtninc Husz. First, the mouth, saying "Film is the perfect medium, the only medium for the age of machines, because it is mechanically made, uses mechanical construction, montage, juxtaposition, not focused on the small inner life but on the grand scale, the whole picture, capable of recording an entire revolution!" Jump to the ear of Husz, deep, empty, listening, filling up. Interior shot, from the ear to the heart. (*Small pause*) In German film studios, nobody listens. (*Beat*) Music!

GOTCHLING: (*Singing*)
No more, tradition's chains shall bind us,
Arise ye poor, no more in thrall.
The earth shall rise on new foundations;
We have been naught, we shall be all!

HUSZ: Three: Dream sequence, like from Hollywood.

(GOTCHLING *starts whistling high-pitched, dreamy* Internationale *chorus.*)

HUSZ:
Map of Europe, borders drawn in black, heavy lines.
Flames eat it up, the map burns;
Behind it, carved in granite, the lovely word
"Internationalism."
The granite
Dissolves.
Cross-fade to a magnificent expanse,

A bowl-shaped valley,
Mountains,
And millions of people, simply millions,
So many that the valley is filled,
Each an infinitely precious part of a glorious entirety,
In complex, dissonant, harmonious voice,
Rising, exploding, singing the song.

(HUSZ *joins* GOTCHLING; AGNES *joins in.*)

ALL THREE:
'Tis the final conflict;
Let each stand in their place;
The Internationale
Will be the human race.
'Tis the final conflict;
Let each stand in their place;
The Internationale
Will be the human race!

HUSZ: End of film.

(*End of scene*)

**Scene Eight: Ich habe eine neue Giftsuppe gekocht (I Made A New Poison Soup)**

([*Slide:* NOVEMBER 6, 1932. LATER THAT NIGHT.] *The room is dark; a hunched figure can be discerned sitting at the table; a grinding noise is heard.* AGNES *enters from the bedroom, turns on the light.* DIE ALTE *is at the table with her mortar and pestle. She looks up at* AGNES, *who is startled.*)

AGNES: Oh!

DIE ALTE: Do you have something to eat?

(AGNES *hesitates, staring, then moves to the cupboard and takes an apple from a bowl. She puts it on the table.*)

DIE ALTE: Something softer. Cheese?

AGNES: Do you live here? In this building?

(*Small pause.* DIE ALTE *looks at* AGNES.)

DIE ALTE: There's an iron stairs outside the window.

AGNES: The fire escape?

DIE ALTE: Do you have something to eat? The price of things. It's unbearable.

AGNES: You came down the fire escape?

DIE ALTE: The wind's strong there. I stand on the stairs on windy days. I press up against the bricks, they're cold, my hair flies loose, my gown whips against the railing, my cheeks burn. (*Small pause*) Bread if you don't have cheese.

(*There is a loud knock in the walls.*)

AGNES: The water pipes.

DIE ALTE: Sounds like knocking. Little penny man. Let him in.

AGNES: (*Going to the cupboard.*) I think I have some rolls.

DIE ALTE:
Just before I fall asleep,
After God has heard my prayers,
Things below begin to creep:
The penny man is on the stairs.

AGNES: Oh, I remember that poem. Years ago . . .

DIE ALTE: The rolls, please.

(AGNES *gives her a roll. She begins to eat, greedily.*)

DIE ALTE: It's a little stale.

(*End of scene*)

**1980–1988 #2**
**Dinner in Bensonhurst**

(*Lights up on* ZILLAH.)

ZILLAH: At least once a month I get schlepped to my parents for a meal which always ends in hysterics. First we eat and talk about pleasant things—why I'm not working, why I'm not married, why my brother Zachary is such a putz (my opinion exclusively), but then someone mentions politics and the niceties are thrust aside. Blood is spilt over unimportant, hardly debatable issues. Like the remotest possibility that the Holocaust bears any resemblance to any other event in history, especially recent history. Or that the current president, who shall go nameless, bears any resemblance whatsoever to a certain fascist-dictator anti-Semitic mass-murdering psychopath who shall also go nameless. My father and my brother Zachary—who really is a putz, by the way; he's become this investment broker who walks on coals on the weekend—they think my problem is a tendency to get over-excited. *I* think the problem is basically that we have this event—Germany, Hitler, the Holocaust—which we have made into *THE* standard of Absolute Evil—well and good, as standards go it's not bad, but now that we have this standard people get frantic as soon as anyone tries to use it. Nothing compares, nothing resembles, well, so he's a little bit like you-know-who but then again he isn't really—and the standard becomes *un*usable, and nothing qualifies as evil with a capital E. Which is understandable, because God, that was all pretty horrible and what do we do if we believe that what America is doing with the contras in Nicaragua is sort of like what Hitler did with Franco in Spain? It would be . . . upsetting, I suppose.

(Zillah *takes out an enlarged photo of Reagan and a black crayon. She scribbles a toothbrush moustache in the appropriate place on the photo. She then holds the photo in front of her and recites, in a hokey German accent:*)

Zillah: "Mr. Roosevelt was much concerned about German intentions in Europe. If Germany inquired about American policy in Central and South America, she would be referred to the Monroe Doctrine and told to mind her own business." (*She lowers the photo.*) Adolf Hitler, April 28, 1932.

(*End of interruption*)

**Scene Nine: Love Scene Without Lemon**

([*Slide:* DECEMBER 4, 1932. THE NAZIS STILL CONTROL A PARLIAMENTARY MAJORITY DESPITE ELECTION SETBACKS. HITLER, WITH THE SUPPORT OF PROMINENT INDUSTRIALISTS, DEMANDS THE CHANCELLORSHIP OF HINDENBURG. HINDENBURG REFUSES.] Agnes *alone.* Kapital *face down on table. Radio on, playing jazz. The music stops and Hitler's voice comes on.* Agnes *switches radio off.* Husz *enters in a hurry.*)

Husz: Now let's have sex.

Agnes: Not now, I don't want to.

Husz: But I need to. I'm anxious tonight.

Agnes: I can't. I'm too anxious . . .

Husz: We have to get together on this.

AGNES: Kiss.

(*They do.*)

AGNES: Did you enjoy that?

HUSZ: Not particularly, no.

AGNES: Husz?

HUSZ: Hmm?

AGNES: I love you.

HUSZ: Inveterate bourgeois. Thank you, comrade Eggling.

(AGNES *goes to him. Another kiss.*)

AGNES: They say he'll be chancellor. Before the year is out. Hindenburg's very old.

HUSZ: (Tired, with little conviction) There'll be uprisings. His government will be short-lived.

AGNES: For a thousand years.

HUSZ: (*Laughs*) Nothing ever lasts that long.

AGNES: Lately I feel like I'm in a film, all the time. A newsreel. I see all these events already on film, not just Hitler, but us: no sex, eating and crying. All public events. There is a title: "PERCHED ON THE BRINK OF A GREAT HISTORIC CRIME".

HUSZ: Indeed.

AGNES: And you want to have sex? At a time like this?

HUSZ: I'm anxious.

(*End of scene*)

**Scene Ten: The Rent**

([*Slide:* JANUARY 1, 1933.] AGNES *alone. It's late at night. The apartment is dimly lit.*)

AGNES:
I can see myself living here
Through a hurricane or fire—
Even if the building was burning
I think I'd stay.
Why?
Do you know how hard it is
To find an apartment in Berlin?

(*As* AGNES *continues to speak, beautiful, intense sunlight begins to stream through the windows.*)

AGNES:
I feel at home.
My friends like it here,
Better than their own apartments.
I'm not a fool.
I know that what's coming
Will be bad,
But not unlivable,
And not eternally,
And when it's over, I will have clung to the least last thing,
Which is to say, my lease.
And you have to admit, it's a terrific apartment.
I could never find anything like it if I moved out now.
You would not believe
How low the rent is.

(*End of scene*)

**Scene Eleven: Oranges**

([*Slide:* JANUARY 30, 1933. PRESIDENT HINDENBURG APPOINTS ADOLF HITLER CHANCELLOR OF THE GERMAN REPUBLIC.] AGNES *and* BAZ. *Night.* BAZ *is kneeling on the floor, praying.*)

BAZ: I see no reason to be ashamed. In the face of genuine hopelessness one has no choice but to gracefully surrender reason to the angelic hosts of the irrational. They alone bring solace and comfort, for which we say, in times of distress, "Hosannah and who needs science?"

AGNES: But then you're saying that it's all right to admit defeat.

BAZ: Well, when one is defeated . . .

AGNES: But see, that's just the problem. How do we know? What if we lay down and give up the ghost just at the moment when . . . (*She's stuck.*)

BAZ: When what?

AGNES: When the whole terrible thing could somehow have been reversed.

BAZ: Do you really think it can? The farmers say, "If we could only grow wheat in the winter then we wouldn't be so hungry."

But does that mean anything to the groundlock and the frost? No. So the farmers wait till spring. What we need is a Meteorology of Human History. Then maybe we could weather the changes in the political climate with as much composure as we weather changes in the weather. Seasons of History. Does it matter if we know why it rains? It just rains. We get wet. Or not. Life is miserable. Or not. The sun shines or it doesn't shine. You can explain these things, scientifically, meteorologically, and we can applaud the elegance of your explanation, but it won't stop the weather, or that telling feeling of being overwhelmed. Because on this planet, one is overwhelmed.

AGNES: Gotchling would call that defeatist crap.

BAZ: Gotchling. Gotchling is out at this very moment nailing posters to telephone poles. But you and I . . .

AGNES: I remember once I was out all day in the rain, and the sky was dark from morning on, but just before night the rain stopped, and between the black sky and the ground there was a small open space, a thin band of day that stretched across the rim of the world. And as I watched, night came and the ground and sky closed shut. I'm overwhelmed. I feel no connection, no kinship with most of the people I see. I watch them in the underground come and go and I think, "Are you a murderer? Are you?" And there are so many people.

BAZ: Yesterday I was on my way to buy oranges. I eat them constantly in the winter, even though they cost so much, because they prevent colds. On my way to the grocer's I passed a crowd in front of an office building; I asked what was going on, and they showed me that a man had jumped from the highest floor and was dead. They had covered the man with tar paper but his feet were sticking out at angles that told you something was very wrong. There was a pink pool of red blood mixed with white snow. I left. (*Pause*) At the grocer's I felt guilty and embarrassed buying these fat oranges for myself only minutes after this man had died. I knew why he had jumped. I thought of him opening the window, high up, and the cold air . . . (*Pause*) On my way home I re-imagined the whole thing, because I felt a little sick at heart. The dead man was sitting up in the snow, and now the tar paper covered his feet. As I passed by I gave him one of my oranges. He took it. He stared at the orange, as though holding it could give him back some of the warmth he'd lost. All day, when I closed my eyes, I could see him that way. Sitting in the snow, holding the orange, and comforted. Still bloody, still dead, but . . . comforted.

Agnes: I'm not very scientific. I really believed once that oranges prevented colds because they store up hot sunlight in the tropical places they grow, and the heat gets released when you eat one.

Baz: I consider that a perfectly scientific explanation, and probably correct. These are cold days . . . not to be believed.

(*End of scene*)

**Scene Twelve: Furcht und Elend (Fear and Misery)**

([*Slide:* JANUARY 30, 1933. LATER THAT NIGHT.] Agnes, Husz, Paulinka, Gotchling, *and* Baz. *The wreckage of an unhappy evening lies scattered about.*)

Gotchling: It's all so much dry rot and fungus! The times are what we make them.

Husz: I grant you that. And we will make them unlivable.

Baz: Touché.

Gotchling: Things may get tough for a bit.

Husz: A bit?

Gotchling: More than a bit. A long time.

Husz: A very long time. To be replaced by something that looks like progress but will turn out to be worse than what it replaced. (*He starts for the bedroom.*)

Gotchling: Where are you going?

Husz: To piss. Out the window. (*Exits*)

Paulinka: I once said to Rollo Jaspers, "If you didn't fill your films with such hateful, stupid people, the world wouldn't look so bad to you." And he said, "I fill my films with the kind of hateful, stupid people the world is full of. Look around you." And at that precise moment, everyone in the vicinity was remarkably hateful and stupid and I had to concede the point. Depressing memory.

Gotchling: Opium is the perfect drug for people who want to remain articulate while being completely trivial.

Baz: I'm off. It's been a lovely wake. Give my best to the corpse. Happy eternity.

Gotchling: You shouldn't go out.

BAZ: I know, but the tea garden, my dear. The night is calling.

AGNES: Stay. The streets are too dangerous.

GOTCHLING: They're celebrating.

BAZ: I want to celebrate too.

GOTCHLING: What is that? Is that some kind of a joke?

AGNES: Celebrate what?

BAZ: The end of a very long and painful struggle.

GOTCHLING: You aren't . . . amusing, Baz. You're straining too desperately for effect. Sometimes . . .

BAZ: Yes?

(HUSZ *reenters from the bedroom.*)

GOTCHLING: (*To* BAZ) Sometimes I could strike you.

(*Silence. Goes to* GOTCHLING, *kisses her on the forehead, and leaves.*)

GOTCHLING: All of you. This elegant despair. It's so comfortable. You pretend to be progressive but actually progress distresses you. It's untidy, upsetting. Fortunately it happens anyway.

HUSZ: So I believed. I journeyed to the home of Progress. I gave it an eye. Progress ate it up, crunch crunch, and said, "You have two eyes, give me another!" And I said, "Oh no thanks, I'm leaving."

GOTCHLING: And so you left and turned into a reactionary.

HUSZ: No. I didn't. I can't become a reactionary because that eye, part of me, is to this day lying in the belly of Progress. And it will never let me go. The eye I have left looks clearly at all the shit in front of it, but the eye I gave to the revolution will always see what it saw then . . .

GOTCHLING: That was the good eye. This one's diseased. Too much Trotsky!

HUSZ: The last true revolutionary, may God keep him! Everyone else has surrendered.

GOTCHLING: Morbid dry rot! I hate arguing with you, Husz. I used to enjoy it, but you've become a bitter old bore.

HUSZ: Sweet Annabella.

Paulinka: We are such rotten people.

Agnes: No. Don't say that.

Gotchling: (*Preparing to leave.*) We may be. History will move on without us.

Paulinka: I'm right. We are frightened and faithless. What's inside is an unstable, decomposing mess. Everyone on the street, looking tidy, just thin-skinned vessels full of grey, reeking, swampy pulp . . . (*She starts to get nauseated.*)

Husz: Listen!

(*Everyone except* Paulinka *is immediately alert.* Gotchling *goes to window.*)

Husz: Do you hear something? Listen, Paulinka.

Paulinka: No, I . . .

Husz: Shut up. Listen.
There is something calling, Paulinka.
If you retain a shred of decency
You can hear it—it's a dim terrible
Voice that's calling—a bass howl, like
A cow in a slaughterhouse, but
Far, far off . . .
It is calling us to action, calling us
To stand against the calamity,
To spare nothing, not our blood,
Nor our happiness, nor our lives
In the struggle to stop the dreadful day
That's burning now
In oil flames on the horizon.

What makes the voice pathetic
Is that it doesn't know
What kind of people it's reaching.
Us.
No one hears it, except us.
This Age wanted heroes.
It got us instead:
Carefully constructed, but
Immobile. Subtle, but
Unfit
To take up
The burden of the times.

It happens.
A whole generation of washouts.
History says stand up,
And we totter and collapse,
Weeping, moved, but not
Sufficient.

The best of us, lacking.
The most decent,
Not decent enough.
The kindest,
Too cruel,
The most loving
Too full of hate,
The wisest,
Too stupid,
The fittest
Unfit
To take up
The burden of the times.

The Enemy
Has a voice like seven thunders.
What chance did that dim voice ever have?
Marvel that anyone heard it
Instead of wondering why nobody did anything.
Marvel that *we* heard it,
We who are unfit for anything
But listening,
And talking,
We who have no right to hear it—
NO RIGHT!
And it would be a mercy not to.
But mercy . . . is a thing . . . no one remembers its face anymore.

The best would be
That time would stop
Right now,
In this middling moment of awfulness,
Before the very worst arrives.
We'd all be spared more than telling.
That would be best.

(*Pause*)

GOTCHLING: The most profound thing about you, Husz, is your irresponsibility. (*She heads for the door.*) Open the windows, clear the air. I have work to do. A broadsheet we're putting out. The United Front. And I'm late. (*Exits*)

(*End of scene*)

**1980–1988 #3**
**Amnesia**

(*Lights up on* ZILLAH.)

ZILLAH: I have been accused of being too free with my use of the word "Nazi". It's true. I have a generous nature. The President is a Nazi. Nazi Nazi Nazi. Nazi Nancy. Nazi Bork. Nazi Oliver North. I mean of course they don't walk around in black leather —not in public, anyway—but MUST we be so literal? How much of a Nazi do you have to be to qualify for membership? Is a 25% Nazi a Nazi, or not? Ask yourself this: it's 1939, the Goerings are having an intimate soiré. If he got an invitation, would Pat Buchanan feel out of place? Are you kidding? Dust off the old tuxedo and be there in a jiffy. Kisses to Adolf and Eva. The differences between their Great Communicator and ours are differences of quantity, not quality: Theirs was crazier, ours is stupider, but is that, I ask you, a reason to relax?

I never relax. For me, R and R doesn't mean Rest and Relaxation, it means Research and Revelation. I can work up a sweat reading *The New York Times*. I gasp. A lot. (*She demonstrates.*) I can clear a corner of the New York Public Library Reading Room in seconds. (*Demonstrates again.*) R and R. Then there's P and P. Paranoia and Panicking. I read, I gasp, I hit the streets at three A.M. with my can of spraypaint: REAGAN EQUALS HITLER! RESIST! DON'T FORGET, WEIMAR HAD A CONSTITUTION TOO!

Remember, in times like these, overstatement is your friend. Use it! And things that sound looney tunes at a cocktail party will go down easy when they're spelled out in four-foot-high dayglo letters dripping down a wall. The writing on the wall. I find myself getting more and more Biblical. Revelation: It's the spirit of the age.

(*End of interruption*)

**Scene Thirteen: Welcome**

([*Slide:* JANUARY 30, 1933. STILL LATER.] AGNES, HUSZ, *and* PAULINKA. *It's now close to dawn.* AGNES *is cleaning up.* PAULINKA *is sobering up.* HUSZ *has been drinking.*)

AGNES: I think we're not going to have any more arguments. Not here. No one really understands what's happening and so everyone just tears at each other out of fear. I hate it. So no more fights, no more evil talk, no more anger. A year ago we were better people. I know the world is falling apart but who says we have to go with it? It's evil, what's happening. Maybe you're right, Paulinka.

PAULINKA: I doubt it. Right about what?

AGNES: About the Devil.

HUSZ: Sssshhhh!

AGNES: What?

HUSZ: I don't like loose talk about . . . that. Especially at night.

AGNES: You're joking. No one really believes in the D. . . .

HUSZ: Want to meet Him?

AGNES: Sure. Why not? You know Him?

HUSZ: Not well, but He'll come if I call.

PAULINKA: You have impressive connections, Husz.

HUSZ: My family comes from the High Carpathians, from a village way up on a wild, barren mountain. Goatherds; mean, tough people. In the fourteenth century nearly everyone in the village was butchered, put to the axe for engaging in intimate congress with the Devil. Since then every Magyar born on the mountain has a special understanding with Him. He's very fond of us. He'll come. Should I . . .

AGNES: I already said yes.

HUSZ: Paulinka?

PAULINKA: Of course. I thought I'd have to wait till I died.

HUSZ: First you both have to cover your left eye with your hand.

AGNES: This is silly, Husz. I don't like this.

HUSZ: Quiet please. It's too late. I've already called Him. Cover up, Agnes. (*He stands suddenly.*) Good. (*Pause*) Music ready?

(*There is an answering blast of music—the finale from Mahler's second symphony* [The Resurrection]. AGNES *reacts violently.* PAULINKA *seems delighted.*)

HUSZ: Lights ready?

(*The lights become dim and, well, infernal.*)

HUSZ: Devil . . .?

(*From offstage and everywhere, a deep voice answers in a whisper—"Ready."*)

HUSZ: Then lights! Camera! Action!

(*Blackout. Then two red eyes appear, glowing. It is the Devil's dog. A strange light begins to fill the room. All the furniture has been rearranged. The largest chair has been moved to the center of the room, and the dog, smoke dribbling from its mouth, is crouching by the chair. The door swings open, and the Devil enters. He is dressed elegantly, walks with a limp [clubfoot] and a cane, and he breathes heavily, almost asthmatically.*)

HERR SWETTS: Why have you called me?

HUSZ: Thank you for coming. I hope your journey wasn't long.

HERR SWETTS: Not long, no. I have taken up temporary residence in this country. Why have you summoned me?

HUSZ: Friends of mine sensed your coming, wanted to meet you. This is Agnes Eggling . . .

HERR SWETTS: (*To* AGNES) Madame. Charmed.

AGNES: Uhhh, ahhh . . .

HUSZ: And this is Paulinka Erdnuss.

HERR SWETTS: (*To* PAULINKA) Ah yes. I've seen your films.

PAULINKA: Monsieur, je suis enchanté.

HERR SWETTS: Et moi aussi. (*To* AGNES) And you, you are also in films?

AGNES: Uhhh, ahhh . . .

HERR SWETTS: Can she speak?

HUSZ: Usually.

HERR SWETTS: Good. Curing mutes is a messy business. What happened to your eye?

HUSZ: Knocked out by a rifle butt. Hungary, 1919.

HERR SWETTS: Ah yes. 1919. (*Small pause*) That I can fix. May I?

HUSZ: Free of charge?

HERR SWETTS: Oh no, no, never that, never that. A small fee, naturally . . .

HUSZ: Thanks, but I think not.

HERR SWETTS: As you wish. (*He becomes slightly more asthmatic, seems a little worried.*) Well! So! You have lovely friends, Husz. May I go? (*Starts for door.*)

HUSZ: Oh please, not so abruptly. Leave us a souvenir.

HERR SWETTS: (*Becoming rather angry*) What? Stink of pitch that clings for years? Hair snarls? I don't dispense souvenirs.

HUSZ: Tell us something.

HERR SWETTS: I don't know anything. (*Again starts for the door, now audibly wheezing and in evident discomfort.*)

HUSZ: A great mystery. The awful secret of these awful times . . .

HERR SWETTS: But really! I know nothing! My ignorance is beyond calculation. It springs from an abysmal font deeper by leagues than the deepest wisdom. I do not know the workings of the Universe. I only know myself.

HUSZ: That, then.

HERR SWETTS: Autobiography? (*The wheezing lessens slightly.*) It's interminable.

HUSZ: Condense it.

PAULINKA: Yes, please.

HERR SWETTS: (*Slight pause; then, to* AGNES) Might I trouble the mistress of the hearth for a glass of wine? (*On the last word he is hit by some kind of intestinal pain. He heads for the chair.*)

AGNES: I . . . I . . .

HUSZ: I'll get it.

HERR SWETTS: Many thanks. And perhaps . . . a little something . . . for my dog. (*Again the pain*)

(HUSZ *pours a glass of wine, brings it to the Devil, who swallows it in one desperate gulp, then drops the glass as he doubles over in terrible pain. He begins to shake and utters a low, dreadful noise, halfway between a moan and a growl. The growl breaks into a shriek as he clutches his heart and begins to speak. His words and his physical pain are a single thing.*)

Herr Swetts:
In brief:
I recall a past, nomads, seeming
To them a desert tyrant, with a petty
Tyrant's heart,
Cruel, greedy, englistered with fat, Fond of the flesh
Of children . . .
(*Again the intestinal pain; he now seems to be having some terrible bowel affliction, alternating between diarrhea and constipation. It gets worse as he speaks.*)
Years pass;
An Agrarian Phase, I am
Rougher, reptilian,
A heart of mildew, dung-heap dweller,
Fly-Merchant, cattle-killer,
Friend . . . of Lunatics, Straw
Demon . . . Excremental
Principle, The Shit King! (*There is some kind of release/relief.*)
Quaint.
Childrens' stuff.
Years pass, more years,
Refinement, Scholasticism,
Increasingly metaphysical inclinations
Shape me as
A negativity, a void,
The pain of loss, of
Irreconcilable separation from Joy, from
God! (*The heart pain returns, worse than before.*)
My heart
A black nullity, dull cavity
From which no light escapes,
Not an "is" so much
As an "isn't". (*The heart pain appears to have stopped.*)

Too ethereal. Lacking bite. (*He stands. He appears to be getting stronger.*)

Years pass, years pile up,
The last century
My heart was a piston-pump,
My veins copper tubing,
Hot black oil coursed through them,
Steam turbines roared,
Very Strong! Very Hungry!
Flesh of children and much much more,
Heady Days! The best in aeons!

(*He is now standing erect, breathing deeply but without difficulty for the first time. He mops his brow, straightens his clothing, pats his hair.*)
Even that grows old.
Even yet, years hurtle by.
And in this century, still new,
When questions of Form
Are so hotly contested,
My new form seems to be . . .
No form at all.
I am simply
Unbelievable. Non-objective.
Non-existent. Displaced.
Stateless. A refugee.
The accumulation of so much,
The detritus of so many weary years,
I have at last attained
Invisibility.
It's not the danger that you see
That's the danger.
I become
Increasingly diffuse,
Like powdered gas taking to air,
Not less potent, but more,
Spreading myself
Around.

(*Slight pause*)

PAULINKA: Excuse me. This is fascinating. Did you ever consider the possibility that you might be the victim of neurotic conflicts? Dr. Bloom says . . .

HERR SWETTS: No. My rejection of investigation is complete. I preserve my wickedness in a pristine form. It is never touched. (*As if confiding a secret of which he is immensely proud:*) I gave birth to myself.

(PAULINKA *laughs, charmed. The Devil laughs with her.*)

PAULINKA: This isn't meant as an insult, but isn't that a little grandiose?

HERR SWETTS: Grandiose? Ha! Ha! Ha! That's good! Ha! Ha ha ha hahahahaha . . . (*His laugh turns into a loud, grotesque, subhuman braying noise which makes everyone move as far from him as they can. When he stops, he has lost some of his polish and is as we first saw him—foul-tempered, slightly asthmatic, uncomfortable. He points his cane at* PAULINKA *and says angrily:*) My dear woman, you cannot possibly begin to imagine how Grand . . . the scope of what's ahead. (*Lowers cane*) I sense great possibilities in the Modern World. The depths . . . have not been plumbed. Yet. (*Pause*) I haven't talked so much in years.

PAULINKA: And you really are the Devil?

HERR SWETTS: I . . . My card. (*Hands her his card.*)

PAULINKA: (*Reading it*) Herr Gottfried Swetts. Hamburg. Importer of Spanish Novelties.

HERR SWETTS: For the time being. (*Pause*) Now please excuse me. I really must go. (*Begins to leave.*)

HUSZ: Of course. Thank you for coming.

HERR SWETTS: (*Leaving*) Not at all. Take care, Husz. Mind the other eye.

AGNES: Wait!

HERR SWETTS: What?

AGNES: I . . . I . . .

HERR SWETTS: What?

HUSZ: Agnes, don't keep Him waiting.

AGNES: I . . . wanted to say . . . thank you . . . for coming and . . . welcome to Germany . . . and . . .

HERR SWETTS: Thank you, madame. And thank you for having me. Most gracious. Goodbye.

(*He exits as the last chords of Mahler's second symphony explode and the lights go to black.*)

*Intermission*

## Part Two

### 1980–1988 #4
### Memories of You

(*Cocktail loungey lights up on* ZILLAH.)

ZILLAH: Music, please.

(*Piano intro to* "Memories of You" *[Razaf/Blake] begins. As* ZILLAH *sings, slides of Hitler flash in tempo behind her. These should be of the* "Beloved Führer" *publicity-shot variety.*)

ZILLAH: (*Sings*)
Why can't I forget like I should?
Heaven knows I would if I could.
But I cannot get you off my mind.
Though you've gone and love was in vain,
All around me you still remain.
Wonder why fate should be so unkind . . .
Waking skies at sunrise
Every sunset too,
Seem to be bringing me
Memories of you.
Here and there, everywhere,
Dreams that we once knew,
And they all just recall
Memories of you.
How I wish I could forget
Those happy yester-years
That have left a rosary of tears.
Your face beams in my dreams
'Spite of all I do;
Everything seems to bring
Memories of you.
(*Music tinkles out as slides fade.*)
Thanks, Mr. Piano Man.

(*End of interruption*)

(*Slides:* JANUARY 30, 1933. ADOLF HITLER APPOINTED CHANCELLOR. JANUARY 31, 1933. HINDENBURG DISSOLVES THE REICHSTAG. NEW ELECTIONS SET. FEBRUARY 20, 1933. TWENTY-FIVE OF GERMANY'S LEADING INDUSTRIALISTS

PLEDGE THREE MILLION MARKS TO THE NAZIS' ELECTION CAMPAIGN. FEBRUARY 24, 1933. HITLER DECLARES THE SA AND THE SS "AUXILIARY POLICE".)

**Scene Fourteen: Der Mensch ist nicht gut—Sondern ein vieh!**
**(Man Isn't Good—He's Disgusting!)**

([*Slide:* FEBRUARY 27, 1933 . . . NIGHT.] *There is an orange glow in the room which is coming through a window, from outside. All other lights are off.* DIE ALTE *is sitting in a chair at the table, grinding away. Two very loud knocking sounds come from the wall.* AGNES *enters, turns on a light, and stares at* DIE ALTE.)

DIE ALTE: Two knocks.

AGNES: The hot water pipe. It pours grey water. They have to fix it.

DIE ALTE: Little goblins, penny-men. Knock knock.

AGNES: Oh that poem. Funny to hear it after all these years; I can still recite it.

DIE ALTE: Memory is like the wind. Tricky. Horrible things forgotten overnight. Pleasant nothings remembered for years.

AGNES:
When the tree is black and bare,
And the barren branches droop,
Don't go to the kitchen where
The penny-man makes poison soup. (*She laughs.*)

DIE ALTE:
When the little penny-man
Bangs the pots and pans about,
No one dares to go downstairs,
No one dares to throw him out.

AGNES: (*Sniffing*) There's that smell again. Have you noticed in your—where you live? It started only recently—something rotten, like egg or sulphur gas—maybe something died in the walls. Maybe the building's infested. At night I hear scurrying. (*Sniffs and tries to locate the smell.*) Tonight it's stronger. Smells . . . burnt. (*She goes to the window.*) Oh. There's a fire. A building's burning, down in the Center. The whole sky's orange. Must be a terrible fire. It's one of the government buildings, with a dome . . . you can't see . . . (*She opens the window to get a better view.*)

DIE ALTE:
When God is good the hours go,
And the sun will melt the snow.
Nothing ever comes that can
Help the little penny-man.

AGNES: (*Closing the window.*) It's the Reichstag.

DIE ALTE: Do you have any rolls tonight?

AGNES: The Reichstag is burning.

(*End of scene*)

**1980–1988 #5**
**The Politics of Paranoia**

(*Lights up on* ZILLAH.)

ZILLAH: The politics of paranoia: First law: During periods of reactionary backlash, listen to your nightmares. Those little grey mice chewing at your stomach have more to tell you about the state of the world than a whole week's worth of the *NBC Nightly News*. Listen to your mice! Give then names! Collect 'em, trade 'em with your friends! It's like Hannah Arendt, back in the thirties, in Germany—she read dectective novels: Stroking the flames of her paranoia, feeding her mice. Her friends thought she was crazy, but Hannah died in her own bed in 1975, and most of her friends probably died in gas chambers. Don't put too much stock in a good night's sleep; during periods of reactionary backlash, the only people sleeping soundly are the guys who're giving the rest of us bad dreams.

Recently when I sleep my dreams are being invaded by this woman dressed in a frumpy hat and coat—and for a change, it's not my mother. This woman—I think she comes out of a book I read—a photograph of a huge crowd, thousands of people, a rally, everyone, and I mean *everyone* giving the fascist salute. But there she is, right in the middle of all these ecstatic people waving their right hands and cheering, there she is, and she isn't cheering, not even smiling, and both hands are clutching her purse and she isn't saluting. I noticed her right off and I guess out of gratitude or something she's come to pay me visits. She's in trouble: she looks old, but she isn't, she's gotten fat and her feet are giving out and her eyes are bad. She hasn't spoken—yet—but I know she will and when she does I think we'll find out we have a lot in common. She's my mouse—one of them—from out of a crowd. The first law of the politics of paranoia: Eat something indigestible before you go to sleep, and listen to your nightmares.

(*End of interruption*)

**Scene Fifteen: Further Demonological Explorations**

([*Slide:* FEBRUARY 27, 1933. LATER THAT NIGHT. THE REICHSTAG IS BURNING.] AGNES *with* MALEK *and* TRAUM. MALEK *has a carton.* TRAUM *is looking out the window.*)

TRAUM: It's still going. They should have it out by now.

MALEK: These are things we found at the Party office. We think they're yours. We wanted them out before we get closed down.

AGNES: They won't dare to . . .

MALEK: Absolutely. Any day.

TRAUM: Arrangements have been made. We're ready.

AGNES: For what?

TRAUM: Exile.

AGNES: And then what?

TRAUM: We continue to agitate for the revolution. From without. We wait for fascism to run its course.

AGNES: Which could take how long, do you think?

(*No one answers her.*)

MALEK: (*Taking the Red Baby out of the carton.*) Look. The Red Baby.

AGNES: Want it?

MALEK: Burn it. Burn everything. But don't be seen doing it. (*Beat*) Why did you stop coming around? Your group? No reproach intended, but I've been wondering why you stopped.

AGNES: I'm kind of a political barometer. When I turn up, you know that lots of people must be hearing you because I'm one of the last to hear. When I disappear, it means you're losing. All of a sudden I didn't want to work anymore. I couldn't even make myself go and pick up this box of junk. That's when I knew we were in trouble.

TRAUM: The history of our party over the past few years has not been a happy one.

MALEK: For which thank the Comintern. For which thank Moscow.

TRAUM: Malek, please . . .

MALEK: For which thank ourselves for being stupid . . .

TRAUM: Malek, stop.

MALEK: For letting the Russians run our revolution!

TRAUM: Enough!

MALEK: Coward!

TRAUM: Not here!

MALEK: Not ever! Doing little errands while the Comintern . . .

TRAUM: You are appalling! Now is not the time to be attacking the only place on earth where a communist revolution has succeeded. Blame it on the German working class. Sheep and cattle! Blame it on our own inability to organize! Blame it on the Social Democrats . . .

MALEK: The Social Democrats, The Social Democrats. They didn't kill the United Front. We did! Everything determined by what would serve Moscow best. "Hitler may be a fascist but so what? He's less likely to attack Russia than a bourgeois government allied with France!" They think.

TRAUM: Right, so I suppose instead that you and I should have voted for Hindenburg. Or we should have followed every thug who wanted to turn the Party into the Left answer to the brownshirts. Fight the Nazis on the streets.

MALEK: YES! YES! NOW! SMITE FASCISM WHEREVER YOU MEET IT! Can't you see that we're already there? Don't you see how completely overdue . . .

AGNES: Quiet, please! I have neighbors. The old woman upstairs is a . . .

MALEK: Sorry. Sorry. Enough.

TRAUM: Excuse us, comrade. We'd better go.

MALEK: Burn everything. Books, pamphlets, everything. (*She picks up* AGNES' *copy of* Kapital. *Puts it in carton.*) But at night. Sift through the ashes. Be careful. (*Exits*)

TRAUM: Were you a Party member?

AGNES: No. Not. I was going to, but . . . no.

TRAUM: Consider yourself lucky. They have the members lists. (*Starts to leave.*)

AGNES: I'm . . . I'm sorry.

(TRAUM *stops, stares at her, and laughs quietly.*)

TRAUM: Don't apologize. It's not your fault, is it? Just do what the comrade says. Burn it all.

(*End of scene*)

(*Slide:* FEBRUARY 28, 1933. THE GERMAN COMMUNIST PARTY IS BLAMED FOR THE BURNING OF THE REICHSTAG AND DECLARED AN OUTLAW ORGANIZATION.)

**1980–1988 #6**
**Sleep for a Thousand Years**

(*Lights up on* ZILLAH.)

ZILLAH: I see her alone at night, in her apartment, and though she used to read other books, calm, clear-headed analyses of what's wrong with the world, now she's turned to darker words, to words with leathery panicky wings, words that flap up like flights of bats to describe the presence of Evil, Evil with a capital E. Revelations. The world has changed and she's reading the Book. Like me. Apocalypse prose for these lost days. We turn the pages together, gasping, as the words fly up in our faces, through the open window and out into the dark. (*She picks up a large Bible, opens it, and reads:*) "I saw a great beast come up out of the ground, and he had two horns like a lamb and he spoke like a dragon. He makes great portents, so that he even makes fire come down out of the sky, and he leads astray the inhabitants of the earth." (*Beat*) She stays awake at night, listening to the city. So do I.

(*End of interruption*)

**Scene Sixteen: Keep You Keep You I Am Gone**
**Oh Keep You in my Memory**

([*Slide:* MARCH 5, 1933. REICHSTAG ELECTIONS. THE NAZIS WIN 288 SEATS, THE SPD 120, AND THE KPD 81. COMMUNIST DEPUTIES WHO CAN BE FOUND ARE ARRESTED.] AGNES *is cleaning.* PAULINKA *is heard rushing up the hallway stairs. She bursts through the door.*)

PAULINKA: AGNES! AGNES!

AGNES: What! Paulinka, what?!

PAULINKA: It's over! Over! Agnes! I'm . . . oh, oh, oh . . . (*She begins to weep and throws herself on the floor.*)

AGNES: Paulinka! Paulinka! Talk to me! What's wrong? What happened?

PAULINKA: The worst, the worst imaginable . . .

AGNES: Who? Who?

PAULINKA: Who what?

AGNES: What?

PAULINKA: Who what?

AGNES: Who's dead?

PAULINKA: Dead? Who said anyone died? No one died.

AGNES: From the way you're acting I assumed that . . .

PAULINKA: No. No one dead. It's worse than that. Much worse. The death of love, the death of trust, is worse than death.

AGNES: What are you talking about?

(PAULINKA *screams, a loud, long wail.* AGNES *rushes over and clasps her hand over* PAULINKA'S *mouth.*)

AGNES: Have you gone crazy screaming like that? Do you want to have me evicted?

PAULINKA: He's gone.

AGNES: Who are you talking about?

PAULINKA: I got there at 11:30. Tuesday morning, 11:30. I rang his bell. Nothing, nothing. Ring, ring, nothing, nothing. The landlady comes out. Waddle waddle. "Oh Miss Erdnuss, it's just too awful, the Herr Professor Doctor. He's gone."

AGNES: Dr. Bloom? He's gone?

PAULINKA: Poof.

AGNES: Oh, Paulinka, how terrible for you. I'm sorry.

PAULINKA: SORRY! Who give two shits if you're sorry! My analyst leaves me without a word, without the courtesy of a final session or a note or anything, right in the middle of everything he just kicks out the tent poles and leaves with his wretched wife and brats and leaves me, *me*! And you can't say anything, just sorry, too bad. That miserable fraud, I'll ruin him. RUIN HIM!

Agnes: Shut up! Think what you're saying. Why do you think he left? Why?

Paulinka: He had no right!

Agnes: Why? Because he's a Jew, that's why! Because Germany's not safe for Jews, because . . .

Paulinka: THIS IS NO WAY TO TERMINATE TWO YEARS OF ANALYSIS!

Agnes: Oh you are being disgusting. Selfish and disgusting. Think about him!

Paulinka: Think about me!

Agnes: No! I don't want to anymore!

Paulinka: Well, thanks so much and to hell with you too! I'll bet he cleared out his bank account. Bet he took his money! (*She hears herself.*) Couldn't he at least have told me?

Agnes: Of course not. Obviously not. He had to leave secretly. It's not easy to get out.

Paulinka: I don't know what I'll do.

Agnes: Smoke a pipe. Kill tonight. It'll look better tomorrow.

Paulinka: No, I don't think it will. (*Beat*) This came in the mail today. It's a letter from the Ministry of Culture.

(Paulinka *offers the letter to* Agnes, *who does not take it.*)

Paulinka: The film industry is going to be . . . what was the word? (*Consults letter*) Oh yes; incorporated. I am invited to meet with the officer in charge, to discuss my plans. They like my work. They think I have a part to play. (*Pause*) Should I go? What should I do?

Agnes: I don't know. Don't ask me that.

Paulinka: Will you work for them? Make films for them?

Agnes: I don't know. No. Maybe. No one will care if I do or not. With you it's different. What would Dr. Bloom say?

Paulinka: Nothing, probably. He never said much. (*Pause*) No, let's see. He'd say, "Run, Miss Erdnuss, run away from them.

You can't live breathing the air they breathe. Meet me in Paris or New York, the strange city they've driven me to. Come find me there. And leave Berlin." That's what he'd say.

(AGNES *and* PAULINKA *look at each other.*)

AGNES: I don't know. I don't know what to do.

(*End of scene*)

**Scene Seventeen: Hic Domus Dei Est, et Portae Coelis (This is the House of God, and These Are the Gates of Heaven)**

([*Slide:* MARCH 12, 1933. PRESIDENT HINDENBURG ABOLISHES THE FLAG OF THE REPUBLIC.] AGNES *is sitting for a portrait that* GOTCHLING *is constructing.* AGNES *holds a red hammer and a carpenter's level.* GOTCHLING *works with a pencil, paper, and a variety of assemblage materials. As she works, they talk.*)

AGNES: I don't feel like doing this today.

GOTCHLING: I know. I appreciate it all the more.

AGNES: I hate sitting still, I'm so full of nervousness, when I sit I start to sink, I'm nervous all the time, except when I'm depressed.

GOTCHLING: Try biting your nails. I do. It soothes me considerably.

AGNES: There's no point to this. No point to making posters, they just rip them down. Don't they arrest people for this?

(*No answer*)

AGNES: I walked to the Studio yesterday. All the way I felt like I was walking through a strange city, not Berlin. It was too quiet, that strange sun not the Berlin sun, too bright. Everything clean and full of danger. I found myself saying an old prayer for protection . . . (*Beat*) I keep thinking that maybe it wouldn't have been so bad to have been a wise old lady-in-waiting for the Kaiserin. In the films I always had lots of well-made objects to handle: a big sturdy clothes brush with fine bristles, Belgian lace, and there were those silver cases with little enamelled hunting scenes on the lids. They were cold but they warmed in your hand and they were heavy. Just holding them made you feel safe. What's so great about democracy? (*Pause*) Want to see a jolly twinkle? (*She twinkles*)

GOTCHLING: Please. That's nauseating.

AGNES: I know you think I'm a reactionary for feeling this way. You judge everyone but I feel it anyway. I feel . . .

GOTCHLING: Feel feel feel feel feel. So much feeling. Hold still. Let me give you something real to worry about.

AGNES: What?

GOTCHLING: We need apartments. Belonging to people who are sympathetic.

AGNES: We who?

GOTCHLING: The Party.

AGNES: The Party's been outlawed.

(*Pause*)

GOTCHLING: As I was saying. We need apartments. All over the city. Way stations to the east. Storage rooms . . .

AGNES: No.

GOTCHLING: Not for storage, then. A waystation. There are people hiding . . .

AGNES: No.

GOTCHLING: Agnes . . .

AGNES: People shouldn't be leaving. They should be staying. Everyone is going. There should be fighting. Who's going to fight? What are people like me supposed to do if people like you just leave?

GOTCHLING: Some of us are staying. Some of us can't.

AGNES: Are you leaving?

GOTCHLING: I can't say.

AGNES: You are. I knew you would. For God's sake, Annabella, what is going to happen to us?

GOTCHLING: I don't know.

AGNES: And still you recklessly ask me to . . .

GOTCHLING: Not recklessly.

AGNES: It sounds dangerous.

GOTCHLING: It is dangerous.

AGNES: Then I won't do it.

GOTCHLING: The Party needs it.

AGNES: There is no Party! There's no more Party! Wake up! You're a painter, not a politician, you always were a painter so start acting like one!

GOTCHLING: How do I do that, Agnes?

AGNES: Leave me alone!

GOTCHLING: No. I've never been that kind of a painter.

(*Pause*)

AGNES: I don't understand you, Gotchling. Paulinka is drugged and unhappy. Baz talks about suicide all the time . . .

GOTCHLING: He just talks.

AGNES: Husz is depressed, I'm miserable, and you . . . you're the only one who's able to navigate this. Why is that?

GOTCHLING: It's because I'm much more intelligent than the rest of you.

AGNES: Then why do you bother with us?

GOTCHLING: I enjoy feeling superior.
Listen, Agnes.
I am working class.
And that really does make a difference.
I know what's useful,
And what isn't.
I know the price of things,
And I know how to give things up.
I know what it is to struggle—
These tough little lessons
I don't think you people have ever learned.
I hold tight, and I do my work.
I make posters for good causes.
Even if they get torn up, I make them,
Even though we live in a country
Where theory falls silent in the face of fact,
Where progress can be reversed overnight,
Where the enemy has stolen everything, our own words from us,
I hold tight, and not to my painting . . . not only to that.
Art is never enough.
It never does enough.
We will be remembered for two things:

Our communist art
And our fascist politics.
Pick any era in history, Agnes.
What is really beautiful about that era?
The way the rich lived?
No.
The way the poor lived?
No.
The dreams of the Left
Are always beautiful.
The imagining of a better world.
The damnation of the present one.
This faith,
This luminescent anger,
These alone
Are worthy of being called human.
These are the Beautiful
That an age produces.
As an artist I am struck to the heart
By these dreams. These visions.
We progress. But at great cost.
How can anyone stand to live
Without understanding that much?
My back is aching. I can't sit like this anymore. I'm getting old.
Think it over, Agnes. We need the apartment.

(*End of scene*)
([*Slide:* MARCH 13, 1933. GOEBBELS SWORN IN AS MINISTER OF PROPAGANDA.]

**1980–1988 #7**
**From the Book**

(*Lights up on* Zillah.)

Zillah: They say that the Book of Revelations is the President's favorite book. This is plausible once you accept the initial premise, which is that the President knows how to read. It is a great thing, this book. You can try to be reasonable as a clam about evil, but in the end, when you get down to La Nitty-Gritty, clams are cold, thick little animals and you just can't find anything more thrilling than some of this stuff: (*Again, reading from the Bible:*) "And He causes all, the rich and the poor, the free and the slave, to receive a mark on their right hand, and none can buy or sell without that mark. The name of the Beast, and the number of that name . . ." Oh, this is great, you all know this one: "Let him who has a mind compute the number of the Beast, for it is the number of a man, and that number is 666." (*Pause*) OK. A little math lesson. They say that Hitler used to spell his name A-D-O-L-P-H and he changed the P-H to an F to make it look less Austrian or more German or something. God knows. Anyway, A-D-O-L-P-H gives you six letters, and H-I-T-L-E-R gives you another six. See where I'm heading? You with me? The problem is that he didn't have a middle name, but not to worry, you can always use F-U-H-R-E-R. Et voila! The name of our own little fuhrer works *much* better, of course, and with no trouble at all you get the winning number. (*She holds up a poster on which this has been worked out: R-O-N-A-L-D W-I-L-S-O-N R-E-A-G-A-N.*) I didn't figure this out myself, I saw it written on the wall of a bathroom stall in Boston. B-O-S-T-O-N. "Do not" we are told, "seal up the words of the pages of this Book, for the time is near."

(*End of interruption*)

### Scene Eighteen: Berliner Schnause (Berlin Lip)

([*Slide:* MARCH 15, 1933.] AGNES, HUSZ, *and* BAZ; BAZ *is standing, wearing an overcoat and cap.*)

BAZ: Three days ago I was arrested by the new police. They marched into the Institute after lunch. We were ordered into trucks. Dr. Henni and Dr. Kunz got into black cars. Henni is out but he won't see anyone. No one knows what happened to Dr. Kunz. He may be dead.

AGNES: Oh my god.

HUSZ: What a drink?

BAZ: Oh, that would be completely welcome. I have a story.

AGNES: Are you all right? Is the Institute closed?

BAZ: The Institute? Boarded shut, looking very permanently sealed and done for. We were accused of printing pornography and abetting illegal medical practices—abortions. Lots more besides; the files were taken. That's bad news. We weren't prepared. Boards on the windows now. Did I say that already?

AGNES: Are you sure you're all right?

BAZ: I cried during the interrogation.

Husz: So what? Lots of people do.

Baz: But it's different when I do it. The mascara runs.

Agnes: Did they . . . do anything to you?

Baz: One of them slapped me. It was more of a shock than painful. They scream a lot. Then they let us go—half of us, just turned us loose on the street, no explanation, no word about the others.

Agnes: When did they let you go?

Baz: Two days ago . . . or three? Yes, three.

Agnes: Three days ago? But where have you been? Gotchling's been looking . . .

Baz: I went to Munich.

Agnes: Why Munich?

Baz: To kill myself. (*Beat*) Really. I'm very much afraid of them. I have been for years, all police, but these are much more frightening. Being alone with them in a room with a locked door is paralyzing. I looked at the carpet the whole time. I thought, good, they have a carpet, they won't do anything that would get blood on the carpet. When the main one grabbed my face and slapped it I started crying. (*Pause*) I have always been terrified of pain. He said to me, "In the woods outside of Munich, do you know what we are building?" I said no, and he said "A Camp. For people like you." (*Pause*) I have a criminal record. I can't get out easily. I expected them to arrest me immediately after letting me go—something they do. So I decided to kill myself.

Husz: In Munich.

Baz: Yes. Munich. You won't believe what happened.

Agnes: What? Why Munich?

Baz: I wanted to go to another city so that none of you would be asked to identify me afterwards. I took the night train. When I got there I bought a revolver and four bullets. Extras. I can't imagine why I thought I'd need extras. Anyway, I wanted to go someplace to do it where it would be convenient for the person who found me, a place where people go who aren't particularly frightened or upset by death. Nuns who care for the terminally ill. Better that than in a café, ruining some waiter's whole day . . .

Husz: You are wonderfully considerate.

BAZ: I try to be. But I felt that killing myself in the midst of a bunch of nuns was probably a much more serious sin than doing it discreetly in a secular location. So I went to the park.

AGNES: And . . .?

BAZ: Agnes, I met a remarkably attractive young Silesian there. I was exhausted. Fatigue makes me easy to arouse . . .

HUSZ: So you did it in the bushes.

BAZ: Husz, you are a man of the world.

HUSZ: After which you decided not to die.

BAZ: Right again. My theory is vindicated.

HUSZ: How so?

BAZ: I realized after my Silesian friend left that it had been nearly a week since my last orgasm. Too much pent-up energy. The result: depression. Add to it the nightmare of the last few days—suicide. One good sojourn under the bushes and my desire to live returned to me in all its hot, tainted glory.

AGNES: And so you came home?

BAZ: No. There's more. The best part.

AGNES: More?

BAZ: Well, here I am in Munich with a little money, a loaded gun, and a whole day to kill before the night train to Berlin. What to do?

AGNES: Hang around the bushes.

BAZ: No, Agnes. Once a day, every day, not too seldom, not too often, balance is everything. I went to the cinema. And you are absolutely not going to believe what happened.

HUSZ: You saw a film.

BAZ: Yes, of course, but not only that. It was a Dietrich film. And there was hardly anyone there, it being early in the day, just me and some old people and some war vets. When all of a sudden into the theatre marches a squadron of brownshirts and guess who else?

HUSZ: Ummm. . . . Adolf Hitler.

BAZ: Right.

(*There is a pause*)

AGNES: You're making this up.

BAZ: I am not. It was him. In a slouch hat and a trenchcoat. And someone else with him, a man I didn't recognize.

HUSZ: I don't believe this.

BAZ: Well I told you you wouldn't but it's perfectly true. Hitler. And he sat down three rows in front of me. The SA sat in back of him but I had a clear view of the back of his head. I could see the oil in his hair.

AGNES: Oh my God.

BAZ: Just what I said. (*Pause*) The film got going and I was thinking to myself, "Life plays funny tricks. Here we are, watching a Dietrich film: ten pensioners, six war-cripples, Adolf Hitler, and me, a homosexual Sunday anarchist with a loaded gun in his pocket." (*He makes the gun with his fingers, aims carefully, and makes a soft "bang".*) So I left.

HUSZ: You what?

BAZ: I left.

(*Another pause*)

HUSZ: Is this true?

BAZ: Yes, it is.

HUSZ: It's true? Adolf Hitler?

BAZ: Yes.

HUSZ: And you left?

BAZ: I left.

(HUSZ *jumps up, runs over to* BAZ, *grabs him by the shirt front, and begins shaking him furiously.*)

HUSZ: WHY DIDN'T YOU SHOOT? YOU HAD A GUN! YOU FUCKING IDIOT! WHY DIDN'T YOU SHOOT!

(AGNES *grabs* HUSZ, *who shoves* BAZ *away and storms to the opposite side of the room.*)

AGNES: Husz! What are you saying?

HUSZ: What am I saying? What am I saying? Why didn't he shoot? *I* would have shot! Why? (*Running back to* BAZ, *but not touching him.*) WHAT IS THE MATTER WITH YOU?

BAZ: Because, Husz. (*Pause*) Because they would have shot me.

AGNES: Baz, you're making all of this up.

BAZ: No. I couldn't get my hand to move, to even begin to move towards the pocket that had the gun. Because I might have killed him, but they would certainly have killed me. And I don't want to die.

HUSZ: Adolf Hitler!

BAZ: I do not want to die.

(HUSZ *turns his back to* BAZ. *There is a pause.*)

BAZ: A friend is arranging a phony passport and visa. They'll be ready in six days. I'm leaving. That's what I came to tell you. I'm leaving.

(*End of scene*)

([*Slide:* MARCH 20, 1933. DACHAU CONCENTRATION CAMP OPENS.])

**1980–1988 #8**
**Epitaph**

(*Lights up on* ZILLAH.)

ZILLAH: I ask her sometimes, when she appears, how she died. An air raid? In the camps? Because I know she's dead, that she died then, unhappily. And she hasn't answered me yet, but I think I know what she's going to say: (*Pause*) "Not in the camps, and not in the war, but at home, in front of a cozy fire, I died of a broken heart."

(*End of interruption*)

([*Slide:* MARCH 23, 1933. A COALITION OF NAZIS, NATIONALISTS, AND CENTRISTS PASSES THE ENABLING ACT, "FOR REMOVING THE DISTRESS OF THE PEOPLE AND THE REICH", GIVING HITLER FOUR YEARS IN WHICH TO GOVERN WITHOUT THE PARTICIPATION OF THE REICHSTAG, WITHOUT REGARD FOR CONSTITUTIONALITY, AND WITH THE RIGHT TO CONCLUDE TREATIES WITH FOREIGN POWERS AUTOCRATICALLY.])

**Scene Nineteen: Der Wildgewordene Kleinburger (The Petit-Bourgeois Run Amok)**

([*Slide:* MAY 1, 1933. VERY LATE AT NIGHT.] *The apartment is dark.* Die Alte *staggers drunkenly about the room, clutching a bottle. She turns on the radio. It warms up, but plays nothing but static. She bangs ferociously on the table, three times, then shouts:*)

Die Alte:
So it's Ho! for the man with the iron nails
And the slippery toungue so black.
With his foul breath and hands, bang bang,
All a-sweat in the damp, dirty bed, bang bang,
As he pulls at your hair, and he claws at your back,
And he tickles your neck and your crack, bang bang,
And he tickles your neck and your crack.

(Agnes *rushes in during this.*)

Agnes: This has got to end! *What do you want here*?

Die Alte: I had a black pillow once . . .

Agnes: (*Heading back to the bedroom.*) I can't listen to this anymore!

Die Alte: (*Yelling*) I HAD A BLACK PILLOW ONCE ON MY BED AND EVERY NIGHT I HAD HORRIBLE DREAMS!

(Agnes *is listening.*)

Die Alte: Horrible, every night. It's the black pillow, they'd warn me, you can't sleep peacefully with your head resting on that. But I loved that pillow. I'd have thrown the whole bed out before I'd throw that black pillow away. I held on to it for years.

Agnes: And the dreams?

Die Alte: Every night for years.

Agnes: What happened?

Die Alte: I wound up all alone.

(*Small pause*)

Agnes: I'm afraid of you.

Die Alte: You look green. (*She holds bottle toward* Agnes.) I'd give you some, but it's mine. Beer. *German* beer. Not vodka like you and your Bolshevik friends drink.

(*Small pause*)

AGNES: My friends aren't . . .

DIE ALTE: (*Suddenly in a rage*) BOLSHEVIK! BOLSHEVIK! FUCKING BOLSHEVIK PIGS, ALL OF YOU! This nest; I know! You'll be reported . . .

(AGNES *grabs a broom, which is standing nearby. She advances toward* DIE ALTE, *who moves away.*)

DIE ALTE: If you hit me with that I promise you you'll wish you hadn't.

(AGNES *raises the broom. There are three knocks. The radio dies.*)

DIE ALTE: It's Him.

AGNES: Who?

DIE ALTE: The rent-collector. Let him in.

(AGNES *goes to the radio, thumps it. It doesn't respond.*)

AGNES: Dead.

(*There is a sharp tearing sound. The radio dials glow. The machine begins to shake, then crack open.* AGNES *screams and jumps back, holding the broom in front of her as a defense. The radio cracks completely and a little figure leaps out.* AGNES *screams again, more with rage than fear, and begins to chase the scurrying figure about the room, swinging her broom, swatting wildly and, in the process, causing considerable damage to the premises. Suddenly the figure stands and faces her. She sees that it is a beautiful blonde-haired little boy in a brown uniform and cloak. She stops swinging the broom, frozen. He scuttles away and out of the apartment through some crevice, like a roach.*)

DIE ALTE: Some dance. Nice music. It's bad to be too much alone.

(*She goes out the door.* AGNES *watches her leave, looks around the room, surveying the wreckage. She picks up an overturned chair, and sits, staring.*)

(*End of scene*)

**Scene Twenty: An Acid Morning Light**

([*Slide:* MAY 2, 1933. WITH MINIMAL RESISTANCE, GERMAN TRADE UNIONS ARE ABOLISHED.] *The next morning. The room is in complete disarray.* AGNES *sits in the middle of the* *mess, holding the broom. There is a soft knocking and a whispered "*AGNES*". She doesn't move. More knocking and another "*AGNES*". She turns, stares at door, and then wearily opens it.* PAULINKA *enters, supporting* HUSZ, *who is limping and holding his ribs.* PAULINKA *deposits him in a chair and goes immediately to the liquor. She pours a stiff drink.* AGNES *stands by the door, and then slowly closes it. She doesn't move.*)

PAULINKA: Shit.

(PAULINKA *and* HUSZ *look at each other and begin to laugh.*)

HUSZ: (*Holding tighter to his ribs.*) OW!

(*He stops laughing, then looks at* PAULINKA *and they start laughing again,* HUSZ *in a considerable amount of pain. The laughter gets mildly hysterical, especially* PAULINKA'S.)

AGNES: (*In a very black mood*) What is going on?

(*The laughter is quieting down;* HUSZ *tries to stand, decides against it.*)

AGNES: Stop laughing. Husz, what's wrong with your foot?

HUSZ: My foot, my chest, my head . . . (*He starts laughing again, makes a courtly salute in* PAULINKA'S *direction.*) Madame Hero.

(PAULINKA *starts laughing, then begins to sob.* HUSZ *begins to sob. She walks to him, he stands, they hug, he screams "OW", sits, they both start to laugh/cry.*)

AGNES: What in the hell is going on here?

PAULINKA: This place is a mess.

HUSZ: Paulinka is a hero.

PAULINKA: Shut up, Husz.

HUSZ: Paulinka saved my life.

AGNES: What are you talking about?

HUSZ: (*To* PAULINKA) You should feel elated!

PAULINKA: (*Putting her head in her hands.*) I feel sick.

HUSZ: You see, there was a little riot . . .

AGNES: A riot? Where?

HUSZ: In the Studio, of all places. We were shooting a quiet scene for the new Frederick the Great film—shepherds and sheep, very pastoral—when there's a loud noise behind one of the drops. Suddenly the drop comes down and there are people fighting—people and security guards—the kind with swastikas. Having a disagreement over whether or not the electricians' union office was going to be closed down. The security men felt one way, the electricians felt another way, and then some Nazis—real Nazis— showed up to reinforce the security guards and it got messy and most everyone left.

AGNES: And you didn't?

HUSZ: I wanted to film it. And I wanted to hit someone. So I kept my camera rolling and I guess I just got caught up in the dance. I wound up getting cornered in the stairwell by a whole gaggle of fascists and we had a very serious discussion about human anatomy . . .

PAULINKA: They started clubbing him.

HUSZ: And they were ready to take me away. At which point there sounds from the heavens above a voice like a trumpet, a huge voice, a voice made mighty in the regional theaters of the fatherland, crying "LEAVE THAT MAN ALONE." All heads turn, mine included, to confront the blazing eyes and marble brow of one of Germany's minor celebrities . . .

PAULINKA: I resent that!

HUSZ: Fraulein Movie Star Paulinka Erdnuss herself! The Nazis drooled and wagged their tails and begged for autographs while I slunk away.

PAULINKA: That's not what happened.

HUSZ: No. It was very interesting, Agnes. She simply scolded them and they left. She said, "Leave him alone. How dare you? Don't touch him. That isn't right. *I know all of you.*" And they went off.

PAULINKA: I was brilliant. It was the performance of my career. Incredible to have wasted it on a crazy Hungarian and three Nazi thugs.

HUSZ: There were five.

PAULINKA: Three, Husz. Three. Five and I would have pretended not to know you. You're a very stupid man, Husz. They're going to come after you for this. (*To* AGNES) That's why I brought him here. I didn't think his apartment would be safe.

(AGNES *nods.*)

PAULINKA: (*Starting out*) God help you. I have to go.

HUSZ: Of course you're terrified . . . it makes sense to be terrified. But to stand up against the terror! That is a great thing. Resistance! People who resist.

(PAULINKA *stops, turns to him, and laughs.*)

PAULINKA: I was there, Husz, at the Studio to tell Special Propaganda Chief Otto Von Muller that I would be interested, yes, in accepting his very generous offer of continued employment within the film industries of the Third Reich. So shit on you and your stupid moral dilemmas. (*Slight pause*) Oh, and here. (*She takes a big kitchen knife out of her purse and stabs it into the table top.*) This is yours. (*She leaves, slamming the door.*)

HUSZ: Germans . . . are full of surprises.

AGNES: (*Looking at the knife.*) What is this?

HUSZ: It's mine.

AGNES: What are you doing with that? What in God's name are you doing?

HUSZ: Regretting a lost opportunity.

AGNES: I don't understand.

HUSZ: Not surprising.

AGNES: I don't understand.

HUSZ: You don't? Really? It's simple. It's a butcher knife. I carry it with me these days. I keep hoping I'll run into someone . . . I don't like and I'll make him see the point, as it were.

AGNES: I don't want that thing in my house. I don't want you here with that.

HUSZ: You still don't understand? History repeats itself, that's Marx, first as tragedy, then as farce. When I was young . . .

AGNES: I don't want you here!

(*Pause. He looks at her.*)

HUSZ: Then I'll leave.

AGNES: Go!

(HUSZ *stands, pulls the knife out of the table so roughly that it splinters the table top.*)

AGNES: My table! You bastard! Get out! Go!

(HUSZ *starts to limp to the door, then sits heavily on the floor, unable to walk.*)

AGNES: Go! Go! Go!

HUSZ: I can't.

(*Pause, then* AGNES *sits on the floor as well.*)

(*End of scene*)

**Scene Twenty-one: Love Scene Without . . .**

([*Slide:* May 2, 1933. LATER THAT NIGHT.] HUSZ *is seated, without a shirt, linen wrapped around his ribs.* AGNES *is pulling the apartment back together.*)

HUSZ: It will not be hard to leave Berlin. (*Pause*) You can't imagine how much I miss Hungary. You can't imagine how much I hate German cooking. You can't imagine what it's cost me to be a castaway here, making German films, churning out the kind of bad dreams a drug addict or a criminal lunatic has before he wakes up and does something terrible. (*Beat*) Justice . . . is vanishing. Like all the air in the earth's atmosphere getting used up, like life's blood running freely on the ground, pouring from a wound too big to stop up; you watch it spill, watching yourself die. Justice precedes beauty. Without justice, beauty is impossible, an obscenity. And when beauty has gone, what does a cameraman do with his eye?

(AGNES *stops cleaning, looks at* HUSZ. *He motions for her to sit next to him. She does.*)

HUSZ: In American movies, when the pioneers cross the big plains west of St. Louis, I have seen expanses as vast and as beautiful as the Hungarian flatlands. Well, not as beautiful, but . . . I have cousins in Chicago. I can get you false papers. I have mine already. I want you to come with me.

AGNES: (*Standing up*) I think we should go to the hospital.

HUSZ: I want you to come with me.

AGNES: I want you to go to a doctor.

HUSZ: When I lost my eye in 1919, it was the doctor who treated it that turned me in. At times like these, best to avoid doctors and hospitals.

AGNES: You're hurt.

HUSZ: You have done extraordinary things with this bedlinen bandage. And I seem to be able to walk.

AGNES: The foot is broken.

HUSZ: No, I don't think so. Just very badly bruised.

AGNES: (*Softly*) I can't go, Husz.

HUSZ: Why not?

AGNES: I don't speak English. I can't function in strange places. It took me years to get a contract, what kind of work would I do in Chicago? Traveling upsets me. Really. I can't move. I can't move. I'm sorry. Later, maybe . . .

HUSZ: This is no time, Agnes, for alliances that aren't portable.

AGNES: Stay.

HUSZ: I can't.

AGNES: Even at this late date, Husz, we can't get synchronized. (*Pause*) Leave, then, throw your life away if you want to, but don't expect to find anything waiting for you when you come back.

HUSZ: Goodbye, dear heart. I promise to write.

(*They embrace, kiss.*)

HUSZ: It will not be hard to leave Berlin. But it will be very hard to leave you.

(*End of scene*)

### Scene Twenty-two: Hands

([*Slide:* MAY 3, 1933.] AGNES *alone, sitting at table.*)

AGNES: (*Holding up her right hand.*)
With this hand
I
Hold water,
Stir the soup,
Crack walnuts,
Turn keys,
Scratch,
Move, divide,
Replace,

Light the light,
Write postcards,
Pay,
Receive payment,
Grasp,
Fill out a ballot, seal it,
Take up a knife,
Make a cut.
The practical hand,
This hand,
Its veins, nerves, tissue
And bones.
Five fingers has this hand.
With five I can . . .
(*Holding up her left hand.*)
Now this hand.
With this hand,
Weak claw, I
Shred shadows,
Brush dust,
Drop glass, let go,
Sense changes in the air by
The subcutaneous twingings,
The shy retirement of heat
To cool inner safety;
This hand to make
A frail moon-cup
Protective patch
Over the weak eye,
The eye that cannot bear to see.
Five fingers has this hand.
With five I can . . .

And this is the hand that betrays me. (*Holds up right hand.*)
And this the hand that holds my life. (*Holds up the left.*)

(*End of scene*)

([*Slide:* MAY 10, 1933. HITLER ADDRESSES THE FIRST CONGRESS OF GERMAN LABOR AND DECLARES HIS INTENTION TO "ABOLISH CLASS WAR". LATER THAT NIGHT, THE FIRST PUBLIC BOOK BURNINGS ARE HELD.])

### Scene Twenty-three: Revelations and Farewells

([*Slide:* JUNE 22, 1933. THE SOCIAL-DEMOCRATIC PARTY IS ABOLISHED.] AGNES *stands near the window, looking out.* PAULINKA *and* BAZ *are dressed for travel.*)

PAULINKA: The train ride to Moscow will take three days. The trip to Hollywood would have taken a month. So I decided to go to Russia. Well, not really. The Americans found out about my old KPD membership.

BAZ: Remarkable.

PAULINKA: Your past catches up with you. (*Beat*) What kind of a world is it where Husz moves to America and I wind up in the USSR? Doesn't that seem . . . backwards, or something?

BAZ: Don't talk about Husz when you get to Moscow. Don't say you knew him. Stay out of politics.

PAULINKA: Easy for me to do. (*Beat*) There was this woman in Wardrobe who used to fold a KPD leaflet very carefully and slip it into the pocket of my costume on the sly. Every once in a while. Then she'd wait for me to find it, and when I did she'd be watching, and she'd wink at me. This went on for years. I hated her. Last week, I guess someone informed on her; they came for her at the Studio. She screamed. But . . . (*Pause*) That was the end for me. I faked a nervous breakdown, or maybe I didn't fake it, who knows. And so on. The end. (*Beat*) You're being ominously quiet, Agnes. You could at least wish me a pleasant voyage east.

(*Pause.* AGNES *looks at* PAULINKA, *then out the window again.*)

BAZ: The winters in Russia have a nasty reputation.

PAULINKA: I packed my furs. And I expect a warm welcome in Moscow. I, too, have a reputation. (*Small pause*) It isn't so terrible. They do make the best films.

BAZ: Not recently.

PAULINKA: Don't be so morbid, Baz! Put a good face on it.

BAZ: Hard to do.

PAULINKA: Apparently. But not for me. (*Pause*) It's frightening, isn't it? What an actor does. Assume the mantle of truth, of courage, of moral conviction, and wear it convincingly, no matter what sort of chaotic mess there is inside. (*Beat*) Agnes, you have to say something.

AGNES: You . . . are going to miss your train. (*Slight pause*) I wish you'd go now. Please go.

(PAULINKA *leaves.*)

Agnes: See? You'd think, when a person goes, a whole person just goes away, it would leave a hole, some empty place behind, that's what I thought, I expected that, but . . . it doesn't. Everyone's going but it isn't like the world has gotten emptier, just much smaller, more closed in. It contracts, the empty places . . . collapse. Goodbye.

Baz:
Do you remember what it was like ten years ago, Agnes?
One red word and a street-full of people would come running.
The Revolution . . .
When I was sixteen, in Leipzig, I joined
A band of young people—we went
Off to the mountains,
Read Wedekind and Whitman the American,
Sang Schubert and Mahler the Jew,
Worshipped the sun, made a God of Nature,
Experimented with each other
In all sorts of ways,
And then . . .
We got crazy,
We got pregnant,
We discovered urges we wished we'd left alone.
We saw the Revolution die.
Everyone fled back to Leipzig,
Back to upholstered furniture, marriage,
Heterosexuality, each
To his or her own prison . . .
We were too frightened
And too young
To see how close we'd been
To something truly free; knocked
On the gates of the Divinity,
Only to retreat in terror.
(*He stands to leave.*)
Today you see platoons of children,
Younger than we were,
Marching as organized as ants
Into the mountains. They wear uniforms.
They plan experiments of a different kind.
They'll dream blood-dreams
Of goats rutting and lions killing,
And they'll sing songs about racial purity.
Their revolution, I think, will succeed.

They'd be the future except
They stand as a guarantee
That no future exists.
Only a long, long nightfall
And then a permanent goodnight.
(*Pause*)
Goodnight. Paris awaits.
(BAZ *goes to* AGNES, *reaches in his pocket, takes out an orange, gives it to her.*)
Weather this, Agnes. And keep the door locked. (*Exits*)

(*End of scene*)

**Scene Twenty-four: All That was Fat and Bright is Perished from You**

([*Slide:* JULY 14, 1933. HITLER DECLARES THE NATIONAL SOCIALIST GERMAN WORKERS' PARTY THE ONLY LEGAL POLITICAL PARTY IN GERMANY.] *Lights up on* GOTCHLING *and* AGNES.)

AGNES: What do you want?

GOTCHLING: That's quite a welcome.

AGNES: I haven't seen you for months. You must want something. I thought you'd gone for good.

GOTCHLING: I have, officially.

AGNES: Officially where?

GOTCHLING: Officially Switzerland.

AGNES: And really where?

GOTCHLING: Switzerland.

AGNES: Lie.

GOTCHLING: You don't want the truth.

AGNES: Lie.

GOTCHLING: It doesn't matter. I need your help. The apartment . . .

AGNES: I knew it. The answer's no.

GOTCHLING: There's no one else. You have to.

AGNES: I do not. You can't make me risk my life. Risk your own.

GOTCHLING: I am.

AGNES: Good for you. How wonderful. I refuse this honor.

GOTCHLING: Tell you what. We'll make a deal.

(*No answer*)

GOTCHLING: You can't save yourself, Agnes. If you make it, you make it, but only because you're lucky.

AGNES: I don't know what you're talking about.

GOTCHLING: You will. (*Beat*) If you say no to this, Agnes, you're dead to me. And we both need desperately to keep at least some part of you alive. Say yes, and I promise to carry you with me, the part of you that's dying now. I can do that, I'm stronger than you. Say yes, and I will take your heart and fold it up in mine, and protect it with my life. And some day I may be able to bring it back to you. (*Pause*) You're very fond of regrets, Agnes, but the time for regretting is gone. I need very much to be proud of you.

AGNES: If I get arrested, Annabella Gotchling, I swear to God I will never forgive you.

GOTCHLING: Three days from now, around six in the evening. Expect her. She says she knows you. Her name is Rosa. (*Exits*)

(*End of scene*)

**1980–1988 #9**
**Tango/Tango/Lullaby**

(*Lights up on* ZILLAH.)

ZILLAH:
There's a terror that skips
Over the mind and out the throat
In one little leap, faster than thinking:
Revelation: We are in danger.
The Beast is awake, capable of anything.
Deep under Berlin, deep under Washington,
In the bunker, in the shelter,
He's singing to us
In a rough voice coarsened with blood:
Dance with me,
Dance with me,
Find the wild joy that makes
The People want to dance.
It's a bad old lullaby,
It keeps you wide awake.

It's not the danger that you see
That's the danger.
Dear Beast, you've waited so long,
Sleepless and pacing,
Capable of anything,
Come out of the ground,
Thousand-year locust,
Beast again, horned again,
Eager to tango.
This time
We're ready. We're waiting
For you. Now.

(*End of interruption*)

### Scene Twenty-five: The Green Front

([*Slide:* July 17, 1933.] Agnes *is alone in the apartment, pacing, checking the windows. There is a soft knock at the door.* Agnes *freezes. The person outside knocks again.* Agnes *goes quickly to the door, opens it a crack, then lets* Rosa Malek *in.*)

Agnes: No one saw you.

Malek: No.

Agnes: How can you tell? There are so many doorways and alleys and windows.

Malek: I don't think anyone saw me.

Agnes: You don't *think*? Oh God in heaven . . .

Malek: You've got to calm down. What if someone saw me? I'm not wearing a red beret and a sign saying "Escaping Communist."

Agnes: But later, when they come looking—I shouldn't have done this, I really shouldn't. It's no joke. Goddamned Annabella. They'll find out. The hateful people in this building. They watch everything. They get money for informing. Calm, calm. I need a drink. Do you want a drink?

Malek: Yes, please.

(Agnes *pours two glasses and gives one to* Malek. *they both sit. They drink.*)

Agnes: But you can't stay here long.

Malek: Just till morning.

AGNES: Morning. Then you've got to leave. And don't give this address to anyone else.

MALEK: No.

(*Pause*)

AGNES: (*Calmer, softer*) Where are you going? After here?

MALEK: I can't say.

AGNES: No, well, no, that's . . . that makes sense. I wouldn't actually want to know. But . . . you'll still be . . . working.

MALEK: I really can't talk about that.

AGNES: No. Please, I'm sorry. You probably think I'm a spy. I . . . I haven't changed that much. (*Beat*) I just need to know that you'll be working. You and Gotchling. You'll keep doing what needs to be done, underground, I couldn't, I'm really not worth much, I suppose . . . the fear is too great, it makes me stupid, but . . . it still matters to me.

MALEK: I know it does, Agnes.

AGNES: And this will pass. Months, not years.

MALEK: There are people working, Agnes. And it will pass. But it could be years.

AGNES: Oh no, not years, I don't think so. (*Pause*) I'm afraid of living alone, here, that something will happen to me. Stupid of me telling you this, you have such real things to be frightened of but . . . I'm lonely. And years frightens me. I ought to do something to help but I'm simply not able. The arrests. Every day they execute . . .

MALEK: (*After a brief pause*) This is important. What you've done for me.

AGNES: (*Suddenly angry*) This is nothing. Don't coddle me. This is shit. (*Beat*) I think we should go to sleep. (*She gets up and goes toward the bedroom.*)

MALEK: Agnes.

(*She stops, but does not look at* MALEK.)

MALEK: On the border, in Karlsbad, there's a house: 30 Erzegebirge Street. Memorize the address, don't write it down. 30 Erzgebirge, like the mountains. The front of the house is in Germany. The back of the house is in Czechoslovakia. The people who live there are . . . friends of ours, and the Nazis don't know about it yet—the system is full of little holes like this. Go there by train, at night, if it gets bad here; knock on the door and tell them you're looking for the Green Front. They'll take you to the back door, and you're out. (*Pause*) If you need to. Ask for the way to the Green Front. The borders are full of holes.

(AGNES *walks slowly to the bedroom without looking back.*)

AGNES: Please be gone by morning. (*She closes the bedroom door.*)

(*End of scene*)

([*Slide:* OCTOBER 14, 1933. GERMANY WITHDRAWS FROM DISARMAMENT TALKS AND THE LEAGUE OF NATIONS. NOVEMBER 12, 1933. REICHSTAG ELECTIONS AND NATIONAL PLEBISCITE RESULTS: AN ALL-NAZI PARLIAMENT AND A 95% POPULAR VOTE OF CONSENT.])

**Epilogue**

(AGNES, *completely alone at kitchen table. She has an orange, which she pushes, causing it to roll off the table and across the floor.* DIE ALTE *enters through the door, picks it up, and begins to peel and eat it.*)

AGNES: I live in a modern flat.
On one side lives nightmare,
On the other, despair.
Above me, exhaustion,
Below me, a man
With the pale face
And red hands
Of a strangler.

DIE ALTE:
I can eat anywhere. I remember
The thick smoke rising from the ruins of home,
Black plumes in an ash-white sky,
The sun transformed
Into a nickel-plated dot
No bigger than a groschen. It seemed
To race through the clouds—
Or was that the moon? No.
The sun. The moon
Was huge and rusted
Like an infected eye.

It moved slowly, and the nights were black.
Rats looked for bodies under the rubble,
So corpses had to torched right in the street:
A piteous sight.
The planes came back
Every day
To bomb the craters they'd created
Only the day before.
The water was oily
And full of typhus.
Everyone was patchy,
delirious, diseased,
And waiting for the end . . .

AGNES:
When God is good
The hours go,
But the world rolls on,
Tumbrel-slow,
And the driver sings
A gallows-song:
"The end is quick.
The way is long."

I fear the end,
I fear the way,
I fear the wind
Will make me stray
Much farther than
I want to stray,
Far from my home,
Bright room called day,
Past where deliverance or hope
Can find me.

DIE ALTE:
But through it all
I never lost my appetite,
And never ceased to look for food,
Just like the rats.
I ate while the bombs fell,
Ate while the bodies burned,
Ate at the funerals, hurried and undignified,
Of people I had loved . . .
Ate

Through days of pain
And nights of terror;
With cracked teeth
And split lips
I kept eating, digesting,
And looking for meals.

When they rounded us up,
And brought us to the camps,
And showed us the mass graves and said
"You
Are responsible for these"
I was thinking, "I
Wasn't here,
Didn't know,
Didn't want to know,
Never pulled a trigger,
Never pulled a switch,
Feel nothing for these beds
Of sleepers, deep asleep,
But only
Look at how thin they are,
And when they let us return to Munich
I wonder what I'll find for dinner."

(*The room begins to grow dark.*)

AGNES:
Club-foot.
Smell of sulphur.
Yellow dog.
No shadow.

Welcome to Germany.

(*Blackout*)

*The End*

Eric Overmyer

# *In a Pig's Valise*

*"A hard-boiled yarn with music"*

ERIC OVERMYER is an Associate Artist at Center Stage, a member of New Dramatists, and the former Literary Manager of Playwrights Horizons. His other plays include *On the Verge, or The Geography of Yearning* (Broadway Play Publishing, 1986), *Native Speech* (Broadway Play Publishing, 1984), *In Perpetuity Throughout the Universe,* and *Hawker.* He has published poems in *The Paris Review, Shankpainter, Shaman,* and *Native Dancer.* Additionally, Mr. Overmyer was a story editor on television's *St. Elsewhere,* and has written for *The Slap Maxwell Story* and *The Days and Nights of Molly Dodd.* A recipient of the McKnight Fellowship and the Le Compte Du Nouy Award for playwriting, Mr. Overmyer recently received a New York Foundation for the Arts Fellowship, a Rockefeller Fellowship for Playwriting, and a grant from the National Endowment for the Arts.



*In a Pig's Valise,* a "hard-boiled yarn with music", received its professional debut at Center Stage, Baltimore, in June 1986, with music by Karl Lundeberg and musical staging by Marcia Milgram Dodge. Mark Harrison directed the following cast:

JAMES TAXI .......................... Jack Kenny
DOLORES CON LECHE .................. Yamil Borges
SHRIMP BUCKET ............... Michael McCormick
PILES ................................ Rico T. Tavi
THE BOP OP ........................ Keith Curran
ZOOT ALORS ......................... Steve Pudenz
BLIND SAX .................... Arnold K. Sterling
MUSTANG SALLY ..................... Sheila Peace
DIZZY MISS LIZZY .................. Pamela Jame
GUT BUCKET .................... Alan Brasington

Hugh Landwehr did the set design; Jess Goldstein, the costume design; Pat Collins, the lighting design; and Janet Kalas, the sound design. Susan Andrews did the props. Stan Wojewodski, Jr., was Artistic Director; Peter W. Culman, Managing Director, and Victoria Nolan, Associate Managing Director.

Special thanks to Del Risberg.

*Characters*

| | |
|---|---|
| James Taxi | a private eye |
| Dolores Con Leche | a thrush |
| Zoot Alors*<br>Root Choyce<br>The Bop Op | denizens of the Heartbreak Hotel |
| Blind Sax | |
| Shrimp Bucket<br>Gut Bucket | the notorious Bucket Brothers |
| Mustang Sally<br>Dizzy Miss Lizzy | the Balkanettes: backup singers |

*The actor who plays Zoot plays Gut Bucket (in a fat suit).

The action takes place in and around The Heartbreak Hotel, at the corner of Neon and Lonely.

> "Don't kid me. My nerves are frayed,"
> I said. "Who's the junky?"
>
> "Come along, Alfred," the big man said
> to his companion. "And stop acting girlish."
>
> "In a pig's valise," Alfred told him.
>
> The big man turned to me placidly.
> "Why do all these punks keep saying that?"
>
> —Raymond Chandler, *The Little Sister*

*Author's note*:
*In a Pig's Valise* is a genre comedy. The genre being simultaneously sent-up and celebrated is the hard-boiled detective novel, invented by Raymond Chandler. The true subjects of this comedy are genre style and language, genre myth and image.

*In a Pig's Valise* is for Mark Herrier and Becky Gonzalez.

## Act One

(*Lots of fog.*)

(*A streetlight. A couple of neon signs. Pale pink 'n blue neon fluid script.*)

(*Heartbreak Hotel. Bar.*)
(*MUSIC:* Opening Titles, *a smoky instrumental, sax solo, something slow sultry sweet sexy sad and blue.*)

(*The music starts and swelllls.*)
(*The fog drifts and swirls.*)
(*The sign flashes.*
Ba Ba Ba Ba Ba Ba Ba)

(*A car approaches. Headlights. Fades away. Brakes screech on rain-slick streets.*)

(*A match is struck. With panache.*)

(*A man steps out of the fog.*
*You know what he looks like:*
*slouch hat, thread-bare suit, five o'clock shadow, no tie. Under his suit jacket he's wearing a pajama top instead of a shirt.*

*And he's very very short.*

*His voice is cool and tired.*)

TAXI: Chaka chaka chaka cha. (*Pause*) Listen, baby. (*He sings* Neon Heart, *a hot and cool ballad about the life.*)

NEON HEART

TAXI:
It was a foggy night
I heard a sax on the soundtrack
Somewhere a neon light
Flashed me right back to you
I walk the lonely streets
Cruisin' clues on bar stools
My heart's got a private beat
So cool it's neon blue

---

You know it's lonely out there
Streets rainy and bare
And the whiskey is starting to pour
I know what you're longing for
Goin' to the Neon Heart
You know that's where the records start
You know that's where they keep the score

I ease the Chevy slow
Ridin' around with the top down
I pay the tab at dawn
And I drive home alone

Money slick changes hands
Honeyed licks from dance bands
And her eyes are dazzling and dark
Going to the Neon Heart

(*Sax solo*)

You know the neon's so fine
The saxophones shine
And the dancers are dreaming in bars
Tell me that it's time to part
Goin' to the Neon Heart
You know that's where the records start
You know that's where the mysteries are

You say "no vacancy"
But I'm gonna make you love me
It'll be yours to take
Turn me off and watch my neon
Neon Heart break

(*Sweet finish*)

(*Sizes up the audience.*)

TAXI: As long as we're here. Let's smash the bubbly.

(*He lights up. The smoke from the cigarette curls up in the blue streetlight, and his cool pose is the essence of a classic Forties album cover.*)

TAXI: It was two-fifty-two in the fretful A.M. I'd been ensconced in the back of my Chevy Bel-Air, dreaming I was a fresh-pressed Sinatra seventy-eight, with classic Forties water-color cover art. *Pastels.* I could've spun that particular platter all night long, until the grooves screamed for mercy. Instead, I found myself shivering in my shoes—scratch that—my *gumshoes,* on one of the worst corners in this quadrant of Western Civ. There were a lot of corners reserved for the criminally insane in this behind-the-eight-ball burg, but this one was special. Neon and Lonely.

(*He drags on his cigarette.*)

TAXI: Neon and Lonely. The co-ordinates of desire. Sax solos. Neon longing. Convertibles. *Stolen* convertibles.

(*An acid belch*)

TAXI: I'd come in from the valley. Forty suck-your-heart-out miles of fast food and neon. Avec shot brakes and smoldering upholstery. I was risking a loitering rap in front of a beanbag hotel. The kind of dive where checkout time sometimes comes when you least expect it. Loitering with intent: to meet some mysterioso-ette. Here. In the shadow of *The Heartbreak.*

(*The neon* Heartbreak Hotel *sign pops on.* TAXI *regards the classic pink and blue sign sourly.*)

TAXI: Fleabag, beanbag, paperbag, scumbag, douchebag, bodybag hotel. Bagatelle. The Heartburn. This place is a case.

(*He sneezes*)

TAXI: It was another damp one. The latest in a series. It seemed like a lifetime ago that I'd gotten her call. The call that had me sucking up bronchial smog and the kiss-me-deadly night air on the corner of Neon and Lonely with red eyes and flat fleet.

(*Beat*)

TAXI: Feet.

(*Beat*)

TAXI: The air was like Liquid Paper. Whoo. My chronic hypothermia was coming on like a hit of purple haze. Cold cojones, pal. I was shaking like a maracas player on the Feast Day of St. Xenophobe of the Green Card. I played a round of pocket pool and kept hanging in. The fog continued to ladle itself on. Like pea soup in a Merchant Marine mess hall. Like interest on an easy-payment credit plan. Like suffering similies in exhausted sub-genres of pop-fic and modern lit. You couldn't hack through it with an M-16. Not that I had one. On me.

(*Beat. Drags.*)

TAXI: All in all, a sweet, sweet set-up for a sap like me.

(*Beat. Drags.*)

TAXI: But I couldn't leave. They'd towed my car. The kiss-me-Wednesday-night air was putting a chill on my bones like jelly on a gefilte fish. I took a moment to strike a match on my eyebrow and set fire to another coffin nail.

(*He strikes a match on his eyebrow, lights a second cigarette, smokes both.*)

TAXI: One more thing. When I face front and talk to you this way—this way! This is the Voice Over voice. The Big VO. When you earn your PI license, they issue you your own VO. Don't let it slow you down. Just pretend that my lips don't move and you can hear my voice surple out over the PA all muffled and crunkly. I'm supposed to be *thinking*, see.

(*He snuffs one cigarette.*)

TAXI: But what I'm really doing is passing on vital exposition as we make an incomplete transition from pulp to performance. In other words, if I didn't tell you, you'd never know.

(*Beat*)

TAXI: It's gotta be how it's gotta be. We're all prisoners of genre.

(*Music*)

TAXI: Warning! If the little voice in *your* head sounds pre-recorded, odds on it's head cold. Maybe sinus.

(*Beat*)

TAXI: The name is Taxi. James Taxi. Mother calls me—when she calls me—Nancy James.

(*He snuffs second coffin nail.*)

TAXI: The voice at the other end of the line had had an Hispanic accent that was sweet as sucre and resonated like dollar signs in my ears. I won't perjure myself and tell you that the prospect of meeting that voice in person wasn't better than a poke in the eye with a sharp forty-five. I needed the job.

(*The phone rings.* TAXI *answers it.* Flashback Music.)

TAXI: Give to me straight.

(*The* Flashback Music *segues into* Kiss Me Deadly, *sung by* DOLORES, *who emerges from a bright red phone booth. It's an Afro-Cuban salsa dance number with lots of percussive spice.*)

(Dolores *dances and sings up a phonebooth storm.*)

Kiss Me Deadly

Dolores:
I'm looking for someone to help me out
No cop no doctor just a private eye
Listen to me Taxi hear me out
I'm looking for a stand-up guy

I need help give me a hand
I need help I'm in a helluva jam
If you heard my story you wouldn't believe your ears
You couldn't conceive it in a million years
International conspiracy global plot
These people are killers ready or not
They want to

Kiss me deadly
Make me quiver and quake
Kiss me deadly, deadly, deadly
Keep me wide awake

They want to mesmerize me

Are you the man to crack this case
Gonna be plenty of danger
You a tough enough guy to be my ace
Can you take a chance on a stranger

It's muy crazy but come to my aid
I need a Phil Marlowe or a Sam Spade
He'll have to

Kiss me deadly
Make me quiver and shake
Kiss me deadly, deadly, deadly
Keep me wide awake

He'll have to mesmerize me

(*Spoken:*)

You're probably just a divorce-case shamus—breaking down motel room doors—flash photographs—lunchtime trysts—perfecting your palm tree crawl—drink your whiskey out of your sloch hat—why do they call them gumshoes, pal—bet you're a dick that cracks so wise—bet you'll be a bachelor the rest of your days—when you gonna get SOCIAL—I'm no little sister from Mar Vista, pal—even if you wanted to you probably couldn't

(*Sings*)

You couldn't
Kiss me deadly
Make me quiver and quake
Kiss me deadly, deadly, deadly
Keep me wide awake

Think you could mesmerize me?

If you could be the guy to ease my grief
You'd trade your forty-four and your sore eye-teeth
For a chance to hang around with me
I got a voice like a frozen daquiri
Take this caper
I'll make it worth your while
You may lose your life
But you'll go with a smile
Aren't you tough enough to

Kiss me deadly
Make me quiver and quake
Kiss me deadly, deadly, deadly
Keep me wide awake
Come on and
Kiss me deadly
Honey don't be shy
Kiss me deadly, deadly, deadly
Be my personal private eye
Come on and mesmerize me

(*Big finish*)

Taxi: Nice pair of lungs, Miss—

Dolores: Con Leche.

Taxi: Con Leche. What you've told me so far is close enough for Cliff Notes. Why don't we get together? You can fill in the fine print.

Dolores: Your place or mine?

Taxi: Let's face off at center ice.

Dolores: Know the Heartbreak?

Taxi: Hotel for mutants?

DOLORES: That's the one. Meet me tonight at the Heartbreak, Mr. Taxi. After midnight. You can catch my act.

TAXI: I'm running a fever already.

DOLORES: It's an eye-opener.

(*She hangs up as lights and music dissolve.* TAXI *hangs up. He burps delicately.*)

TAXI: Those dissolves always make me motion sick. Whoever she was, she gave great phone. After I hung up the horn, I closed the office for the afternoon. I gave my faithful amanuensis, "Legs" Lichtenstein, the rest of the week off. She'd earned it. I hadn't paid her since fiscal '57. Legs. What a word jockey. But that's another story. I sauntered over to my local gin joint and tossed down a couple of muscles. For you rookies out there, a muscle is standard-issue detective drink: Kahlua and Maalox. Then I grabbed some shut-eye in the back of my Chevy. (*Beat*) Con Leche's voice haunted my dreams like guava jelly. Spread sweet and smooth. I was stuck on that voice. Like enamel on a molar. (*Shivers*) If I come down with something. Neon and Lonely. The Heartbreak Hotel at Neon and Lonely. Love it.

(*A throbbing bass line is heard.* TAXI *snuffs his cigarette and turns up his collar.*)

TAXI: Something funky this way comes.

(TAXI *slides into the shadows.* ROOT, ZOOT, THE BOP OP, SALLY, LIZZY, *and* BLIND SAX *juke in.* ROOT *and* ZOOT *are carrying what looks to be a body, wrapped in plastic and frozen solid.*)

(*The others are loaded down with funky tube gear and strange devices. All are heavily and obviously disguised. They do* The Skulk, *an instrumental dance number. The music is threatening and insidious, and the dancing slinky. Eventually they all skulk on into The Heartbreak.*)

(ROOT *and* ZOOT *have a little trouble negotiating the stiff through the doorway. One of the Heartbreakers*—THE BOP OP—*drops something.*)

(TAXI *steps out of the shadows and picks it up. It's a white, plump, three-fingered glove, the kind Disney characters wear.*)

(*The music seques into* Three-Fingered Glove.)

Three-Fingered Glove

Taxi: Is this a clue
Maybe not
A piece of the puzzle
A part of the plot
Or just an accident
A meaningless event
Not worth caring about

Well you can never tell
I'll put it away
It may be a clue for a rainy day
Wait and see

Three-fingered glove
What's it good for
Three-fingered glove
Who's it belong to
You'd have to be
A digital amputee
A sawmill worker or such
It's not much to go on

But oh what the hell
You never can tell
I'll put it away
It may be a clue
For a rainy day
Wait and see—

(Dolores *steps out of the shadows.*)

Dolores: Nice pair of—lungs, Mr. Taxi.

(Taxi *hastily stuffs the three-fingered glove in his pocket.*)

Taxi: (*In the VO*) I had egg roll all over my kisser. An Hispanic hallucination was hovering nearby like heat on a desert highway.

Dolores: You talking to me? And why the past tense, pal?

Taxi: It's a convention, sweetheart. You ain't supposed to hear, dig? It's for them. (*Indicates audience*) The Big VO. Keeps 'em au courant.

Dolores: Is a VO anything like an MO?

Taxi: (*Warily*) Maybe. Who wants to know? Let's just say I'm cogitating a capella.

DOLORES: It's a free country.

TAXI: Don't kid yourself. Say, you got a Dramamine, sister? I got a case of dissolve sickness. I feel like a side o' slaw strewn on a soggy paper plate.

DOLORES: Those hard-boiled similies get pretty thin. As thin as the skin on a cup of hot cocoa.

TAXI: As thin as the crust on an East Coast pizza pie.

DOLORES: Neon and Lonely. Great spot for a rendezvous.

TAXI: This corner is seedier than a strawberry.

DOLORES: And darker than a landlord's heart. Thanks for showing up, Mr. Taxi.

TAXI: My pleasure, Miss Con Leche. Sleep is out of style this season. Let's get down to the storyline. What's the drumbeat, baby?

DOLORES: I want you to locate something for me.

TAXI: Is it yours?

DOLORES: Yeah.

TAXI: Sounds legal. Maybe we can do business. I have irresistible charm. Once you meet me, you never want to let me go.

DOLORES: I find that difficult to swallow. Although I can believe the vice squad feels that way.

TAXI: They refer you?

DOLORES: As a matter of fact, Mr. Taxi, I picked you at random from the *Yellow Pages.* I was trying to call a cab.

TAXI: I've heard that one. If I had a thousand bucks for every time I've heard that one, I wouldn't be here now.

DOLORES: I just assumed that all private dicks were alike—

TAXI and DOLORES: (*In unison, more or less*) In the dark.

TAXI: Let's eighty-six the bright banter, shall we? And enough with the dick jokes. I hear enough dick jokes in the course of a day—

TAXI and DOLORES: (*In unison, more or less*) To choke a horse.

TAXI: Okay, Con Leche. Lay it on me with a trowel. This missing something—stolen?

DOLORES: Repeatedly.

TAXI: Once rabid, twice shy. Valuable?

DOLORES: Priceless.

TAXI: Sure, sure, they all say that. I'm not your insurance company, lady.

DOLORES: Uninsurable.

TAXI: No kidding. Description.

DOLORES: Dreams.

TAXI: (*Sighs*) Could we be specific, Miss Con Leche? What are we talking about here?

DOLORES: Dreams. Someone is stealing my dreams.

TAXI: Dreams.

DOLORES: Stolen. Lifted. Light-fingered. Long gone.

TAXI: Let's get literal, Miss Con Leche.

DOLORES: (*Touching herself*) This is as literal as I get, Mr. Taxi.

TAXI: Metaphor is for poets, kid. We hard-boiled guys go for palpable factology. We like simile. Like or as. Like a dream. As if in a dream. But not a dream dream. I don't believe in dreams. Except the kind that exist out there in the zeitgeist. You can put your meathooks on 'em.

DOLORES: Zeitgeist?

TAXI: Like, my dream is a pair of center-court season tickets. My dream is a condo in the clouds. My dream is a garnet-colored Jag with custom plates.

DOLORES: You're slow, Taxi. I'm hablando-ing straight. Someone is stealing my dreams. My brain's being boosted. Look.

(*Flashback music*)

DOLORES: It all began a month ago. I answered an ad—

TAXI: (*Detecting ferociously*) What ad? Where?

DOLORES: Cool your jets. This ad for folk dancers. Ethnic folk dancers. That's my profession. They were hiring ethnic folk dancers down at The Heartbreak Hotel.

TAXI: Flashback me back, baby, and don't edit the tape. Sure you don't have a Dramamine?

DOLORES: Watch my tracks, hard guy.

(*Music. The front of The Heartbreak opens up.*)

(*Seedy. Pathetic palms and pink flamingos.*)

TAXI: Wow. Spiff City. Turn down the ambiance.

DOLORES: It grows on you.

TAXI: I'll bet.

DOLORES: The ad said ask for a Mr. Bucket. So I did.

(*She walks in.* TAXI *remains outside, watching the flashback.* ROOT, ZOOT, BOP, *and* BLIND SAX *are in the lobby:* ZOOT *sits at the desk,* ROOT *polishes the flamingos, and* BOP *does his nails.* DOLORES *lingers in the lobby.* ZOOT *hits the desk bell: The guys snap to and harmonize.*)

PUT YOUR LEGS ON MY SHOULDERS

BOP: Put your legs on my shoulders
Put my head in your lap
Wrap your kneecaps 'round my earlobes
And we'll do it just like that

Put your legs on my shoulders
Honey drive me 'round the bend
Honey dive right in
Wake the neighbors up again

ROOT and ZOOT:
Honey your legs, ba doom, ba doom, ba doom
Honey your legs, ba doom, ba doom, ba doom

(*Continues under*)

BLIND SAX: Oh darling when you kiss me
And we get so moist and slick
Remember when you miss me
To give me one last lick

ALL: Put your legs on my shoulders
Don't tell me I just ate
You know I always told her
Grab my ears and aim me straight

Put your legs on my shoulders
Put my head in your lap
Wrap your kneecaps 'round my earlobes
And we'll do it just like that

ROOT and ZOOT:
Honey your legs, ba doom, ba doom, ba doom

(*Continued under*)

BLIND SAX: Oh darling when I meet you
And we go to bed in haste
Oh darling when I eat you
I long for one last taste

| ROOT, ZOOT and BLIND SAX: | BOP: |
|---|---|
| Put your legs on me | Put your legs, put your legs, put your legs |
| Put your legs on me | Put your legs, put your legs, put your legs |
| Your legs on me | Put your legs, put your legs, put your legs |
| My shoulders | On my shoulders |

ALL: Oh oh oh oh oh ahhhhhh

(*Big finish*)

ROOT: Needs work.

TAXI: (*In the VO*) Those guys weren't the Four Horsemen of the A Capellalypse, but they weren't bad. Their harmonies were closer than a skin graft. (*Waves* DOLORES *in.*) Don't stop now. It's just getting interesting.

(DOLORES *walks in.*)

ZOOT: Yez? Mai ah elp yew? Dew yew ruchoir un rheum?

DOLORES: Pardon you?

ZOOT: Dew yew ave un reservasion?

DOLORES: No habla whatever language that is.

BOP: Reservations, ya need 'em?

DOLORES: No, thanks, I got plenty already. I'm looking for Mr. Bucket.

ZOOT: Wheech Monsieur Boockette? Oui ave deux Monsieurs Boockettes.

DOLORES: I want to speak to the Mr. Bucket who's looking for ethnic folk dancers.

BOP: She wants Gut, Zoot. Give him a ring.

ZOOT: Honkey dorey.

(*He rings.* BOP *cruises* DOLORES.)

BOP: What kinda ethnic dancing you do, Miss—

ZOOT: Allo, Monsieur Gut ou Monsieur Shreemp?

DOLORES: Con Leche. Call me Dolores.

ZOOT: Zere ees une dancair ethnique en zuh lowbie, Monsieur Shreemp.

BOP: Okay, Dolores, call me Bop. Everybody does.

ZOOT: Oui. Oui. Bon temps roulez, Monsieur.

(ZOOT *hangs up.*)

DOLORES: Okay, Bop. I do all kinds.

BOP: No wheezing.

DOLORES: You name it.

BOP: Slavic?

DOLORES: Slavic, Serbian, South Philly—

ZOOT: Monsieur Boockette ees on iz whey.

DOLORES: Que?

BOP: Hang ten, the boss is on the lam.

DOLORES: The ad didn't say I'd need simultaneous translation.

(SHRIMP *enters. Very bad taste: polyester and velvet.*)

SHRIMP: May I help you?

DOLORES: I hope so. I'm here about the ethnic dancing ad.

SHRIMP: (*Sizing her up.*) Yes, yes, you look the part. Of course, I don't hire the dancers, I just run the audition.

DOLORES: (*Alarmed*) Mr. Bucket?

SHRIMP: I'm Mr. Shrimp Bucket. My brother, Gut Bucket—

(*Ominous underscoring from* BLIND SAX *whenever* GUT'S *name is mentioned.*)

(TAXI, *watching the flashback, pricks up his ears.*)

TAXI: Hmmm. Ominous underscoring.

SHRIMP: —has final say-so on the ethnics. I do the local talent. Yo-yo artistes. Geeks. Talking dogs. Doctor Gut—

(*Ominous underscoring*)

SHRIMP: —is tied up in the Ice Bucket at the moment. If you'd care to wait, Miss—

DOLORES: Con Leche.

SHRIMP: Con Leche. Zoot, ring Root. Been dancing long?

DOLORES: Yeah.

SHRIMP: Good. Good. That's swell.

ZOOT: (*Into phone.*) Root? Zoot. Toot Sweet.

DOLORES: (*Overly casual*) You feature ethnic dancing? Or is this a new thing?

SHRIMP: Ethnic dancing? Are you kidding? We're famous for it. The Clam Room: Tops in Ethnic Dancing. The Best Ethnic Dancing in Town. Wow. We just lost our lead ethnic dancer. She'd been with us for quite some time.

DOLORES: Why'd she leave? Didn't she like it here?

SHRIMP: She loved it. But she had to get out of the business.

DOLORES: Have I heard of her?

SHRIMP: You ask a lot of questions. For a dancer. Mitzi Montenegro. Know her?

DOLORES: No.

SHRIMP: I find that hard to believe, Miss Con Leche. Small world, ethnic dancing. Let me intro the leftover staff. That's Zoot Alors. He's—the night man.

DOLORES: We met.

ZOOT: Yew bet. Enchante. Pairhops Ah could interest yew in un course of stoody a L'Ecole Maurice Chevalier?

SHRIMP: Peddle your accents agues on your time. This is the Bop Op. The Bop Op is wearing a brown pin-stripe suit, a brown button-down shirt from Brooks Brothers, brown socks, brown tie, brown Florsheim shoes, and chocolate brown Bill Blass boxer shorts. He's a very conservative dresser, but that's okay, we love him.

BOP: Hotel Security. How ya doin'?

SHRIMP: And don't mess with him. He's a brown belt.

(ROOT *enters.*)

SHRIMP: This is Root Choyce, Third World piano bar piano player and part-time ponce. Root tickles the ivories in the Clam Room.

ROOT: I don't take requests.

(BLIND SAX *plays a riff.*)

SHRIMP: Oh, yeah. Out of sight, out of mind. This is Blind Sax.

DOLORES: Nice to meet you, Mr. Sax.

SHRIMP: Be kind when you call him blind, Miss Con Leche. He's super sensitive. We here at the Heartbreak like to say Blind Sax is "visually challenged."

DOLORES: Okay, I can relate to that.

SHRIMP: I thought you could. Zoot, Cherchez les femmes?

ZOOT: Les gals are in rehearsal, mon boss.

SHRIMP: A real duo, know what I mean? Well, now that you've met the suspects—

(*Everyone laughs, "heh, heh."*)

SHRIMP: —why don't you cool your heels? Your audition's tonight, right here in the lobby. Root, show Miss Con Leche to her room. My brother, Doctor Gut—

(*Ominous underscoring*)

SHRIMP: —will be with you shortly. I do hope it works out.

DOLORES: So do I. Thanks a lot, Mr. Bucket.

SHRIMP: Don't mention it. In fact, don't ever mention it again. To anyone. Blind Sax, a little traveling music, please.

(ZOOT *rings bell.*)

ZOOT: Root.

ROOT: Zoot. Walk this way.

(BLIND SAX *plays ominous underscoring as* DOLORES *tries gamely to walk like* ROOT *as he wends his way to her room.*)

DOLORES: (*To* TAXI) That was easier said than done. This weird music was following me and I had a creepy feeling about the whole set-up.

TAXI: Could be the ominous underscoring. Hard-boiled tip number one: Trust your underscoring. Did you know Mitzi Montenegro?

DOLORES: (*Suspiciously evasive*) Why?

TAXI: I thought we might ring her bell. Check her pulse. Scan her polygraph.

DOLORES: Never heard of her.

(DOLORES *returns to the flashback and walks into a pool of light.* ROOT *hands her a key.*)

ROOT: Enjoy.

(*He exits.*)

DOLORES: This isn't the Holiday Inn, Toto.

(*She unwraps a hotel drinking glass and pours water into it from a pitcher. It foams madly.*)

DOLORES: I'd have to be stupid to drink this.

(*She drinks. Lights and music as she swoons dead away. The room crackles and glows.*)

(*Blackout*)

(DOLORES *re-appears in a pin spot.*)

TAXI: You blacked out.

DOLORES: Like there was no tomorrow. I knew the tap water in this town was muy malo agua, but oh man! When I came to, I staggered over to my audition. I had the strangest feeling I'd been dancing in my sleep. I was so tired my legs felt like Spandex.

(*She meets* SHRIMP *in the lobby.*)

SHRIMP: Miss Con Leche. Have a nice nap? You look so fresh.

DOLORES: Is it safe to drink the water?

SHRIMP: Don't be ridiculous.

(MUSTANG SALLY *and* DIZZY MISS LIZZY *saunter in. They wear Balkan folk dancing outfits: full skirts, peasant blouses, beaded vests, braided hair, the works.*)

SHRIMP: Meet the Balkanettes.

SALLY: This is the last time I wear these duds.

SHRIMP: Mustang Sally and Dizzy Miss Lizzy. Ladies, this is Miss Con Leche. She's here to audition for lead ethnic dancer.

SALLY: Shrimp, you mollusc meat. You promised to bag this ethnic dancing bull when Mitzi bit the bullet.

DOLORES: Mitzi Montenegro?

SALLY: She a friend a yours, softball?

DOLORES: Never heard of her.

SHRIMP: Clam down, Sal. Let's do this audition.

SALLY: Crustacean face.

(*The* BALKANETTES *do a little "Balkan Boogie", a discofied Balkan folksong.* DOLORES *picks it up with no problem.* SHRIMP *applauds.*)

DOLORES: You call that ethnic?

SHRIMP: (*Hurt*) I do.

LIZZY: (*Sotto voce*) He's the choreographer.

DOLORES: Oh, it's good. But try this.

(*She signals the band. The music changes to liquid Latino. She does the sinuous steps of* "Mango Smoothie." SALLY *and* LIZZY *try to follow suit.* SHRIMP *even does a little impromptu choreography:*)

SHRIMP: Oh, that's nice! Try this! And this! Oh, I like it like that! Look at that cake action!

(*Flamboyant finish*)

SHRIMP: That was extra, extra special. I'm impressed. What do you call that?

DOLORES: Mango Smoothie.

SHRIMP: I have to check with my brother, Doctor Gut—

(*Ominous underscoring*)

SHRIMP: —but I think we might have a relationship here.

DOLORES: Oh, Mr. Shrimp, thank you so—

SHRIMP: Don't mention nada, I told you.

SALLY: Not too shabby.

LIZZY: I liked it.

SALLY: Hey, Mex.

DOLORES: Que hey, Tex.

SALLY: You're good. Let me give you some unsolicited advice.

SHRIMP: Sally—

SALLY: Clam up, bivalve. I've seen your type before, Ceviche—

DOLORES: Con Leche.

SALLY: At least once. Take it from me. Watch your steps.

LIZZY: See you at show time. It's going to be great working with you. Can't wait. Bye.

(*They exit, cake-walking.*)

DOLORES: What did she mean? Watch your step?

SHRIMP: Isn't that something you dancers say to one another? Maybe she's afraid she can't cut the con carne.

DOLORES: Oh no, she's good. Well, not that good.

(*A phone rings.* SHRIMP *answers, listens a moment.*)

SHRIMP: I couldn't agree more.

(*Hangs up.*)

SHRIMP: Miss Con Leche, you start tonight. My brother, Doctor Gut—

(*Ominous underscoring*)

SHRIMP: —was most impressed by your audition. He ate up the tape with a spoon. Beautiful superb and I loved it. His exact words.

DOLORES: Oh, that's bueno, Mr. Bucket.

SHRIMP: Keep it under your fruit bowl, kid.

DOLORES: Carmen Miranda couldn't carry my maracas!

SHRIMP: I'm sure she couldn't. See you tonight in the Clam Room. And, Miss Con Leche—

DOLORES: Yes, Mr. Bucket?

SHRIMP: Try and get some rest. Heh heh.

(SHRIMP *cackles and exits. Lights and music dissolve* DOLORES *re-joins* TAXI.)

TAXI: (*In the VO*) It looked like a cut-and-blow-dried case of Mickey One, pure and simplex. I didn't put much stock in her yarn about sleep dancing and dream stealing. It was my job to soothe her fevered brow. Taxi, the human tranq.

DOLORES: Don't do that. It makes me nervous.

TAXI: Sorry. I didn't make the mysterious Doctor Gut's mug in the flashback lineup.

(*Ominous underscoring*)

DOLORES: I've been here for months, and I still haven't seen him. He's elusive.

(*Ominous underscoring swells.*)

DOLORES: You gotta help me, Taxi. I need my dreams. And my legs feel like paella.

TAXI: Why? Why you? Why dreams?

DOLORES: That's why I hired you, Mr. Taxi. That's your bag.

TAXI: That's my racket, Miss Con Leche, and I'm gonna bag it. Lookee, Miss Con Leche, dreams aren't my limo. Hot merch, that's my feedbag. Your basic electronic tube gear that's taken a stroll in felony shoes. The spouse that's a louse, fun on the run. Dreams? I wouldn't know where to begin. I'd be standing there in my flat feet with this big black cartoon balloon coming out of my mouth—and eggnog all over my mugshot.

DOLORES: I'll give you a hand. How hard can it be?

TAXI: I told you, knock off the dick jokes.

DOLORES: Really, you're too sensitive.

TAXI: It's my tragic flaw.

DOLORES: Mr. Taxi, someone is running a number on me. I wanna know who, and I wanna know why. Somebody's trying to cash my ticket. You think I'm meshuga, Mr. Taxi?

TAXI: Murder by exhaustion and bad choreography? Meshuga? No. Exotic, but not meshuga.

Dolores: I feel like I'm the star of a creature feature, Mr. Taxi. I want some relief from these drive-in movie scenes.

(*She sings* I'm Not Dreaming, *an overwrought ballad.*)

I'm Not Dreaming

Dolores:
I'm not dreaming anymore
Gave it up don't know what for
I'm not dreaming por favor
No I'm not
I got no dreams to dream to amaze me
Is this a scam or scheme to aphase me
Fluster or haze me
Make me muy crazy

I'm not dreaming the dreams I once had
I'm not dreaming it's making me sad
I'm not dreaming when I say
I'm not dreaming

If dreams were money
I wouldn't have a dime
If dreams were dialogue
I'd be quiet as a mime
If dreams were liquor
I'd be sober all the time
I'm a plain glass of tonic
and I can't find a lime

I'm not dreaming the dreams I once had
I'm not dreaming my nights are all bad
I'm not dreaming when I say
I'm not dreaming

(*Poignant finish*)

Taxi: Sleep dancing. Dream stealing. Homicidal insomnia. (*Snaps fingers*) Somebody trying to flip your hotcakes. Now that's an old-fashioned celluloid motive I can get next to. They say, Miss Con Leche, that if you don't dream you eventually book yourself a cruise on the Big Banana Boat. Let's say somebody decides to *interfere* with your sleep. They convince you your dreams are being stolen. Try telling the cops somebody's stealing your sleep. You'd be a wasp-waist cinch for certification as a solid-gold paranoid.

DOLORES: You're not such a slouch after all.

TAXI: It's a pretty-out scenario, Miss Con Leche. Who'd buy a set-up like that?

DOLORES: You would.

TAXI: You're right. I would. Look, before I dip my wick any further, let's get something straight between us. I get fifty clams a day. Plus plenty of sauce for expenses. Boil or steam, no fry. Doctor's orders. A hundred in front, before I even start breathing.

DOLORES: No dinero. No habla B-movie lingo.

TAXI: Look, sis, you're cute and Hispanic as hell, and when I look down into the depths of those lucious dark eyes I get vertigo and calico and Monaco and like that, but your good looks won't pay my bar bill—

DOLORES: Chew on this.

TAXI: American Express Gold Card!

DOLORES: A movie mogul passed out in his Sumatra Slush. I lifted it lightly.

TAXI: Never even fondled one before.

DOLORES: Ought to be kosher 'til Monday.

(TAXI *gets suave.*)

TAXI: I'm a sucker for a pretty face. Miss Con Leche, I didn't catch your moniker.

DOLORES: Not Monica. Dolores.

TAXI: Dolores. Dolores Con Leche. Sorrows with milk.

DOLORES: I didn't know you were quite the linguist, Mr. Taxi.

TAXI: Hang around. I may surprise you. Since I'm on the payroll—may I call you Dolores?

DOLORES: Not a chance.

TAXI: You're on. So, who wants to scramble your sweetbreads, sweetheart? Why such a screwy way of driving you batshit?

DOLORES: Grill the Balkanettes. They hate ethnic dancing. They want Shrimp to feature Nuevo Huevo music in the Clam Room.

TAXI: Nuevo Huevo? New Egg?

Dolores: They call themselves the Omelettes.

Taxi: (*Sighs*) If only this were a Ross McDonald. Family skeletons. Criminality recapitulated in blood. Classy shit. (*Beat*) New Egg music seems like a kinda slim motive to hang a scam like this on. I got a million questions, Miss Con Leche, and no answers. And in my book, that just doesn't add up. We're going to have to go back in.

Dolores: Walk this way.

(*She starts off. What a walk.*)

Taxi: (*In the VO*) But there was no way I could walk that way. She had a walk that made my circumlocutions look like straight talk. And a pair of gams that could raise gooseflesh on a tossed salad. And they went all the way up to the top of her legs. I didn't exactly put a down payment on her story—but her walk had me more than a little intrigued.

Dolores: Will you stop talking like that?

Taxi: Sorry. Bad habit. Too many years living alone.

(Dolores, *mock sultry, puts her arms around* Taxi.)

Dolores: Taxi, tell me. What's so private about a dick?

Taxi: It's not fair, you know. I'm an innocent victim of slang warp.

Dolores: I've been dying to know, why do they call them gumshoes?

Taxi: Can the snappy patter with syrup, sister. I don't even understand it. Let's make waves. We'll look into this—(*Beat*) dream snatch.

(*Pause*)

Dolores: Okay. Truce.

(*As they start into the Heartbreak,* Taxi *checks his gun.*)

Taxi: Rod. Roscoe. Gat. Heater.

(Root, Blind Sax, Zoot, *and* The Bop Op *appear.* Taxi *sniffs.*)

Taxi: (*In the VO*) The Heartbreak was a definite sushi bar, crawling with once and future co-defendants.

(*Hostile stares from* The Heartbreakers.)

BOP: House rules. No private moments. Talk to yourself again, buddy, you're history. You're a silent flick that's been sliced into guitar picks. Got me?

TAXI: Yeah. Yeah. I got ya.

DOLORES: Chill out, you guys.

(SHRIMP *enters.*)

SHRIMP: Dolores. Looking forward to the show tonight, sweetheart. Those new steps are—what's the word? Crepuscular.

DOLORES: Crepuscular?

SHRIMP: Why not? Who's your little friend?

DOLORES: Mr. Shrimp, this is James Taxi. He's here for the show. James Taxi, Shrimp Bucket.

SHRIMP: What's your racket, Mr. Taxi?

TAXI: Talent scout. Really. How about you, Mr. Bucket?

SHRIMP: This joint is chez moi.

TAXI: My condolences to the chef.

SHRIMP: You write your own stuff. I like that in a man. Let me intro the leftover staff. This is the Bop Op.

BOP: Hotel security. Got any valuables?

TAXI: Yeah.

BOP: Hand 'em over.

(THE BOP OP *pockets* TAXI'S *wallet and watch.* SALLY *and* DOLORES *enter.*)

SHRIMP: A real duo, Mr. Taxi. Mustang Sally and Dizzy Miss Lizzy. Root Choyce palpitates the eighty-eights in the Clam Room.

ROOT: I don't take—

TAXI: Requests. But I got a request right now. Fast forward through the intro, pal. I caught 'em in the flashback.

SHRIMP: Miss Con Leche's been filling you in?

TAXI: In a manner of speaking.

SHRIMP: Good things I hope.

DOLORES: Nothing but the best.

Shrimp: Well then, you already know that Professor Alors runs L'Ecole Maurice Chevalier.

Zoot: Yew mai call moi Zoot. Pairhops I can interest yew in a course of stoody a L'Ecole Maurice Chevalier?

Shrimp: God, I love the way you say that.

Taxi: You don't get French lessons at the better hotels. I find that comforting.

Shrimp: We aim to be a full-service hotel. Professor Alors does not teach French, he teaches French accent.

Zoot: Yew nevair know when an accent ague mai sev yewour life.

Taxi: (*In the VO*) Professor Alors' accent smelled like brie, and the whole joint gave off an over-ripe odor like a bistro on a bad day.

Bop: I warned you about that, fella. Don't make me have to get litigious with you.

Zoot: Why yew talk lak zat? Lisson, yew should talk lak zees. Lak moi. An yew can. Zo easy. Zhust enroll at L'Ecole Maurice Chevalier, ze worl will be your camembaert.

Taxi: Tres bibliotheque, pal, but I'll pass.

Zoot: Zoot yourself.

Shrimp: He also slings slang. You oughta take from him, Taxi. Be good for business.

Taxi: I don't follow you.

Shrimp: You could use some work on your lingo noir, Mr. Taxi.

Taxi: Lingo noir? I'm a talent scout, Mr. Bucket. I told you.

Shrimp: I know you did.

Sally and Lizzy: A talent scout? A talent scout? Really?

Taxi: (*In the super sincere showbiz manner*) Really. Trust me.

(Taxi *sings* Talent Scout, *a snappy number with a calypso/soca flavoring.* Sally *and* Dizzy *sing backup.* Dizzy *is really smitten.*)

Talent Scout

Taxi:
If you do your thing in dry ice fog
You call my number and I'll be there
I get the chills for a talking dog
You can trust my guts I'm on the square.

'Cause I'm a talent scout
        Talent scout
Now hear me out

If you doff your duds or don a drag
I'll break a leg to catch your act
Got a kinky twist or a twisted gag
I'll go anywhere and that's a fact

'Cause I'm a talent scout
        It's in the bag
Talent scout
        Without a doubt
Talent scout
        He's got the clout

TAXI: All the tappers and the rappers and the breakers and the fakers and the strippers with their zippers say get a load of this you
Talent Scout
All the over actors and the Green Bay Packers and the substance smugglers and the chainsaw jugglers and the wheeler dealers and the touchy feelers say hey look at me you
Talent Scout

Everybody wants to be in show business!

I'm a
        Talent Scout
Oh twist and shout
        A Talent Scout
Come on talk about
        A Talent Scout
Now hear me out
        A Talent Scout
Everybody wants to be in show business!
Not sauerkraut
        A Talent Scout
I got the clout
'Cause I'm a talent
I'm a talent
I'm a talent
I'm a talent
        Oh what a talent
Talent Scout!

(*Big finish*)

SHRIMP: Big hands! Big hands! Aren't they lovely, superb, and extra extra special?

TAXI: Nice job, girls, really.

BOP: Local talent.

LIZZY: Don't get cute, Boppo. You here for the show, Mr. Taxi?

TAXI: Looking forward to it.

LIZZY: So am I.

TAXI: What do you do? In the show, I mean.

SHRIMP: The Balkanettes sing backup for Dolores.

SALLY: Temporarily. That is strictly a temporary arrangement.

SHRIMP: We'll talk about it later.

SALLY: You bet we will, prawn prick.

SHRIMP: Ladies, meet me upstairs in my office. If you'll excuse us, Mr. Taxi.

(SHRIMP *and* THE HEARTBREAKERS *turn to go.*)

TAXI: Is Mitzi Montenegro still on the bill?

(*They all wheel around and stare at* TAXI.)

SHRIMP: You know Mitzi like I know Mitzi?

TAXI: It's my business to know, Mr. Bucket. Every aficionado of ethnic dancing knows Mitzi Montenegro, the Balkan Bombshell.

SHRIMP: Miss Con Leche said she'd never heard of her. Which led me to believe that Mitzi was—obscure.

TAXI: Oh. Well. Dancers. What do they know? Where's Mitzi boiling her bulgar these days? I'd like to catch her act.

SHRIMP: You're out of luck, Mr. Taxi. The Balkan Blockbuster said so long to the ever-sweaty world of ethnic dancing some time ago. In fact, Mitzi's in—home appliances now. She's cool. Heh heh.

HEARTBREAKERS: Heh heh.

(*They all exit.*)

TAXI: I guess Mitzi wasn't, you know—well-liked.

DOLORES: Take it light, Tax. Cool the monologues.

TAXI: Don't tell me my business.

DOLORES: I gotta go warm up.

TAXI: I'll take a quick snoop see. Glom some loose threads.

DOLORES: Check out my room. Maybe you'll pick up something.

TAXI: That's what I'm afraid of. Just kidding. Don't hit me.

DOLORES: Meet me in the Clam Room.

TAXI: Right.

(DOLORES *exits.* TAXI's *alone.*)

TAXI: (*In the VO*) Something Shrimp said had me sweating like a bad paint job. That crack about lingo noir. Were the flats of my feet showing? And Dolores. The name meant sadness en Español. And I had a hunch this case was gonna bring me more than my share of grief. Why didn't she bag this gig? Something was keeping Con Leche tied to this clip joint. Was it Mitzi? What is Mitzi Montenegro to her, or she to Mitzi Montenegro?

(THE BOP OP *has entered quietly behind* TAXI.)

BOP: That is the question.

TAXI: (*Screams*) Hah!

(*He turns around, hands in the air. Looks at* BOP, *looks at his own hands up, covers by pointing with both index fingers still above his head.*)

TAXI: What's your racket?

BOP: Hotel security. What's yours?

(BOP *frisks* TAXI, *who still has his hands in the air.* BOP *removes* TAXI's *rod.*)

BOP: Talent scout, huh?

TAXI: Show business is the toughest business there is, Mr. Op.

BOP: Don't get cute. I'll just keep this for you. Until you check out.

TAXI: Where do I find Doctor Gut?

(*Ominous underscoring.* TAXI *starts.*)

TAXI: Geez, do you ever get used to the soundtrack shadowing you all over the set?

BOP: It's like traffic. I don't even hear it anymore.

(TAXI *ostentatiously picks his teeth with a dollar bill.*)

TAXI: What's your alias?

BOP: What's yours, big boy?

TAXI: Taxi. James Taxi.

BOP: Oh, right. Well, Mr. Taxi. Why don't you—why don't you—(*Barely suppressed hilarity*) call me a cab?

TAXI: I've heard that one.

BOP: I'll bet you have.

(TAXI *picks his teeth with a second bill.*)

BOP: You couldn't pry it out of me with a crowbar—

(TAXI *adds a third bill.*)

BOP: —that Doctor Gut—

(*Ominous underscoring*)

BOP: —is tied up in the Ice Bucket.

(TAXI *hands* BOP *the bills. He shakes them dry.*)

TAXI: How do I get to the Ice Bucket?

BOP: You don't. Off limits.

(TAXI *writes him a check.*)

BOP: Got two pieces of I.D.?

TAXI: My wallet's in your pocket.

BOP: And it's gonna stay there. Make an isosceles triangle and take the first fire escape on the left. All the way to the top. (*Looks at check.*) Add a zero to this, I might get careless with my pass key.

(TAXI *changes the check.* BOP *tosses the key.* TAXI *catches it.*)

BOP: Have it back in an hour.

TAXI: Beat it, thumbprint. I gotta talk to myself.

BOP: Whatever gets you off.

(BOP *exits.*)

TAXI: (*In the VO*) I kept a gimlet eye open for the nearest fire escape. Now that I had the keys to the kingdom, I decided to take the grand tour.

(*Lights and music.* TAXI *in a spot.*)

TAXI: (*In the VO*) My first stop was the Ice Bucket. It didn't take a detective to find it. I just followed the dry ice to the door.

(*He travels. Clouds of dry ice.*)

TAXI: (*In the VO*) The fire escape was slicker than sea urchin roe.

(*He arrives at the Ice Bucket just as* DOLORES *appears and knocks on door.* SHRIMP *answers. Dry ice and sax music seep out of the Ice Bucket.*)

SHRIMP: Dolores. What a treat.

DOLORES: (*Checking out dry ice.*) Hey! Muy hielo seco!

SHRIMP: I thought dry ice en Español was hielo carbonico.

DOLORES: Could be. Is Doctor Gut here?

(*Ominous underscoring*)

SHRIMP: No. But he left these for you. (*Hands her a vial.*)

DOLORES: Gracias so much.

SHRIMP: How's your insomnia?

DOLORES: I'm syncopated. I think I've got anemia, too. I'm beat.

SHRIMP: You do look run-down. I'll have—

(*Ominous underscoring starts.* SHRIMP *cuts it off.*)

SHRIMP: You know who—prescribe some animal vitamins.

DOLORES: Well. Okay.

SHRIMP: Trust me. They'll do you a world of good. Ciao.

DOLORES: Later.

(*He ushers her out. As she leaves,* BOP *joins* SHRIMP.)

BOP: Dolores. What a dream, huh? (*He laughs uproariously.*)

SHRIMP: Don't wear it out. Who's her friend?

BOP: Half-baked hawkshaw. Bargain-basement shamus. (*Takes out gun.*) I relieved him of this antiquated armament.

SHRIMP: (*Gives* BOP *a look.*) I knew it. I've got an instinct for these things. Why would our milky señorita bring a hawkshaw into the Heartbreak?

Bop: Maybe she's got wise. (*Smiles*) Mitzi got wise, too.

(*They share an unpleasant laugh.*)

Shrimp: Take care of him after the show. He mustn't muck up our meeting with our little Asian muckamuck.

Bop: In my mind, he's already relegated to the dustbin of history.

Shrimp: (*Gives him a look.*) See how they're doing downstairs.

Bop: You're the boss.

Shrimp: Yes. Yes, I am.

(*Lights and music.* Shrimp *fades.* Taxi *follows* Bop.)

Taxi: (*In the VO*) I followed Bop to the laundry. Zoot was doing a quick starch and steam. He didn't seem too happy about it.

(Bop *enters laundry.* Zoot *holds up a three-fingered glove.*)

Zoot: Cherchez eets mate? Zere ees anozer one of zees. Ahve yew seen eet?

Bop: Uh-oh. Check his coat pockets?

Zoot: Oui. Oui. Bon idear. Oh, eef Ah don't find zat glove, zee boz weel be furryous.

Bop: More than furryous. Livid, positively. Shrimp wants him to look his best for the Big Noise from Nauru. That means both gloves, babe.

Zoot: Ah! I am un dead man! Monsieur Croque!

Bop: Relax. You don't want to hyperventilate down here in all this humidity. I'll take a look around outside.

Zoot: Merci, merci. Yew are un lumberjacques of un prince.

Bop: For you, Frenchie.

(Bop *blows him a kiss, and fades. Lights and music.* Zoot *exits, singing* Three-Fingered Glove *in French.*)

Taxi: (*In the VO*) Bop's passkey was solid gold. It was making things easy. Maybe too easy. My next port of call was a bug on the pay phone.

(*Lights and music.* Taxi *puts a transistor in his ear, as* Root *appears in a pool of light talking on the phone.*)

Taxi: (*In the VO*) Bingo.

ROOT: (*On phone*) Hey, this is a sophisticated device. State of the art. He's gonna get a look at their very very special stuff. They're gonna pull out the stops, kick out the jams, and boogie their sneakers away for this hombre. Where is Nauru anyway? I heard bird guano. The whole lousy island, nothing but bird guano. Bird guano is what I heard, chucko.

(*Lights and music.* ROOT *out.*)

TAXI: (*In the VO*) Suddenly there was more thickener in the plot than corn starch in a coffee shop cherry pie. The meter was still running on Bop's passkey. On my way to the Clam Room, I stopped off to chat up the Balkanettes.

(SALLY *and* DIZZY *in a spot.* SHRIMP *enters.*)

SALLY: If it ain't the invertebrate.

SHRIMP: Five minutes, girls. It's showtime! You remember the new steps?

SALLY: They suck gazpacho, Shrimp head. Stupid steps.

LIZZY: Stupid costumes.

SHRIMP: (*Hurt*) I designed those myself. You ought to be nicer to me. Remember, ladies. Mitzi Montenegro!

(*He stalks out.* TAXI *steps in.*)

LIZZY: Remember what happened to Mitzi Montenegro.

TAXI: Just what did happen to Mitzi? How are you, ladies?

LIZZY: Better and better.

SALLY: Her career didn't work out. The way she planned.

TAXI: She's not happy in home appliances?

SALLY: Why are you so interested in Mitzi, Mr. Talent Scout? She was a lousy dancer.

TAXI: Mitzi was my client. I was her agent. That's a sacred relationship.

SALLY: We don't know where she is.

LIZZY: Honest. Hope you like the show, Mr. Taxi.

TAXI: I have my doubts. Eastern European ethnic dancing.

SALLY: Stand back!

(*They tear off their Balkanettes costumes: amplified Velcro! Underneath, they are wearing black leathers, black boots, nylon wigs, switchblades. From Balkanettes to Ronettes.*)

SALLY: The Balkanettes are as passé as Raisinettes. From now on, it's The Omelettes!

TAXI: I take it you're ready to rock 'n roll all night.

LIZZY: All night. Wanna join us? We could go dancing after the show. New Egg music's gonna be the next big thing.

TAXI: I can definitely say I'm not altogether uninterested. We'll talk. After the show.

(*Lights and music.* DIZZY *and* SALLY *fade.*)

TAXI: (*In the VO*) The questions were mounting up like a stack of unpaid utilities bills, and I had to find the answers before somebody turned off the lights. I had a feeling this case wouldn't be brief. Brief. Brief.

(*Rescued by the band: music.*)

TAXI: Showtime?

BAND: Showtime!

TAXI: (*In the VO*) That was my cue to cut to the chase.

(*The lights come up full on The Clam Room. A couple of tables. Chase lights.* THE BOP OP *is the maitre d'.*)

BOP: This way, Mr. Taxi.

(*He seats* TAXI *at one of the onstage tables.* TAXI *is the only customer.*)

TAXI: Is it always this slow?

BOP: It's been better. What'll you have?

TAXI: Ramos fizz. Do I have to be this close? I'll get sequin burn on my retinas.

BOP: You're the talent scout, aren't ya?

TAXI: Right. Right.

(BOP *exits. Music! Chase lights! Spots!*)

(*THE CLAM ROOM: a gaudy sign.* SHRIMP *bounds on, mike in hand, big fanfare, his theme music:* Shrimp Louie.)

(*The Band shouts the refrain from offstage:*)

SHRIMP LOUIE

SHRIMP:
I'm a burnin' burnin' hunk of Shrimp (Shrimp Louie o Shrimp Louie)
I'm a burnin' burnin' hunk of Shrimp (Shrimp Louie o Shrimp Louie)
Don't fuss with the dressin'
'Cause you know you ain't messin'
(Shrimp Louie to go Shrimp Louie)

(*Repeat*)

(*Big finish*)

Shrimp Louie—
Eat it every day!

(*Big resolving chord from band.*)

SHRIMP: Thank you. Thank you. Thank you. So sweet so sweet so really nice 'n neat. (*Waves to* TAXI.) Our special guest tonight, ladies and gentlemen, Mr. James Taxi, a big-time talent scout. Thanks for joining us, Jimmy, here in the ever-humid Clam Room. You're gonna get an eyeful of local talent tonight, I guarantee it. You slay me, Jimmy, just slay me. Right off the old drugstore rack. (*Sincere beat*) Hi. I'm your host, Shrimp Bucket. Welcome to the always nectarious Clam Room and our show, Crack of Dawn, I know you're gonna just cream all over it—saaaaaaaaaaaaaaaaaaaaay (*Pointing to lights out front.*) Those mixed fruit gels are really something. Talk about your saturated color! Wow! What is that? Vacation pink! And lavender surprise! And over there a hot rod cherry red! All the way from Vegas, these guys do a super job, ladies and gentlemen, big hands! Big hands! Aren't they beautiful superb and extra extra special? Say, welcome to the ever-livid Clam Room! The temperature's rising we're getting hot hot hot! While we're waiting for our opening number here in the ever-hepatatic Clam Room—(*Sings á la Johnny Mathis*)

Let me entertain you
Let me conk your hair

SHRIMP: (*Toothy smile*) that's just a teaser, folks. More of me anon.

And speaking of digits—direct from their record-breaking engagement in the attic of the Heartbreak, where they've been going at it hammer and tong—here to smash some of their very own platters, and spread sunshine and broken petro-chemical plastic all over the place—let's give a hot chowder Clam Room wilkommen to—The Four Freshpersons! Doing their latest—look out it's hot—*Vegetable Medley! Vegetable Medley!* The Four Freshpersons!

(ROOT, ZOOT, BOP, *and* BLIND SAX *in matching jackets, do an all-purpose soul medley: wonderful harmonies, dramatic shifts in rhythms, great synchronized dance steps.*)

VEGETABLE MEDLEY

BOP, ROOT, ZOOT, and BLIND SAX:
(*Caffeine*)
Early in the morning and all through the night
Mainline mainline straight to my heart
Caffeine caffeine
Caffeine caffeine
Mainline mainline straight to my heart
Put the spike to my heart and shoot it right in
Put the spike to my brain and shoot it again
Give it to me baby hot and black
Give it to me baby don't hold back
Grab an available vein (grab an available)
Grab an available vein (grab an available)
Grab an available vein (grab an available)
Free refill free refill free refill free
Free refill free refill free refill free
Free refill free refill free refill free

(*Into:*)

THE ECHELON OF SCUM

I'm going up and down
On the carousel of crum
I'm floating on the top
Of the echelon of scum
Cause I'm a bad guy
Don't need no alibi
I'm the cream of the crop
And I'm floating to the top
Of the echelon of scum (of the echelon of scum)
I'm a nasty man
That's what I am
I got crime in my bones
I put slime on my scones

You know I do as I please
I'm the crown prince of quease
I'm the créme de la crum
I'm the sultan of scum
I'm the cream of the crop
And I'm floating to the top
Of the echelon of scum (of the echelon of scum)

(*Into:*)

Ethnic Jokes Broke My Baby's Heart

(Zoot *sings lead on* Ethnic Jokes.)

Didja hear the one
That's what they say
Didja hear the one
Every single day

Those ethnic jokes
About my baby
Those ethnic jokes
They drove her crazy
Those ethnic jokes they broke my baby's heart

I heard that one, sucker
It ain't funny
I heard that one turkey
You'd better run for your money

They'd tell those jokes
About her brother
They'd tell those jokes about her mother
Those ethnic jokes they broke my baby's heart

Zoot: (*Spoken*)
She's gone away now I don't know where
To a place where they don't tell those kind of jokes
To a better world—somewhere

(*Bass:*) The melting pot ain't so hot

Ethnic jokes about my baby
Ethnic jokes they drove her crazy
(*Repeats twice*)
They broke my baby's heart

(*Into:*)

PUT YOUR LEGS ON MY SHOULDERS
Put your legs on my shoulders
I'll drive you round the bend
I know you're feeling bolder
Wake the neighbors up again
If you're feeling colder
Put your legs
Put your legs
Put your legs
On my shoulders
Yeah!

(*Big finish and choreographed exit*)

SHRIMP: The Four Freshpersons! The Four Freshpersons! Aren't they beautiful superb and extra extra special? We'll continue with "Calamity in the Clam Room" in just a few days, but first—I want to speak to you directly. Mano a mano. That's the great thing about live theatre. That communication—can I have the house lights please?

(*House lights come up.* SHRIMP *surveys audience.*)

SHRIMP: Great. That communication between us—and you. That living, breathing, okay mistakes *can* happen kind of communication. The theatre is the last bastion of *live* entertainment. As you may not know—or even believe—the price of a ticket doesn't begin to cover costs. Not even close. There's what you see—lights, costumes, sets, actors. The band. And there's what you don't see. Hidden costs. Limos, lunches, lingerie. Ludes. Union kickbacks. Just kidding, fellas. Don't turn off the lights. But seriously, there are hidden expenses. And sometimes we just can't hide them any longer. I don't think I have to tell you folks—(*To audience member*)—Try to work with the drug. *With* it. (*Back to audience*)—I don't have to tell you about inflation. A show like this one, expenses have just gone through the roof over last season. You know, if we were to cover costs through ticket sales alone, we'd have to sell each seat five times. Five times. And that would be mighty uncomfortable. Think about it. (*To audience member*)—Keep clam, keep clam. It wasn't that good. (*Big*) Hey! We're having some fun now! And now—accompanied by the ever-lactating Balkanettes—the star of our show—the filibrating thrush herself—the Hispanic Hyperventilator—Dolores Con Leche!

(DOLORES, *with* SALLY *and* LIZZY. *Splashy entrance, gorgeous gowns, wigs. Motown heaven. They sing* Never Judge a Thriller.)

NEVER JUDGE A THRILLER BY ITS COVER

DOLORES WITH SALLY AND LIZZY:
Never judge a thriller by its cover
Never judge a thriller by its cover
Never judge a thriller by its cover
No no no

DOLORES:
I'm a thriller baby
I'm a paperback broad
I'm a killer baby
Read me out loud
Turn my pages sweetheart
And follow my plot
Don't skip a single chapter
'Cause I'm hot hot hot

Never judge a thriller by its cover
Never judge a thriller by its cover
Never judge a thriller by its cover
No no no

I'm a chiller baby
I'm a drugstore dame
I'm a killer baby
That's my claim to fame
Don't quit till you finish
Till we get to the end
Then we can start all over again

(*Refrain*)

(*During an instrumental break,* BLIND SAX *wailing,* DOLORES *transforms herself into the classic image of a pulp covergirl: strap down over on shoulder, cigarette, smoking derringer. Thus transformed, she sings:* "I'm a Spine-Tingler, Baby"—*but the lights suddenly go out, and the sound grinds down, like a record player whose plug has just been pulled. Then, just as suddenly, the lights come back on, and the music whirls back up to speed. In the blackout,* TAXI *has gotten up and is standing in the middle of the stage. He attempts to speak to* DOLORES, *but she ignores him as the* BALKANETTES *finish their set:*)

DOLORES:
I'm a spine tingler baby
I'm a pulp coquette
Be a hard guy with me baby
You will never regret
Got a tiny forty-four

Got a hot Corvette you bet
Better go for my cover baby
What you see is what you'll get

Never judge a thriller by its cover
Never judge a thriller by its cover
Never judge a thriller by its cover
No no noooooooooooooooo . . .

Never judge a thriller by its cover
Never judge a thriller by its cover
Never judge a thriller by its cover
No no no no no

(*They exit in a furious finish, leaving* TAXI *alone on stage.*)

(SHRIMP *bounds back on and stands in front of* TAXI.)

SHRIMP: Dolores! Dolores! And the Balkanettes! They'll be back later with some authentic ethnic folk dancing! I guarantee it! Dolores and the Balkanettes! What a warbler! Now that's ornithology! And the dance steps! Don't you just love them? Better than synchronized swimming! They don't call them Balkanettes for nothing! Okay! Kung Fu fighting next! (*To* TAXI) Take your seat, fella. Hey! We're having some fun now! (*To audience member*) I spoke to you earlier about that. Work *with* the drug. The band does.

TAXI: I got a coupla plot points I'd like cleared up.

SHRIMP: You came in late, fella.

TAXI: That's where you're wrong. I've been over my neck in this from the very beginning.

SHRIMP: Come back tomorrow night. I'll flush the rust out of my pipes.

TAXI: I'll pass. I wanna know the whereabouts and general prognosis of Mitzi Montenegro.

SHRIMP: What's it to you?

TAXI: Mitzi was my client.

SHRIMP: Tell me another one, shamus.

(TAXI *grabs* SHRIMP *by the lapels, and being so short lifts himself off the ground.*)

TAXI: Why don't you buy my cover? What's your trick bag, sleazeball? Sing.

SHRIMP: Clam down, fella.

TAXI: And what was that little blackout about? Sounded like somebody pulled the plug.

SHRIMP: You wanna know a lot for the price of admission. Okay, I'll tell you. Yes, what you suspect is all too true. We lipsynch.

TAXI: Very nicely done.

SHRIMP: Thank you. Now you know our nasty little secret. How about you stop wrinkling the merchandise.

TAXI: How about you give me the straight dope on Mitzi Montenegro. If you wanna be around for your encore, pal.

SHRIMP: Since you put it that way, let me put it this way. And this way. And what about this way.

(*As* SHRIMP *puts it various ways,* BOP *brings in* TAXI's *drink. It's foaming madly.*)

TAXI: You're a literal kind of guy, Mr. Bucket. Where's your brother, Doctor Gut?

(*Band plays ominous underscoring Las Vegas big-band style.*)

TAXI: I wanna have words with him.

SHRIMP: My brother is a busy man, Mr. Taxi. He doesn't have time to play private eyes.

BOP: Your Ramos fizz, sir.

TAXI: Oh, no. I'm hip to this motif.

SHRIMP: You make it hard on yourself, Mr. Taxi.

(BOP *saps* TAXI. TAXI *crumples.*)

BOP: Later for you, lightweight.

SHRIMP: (*To* BOP) You young squid you. Let's blow this clam bar.

(Shrimp Louie *reprise,* SHRIMP *booming out his best rock voice:*)

SHRIMP:
I'm a burnin' burnin' hunk of Shrimp (Shrimp Louie o Shrimp Louie)
I'm a burnin' burnin' hunk of Shrimp (Shrimp Louie o Shrimp Louie)
Don't fuss with the dressin'
'Cause you know you ain't messin' with me

Of all the Louies which is the best (Crab Louie?)
No way (St. Louie?)
Get real (Louie Louie?)
Even Louie Louie bites the bag with
Shrimp Louie
Shrimp Louie
Shrimp Louie

Eat it every day

(*The* HEARTBREAKERS *boogie on out, leaving the comatose* TAXI *on stage.*)

(*A blue spot on* TAXI, *face down and unconscious. The spot narrows to a pencil point, then extinguishes. When the house lights come up for intermission,* TAXI *is gone. But left behind is a chalk outline of his body on the floor.*)

*Act Break*

## Act Two

(*A bare stage. Three pools of light. A wooden barstool in one.* TAXI *saunters out, jacket over his shoulder, cool as can be, and sings* Prisoner of Genre.)

PRISONER OF GENRE

TAXI:
I take my coffee black
With a slug of rye or three
I call my mother—"mac"
And you can make all my moves—"B"

I'm addicted to the style
And all my moves are noir
I'm a sucker for a smile
Across a crowded bar

I'm just a prisoner of genre, baby
I guess I've found my niche
I'm just a prisoner of genre, baby
A lonely captive of kitsch

I've surrendered to the slang

I make all my moves in raincoats
I got a roscoe in my pocket
If I thought I had a future
I'd run right out and hock it

I'm just a flat-out flake
I make out in smoky rooms
I'm dying for another take
And living for those zooms

I'm just a prisoner of genre, baby
I guess I've found my niche
I'm just a prisoner of genre, baby
A lonely captive of kitsch

J'adora my fedora

Tap City is my address
Where all the bulbs are bare
My haute cuisine is rice and beans
But I'll do it for the dare
(*Spoken:*)—plus expenses

I've been drugged and sapped
And slugged and slapped
I got neon on the brain
I risk my skin for pocket money
I'm a sucker for a dame

I'm just a prisoner of genre, baby
I'm addicted to the style
So make it confidential
And slip it in your file
I'm just a prisoner of genre, baby
A prisoner, a prisoner—In style.

(*Sweet finish. Lights dissolve to:*)

(*In front of the Heartbreak* TAXI, *out like, well, like the classic sapped hard-boiled gumshoe.*)

(*A reggae bass beat*)

(TAXI *woozes to his feet.*)

TAXI: (*In the VO*) I came to with a Mafiosa construction company slapping together a condo in my back brain. They were working overtime and pounding plenty o' nails. Two brothers, Guiseppe and Antoine. I clawed my way up through concentric spinning circles of trauma, dread, nausea, pain and primary motor dysfunction. (*Staggers*) I was dizzier than a dose of peroxide, and as feverish as a bottle of aspirin. Detective with eggcream all over his punim. C'mon, Taxi. Do something really tough—like get on your feet. You got a New York City driver's license. Prove you deserve it.

(*He swoons.* DOLORES, *entering, catches him.*)

DOLORES: What's so macho about a New York City driver's license?

(*She props him back up.*)

TAXI: License to kill, sweetheart. License to maim.

DOLORES: Natty Taxi. Someone caught you looking uptown instead of down.

TAXI: Just as I had your shrimp-faced boss squirming like aquarium meat. Whoo. I feel like a short chunk of beef jerky. Chewed. I'm fading faster than a forged check.

(DOLORES *straightens him by the lapels.*)

DOLORES: My dreams can't wait until tomorrow.

TAXI: Listen, as far as I'm concerned, your dreams can wait until Jimmy Hoffa shows up to claim his Social Security.

(*She slaps him. He revives.*)

TAXI: Thanks. I dreaded that.

(*Reggae bass beat goes out. He starts off.*)

DOLORES: Where are you going?

TAXI: Home. I've had it. I've had it being pushed around on no sleep, and I've had it being conned by my own client. There are easier and cleaner ways to make a buck, and I'm gonna go find 'em. Right now.

DOLORES: Taxi, you can't leave me. Okay, what do you want?

TAXI: I want you to level with me. Who is Mitzi Montenegro?

DOLORES: Just another ethnic dancer.

TAXI: Sure, sure. They all say that. Say, I caught the show tonight. Boffo charisma, mucho melisma.

DOLORES: What?

TAXI: You're a thrush. You may be an unreliable witness, but I dig the way you warble.

DOLORES: Taxi, I didn't do the show tonight.

TAXI: Don't kid me. I was this far away from you. I may have trouble picking a perp out of a lineup—

DOLORES: No way. I dropped one of Dr. Gut's brain bombers—

(*Ominous underscoring*)

DOLORES: —to pep myself up, and I was out before you could say Tito Puente.

TAXI: Either you've got schizoid amnesia, or the Bucket Brothers have a first-class female female-impersonator. Remember the blackout?

DOLORES: How could I? I told you—

TAXI: Onstage. Somebody tripped the breaker. I got up and whispered to you. You didn't whisper back.

DOLORES: Taxi, I'm telling you. It wasn't me.

TAXI: Mitzi Montenegro—what's she look like?

DOLORES: How should I know?

TAXI: Come clean, Con Leche. She's as familiar to you as a hangnail. Who is she?

DOLORES: My sister.

(TAXI *slaps her.*)

DOLORES: My sister!

(TAXI *slaps her again.*)

DOLORES: My sister!

(TAXI *slaps her again.*)

DOLORES: My sister! (*Slap*) My sister! (*Slap*) My sister!

TAXI: Not your daughter?

DOLORES: My sister!

(*She knocks him down with a right hook. He picks himself up.*)

TAXI: I believe you. Don't hit me again. How long's she been gone?

DOLORES: More than a month.

TAXI: Was Mitzi the type to take a powder and not leave a forwarding address?

DOLORES: Mitzi knew something wasn't on the level. She was just about to go to the authorities when she disappeared.

TAXI: Cops?

DOLORES: Health department. She's my kid sister, Taxi.

TAXI: Say no more. Where I come from, that counts for something. Don't worry, kid. I'll find your dreams.

(DOLORES *grabs him and kisses him three times.*)

DOLORES: Oh, bueno! Mucho! Muchacho! Muchisimo!

TAXI: (*In the VO*) Her lips were a palpable lip batido—

DOLORES: Don't do that in front of me, Taxi. Na Khazan.

TAXI: Que tengo, Con Leche. Whatever you do, don't nod off. Get a cup of joe. Trust me.

DOLORES: I'll take my bombers.

TAXI: Don't you learn from experience? You're strung out like laundry. Fork 'em.

(*She hands him the vial* SHRIMP *gave her.*)

TAXI: Non-prescription speed only. Get the guys to take a long coffee break with you. Then meet me in your room. I have to make a phone call.

DOLORES: Bueno! Let's locate Mitz, Tax! Undulate! Undulate!

(*She exits. He looks after her wistfully.*)

TAXI: (*In the VO*) I would have given a lot to undulate with Con Leche right about then, but time was short and talk is cheap. I had a hunch if I could find Mitzi, I'd clear up this caper like linament on a charley horse. (*Beat*) Well, they can't all be gems. To reorient myself, I did a quick mental hit and run.

(LIZZY *and* SALLY *in a spot.*)

SALLY: Her career didn't work out—

LIZZY: —the way she'd planned.

(SHRIMP *in a spot.*)

SHRIMP: My brother left these for you, Miss Con Leche.

(DOLORES *in a spot.*)

DOLORES: I'm not dreaming the dreams I once had.

(ROOT *in a spot.*)

ROOT: This is a sophisticated device. State of the art.

(ZOOT *in a spot. Holds up a three-fingered glove.*)

ZOOT: Zere ees anozer one of zeez. Have you zeen eet?

(SHRIMP *in a spot.*)

SHRIMP: Doctor Gut—

(*Ominous underscoring*)

SHRIMP: Dug the tape. Beautiful superb and I love it. His exact words.

(BOP *in a spot.*)

BOP: Comidas chinas y criollas! Mofungo!

(TAXI *shakes his head.* SHRIMP *in a spot.*)

SHRIMP: She's in home appliances now. She's cool. Hey, Tax—You're beautiful, baby. Don't ever shave.

(*All begin repeating their lines at once as the lights swim. A babble.* TAXI *cuts it off and everyone disappears.*)

TAXI: (*In the VO*) Those mental hit and runs were tough to take on no sleep. And I wasn't any closer to finding out if Dolores' dreams were being stolen, and if they were, why. But I wasn't born yesterday. I've heard enough ominous underscoring in my time to know that at the bottom of it all was Dr. Gut . . .

(*Ominous underscoring*)

TAXI: Bucket. (*Pats pocket*) What? (*Pulls out his gat.*) Why had the Bop Op given me my gat back? It was time to recherchez the Heartbreak.

(*Goes to phone booth. Dials.*)

TAXI: Bucket. Shrimp. Residence. Same to you. (*Dials*) Bucket. Taxi. *Taxi.* I got something you want. Something that you're looking for. Oh no? I wouldn't be too sure about that. Ask Professor Alors. Yeah.

(SHRIMP *puts him on hold. Tinny Muzak comes out of the phone.* "Shrimp Louie.")

TAXI: Gee, I oughta get this for the office.

(*Muzak stops.* TAXI *gets back on the line.*)

TAXI: Surprised? What about this? Earlier tonight you smuggled a stiff into the Heartbreak. Isn't that the reverse of the house rules? My pleasure. You'll see me when you see me.

(TAXI *hangs up. The Heartbreak opens up and* TAXI *walks in.*)

TAXI: (*In the VO*) I took the shortest route to Con Leche's room.

(*Elevator light and music effect.*)

TAXI: (*In the VO*) It was an old elevator, and every jolt told me it had been a long night. And was gonna get longer.

(*Elevator effect grinds to a halt.* TAXI *steps off.* ROOT *is lounging on* DOLORES' *bed. The shadow of venetian blind slats falls across the room.*)

TAXI: Staff discount?

ROOT: Too steep for your gear-ratio, Taxi.

TAXI: Split, rapsheet.

ROOT: Got a snort of salsa up your snoot, snooper? Con Leche ask you up here for a dash o' tabasco? Nogales nightcap?

TAXI: I want any lip from the help, I'll ring room service. Now make waves. Or I'm gonna get very very short with you.

(ROOT *gets off the bed and looks down at* TAXI. *Sneers.*)

ROOT: Riiiight.

(*He exits.*)

(TAXI *holds* DOLORES' *vial up to the light. He reads the Rx.*)

TAXI: Take as needed for instant sleep. Catnap, one cap. Two caps: Sleep soundly through sirens, heavy construction, marital discord, civil disorder, and decade's major cultural events. For the Long Goodbye: Scarf as many as fast as you can. Caution: Do not ingest while vertical. (*In the VO*) It did not seem like such a half-baked bad idea once I thought about it. I was dragging bun. I needed forty winks like a Chinese restaurant needs MSG. I could lie down on the job and do a little field research at the same time. The place to start putting the handcuffs on this sleep snatch was Con Leche's pillow (*Investigates bed wiring.*) Kinky. (*Tries to open vial—can't.*) Detective-proof bottle.

(*Gets it open. Still standing, he shakes out a pill and pulls out a pint:*)

TAXI: (*In the VO*) I crossed my palm with a logsawer, and tossed down a slug. Then a distant bell rang in the back of my cerebellum. Something about doctor's orders. Something about verticaallllllluuuuuuu—

(*His eyes roll back in his head and he's out in a dead faint. The bed crackles and glows.*)

(*Huge arc of blue light.*)

(*Honk and wail from* BLIND SAX.)

(*Weird greenish light up on* TAXI, *who is standing looking down at his sleeping self. Dream music, underscoring and special effects.*)

Taxi: (*In the VO*) I was dreaming I had my own weekly series. The James Taxi show. Starring James Taxi. Beaucoup buckage. Endorsements. Fan mail. In the series, I'm the divorced father of three teenage private detectives. Two girls and a boy. It's a good premise. Comedy-suspense. I was just sitting down in my agent's office . . .

(*Lights! TV Theme Music!*)

Lizzy's Voice: (*Amplified; sexy*) It's the James Taxi Show! Starring James Taxi! And his Teenage Detective Kids!

(*Lights!* Taxi *is standing center, mixing pancake batter in his slouch hat.*)

Sally's Voice: (*Amplified*) In tonight's episode Sally tracks down those lacrosse killers, Dad tells Placebo why they call it dope, Liz gets a hickey, and Rico borrows the car.

(Lizzy *and* Sally *skip on, sneaks and jeans, typical TV teens.*)

Sally: Hi Pop.

Taxi: Hi Sal. Where's your brother?

Sally: Flattening his feet.

Taxi: Liz, what's that on your neck?

Lizzy: Oh, it's just—

Sally: What's for breakfast?

Taxi: Dutch babies and apple pancakes.

Lizzy: No cereal?

Taxi: Seen your mother lately?

Lizzy: She says you're behind on your alimony.

Taxi: It's been known to happen.

Lizzy: She's talking to a lawyer.

Sally: Speaking of money, this case I'm working on is getting expensive. Can you loan me a gee? I have to fly to Kuwait this afternoon.

Taxi: How much is a gee?

Sally: Daddy, I don't know.

Lizzy: We get all this tough guy jargon from you in the first place.

SALLY: Nobody at school knows what we're talking about half the time.

LIZZY: It's embarrassing.

SALLY: Well?

TAXI: I'll work on it.

SALLY: (*Kisses him on the cheek.*) Thanks. Gotta run. Safeway's having a special on slouch hats. Bye!

TAXI: What about your breakfast? Liz, is that a—

LIZZY: Bye, Dad!

(*They exit. Lights swim. Music swims.*)

TAXI: (*In the VO*)—when suddenly there was a blinding jagged flash—nothing but late night snow on the small screen—purple and green afterburn on the backs of my eyelids like I'd had a flashcube go off in my face—cauterized cortex! My brain was being processed like Spam!

(TAXI *dances back to the bed, jerking and twitching, a thousand volts of pure energy coursing through his body. He flops on the bed.*)

(*The lights stop swimming as* DOLORES *enters.* TAXI *sits bolt upright.*)

TAXI: I'll take the pigs with me!

(DOLORES *slaps him.*)

TAXI: (*Shakes out cobwebs.*) I gotta get a day job. What a night. What a head. Like a guacamole avocado.

DOLORES: Taxi, what are you doing in my bed?

TAXI: Sacrificing my body to detective science. I downed one of these.

DOLORES: My pepsters from Doctor Gut.

(*Ominous underscoring*)

TAXI: How do they do that? Yeah, these pepsters are first-class dozers, sweetcakes. Always read labels.

DOLORES: Did you dance in your sleep?

TAXI: Like a linebacker. Jétés somnambulés.

DOLORES: Qué pasa, Tax?

TAXI: When my head hit the pillow, the Buckets siphoned off my dream faster than a vice cop on the take.

DOLORES: Why you?

TAXI: Not me—you. They didn't expect anyone else to be using that futon.

DOLORES: (*Outraged*) Taxi! What do you take me for—a nun? Just because you don't have any social life—

TAXI: Here's the scam—they've got Mitzi in the hotel somewhere, and she's doubling for you in the show. That wasn't you I saw out there tonight, it was your sister.

DOLORES: My kid sister.

TAXI: Your kid sister. And believe me, where I come from, that counts for something.

DOLORES: Why are they doing that to Mitzi?

TAXI: I don't know. But there's got to be major-league clammage in this dream snatch. Hotel do well?

DOLORES: Get real. This place doesn't do business on New Year's Eve.

TAXI: Go downstairs and stake out the lobby. If this jaspar from the Far East shows up, tip me. Jiggle the wiring.

DOLORES: I don't care what they say about you, Tax. I think you're jake.

TAXI: James. And just what do they say about me?

DOLORES: Oh hombre, por díos, no me hagas rerir! (*She exits.*)

TAXI: (*In the VO*) I've always been a sucker for the enigmatic kind. I was overdue for a shrimp fry. I had something he wanted.

(*Traveling music.* TAXI *arrives at the Ice Bucket anteroom. Dry ice seeps. A rattan fan chair.* SHRIMP *is practicing some moves with an imaginary mike for* Shrimp Louie.)

SHRIMP: (*A capella*)
I'm a burnin' burnin' hunk of Shrimp
I'm a burnin' burnin' hunk of Shrimp
Don't fuss with the dressin'
'Cause you know you ain't messin' with me—

TAXI: Brushing up your act, Mr. Bucket?

SHRIMP: What's your professional opinion, Mr. Taxi?

TAXI: Don't quit your day job.

SHRIMP: I think I sound pretty good without the band. *Shrimp Louie*—a ca *paella. Heh heh.*

TAXI: I get the driftwood. You're one bad egg.

SHRIMP: Your use of the idiom is dazzling. Of course, you show folk. Life in the demi-monde. Sit down, sit down. Take the Huey Newton Chair.

(SHRIMP *indicates the rattan fan chair.* TAXI *sits warily.*)

SHRIMP: Drink?

TAXI: Whiskey. Three fingers.

SHRIMP: (*Beat*) Three fingers, eh? Chaser?

TAXI: Neat. No attitude.

(ROOT *appears and hands* TAXI *a drink.*)

TAXI: Swift. I like that it's not foaming. What's the call brand?

ROOT: Heart of Darkness. The White Man's Bourbon. (*He exits.*)

TAXI: Why does he get all the good lines?

SHRIMP: Affirmative action.

TAXI: Affirmative action. The Huey Newton Chair. You make the Heartbreak Hotel sound like a museum, Mr. Bucket.

SHRIMP: How perspicacious of you, Mr. Taxi. Yes, the Huey Newton Chair is part of our American Icon collection. Huey endowed it.

TAXI: An endowed chair in a hotel?

SHRIMP: We're a non-profit hotel. Huey was kind enough to leave us the chair.

TAXI: I'd like to take a gander at the rest of your collection.

SHRIMP: Not a chance. By appointment only. We're not a wax museum, Mr. Taxi.

TAXI: Oh? I thought maybe you were. What was that package you had delivered this morning? A new exhibit?

SHRIMP: A very old exhibit, Mr. Taxi. We'd sent it out for a little restoration. Now, Mr. Taxi, I'm a busy guy. Belly up to the point.

TAXI: With pleasure. I decided to wink out in Con Leche's room. I popped a dubious dozer, and was out like a golfing doctor. While I was sawing my sheep, somebody lifted my dreams.

SHRIMP: Your—heh heh—dreams, Mr. Taxi? What would anyone want with your dreams? Dreams are so personal. Like underwear. You never have to worry about having your underwear snatched from the laundromat. They're too personal. They wouldn't fit. (*Beat*) Dreams are the underwear of the mind, Mr. Taxi. Why take somebody else's? No deposit, no return. That goes double for sordid, soiled, soggy, no starch, sewer-snooper dreams like yours—the grubby shorts of a truly short subject.

TAXI: If you were in my line of work, Mr. Bucket, you'd know there are plenty of creeps—right out there—who'll go for somebody else's boxers. But I'm not here to argue eschatology with you. I wasn't the intended. Nobody expected me to be on that futon. You were after Con Leche. You siphoned off my dreams because you thought they were hers. You're sucking up Con Leche's dreams like plankton. You've got her doped to the gills. Whatever you're using has a nasty side effect. It makes her dance in her sleep. She's no good in the act anymore, so you've got the supposedly missing Mitzi Montenegro doubling Dolores! You're an ethnic dancing junkie! Admit it! You're hooked!

SHRIMP: You're raving. How is such a thing possible?

TAXI: We may never know. But I intend to find out.

SHRIMP: If you'll excuse me, I've had enough of this bizarre conversation.

TAXI: Thanks for the gut bomb.

(*Ominous underscoring from* BLIND SAX)

SHRIMP: Aren't you forgetting something?

TAXI: Am I?

SHRIMP: You have something that belongs to me.

TAXI: Oh, you mean—(*He pulls the three-fingered glove out of his pocket.*)—a three-fingered glove?

(SHRIMP *lunges for it, but* TAXI *pulls his gat.* SHRIMP *puts his hands up. They sing a reprise of* Three-Fingered Glove.)

THREE-FINGERED GLOVE

(TAXI *and* SHRIMP)

TAXI: Three-fingered glove

SHRIMP:
Where did you find it

TAXI:
Three-fingered glove

SHRIMP:
What good can it do you

TAXI:
Why don't you tell me?

SHRIMP:
You're not a digital amputee—yet

TAXI:
Are you threatening me

SHRIMP:
It was my grandpa's
An heirloom you see
He lost a pinkie in a bandsaw
It means bupkes to me

TAXI:
Well, you never can tell
I'll put it away
It may be a clue for a rainy day

SHRIMP:
Wait and see

(*Music out*)

TAXI: I'll do that.

SHRIMP: There's a reward.

TAXI: How much?

SHRIMP: Two C's.

TAXI: Two G's.

SHRIMP: Okay.

TAXI: A G is worth more than a C, right?

SHRIMP: Where I come from.

TAXI: How do I know this is really yours? It may belong to some digitally challenged person.

SHRIMP: I'll show you the mate.

TAXI: Sealed deal.

SHRIMP: Meet me in the laundry in ten. You drive a hard bargain, Mr. Taxi. I'm not used to negotiating at gunpoint. The security at this hotel is terrible. My apologies.

(*The lights blink conspicously. Ominous underscoring. Lights restore to full and the underscoring phrase revs back up to speed and finishes.*)

TAXI: You oughta do something about your dry ice, it's death on wiring.

SHRIMP: A beintot, Mr. Taxi. A pleasure doing business with you.

(SHRIMP *fades.*)

TAXI: (*In the VO*) I was in the vichyssoise no doubt about it. I had to make waves and fast. That power failure was a signal from Con Leche that the guest of honor was on his way.

(TAXI *steps onto the elevator. Elevator effect.*)

TAXI: (*In the VO*) The elevator wasn't getting younger, and neither was I. I was as jumpy as a bad print.

(*Elevator stops. He steps outside into the lobby.* DOLORES *is waiting.*)

TAXI: Where is he?

DOLORES: (*Pointing*) Incoming at nine 'o clock.

(MR. BATSUMASHBALL *enters. [Played by* ROOT *in dark glasses, turban, and sarong.]*)

MR. BATSUMASHBALL: Sorry, so sorry, I am looking for Mr. and Mr. Bucket—

DOLORES: Oh yes, aren't you uh—

MR. BATSUMASHBALL: Yes, I am Mr. Batsumashball, from Nauru.

DOLORES: Right. Mr. Batsumashball, it was on the tip of my tongue.

(TAXI *slips up behind* MR. BATSUMASHBALL *and sticks a gun in his ribs.*)

MR. BATSUMASHBALL: I knew it! I knew America was a dangerous country! Take my travelers' checks! Take my Rolex!

DOLORES: I'll settle for your sarong.

MR. BATSUMASHBALL: Kinky perverts.

(DOLORES *takes* MR. BATSUMASHBALL'S *turban and puts it on* TAXI.)

DOLORES: Chicks dig turbans.

TAXI: I'll remember that. (*To the band*) Boys can you help me out here?

(*The* BAND *plays strip music, as* TAXI *takes off his clothes and puts* MR. BATSUMASHBALL'S *sarong on. He puts on* MR. BATSUMASHBALL'S *dark glasses and sandals, as* DOLORES *holds the gun on him. They regard* MR. BATSUMASHBALL'S *outrageous tropical boxer shorts*.)

DOLORES: You want his shorts?

TAXI: No thanks. Boxer rebellion.

DOLORES: Take a brain bomber, pal.

(*She stuffs one of her instant sleep capsules into* MR. BATSUMASHBALL'S *mouth—he's out on his feet instantly*.)

TAXI: Think of this as jetlag.

(*They stash him behind the palm*.)

DOLORES: You look good. Your turban is crooked.

(*She straightens it. They get tangled up*.)

TAXI: You got narrative structure, sister. You got plot points galore.

(*They're about to get into a heavy clinch when they hear voices*.)

ROOT: I don't care how blasé you are, no one sleeps through the Big O.

(ROOT *and* BOP *enter*.)

BOP: (*To* DOLORES) I gotta question your taste in men. That's sharp chapeau, fella. I got an extra lampshade upstairs if you're still in the market for headgear. You the big noise from Nauru?

TAXI: I'm not Jackie O.

ROOT: The boss is waiting, Mr. Batsumashball.

BOP: Batsumashball?

ROOT: Walk this way.

(*They start to walk.* DOLORES *tries to tag along but* BOP *stops her*.)

Bop: Not you, Miss Au Lait.

(Dolores *and* Bop *fade as* Root *and* Taxi *take the elevator effect.*)

Taxi: Is this elevator safe?

Root: As yo' mama's yo-yo.

Taxi: Is that a colloquialism?

Root: The colloquialest.

(*They arrive at The Ice Bucket. Lots of dry ice and neon tube gear.*)

(Shrimp *appears.*)

Shrimp: Ah, our distinguished guest. Mr. Batsumashball, I presume.

Root: Mr. Shrimp, meet Mr. Batsumashball.

Shrimp: Mr. Batsumashball. Delighted.

Taxi: Mr. Shrimp Bucket. So nice to be here.

Shrimp: Cool your cuticles, Root. If you go down to the laundry, I think you just might locate that missing—item. And be sure to give our little friend a nice big tip for his trouble.

Root: You got it. (*He exits.*)

Taxi: Ah, Mr. Shrimp. It is my understanding there are—Brothers Bucket.

Shrimp: (*Chuckles*) You're in for a treat. Allow me to introduce my distinguished brother. Doctor. Gut. Bucket.

(*Ominous underscoring. The Huey Newton chair, which has been facing upstage, now swivels around. It is* Gut. *He is dressed like Huey Newton in the famous photograph: black beret, black leather jacket and pants, black boots. He has a black glove on one hand and is holding a spear in one hand, and a machine gun in the other. Almost the spitting image of Huey—except that he's white and very overweight.*)

(Blind Sax *plays* Gut's *Theme. When he finishes,* Taxi *applauds.*)

Taxi: Is that a single or anything? It's very catchy.

Gut: Welcome to our humble hotel, Mr. Batsumashball. Where we pursue our studies in American iconography and contemporary mythology.

TAXI: Your work is well known.

GUT: I certainly hope not. That would be—unfortunate.

(GUT *and* SHRIMP *share an unpleasant laugh.*)

GUT: Perhaps we should proceed directly to the demonstration.

(SHRIMP *wheels out the Dream Device.*)

GUT: As you know, Mr. Batsumashball, we have only to perfect our delivery system to begin global operations.

SHRIMP: After that, it's clear scaling.

GUT: That's right, Shrimp.

SHRIMP: You got it, Gut.

TAXI: That's what I'm here for.

GUT: Your world-wide electronics empire should solve all our problems.

TAXI: It should, shouldn't it?

SHRIMP: With a nice piece of change for you, Mr. Batsumashball.

GUT: This is the Dream Device, Mr. Batsumashball. A dream recorder and projector. It records on these discs—(*He holds up a shiny disc and inserts it:*)—and projects a holographic image. The apparatus is a complete package. It transcribes the dreamer's dream, records it, and plays it back. We got some help on this from SONY.

TAXI: You should have come to me.

GUT: We've been working with a guinea pig. Stealing and recording her dreams. An exotic dancer.

SHRIMP: Please Brother Gut. An ethnic dancer. She's a narcoleptic. She's a dreamboat of a dreamer. Wanna see one?

TAXI: I didn't come all the way from Nauru to see *Police Academy III**

(SHRIMP *flicks a switch on the Dream Device.*)

SHRIMP: You won't believe the fidelity on this. The three-D is stunning. One floppy disc to go! Check it out. This is her favorite. "Fantasia Carmen Miranda."

---

*Substitute topical B movie.

(*Lights! Music!* DOLORES *appears, dressed in the full Carmen Miranda, inc. fruit bowl.* Fantasia Carmen Miranda *is a lavish nightclub number, with the Balkanettes as chorus girls, and* ROOT, ZOOT, *and* BOP *as chorus boys. The music is* Mango Smoothie, *lavishly orchestrated and it swirls. Lots of flashing lights, big and brassy.*)

(*Big finish and blackout!*)

(*Lights up on* TAXI, GUT, *and* SHRIMP.)

TAXI: It's so real.

SHRIMP: It's patented. Our trademark: Palpable Image.

TAXI: That girl's got a Carmen Miranda fixation. How do you get her to do that—dance in her sleep?

GUT: A side effect of the medication we have prescribed for her. Now, Mr. Batsumashball. You're probably wondering why. Why collect dreams?

TAXI: It had double-crossed my mind.

GUT: Why not cash? Gold? Precious gemoids? Negotiable securities and other instruments of financial torture?

TAXI: Why not?

SHRIMP: Profit.

GUT: And power.

TAXI: How do you get profit and power from dreams? Mr. and Mr. Bucket, I still don't smell those greenbacka dollahs.

GUT: Yu have an extraordinary command of the American idiom, Mr. Batsumashball.

SHRIMP: The aboveboard legal side of the market is enormous, Mr. Batsumashball.

GUT: We'll be selling a modified version of this machine to psychoanalysts, therapists of every persuasion, and so on.

SHRIMP: Huge market.

GUT: And a home-use model—for the self-involved.

SHRIMP: Gonna be the biggest thing to ever hit Manhattan.

TAXI: You want me to perfect your long-range dream stealer—

SHRIMP: You'll get a share of the gross.

TAXI: (*Snaps fingers*) Dream piracy. On a global scale. The legal stuff for therapy will be chump change if you can pry open anyone's head in the world and extract their dreams like a gherkin.

SHRIMP: Go for it, Mr. B. Figure the angle.

(SHRIMP *and* GUT *light cigars.*)

TAXI: Gotta be cable. Mondo Video.

GUT AND SHRIMP: Video Mondo!

TAXI: Thousands of new channels. They all need material. You tap into hot sources surreptitiously. Writers, artists, real DREAMERS. You suck out their dreams, record 'em—and either screen the stuff raw, or send it out for development.

SHRIMP: Now you're cooking with canned heat.

TAXI: Stealing dreams is much safer than stealing scripts.

SHRIMP: Hey, you can't copyright dreams.

GUT: Scripts for the insatiable maw of popular entertainment. The demand is endless, the supply anemic.

SHRIMP: And writer's block. You know how many writers out there got block? *Many*. Heads full of great plots and no way to get them out. It's like having a copper mine without a railroad.

TAXI: That simile makes about as much sense as a Sophia Loren voiceover.

SHRIMP: You should talk, Mr. Batsumashball. Gherkins?

GUT: A class scam. Worth billions.

SHRIMP: That's conservative.

GUT: We should capture all markets. Cable is just the beginning. Today, cable. Radio. Television. Hong Kong.

SHRIMP: We're grooming Root to be the second coming of Bruce Lee.

GUT: After Hong-Kong—Hollywood. It's the great big banal American dream, Mr. Batsumashball: the conquest of Hollywood. The Heartbreak will replace Hollywood as the worldwide center of self delusion and primary source of prefabricated dreams. Brother Shrimp. If you please.

(SHRIMP *wheels in a portable deep freeze: rhinestones and neon trim. Clouds of dry ice.*)

GUT: I'm sure you've heard all the classic American myths.

SHRIMP: Every kid knows 'em.

GUT: About this or that legendary artifact.

SHRIMP: It's a government secret. Some old lady has Custer's scalp in a hat box.

TAXI: The saucer people who live in the top of Mt. Shasta.

SHRIMP: Excellent, Mr. Batsumashball.

GUT: That particular myth is indigenous to California.

TAXI: Roy Rogers and Trigger. Stuffed and mounted. Dale, too.

SHRIMP: Dale and Bullet, I think it is. And of course, the ever-popular white alligators in the sewers of New York City and the Colonel's french-fried rat, in a barrel or a bucket. Heh heh.

GUT: My personal favorite is the poodle in the microwave.

TAXI: They put the poodle in the microwave to dry it off. And blew it up.

SHRIMP: I heard it was a wet cat.

TAXI: What's your position on Bigfoot?

SHRIMP: Bigfoot's one of the best.

GUT: Do you ever wonder how these Native American myths germinate?

TAXI: Every day.

GUT: Metastisizing into myths of Bunyanesque proportions? For one simple reason, Mr. Batsumashball—they're true.

TAXI: You got Bigfoot? I wanna see Bigfoot.

GUT: Perhaps this will convince you. (*He opens the deep freeze.*)

SHRIMP: We keep our extra extra special stock in here.

(GUT *pulls out a hatbox, open it, and displays a mangy, moth-eaten blonde wig.*)

TAXI: Custer?

SHRIMP: Who else?

TAXI: Your mother, maybe.

GUT: A hard sell, eh, Mr. Batsumashball? Try this.

(*From the deep-freeze* GUT *extracts and brandishes a thin metal cylinder, three-feet long and shaped like a cigar. He tosses it to* TAXI.)

TAXI: (*With reverence*) Dillinger.

GUT: The one and only. According to popular mythology, Dillinger's—distinguishing anatomical peculiarity was detached after his demise and preserved. Pickled. In a jar.

SHRIMP: Smithsonian.

TAXI: I heard Walter Reed Hospital.

GUT: The value of this item only increases over the years as the stories grow more elaborate.

TAXI: Hard to exaggerate about something like that.

SHRIMP: One item that lives up to its billing.

GUT: And now, the pièce de resistance. Mr. Batsumashball, if you would be so kind.

(TAXI *goes to the deep freeze.*)

TAXI: Dillinger, I never bought. Jealous, I guess. But Bigfoot—I gotta hunch about Bigfoot. Oh, boy, Bigfoot!

(*He looks down into the deep freeze. He drops his jaw. Finally, he speaks in an awed whisper.* When You Wish Upon a Star *plays under in a minor key.*)

TAXI: Uncle Walt.

(GUT *and* SHRIMP *chuckle nastily.*)

GUT: Isn't he gorgeous?

TAXI: He looks better than he did on his last season.

SHRIMP: He was planning a comeback.

GUT: Those stories started just after Uncle Walt—after Uncle Walt—after he—went away. They said he was terminal, so he had himself freeze-dried while he was still alive. Cryogenically preserved in a state of icy grace. In a tube in a tower of Sleeping Beauty's castle. Ready to return to us the day a cure is found. To create new and better Magic Kingdoms! The Second Coming!

SHRIMP: One of our better heists. And not easy. That Tinkerbelle was a bitch.

GUT: Our interest in dreams and icons led us inevitably to Uncle Walt. The greatest purveyor of myth the world has ever known. Uncle Walt—what a dreamer.

Shrimp: There are only so many emeralds in the world. We decided to secure a monopoly on the source.

Gut: Once we've found a cure for what ails Uncle Walt—

Shrimp: We'll bring him back to dream for the Bucket Brothers on an exclusive basis.

Gut: Tickle those ivories! Palpitate those eighty-eights!

(Gut *and* Shrimp *sing* No More Magic Kingdoms, *an anthem of incredible evil.*)

No More Magic Kingdoms

Shrimp and Gut:
No more Fred MacMurray
No more Peter Pan
No more Pluto furry
No more Pollyann—
—a
No more Cinderella
No more haunted house
No more Tinkerbella

No more Mickey Mouse

No more Magic Kingdoms
No more Magic Kingdoms

No more boring nature flicks
No more prime time swill
No more Son of Flubber tricks
No more Haley Mills

No more Jiminy Cricket
No more *Song of the South*
Give me Wilson Pickett
Instead of Donald's mouth

Shrimp:
Quack!

Gut:
Quack!

Shrimp:
Quack!

Both:
No more Magic Kingdom!
No more Magic Kingdom!

Gut:
No more Annette in her sweater
to give us our afternoon thrill
If Daisy and Don don't get it on
Snow White and the Seven Dwarves will

BOTH:
No more Magic Kingdoms
No more Magic Kingdoms
No more Magic Kingdoms
No more Magic Kingdoms

(*Big nasty finish*)

TAXI: Say, he's missing one of his cute little white three-fingered gloves.

SHRIMP: (*Darkly*) Lost in the laundry. So embarrassing. We always try to have Uncle Walt freshly pressed for visitors. Now, Mr. Batsumashball, what about a little ethnic dancing? I'm sure the girls would be happy to oblige. Speciality of the house.

TAXI: I'd like to see another sample.

(*A little miffed,* SHRIMP *goes through a few discs.*)

SHRIMP: Let's see. *IRS Chainsaw Massacre*—revenge—*The Slattern of Soho*—that's one of mine, look out, it's hot—let's see, here's a dud, *The James Taxi Show*—

TAXI: That sounds good.

SHRIMP: No, it's a sit-com.

TAXI: I heard it was action-suspense.

(GUT *and* SHRIMP *exchange glances.*)

GUT: Where did you hear that, Mr. Batsumashball?

TAXI: Word on the street.

SHRIMP: Word travels fast to Nauru.

GUT: Word on the street. I am continually dazzled by your grasp of the American idiom, Mr. Batsumashball. And come. Tell me. How is it you know so much about the Mt. Shasta saucer people and Bigfoot?

TAXI: We keep in touch on Nauru. We have television.

(ROOT *and* BLIND SAX *enter.*)

ROOT: Taxi never showed. Boss.

SHRIMP: What a surprise. So you heard his dream was action-suspense, did you, Mr. B.?

TAXI: A real nail-biter.

(TAXI *is sweating. He pulls the three-fingered glove from his pocket, and mops his brow.*)

GUT: I doubt that your high opinion of your own dream is shared by a significant portion of the viewing audience, Mr. Batsu-Taxi.

(SHRIMP *pulls a gun.*)

SHRIMP: And unhand that glove.

(TAXI *takes off his dark glasses and turban, and hands* SHRIMP *the glove.*)

TAXI: (*In the VO*) I had heuvos rancheros all over my mugshot. I'd meant to grill Shrimp like a souvlaki. Instead, I'd skewered myself seven ways till Sunday. I'd always wanted my own weekly series, but action-suspense, not sit-com. What the hell, you can't sneeze at residuals.

SHRIMP: You're the only residual around here. You're a guy with no secrets, talk to yourself like that. Stay for dinner. Gracie's made extra.

TAXI: I'd like to, but I gotta run.

(GUT *twists* TAXI'S *nipple,* TAXI *screams silently.*)

GUT: Manners, young man.

(SHRIMP *relieves* TAXI *of his gun, and hands it to* BLIND SAX, *who points it at the audience.* SHRIMP *re-directs him at* TAXI.)

TAXI: You really think he should have that?

SHRIMP: The NRA supports the constitutional right of blind people to bear arms.

(*He motions* TAXI *toward the deep freeze.*)

SHRIMP: You're such a fan of the maestro, I thought you'd like to join him.

TAXI: I'd like to, but I left the top down on my convertible. I look forward to Uncle Walt's comeback.

SHRIMP: He'll make his before you make yours, Taxi. Root, zip him up.

(ROOT *drags* TAXI *to the deep freeze.* TAXI *glances in.*)

TAXI: Hey! What goes on here? There's no life support systems hardware. Nothing to keep him hibernation fresh.

(THE BUCKET BROTHERS *grow very grim. A sour strain of* When You Wish Upon A Star.)

TAXI: (*In the VO*) The look on their faces told me I'd hit the bull's eye. It also told me I should have bitten my lips off.

GUT: An accident.

SHRIMP: The support systems were unintentionally destroyed during the heist.

TAXI: But that means now he's worth less than a frozen fish stick.

GUT: We trust you can keep our little secret.

TAXI: My lips are seals.

GUT: I will miss our repartee, Mr. Taxi.

SHRIMP: It was very, very special.

(TAXI *elbows* ROOT *in the stomach. He makes a grab for* SHRIMP'S *gun. Action-suspense underscoring. Big fight. Finally,* SHRIMP *pistol-whips* TAXI *across the bridge of the nose.* TAXI *crumples to his knees. He passes a hand over his face and looks at the wet stuff on his fingers.*)

TAXI: God. Real blood.

(*Reggae bass line*)

TAXI: (*In the VO*) I was about to join Uncle Walt in the Deepest Freeze of All. My reggae headache was taking an encore. Days like this made me think I should have stayed in grad school. All in all, I had a clam's chance on Mt. Everest. Then it hit me.

(*Flashback music.* SHRIMP *is caught in a blinding spot.*)

SHRIMP: Mitzi's in home appliances now. She's cool.

(*Music and spot out.* SHRIMP *rubs his eyes..*)

SHRIMP: I haven't had a flashback like that since Tim Leary and I went barbecuing with Bobby. How do you do that?

TAXI: How do you do the underscoring?

SHRIMP: Trade secret.

TAXI: Flukey ditto.

SHRIMP: Enough shop talk. Hook him up.

(ROOT *pushes* TAXI *into the freezer and begins to attach him to some ominous-looking machinery.*)

TAXI: Mitzi's gotta be in the Ice Bucket. But where?

SHRIMP: You're the detective.

TAXI: Yes, yes I am. Over there. The walk-in cooler.

SHRIMP: How terribly perspicacious of you, Mr. Taxi.

(SHRIMP *opens a closet.* MITZI [DOLORES] *is in a tube.*)

TAXI: Is she in the same shape Uncle Walt is?

GUT: Her pulse is glacial, but rock steady. As long as we defrost properly, she'll be good as new.

(SHRIMP *closes door on* MITZI.)

TAXI: (*In the VO*) It was all beginning to fall into place, like pecs and mams on a fortieth birthday. Mitzi on ice. So she wasn't doubling Dolores on-stage. The Bucket brothers' hologram fooled me, and I was ringside. Mitzi Montenegro, the Balkan Bombshell. Dolores' kid sister. Or was Dolores Mitzi's kid sister? Short-term memory is the first thing to go.

SHRIMP: I'd like to stay, but too much denoument always gives me gas. Speaking of gas—(*To* ROOT) Turn on the liquid nitro. A bientot, Mr. Taxi.

(DOLORES *enters, armed with a Dirty Harry-sized magnum, followed by* DOLORES *and* SALLY.)

DOLORES: Hands up, Bucket.

(GUT *points machine gun and spear at* DOLORES.)

GUT: Likewise, Miss Con Leche, let me urge you to do the same.

SALLY: Shrimp, your ass is filé gumbo now.

SHRIMP: Is this what they call a Mexican stand-off?

DOLORES: I think I'm gonna ventilate you.

SHRIMP: A tough-talking woman with a magnum always turns me on.

DOLORES: You are one sick Shrimp, you know that?

SHRIMP: Since you put it that way—let me put it this way. And this way. And what about this way?

(*As* SHRIMP *puts it various ways,* ROOT *sneaks up and disarms* DOLORES.)

DOLORES: Oh! You! You! You Buckets! Ow!

SHRIMP: In you go. Join your flat-footed friend.

DOLORES: Sorry, Tax.

TAXI: I fell for it too.

(ROOT *puts* DOLORES *in the freezer with* TAXI.)

SHRIMP: Balkanettes too. You don't want to dance ethnic, I'll find somebody who does.

SALLY: Shrimp, I hope you deep-fat fry in fast-food hell for this.

SHRIMP: And after all I've done for you.

(ROOT *stuffs the* BALKANETTES *in the freezer.* DOLORES *looks down.*)

DOLORES: Who's that?

TAXI: Uncle Walt.

DOLORES: My God.

TAXI: Mine too. (*To* SHRIMP) Put his other glove on, will you? He looks naked without it.

(SHRIMP *tosses the glove to* TAXI, *who puts it on Uncle Walt.* ROOT *and* ZOOT *attach* DOLORES, LIZZY, *and* SALLY *to the cryogenics wiring.*)

DOLORES: You dream-sucking Buckets! Why are you putting the snatch on my dreams? Why're you making me dance in my sleep?

TAXI: Allow me.

SHRIMP: Go ahead, Tax. I just love it when you detect.

TAXI: The whole enchilada?

SHRIMP: Be incisive. Relentless. We'll just wither.

TAXI: Everybody ready. Okay. Don't stop me if I leave anything out. The Buckets invent the Dream Device. They swipe Uncle Walt, The Biggest Dreamer of Our Time. But they waste him by mistake. They need guinea pigs to work the kinks out of Doctor Gut's—

(*Ominous underscoring from* BLIND SAX, *who plays and waves gun wildly. Everyone ducks*)

TAXI: System. Shrimp has a thing for ethnic dancers, so they hire Mitzi. They dose her with nuclear downers and suck up her dreams. She dances in her sleep. She's beat. They keep on sucking. It's a vicious spiral. They wear Mitzi out. Or she starts to get wise—whichever comes first. So the Buckets put her on ice.

DOLORES: Oh, you Buckets!

TAXI: You advertise for a new thrush. Dolores shows up. She's looking for her sister. You start the whole sleazy scam over from the top.

SHRIMP: Now that's private detection!

TAXI: Dolores hires me to find out what's what. I glom onto a three-fingered glove outside the hotel.

SHRIMP: Where is Professor Alors? Nitwit. I'll settle his hash later.

TAXI: He's right in front of you. Your brother, Dr. Gut—

(*Ominous underscoring from* BLIND SAX—*everyone ducks.*)

SHRIMP: Don't be ridiculous.

GUT: You're hallucinating.

TAXI: Have you ever seen them together at the same time? Think about it.

SHRIMP: It's a theory. Finish your Perry Mason.

TAXI: I always get suspicious when I see a stiff being carried *into* a hotel. In this case, it was a frozen stiff. Uncle Walt.

GUT: We'd sent him out to a specialist. But there was nothing to be done.

TAXI: I snooped around, intercepted Mr. Batsumashball—and the rest you know.

SHRIMP: Where is Mr. Batsumashball?

TAXI: Behind the palm in the lobby.

SHRIMP: Sheer clam nectar, Tax. Hey, we're having some fun now. Okay! Enough denouement! Let's ice these turkeys! Liquid nitro and lots of it!

(ROOT *turns on the liquid nitro. Dry ice billows.* THE BOP OP *bursts through the door, wearing a tatty Blackglama mink. He has a gun and he flashes a badge.*)

BOP: Special Agent—Lillian Hellman! You're now on ice, Buckets. Freeze! (*To audience*) The first time I met Dashiell Hammet, he arrested me for shoplifting costume jewelry at Lamston's. He was a Pinkerton, I was a Pulitzer Prize winner. We laughed about it later—the little fox.

TAXI: (*In the VO*) Meanwhile, in another part of the forest, The Bop Wop was undercover, stringing the Buckets along like a couple of sausages.

DOLORES: When did you know the Bop Op was a cop?

TAXI: Just now, when he flashed his badge.

BOP: Drop 'em, Buckets. Untie 'em.

(ROOT *unties everyone, while* SHRIMP *and* GUT *drop 'em.* BOP *turns* BLIND SAX *and points him at the* BUCKETS.)

BOP: Special Agent Lillian Hellman. Investigating the theft of Uncle Walt from Sleeping Beauty's castle. Your name is mud, Buckets. What else is in there with Uncle Walt?

TAXI: This.

(*He hands* BOP *the cylinder.* BOP *gets awe-struck and sensual.*)

BOP: Dillinger. Do you know how long the Bureau's been after this? (*Takes it from* TAXI *and hefts it.*) What becomes a legend most.

TAXI: I suspected you might be on our side.

BOP: Special Agent Lillian Hellman. FBI and Copyright office.

SHRIMP: Hey! You can't copyright dreams, I'm telling you.

BOP: When did you start to catch on?

TAXI: The passkey. Putting my piece back in my pocket.

BOP: And who says private dicks are slow?

TAXI: I want my wallet and watch back, brown belle.

(BOP *gives* TAXI *his wallet and watch.*)

DOLORES: Sure is complex.

TAXI: If you're experiencing narrative motion sickness, don't let it get you down. It comes with the territory. By the time we close the covers on this one, you won't remember which ends are loose. (*He takes a sad look at the thawing Uncle Walt.*)

TAXI: He's starting to melt. How could you?

SHRIMP: We didn't mean to break him.

GUT: Obviously. His resale value in this condition is nil.

SHRIMP: We even had to refreeze.

TAXI: (*Aghast*) You're never supposed to refreeze. (*Near tears*) Poor Uncle Walt. No comeback now. Entertainment as we know it will never be the same.

GUT: No more Magic Kingdoms, Mr. Taxi.

TAXI: Lillian!

BOP: Yeah, Nancy?

TAXI: Put these perverts where the sun don't shine!

BOP: You got it.

(*He starts to herd off* ROOT, ZOOT, SHRIMP, *and* GUT.)

TAXI: You don't look very worried.

SHRIMP: (*Laughs*) Me? We have more lawyers than the District of Columbia. I'm about as worried as Standard Oil at tax time.

TAXI: Don't plagiarize my style, Bucket.

SHRIMP: Hey! You can't copyright style, I'm telling you.

GUT: We'll meet again, Mr. Taxi. In the sequel.

LIZZY: Don't forget, Mr. Taxi—the Take It EZ Trailer Park.

SALLY: Come catch our new act, Mr. Taxi.

TAXI: Wouldn't miss it.

(LIZZY *and* SALLY *exit.*)

BOP: This will make a great chapter in my eleventh best-selling volume of fictional memoirs: *I Was A Bride Of Stalin.*

TAXI: Thanks for your help, Lillian.

BOP: My pleasure, Nancy. Call me. We'll have lunch. (*Laughs girlishly*) We'll leave you two flamingos alone.

(*Everyone exits.*)

DOLORES: Taxi! What about Mitzi?

TAXI: We'll come back for her tomorrow. One more night—she'll never know the difference.

DOLORES: Taxi, she's my kid sister.

TAXI: I know. And believe me—where I come from, that counts for something.

DOLORES: Listen, there are still a lot of things I don't understand.

TAXI: Don't sweat it. The genre teaches us to accept the inexplicable. It's a very metaphysical genre.

DOLORES: If you say so. Listen, Taxi. Thanks. No, seriously.

TAXI: All in a night's work.

DOLORES: I guess I've seen the last of you.

TAXI: In a pig's valise, sister.

DOLORES: (*Laughs*) I never thought you'd work that in.

TAXI: It came to me in a dream.

DOLORES: I like your style.

TAXI: Likewise, in spades.

DOLORES: May I call you Nancy James?

TAXI: I wish you would.

DOLORES: Besame mucho!

(*She grabs him and kisses him hard, bending him over in a tango swoon. In the middle of the kiss, he breaks off:*)

TAXI: (*In the VO*) She had lips as sweet and full as ten pounds of sucre in a five-pound sack. They turned my spine to flan. I was diving head-first into a pool of passion-fruit punch, hoping I'd never have to come up for air.

(DOLORES *drops him on the floor.*)

DOLORES: You gotta see somebody about that. I'm not spending the weekend with somebody who talks to himself in the past tense.

TAXI: Promise.

(*He picks himself up. They lock eyes and get steamy.*)

DOLORES: I don't care what they say about you. I think you're muy picante.

TAXI: What exactly do they say about me?

DOLORES: That you're fast as a claims settlement.

TAXI: Irony. I like that in a woman. You know, Con Leche, you're about as subtle as a pitcher of sangria.

DOLORES: Tell me more, big fella.

TAXI: You come on strong, like you're a double shot of tequila with a brew back. But you're really about as tough to take as a spring day.

DOLORES: Sweet. You hard-boiled guys have maple sugar in your veins.

TAXI: Don't stop now.

DOLORES: Taxi, you come on like a mouthful of razor blades, but you're really as hard-edged as a flour tortilla. You're as sweet as a sopapilla.

TAXI: I've mixed metaphors with mugs from Malibu to Cahuenga Boulevard but you're something special.

(*They sing* The Simile Duet. *It's upbeat, and they're falling in love.*)

THE SIMILE DUET

TAXI:
I like a gal who can spin a phrase

DOLORES:
I like a guy who can torture all day a figure of speech

TAXI:
Not to mention syntax

DOLORES:
A well-turned simile puts me in a daze

TAXI:
A simile makes me smile and that's the facts

Just the facts, ma'am

DOLORES:
Like or as is the key
It's as easy as

TAXI:
As easy as

DOLORES:
As easy as Mata Hari

TAXI:
Remember a metaphor is something too subtle
For lowlifes like you and like me

DOLORES:
With your mind like a trap
You'll be played for a sap

BOTH:
Better stick with a quick simile

It could be mighty like the blues
Or taste as stale as yesterday's news
It could be as passé as a Jazz Age flooze
Or as lousy a hand as a couple of twos

TAXI:
I'm out like a tenant behind on the rent

DOLORES:
Out like an agent who won't return your call
Out like a deadbeat to whom you have lent

TAXI:
Out like an ever-loving spouse on the prowl

I feel like a fried banana

DOLORES:
You're smoother than a smoggy day
You're as hip as Missoula Montana

TAXI:
And I feel like a shit soufflé

BOTH:
When the plot has taken a turn for the worse
And your brain is like a chocolate fondue
Turn a phrase so it pays for the rest of your days
And retire to Honolulu

DOLORES:
You can take a figure of speech and torture it all day

TAXI:
But when she says

DOLORES:
You're like a day at the beach

TAXI:
I tell you by me pal that's okay

Both:
It could be mighty like the blues
Or be as passé as a Jazz Age flooze
So throw 'em a curve with your simile swerve
Give 'em a shot with a savvy bon mot
We like like and we like it a lot
We just like a simile hot
Like like like like like like like WOW mannnnnnnnnn!

(*Big finish*)

(*They lock eyes and get steamy again. Fog swirls.*)

Taxi: Chaka chaka chaka cha. Come here, baby.

(*A sizzling kiss*)

Dolores: Let's blow this clam bar.

Taxi: Which way out of Dodge?

Dolores: Scrape the gum off your shoes and walk this way. (*She starts off.*)

Taxi: Not a chance. Wait. I have something for you.

(*He pulls the cylinder out of the deep freeze. She takes it from him.*)

Dolores: Dillinger.

Taxi: It ain't Bigfoot.

(*She sizes them both up.*)

Dolores: I may need this. Let's go find out. Undulate, Tax! Undulate! (*She undulates off.*)

(*He lingers to take one last look at Uncle Walt. He pokes.*)

Taxi: Uncle Walt. Poor fella. He's thawing fast. Hold on. Who's that? (*Pokes*) Holy mugshot! It's Huey. And I don't see Dewey or Louie. Soul on ice. Wow. If Uncle Walt only knew who he was sleeping the Big Sleep with. He'd be fucking Goofy. (*To audience*) I wonder where you buy those little white three-fingered gloves?

(*End Credits music up.*)

(Dolores *and* Company *come back and sing a reprise of* Never Judge a Thriller.)

DOLORES:
I'm a thriller baby
I'm a heroine
I'm a killer baby
Aren't you glad you came in
You skimmed my pages baby
And you followed my plot
You found all the good parts
'Cause I'm hot hot hot

COMPANY:
Hot hot hot hot

Never judge a thriller by its cover
Never judge a thriller by its cover
Never judge a thriller by its cover
No no no

SALLY AND LIZZY:
I'm a best-seller baby

BOP:
Read me straight through

ROOT AND ZOOT:
I'll give away the ending

DOLORES, SALLY, AND LIZZY:
I'm gonna thrill you

GUT AND SHRIMP:
I know you're a mystery buffer

DOLORES:
I'll make this old pose new

TAXI: (*Spoken*) Old prose, old prose new

(*Instrumental break*)

COMPANY:
Never judge a thriller by its cover
Never judge a thriller by its cover
Never judge a thriller by its cover
No no no

(*Repeat as needed.*)

*Big Finish*

Gillian Richards

# *In His 80th Year*

## *A Poem for the Theatre*

GILLIAN RICHARDS began her career in theatre as a playwright in England. Her radio verse-play, *The Dreamers,* was broadcast by the BBC Third Programme in 1955. Her second play, *Sense of Direction,* was directed by Duncan Ross with students of the Bristol Old Vic Theatre School in 1958 while she was Fellow in Playwriting at Bristol University. A short sketch, *Red Brick,* was presented at the Royal Court Theatre on a program of work by new writers in 1959.

She subsequently stopped writing and went into theatre administration, emigrating to America in 1966 and becoming a citizen in 1975. She spent ten years as administrator of the Iowa Theater Lab (1971–81) and currently works in the Literary Services Department of Theatre Communications Group.

In 1979 she began writing and performing dramatic-narrative poetry. Since completing *In His 80th Year,* she has been working on a large (prose) play, *Americas,* about a group of filmmakers who get themselves embroiled in the politics of a small Central American country.



The first production of *In His 80th Year* was presented by BACA Downtown, Brooklyn, N.Y., co-produced by Heat and Light Co., and directed by Anne Bogart, in November 1987. The set was designed by Sarah Edkins; the lighting, by Carol Mullins. Nina Mankin was stage manager. The performers were Peter Guttmacher and Lori Wilner.

For purposes of production, it should be noted that, in the mind of the writer, this poem takes place in an old country house in upstate New York. The woman in the poem is of British origin; she is aged about 40. The man is a year or two younger; he is from Manhattan.

*In His 80th Year* is dedicated to Ric Zank and the Iowa Theater Lab.

## Act One

She sees it caught exactly in the crosshairs of the window:
A cocky little snub-nosed car.
It's crouched at the foot of the tallest tree in the driveway,
Mud-splashed but
Urban still, aggressively spit-polished.
It makes a cherry-red gash in the landscape.
Everything else is muted grays and browns,
Deep-frozen for a week now,
As indifferent to her as a sitter in an old photograph.
Two winters ago, she was telling him,
The stables collapsed spectacularly in a
Welter of cracked timber, buckled sheet metal and
Bent, rusty nails.
That's why the roof's off the summerhouse,
So the weight of the snow wouldn't crush it.
She's let her forehead fall against the cold glass.
Three inches from her chin she
Glimpses his elbow propped upon the windowframe.
But perhaps because she guesses how he stares out at the
  unfamiliar scene
With a small absent frown on his face
(His leg pressed against hers, also absently),
She's as relaxed as if she were alone in the old house.
She feels the heat rising from the radiator.
She sees, through his eyes,
A path half-buried in dead sycamore leaves,
Successive backdrops of gray tree trunks, bare branches,
A white gleam in the sky.
And she's thinking of things not directly related to him that she
Can't much help much like
Time and distance.

### i.

Right in the middle of the bed he throws down his bag.
He straddles beside it,
One arm laid over it. He looks
Quiet but keyed up like

---

Somebody about to be ordered into action
Who's conserving his energy.
Only his eyes move, following her movements.
Here he is, she says.
She brings the picture from the dresser:
It's my Daddy in the Matto Grosso in Brazil—
He's helping them to get the jungle charted before the bulldozers arrive.
He glances at the photograph.
In the middle of a dusty blue-gray underbrush
A lean, stoop-shouldered man
Pauses among the white thorn bushes.
He's got a butterfly net in his hand.
Look at him, she says.
She holds the photograph up in front of her visitor's face.
He's eighty this year.
See how his head's cocked on one side?
He's probably listening for the hum of some new species of bee.
The lounger on the bed raises himself on his arm.
He grins demurely at the photograph and
Passes his hand over her ass.
Doesn't he look the complete insect man? she asks him.
He must have cut the strangest figure in the old days
Crunching towards us over the shingle beaches,
With his butterfly net,
In his heavy black lace-up shoes and his
Thick socks that were
Knitted for him up in some croft in the north of Scotland.
You'd know he's coming
By the rattle of his haversack filled with glass tubes.
Her fist, with the photograph still clutched in it,
Falls in his lap. He waits for her to continue.
She remains motionless, lost in thought. Discreetly
He leans sideways and
Pushes an exploratory hand between the bed and her ass.
All his old clothes smelled of ethyl acetate.
You know what that's like? She
Turns her face against his shoulder.
All the sandflies and the little bees
Would get a whiff of it as he tipped the cork up deftly with his thumb.
Then they'd fall back down the glass sides of the tube
And their legs would curl up . . . .
She's on her feet again suddenly and is

Off across the other side of the room from him.
He opens his eyes with a start.
Look, she says.
She carefully lays the second photograph in the palm of his hand.
It's a smaller one. It shows
A doe-eyed young man standing with a woman in a white dress.
Oh, he says. He looks like you. Tall.
She lolls against the dresser
And, studying his bent head as he
Broods irritably over the photograph,
It comes back to her how at
His place he sat recently,
Just like that,
Holding the picture she'd given him on his knee.
She'd pretended not to notice how he
Rubbed the surface of her photograph abstractedly with his thumb
And appeared troubled somehow, or perplexed.
The picture was nowhere to be seen after that morning,
But in her mind's eye
He reached out his hand,
As he stood alone in his room late at night,
And her face stared back at him
Out of a clutter of old razor blades, cough lozenges
And letters ripped hurriedly open,
Pens that don't work anymore,
Or whatever it is
That he keeps in the small top drawer of his dresser.
She says: He was handsome then, wasn't he?
Over six foot, and dark, with that blunt Welsh nose.
The visitor swings one of his booted feet across the other.
He leans away from the photograph,
Viewing it with a deadpan expression,
With his head on one side.
He twists smartly around when she barges against him on the bed,
Fending her off with his elbow. She
Folds her fingers around his hand till
The photograph in his palm bends slightly.
Yes, she says. Friends we brought home for tea
Thought he was quite a looker.
His shyness would intimidate them though. To
Make himself agreeable he would

Reel off remarkable facts and statistics,
Emphasizing the main points with a
Stabbing gesture with the flat of his hand.
It seemed so incongruous then
That the ones he liked best were plump and sexy—
They weren't afraid of him, would even flirt with him a little—
Chastity, the Quaker, who
Later married a German and got a raw deal and Liz
Who put green and pink stripes in her blonde hair.
Her companion on the bed turns an impassive eye on her.
She kicks at the heel of his boot half-viciously,
Trying to get a rise out of him. He
Traps her foot between his shin and the bed.
Of course I could never see him that way myself.
She lifts her gaze scornfully to his:
Even though I've got a thing about
Lee Marvin/James Coburn (whichever it is)—
Guys who look tall and rangy on screen
And have thick sensual lips and a thatch of gray hair
And a little tension of cruelty in the face.
I say they remind me of my father.
The visitor continues to stare in the woman's eyes without so much as
Moving a muscle, his
Knee pressed to hers,
His eyebrows raised slightly.
She cracks up first. She
Falls back on the coverlet laughing. His smile
Reveals a row of reassuringly solid, even-sized teeth.
She relieves him of the photographs.
She sweeps them off the top of the dresser and into the drawer
And she closes the drawer with a bang.

He runs a hard shower.
Abandoned in the chilly room,
She feels as if
All that was left of him was
A bag tossed down on the bed (not hers),
The splatter of the water and a
Thin line of light under the bathroom door.
She finds a deep scratch in the leather of the bag
Scored by a sharp instrument,
A place where the stitching's come loose.
The torn and crumpled label which she unrolls reads

London, Heathrow to JFK.
London, Heathrow to JFK.
She thinks, on the road to London, Heathrow,
It's always the same story:
Back home, they sit in their little cars like driven men,
Obsessively tailgating,
Changing lanes without signalling . . . .
She tugs at the bag's zipper and the shower door
Screeches open like a knife slipping on a metal plate.

**ii.**

In the whole of the war the Germans dropped three bombs on
Slough.
No one got hurt. No doubt
There was a lot of dust, some broken glass,
Some bushes and trees were flattened . . . .
The sound of his bedmate's voice
Washes in the visitor's ear, then recedes, her
Restless foot worming its way between his ankles.
Uh . . .huh . . .he says. (The heel of his hand
Moving a little on her belly.)
Sometimes today I wonder
If my father's missions to the London docks were dangerous
When he went to inspect the sacks of grain and flour for weevils.
Was it in the middle of the blitz?
Did he wear a tin hat? But
Back then what did I know or care,
Lying on my stomach in my warm bed in the dark,
Making it come in stars and flashes of white light
(She never had it so good again),
Cute little bob-haired kid, look at her, totally out of it.
His head shifting toward her a little on the pillow, effortfully,
G' t' sleep, he says, sweetheart.
His mouth's propped on her shoulder too heavy to close.
Saliva gathers at the corner of his lip.
Are you listening to me? Mm . . .hm.
Stay awake a little longer. Angel.
You want me to hold your eyelids open for you?
(Poking at his face with her fingers.)
Christ, he complains. His upper body
Heaves among the bedclothes like a beached whale.
She rolls over to him, feeling for his

Still half-hard cock in the darkness. I
Lost you, she says to him.
Serves you right, he murmurs.
Whenever we would hear that
Steady uphill whine of the air-raid siren
(Bit by bit fitting herself
Back into the hollows of his body),
Then our parents would move down and
Sleep with my sister and me in the one big room,
In our room with the yellow splintery planks to
Prop up the ceiling so it wouldn't fall on us, and
Outside the French windows, under the bamboo tree which
Hung down its long leaves in the angle of the wall,
The barricade thrown up to protect from the blast with
Bricks and sandbags, heavy boxes . . .
Useful for cops and robbers, ambushes,
Battlements in the desert. It was
Back there that the neighbor boy,
Right in the middle of the game,
Peed his pants for no good reason.
Freaked me out utterly. She feels, with her face
Laid to his chest under the blankets, the
Tremor of a laugh start in the muscles of his belly and
Peter away beneath her cheek somewhere
Before any sound can come out of him. His
Forearm falls across her shoulder, inertly.
Through all that time
The only terror I remember is
My father's face
Coming at me like a clenched fist out of the dark,
Perfectly malevolent.
It wasn't solid but it
Glittered blackly
Like the colors when you grind your eyeballs with your thumb,
With beetling brows, bared teeth,
(He's going to get me, save me).
I imagine my mother snatching me up in her arms as I surface
Yelling in the middle of the bed in my crumpled flowery pyjamas, and
How does it feel,
Daddy, when your little girl
Meets you in her early Christmas morning dreams
And wakes up screaming?
The limp arm weighing on the woman's shoulder

Slips off her back.
Emerging from beneath the coverlet,
She sees that her guest is abandoned to sleep totally,
His jaw hanging open and his head
Half off the edge of the bed. He looks
Dead to the world, sprawled as
Carelessly as a kid tired out after an active day.
She thinks, like a kid
With its hair sweatily damp at the roots, with the
Smell of your cunt on its fingers.

That night she dreamt the house burned down.
She'd intended to wake the city visitor who was
Sprawled on his stomach next to her and whose
Hair had turned white as snow,
But when she opened the bedroom door
She found herself in a place that she didn't recognize
And she couldn't get back.
She remembered sitting on the floor by an elevator and even in
  that
Hushed corridor
With the urns of fresh-cut flowers and the deep-pile carpet,
The roar of the flames was deafening.
She buried her head in her arms and she thought,
Well, that's that.
She worried how they'd ever
Know who the dead man was in the second-floor room, if they'd
Figure it out from the small dent in the bone above his eye socket
Or the work he'd had done on his teeth.
She covered her ears with her hands
And the sounds that she heard were
Four-foot icicles, engulfed in fire, which
Melted from the eaves of the house and crashed to the ground,
One by one.
Up in the meadow
The deer kept their distance,
Snuffing at the smell of smoke in the sub-zero air
And showers of sparks flew over the maple trees.

**iii.**

It's fucking cold in here, says the visitor.
What warmth there is
From their bodies or their breath or the steam of the kettle

Has formed patterns of frost
Inside the panes of the kitchen windows.
The visitor tips up his chair, balancing himself with the palm of
One hand braced against the table edge,
His coffee mug clutched in the other.
He hangs there, interrogatively
Focused on the hunched figure muffled in a woolly jacket next
to him.
No response.
He throws out at her finally:
How can you live like this?
Her head rears up from the woolly collar of the jacket, scattering
Swatches of uncombed hair off her shoulders.
She stares past the left cheek of her last night's partner.
He tips the chair to a more precipitous angle.
When I catch pneumonia and end up in the hospital,
You'll be sorry, he says, with a grin.
Pretty bastard, she thinks to herself.
She gazes at his bent face which is
Wreathed in steam as he coughs sepulchrally into his coffee
mug.
The tip of your nose is pink and your
Eyes are puffed up and you
Still look good. She
Keeps her mouth tight shut. At length her
Friend lets down his chair. Coffee
Slops on the clean kitchen floor scrubbed for his benefit.
He leans expansively across the corner of the table.
C'mon, c'mon, c'm
On, he coaxes her.
He pushes the toe of his boot under her instep.
What are you sulking about?
Fuck it, he demands, after she's
Stubbornly stared down in her lap for a
Full minute, but it feels like longer,
Did I, or did I not, straight off the plane,
Drive one hundred miles in this godawful freezing weather just
to be with
You? Was it or was it not
Me who fucked you last night, sweetheart, until I was quite
played out?
What is your problem? he says.
I've been perfectly nice. Oh,
She bursts out, and she

Crumples up her little cotton table napkin in a heap by her plate,
All of these however many
Months it's been now you've been
Nice! He
Hesitates, still
Hanging halfway across the table towards her. His eye
Falls on the carved silver napkin ring sitting by her plate.
He studies the inscription on the back of the keepsake. Two
Deep lines form down the middle of his forehead.
The corners of his mouth start to turn up.
Is that your date of birth? he asks her.
She pounces on her pretty napkin ring, but he's
Shot out his hand and scooped it up from under her.
He spins it around on his finger.
Put it down, she advises him.
Oh, this is so
Genteel, he exclaims. There she sits,
As good as gold with her little linen table napkin spread on her lap,
Just like a lady, and you
Can't get a civil word out of her. Did your old
Dad teach you these nice manners? he asks her.
Like this, she says.
She leans over, she swings up her hand, and she
Slaps the back of his wrist as hard as she can.
The silver napkin ring
Bounces off her lover's finger. The blower on the wall behind him
Roars into action. Currents of warm air
Ricochet around the kitchen,
Lifting up the hair from the back of the visitor's head.
An empty butter packet skims across the tabletop.
Sunday breakfasts! she says. She
Raises her voice above the gusts of the blower.
How it all comes back to me! She's
Sweet seventeen and she's
Sitting at the right hand of her Daddy, with the
Yellow and the blue-check dusters
Hung on the rack over her head to dry.
He's fathered a pet monster all of his own, poor Daddy.
The visitor lowers his hand, palm down, on the table in front of him.
The flush in his cheek is
Fading as fast as the fiery patch of red skin glowing on his forearm.

Poor Daddy, she says, he's sheltering behind his Sunday paper,
But he knows that it's sitting there,
He can hear it swallowing.
This creature of his sits at his righthand side each Sunday morning.
Its bony wrists encircle its plate.
It makes a small scratchy sound
Rubbing at the seersucker cloth with a split fingernail.
Under the table
The creature twists its big sandalled feet together.
It slumps as low as it can in its chair,
Its spine in a hoop.
It wants to be small enough to be cradled in the palm of your hand, but
Each day it goes on growing.
The creature is hard to train.
Seventeen years and it
Still doesn't use a butter knife.
It resists looking things up in maps and dictionaries.
It plunges into passionate arguments,
Recklessly supported by half-remembered facts and insignificant statistical data,
It doesn't take its table napkin—
Slap it around a bit! says the visitor. He
Scrapes back his chair till it
Jars on the metal edge of the sink at his back and she
Gleefully follows his gaze as it
Veers upwards and
Curtly alights over her head where,
Fixed forever in his glossy poster, with his
Jangling elbows and the sexy creases in his trousers,
Travolta prances, pleased as Punch—
Slap it, Daddy! she exclaims above the roar of the blower.
Slap its wrist and yank it from its reverie. See how it
Flexes its long neck in a fury of humiliation.
Its bony fingers tear at the seersucker tablecloth. It lets out a
Howl of thwarted rage,
And before he knows it, poor Daddy's
Slammed down his fist in the middle of the fractious creature's back,
Half-knocking it into its plate, so it chokes and it gasps
And the room erupts in plaintive cries and shouts around him.
Daddy, Daddy,
Broods his seventeen-year-old monster,

I'm going to back off from you and
Sink down my paws in the mud.
I'm going to lurk with the water lapping at my gnarled eyelids,
Breathing and watching you.
One day I'll be able to knock over a tree with a switch of my tail.
One day I'll be able to take off a man's leg with one bite.
One day I'll learn to be beautiful in spite of you.
One day you'll need my love and I won't need yours.
The woman's voice has fallen to a whisper. Silence
Descends all of a sudden. It feels
Violent as if the room had
Tilted and settled down on its base with a crash.
The blower cranks to a stop.
She watches the knuckles on the visitor's hand turn
White, as he sits regarding her and
Grips the handle of his coffee mug. For an instant
She sees, as vividly as if he did it,
The coffee mug fly through the air and
Shatter on the panelling opposite. Jagged
Shards of it explode back in their faces.
Coffee runs down the wall.
He sets the mug on the table.
What do you want? he enquires of her.
He's standing with his thumbs
Jammed in the pockets of his jeans. He
Shoves in his chair with his knee. He looks
As frosty as the panes of the kitchen windows.
You want me to string you up from the ceiling and beat on
  the soles of your feet?
Where are you going? she asks him.
I have to take a shit, he says, and he
Walks out of the room.

**iv.**

I'd almost forgotten the dog.
An hour had passed by, two maybe.
I fell over him practically,
Sitting there all by himself in the gloom of the hallway.
I got down on the floor by his cushion.
Listen, I say to him. He
Lifts up his ears helpfully. Did you see a
Blond fellow go by you here, about medium height, wearing
A pissed-off expression and a gray sweater and a pair of
Nearly new cowboy boots, brown ones? If only

The dumb dog would look my way but he
Crosses one elegant front paw over the other and
Stares past my face with large, indulgent, ginger eyes.

On the second-floor landing I stood with my back to the wall,
Listening. Dead silence.
All of the doors are pulled shut but
Mine. My friends are all gone.
If it wasn't for the glimpse of the little red car from my window,
The wallet and keys which he's
Carelessly tossed on the dresser, I'd
Think that my darling's skedaddled again.
Maybe we'll go back to bed and forget it.
Who me? I'd never hurt you.
I didn't mean a word of it, angel. Hold me.

As soon as my eyes drew level with the third-floor landing
I caught sight of my visitor.
He's sitting cross-legged on somebody else's mattress,
The one with the green coverlet.
A book is lying open in his lap.
Whatever it is, he's staring down at it with such
Fanatical attentiveness,
His head propped on his palm, that I
Start to wonder if he's really reading it, but
Just at that moment he
Flips over the page
And flattens it down with his thumb in a businesslike fashion.

Finally he acknowledges I'm standing in the doorway.
The look that he gives me is
Meditative, distant.
I'm a face he remembers from somewhere.
He doesn't think he wants to meet me again.
I'd like to knock the book out of his hand. Instead I
Move over and kneel down on the carpet in front of him.
I follow his obsessive gaze to the bottom of the page and up again.
What are you reading? I ask him. I can see him
Stall in mid-paragraph but he doesn't answer me.
What is it, what is it, what is it? I say to him. Words,
He replies, and he covers the page with his hand.
I push my face close up to his. Miniscule
Gray flecks swim in the blue of his eyes.
Wish I could go where those words go, I say to him.
Where's that? he says, guardedly.
Inside your head.

There's a look in his eye but it
Vanishes, quick as a flash, like a small animal
Kicking up its heels and diving for the undergrowth.
The corners of his mouth curl slightly, it seems
In spite of himself.
I feel, in a rush,
Something—contrition, tenderness, panic,
Impatience to make everything right instantly—and
Without stopping to think which, I
Fall forward onto him, my
Face slipping past his cheek and my arms
Grabbing for his waist and his neck as if I'd
Drown otherwise, and he lets out a
Startled grunt, half collapsing backwards on the pillow, and the
 book gets
Trapped somewhere between us: I can feel
The corner of the cover sticking in my belly.
His voice is smothered in my woollen jacket: Get
Off of me! he explodes into my shoulder.
His whole body's rigid as a board but I
Hang onto him however I can, repeating
His name over and over (his
Face is ice cold). I've got to
Talk to you, I mutter to him as my
Mouth skids past his ear. How can I
Talk to you when you're thrashing around like this? Talk, my
Ass! Haven't you been
Talking a blue streak ever since I got in the door? What did I
Do? he demands, with a lethal jerk of his knee. Why should
I be the one who gets to take the flak for your old dad? It isn't
That, it isn't
Him, I say. (I'm stuttering and stammering.)
I'm scared to death I'll never get it up to tell you—to
Ask you to . . . .Help me a little bit!
Talk to me. He gives a sudden heave.
Talk to your shrink. Talk to your dad.
I've had enough of this! He
Wrenches his leg free, then his shoulder, and
Starts trying to roll over on top of me. You never
Listen! I protest as we're jolting about inconclusively.
(He extricates the book and chucks it on the carpet.)
Things change! You think the whole world's going to stand
Still, I exclaim
Breathlessly, just for your convenience . . . .

I'm getting throttled by his elbow. He's
Lunged sideways across me from his waist up. He's got his
Teeth pressed in my neck. Three cheers!
Here he is again, lover boy—a
Gift out of the blue . . .and I
Squeeze both my hands under his chin,
Arch up my whole body, prize his head loose,
Push him back a few inches till we
Hang there, face to face,
Eyeball to eyeball,
Rigid, our
Mouths touching nearly.
Total stand-off.
He falls back on the bed with a curse.

At least it feels a little warmer in the room.
I'm lying with the
Weight of my knees and my belly and my chest
Relaxed onto those of my lover,
And my face in his shoulder.
It shocks me—
It's hard not to roll off him,
Everything about him is so tense (I imagine him
With his teeth gritted, staring at the ceiling)—
Then I realize he's resting his hand on my head suddenly.
I lie there, not daring to breathe, feeling this
Mild pressure of his fingers on my hair,
Anger rising in me,
Utterly unable to fathom
How a gesture like that could come from him right at that
moment.
I try to anchor myself,
Flattened on his body in the little room, but
The weight of his hand carries me back
To another place and a different
Occasion altogether, which is present for me unexpectedly:
The walled garden with the railway cutting running by it,
With the one peach tree,
Too old now to bear much fruit, with
The wooden bower, leaning all to one side but
Sturdy enough to climb on,
Hung with clusters of tiny white polyginum flowers,
Delicious apples rotting in the grass . . . .
My father says it doesn't matter. He says
They don't care if I do badly in my exams.

The world won't end.
He's sitting in his deck chair, wrapped in a rug,
Straight out of the hospital, and he
Places his hand on my shoulder.
In all of my then twenty-two years, this has to be
The only impulsive, tender gesture I remember from him
(Maybe the last) and I think to myself that he had to
Die, almost, before he could make it.
I kneel in the overgrown grass under the apple tree,
Stiff with embarrassment,
Totally absorbed in my own worries.
How am I supposed to respond,
Now, to whatever, conceivably, he might have been feeling
All of those years that are gone, as I
Stare at the purple buddliah hang down its blooms by the wall?

I feel like a tomb that she's lying on in this
Little room with invisible animals (rats,
No doubt) scuttling about overhead in the rafters.
I fantasize that she isn't breathing anymore but when I
Grasp hold of a handful of her hair and I
Tug down on it, harder than I had intended,
A small, pained sound comes out of her.

I lie and listen to the scratching (or the
Gnawing, is it?) in the rafters. She's
Rolled her head sideways slightly. It
Balances there in the palm of my hand but I can tell
She isn't giving it to me really.
She's ticking over perceptibly, resisting me probably.
I haul her up a little by her armpits.
I'm suddenly determined to put an end to this whole business and I
Fold my arms around her real firmly.
I press my mouth against her face. I find
Her cheek is all wet. What now?
I try hard to kiss her on the lips. She
Squirms her mouth aside and I
Pull her against me more tightly anyway, as if I could
Squeeze whatever it is out of her.
You'd better stop crying, I say to her,
Or I'll get in the car and go back to the city.

The minute I loosen my grip on her she
Slaps one hand over her face and starts
Crying in real earnest, sobbing and choking and

Mashing her fingers in her eyes.
Did you ever write to me? she gasps
Vehemently, wiping off tears on my sweater.
One line, one line, one line, a
Postcard of Buckingham Palace? Are you
Kidding? I say to her. My head
Bounces an inch off the pillow. I stare,
Mesmerized almost, at all that moisture leaking through her fingers.
Presentiments of disaster
Flash through my mind. Also
Irrelevant memories of some past meeting . . . her
Blouse is half undone, I can smell
Perfume and sweat, faintly, and sex, and she's
Running her hand lovingly up and down the crack of my ass . . . .
Don't tell me! she says. She pushes her sleeve
Violently over her wet face, this
Gesture appearing to shut off her tears with
As little warning as they began. Ridiculous,
She rages at me, and her elbow jabs
Right in my diaphragm. Even if you ever
Thought of me you didn't have the proper stamps. Besides,
You didn't have a minute, did you? Poor baby, poor baby, he
Fell into bed in the evenings and was out like a light. What
Did you ever give a shit about but your work anyway? Jesus
Christ. I cover my eyes with my forearm.
Back home, the mail on the bureau is piled
This high. Who
Else would like to have a little piece of me? And
Telephone messages.
Decisons, decisions are needed. I
Count to ten, breathing
(As far as I can with her elbow still jammed in my ribs)
Evenly. Sweetheart, I say do:
Both of us a favor. Go downstairs. Wash
Your face, put on your pretty dress.
You'll feel like a million.
Then we'll light the candles, we'll
Open the bottle of wine which was much too expensive to waste,
And as soon as we're tipsy and mellow.
We'll creep right back in your nice, cozy bed where I
Said to you, didn't I?—we never should have been in such a
Hurry to jump out of it in the first place. Now you just tell
Me, sweetheart, if that wouldn't be better than quarreling?

I think she's going to belt me one for a minute Then she
Gradually lowers her head onto my chest,
Whether out of submission or obstinacy, I can't tell.
When did you ever go crazy like this when you visited
My place? I'm
Massaging the back of her neck with my hand, as I speak,
Cautiously, and I'm just
Willing her to come up with some friendly response.
This gloomy old house of yours is even making
Me morbid. I keep telling you,
You've no money and no fun.
Why don't you move down to the city? I ask her. Oh,
Darling, she murmurs. Up comes her
Chin like the turret of an enemy sub breaking the surface.
What would I do in the city?
I'd sit by the phone all week and wait for you to call?
I flip my head sideways on the pillow, and it hits me:
Some complacent, touched-up bastard, tacked to the back of the
door, is
Staring himself out in the washstand mirror. Men, men
Wherever you look in this damn house of hers. Other people's
Razors in the bathroom. Even the dog has a prick.
Stupid woman . . . .Well, to hell with it then, and I
Upset her expectant pose,
Half hoisting myself up into a sitting position.
I don't feel comfortable in your lousy, godforsaken home, I
Shout at the guy in the picture.
This house spooks me!

When I look at her again, she's
Hunched over on the coverlet beside me. She
Squeezes the folds of her skirt between her knees.
I lie back there and watch her rock herself a little to and fro.
All this torment!
How will you ever understand how I love it here? she
Blurts out suddenly. Your
Place doesn't have any ghosts, she accuses me. If
One ever dared raise its head, you'd
Zap it like a cockroach.

I tell her at least
I don't live in a houseful of other women, but
She isn't listening. She's
Crept right up to the head of the bed and she's got her
Mouth against my ear. Her

Hand's on my waist and she's
Moving it up and down a little as she talks.
She's telling me some story about
The beautiful young man who lives in the attic, who
Comes down through the trapdoor at night,
Barefoot, catches rats and chipmunks.
He whispers in the ears of the boys on the third floor.
I mutter to her not to quarrel with me any longer.
I haven't got the least idea what she's up to now, and I
Shift myself impatiently against that restless hand.
She tells me how they open up the curtains and
Spy on the third-floor bathroom, their
Faces pressed against the glass. She describes
Guttering candles,
Melted red wax dripping on the wet tiles.
She says the mirror on the wall is tilted forward.
The woman in the bath floats in the mirror too.
The rosy stain sinks like crimson smoke through the bathwater.
Nobody knows, she says, if it's
Menstrual blood or if somebody offed her.
Either way, the woman looks serene.
I tell her we should go downstairs to her room. I
Twist my head around till her mouth
Slips off my ear. She
Lays her hand on my cheek and pulls me back to her gently.
One summer, she says, when the skylight in the third-floor bath-
room is
Propped open, somebody eases her way through,
Feet first, then her calves and her thighs, the
Black V of her pubic hair stark against her white belly.
Clutched to her breast, she says the woman's got a big coffee can
Stuffed with flowers from the meadow
(And she lists them:
Meadowsweet, buttercups, loosestrife, purple and white
Phlox), a gift for her friend who's
Sitting in the bath laughing, she says, and soaping her knees.
Why is she fighting me? I
Jerk myself furiously half up from the pillow.
Don't you remember lying on the rug,
Not so many months ago now, maybe six, maybe seven, not
Caring if somebody or other
Loved me like this last evening or will love me tomorrow, and
it's the
Best, you say, with me, baby, baby, baby . . .?

Her women are kneeling together in the little attic room.
They're lighting perfumed candles . . .and I'm
Pulling her down on me a little, my
Arm around her waist. She doesn't seem to notice.
The women are lifting the silk camisoles over their heads.
Exchanging, she says . . .
Now I've lost track of this story,
Of the bare breasts and the straps of the silk camisoles. I
Take hold of her hand and pull it against me.
I hold it there against my crotch.
I think she isn't going to fight me. Her
Eyes have closed. I'm closing mine . . . .
She's trying to squeeze her hand free.
Don't fight me, I say to her. It's
Monday tomorrow. There's so little time. And I'm
Dragging on her wrist real hard, and I'm
Begging her (yes!) as near as makes no difference . . .

Bastard! the woman screams at him. She
Jerks herself up on her knees so fast
Her head and the low slope of the ceiling meet with a crack.
Ah . . . ha . . . she moans,
Biting at her hand. She
Cradles her head in her arms.
If you had a knife at your throat, if someone had you
Hanging from a precipice by your fingernails, if it was
The Day of Judgment and St. Peter himself was
Facing you at his pearly gate, you would change the subject!
The visitor's big eyes have sprung wide open.
He's kneeling on the coverlet.
He grins at her, white about the gills.
What subject? he says. There is no subject.
You and me, you and me, you and me!
You pretend to be stupid, she says, but I
Know when you're hiding.
He sways slightly towards her. He doesn't blink.
Coward! she spits out at him.
I'll kill you, he whispers to her.
His knees are digging in the coverlet. His arm is
Half-raised, awkwardly, as if it was
Somebody else's. . . . She's still
Poised, looking at the blank wall, when
All in one split-second spasm, it seems, he's
Upright, exploded off the bed,
Bursts through the door headlong—she hears the

Heels of his boots thudding on the staircase. . . . Wait!
She erupts out of the little room as he
Hits the second-floor landing, bent
Double like a man under fire. Come
Back! and she's after him as fast as she can. He's
Taken the stairs two at a time,
Misses the last three steps, spreadeagles
Up against the big porch door with a crash. The dog
Slithers down the corridor at his heels, its nails
Clicking and slipping on the floorboards. You're
Crazy! she screams at him as the screen door
Swings in her face and she
Slams it open again.
Momentarily the shock of the cold
Knocks all the breath out of their bodies. He
Stumbles back against the white picket fence.
Prickles of ice form in his nostrils.
Come back, come back!
Get in the house. You're insane!
He rights himself, one foot
Landing in the flowerbed. The dog
Races to and fro between them, barking frantically.
The visitor flings out his arms: Come on, he
Yells, it's great out here,
His fingers turning blue.
Are you crazy? she asks him. He
Ducks his head suddenly, dragging at his sweater.
That's what you want, isn't it? he says to her.
His head has vanished in the sweater. A
Quick twist of his shoulders—
The air burns on his bare skin like fire.
What are you doing? she cries, as the sweater
Lands in a heap at her feet.
You'll die, you'll die, you'll die, she moans.
She batters at the screen door with her fists.
I will if I like, he says. He
Hops on one foot, tugging at his boot with
Both hands. The dog is snapping at his ankles,
Crouching, its belly slung low to the ground. Oh,
Please stop! she entreats him.
What do you care? Fuck you,
He shouts back at her, doubled over, his
Teeth gritted. The boot
Shoots off his ankle, and the sock along with it.

Here, baby, he calls to her. The boot
Crashes on the screen door.
Dodging it, she exclaims:
Then why don't you go back to the city, you fucker?
I hope you have a blow-out, run in a ditch,
Kill yourself. Don't you ever come back again!
He lowers his foot gingerly onto the gravel.
Go to hell, she hisses at him. Freeze to death!
And she slams shut the inner door with a crash.

The man and the dog look at one another.
Approaching with its nose to the gravel, the dog
Snuffs at the visitor's naked, bone-white foot.
Go away, says the man.
The animal's tongue is warm and rough.
Over the roof of the old frame house the sky looks like
Lead. Almost all the daylight has drained out of it already.

## Act Two

### i.

His grip tightens on
The neck of the half-empty whiskey bottle which is
Hanging from his left fist.
Easy does it, the visitor says.
He thinks to himself:
If I stretch out my arm,
My clock radio will be sitting in its proper place on the night
 table.
My watch will be next to it, and the book I was
Halfway through reading, whenever that
Was—before my trip.
He opens his eyes and of course it's still
The same unfamiliar living room with a smell of (what is it?)
Long-closed trunks in the attic, dried flowers,
Sunday mornings with stale cookies and coffee like
Your grandmother's house in the country.
He's still on his knees on the cushiony, rough-pile carpet, and he's
Still transfixed
By the sight of a good dark suit (his own)
Considerately pressed and draped over a strange chair in a
 strange room;

His green silk shirt; his
Shoes, which he hadn't unpacked, tucked
Neatly together under the coffee table with
The laces ready loosened, side by side. That
Really bugs me, I used to say to my ex-lady, when you
Mess around with my things, I can't help it.
What glitters in the dim glow from the fringed Victorian lamp?
When he puts out his hand
A thin gold chain (it was
Hanging round the second button of his shirt)
Slithers like a live thing through his fingers.
He jumps and it
Lies there, glinting, half hidden in the pile of the rug.
He thinks to himself: I
Could leave. But I'm
Chilled to the bone. Except in her bed,
I haven't been warm for twenty-seven hours and it's
Warm in here. It's real warm. It's cozy. It's
Warmer than you need it like it is at Mother's place.
He changes clothes slowly.
He pulls on his shoes, propped
With his shoulder to the door of the adjoining room
(The one she wouldn't let me into. Later
She said to me, maybe). He's tied
A nice tight knot in his laces. He thinks:
Yes, whatever you've got
Planned, I'm good and ready for you.
You think I turn my back on trouble but I'm
Damned if I'm going to run out on you now, little lady. No
Such luck! He reaches for the doorknob, then
Releases it. Impulsively,
He's back down on his hands and knees,
Feeling for the thin gold chain in the carpet.
He's lowered his neck, raises his hands to his head:
I'll be with you in my own good time. . . .
Suddenly he's plunged into pitch-blackness.
He fumbles for the lampswitch, presses on it.
Nothing happens.
Antique junk, he mutters, violently
Lurching to his feet in the darkness.
The metal of her pretty gift to him
Swings against his collarbone, cold as ice.
His shins bruised and his palm
Finally closing again over the doorknob, he

Stoops and brushes off the knees of his good suit.
Back in the city
Everything is waiting for me still, my
Friends, my life, my work, he thinks.
Then he throws open the door and goes in.

Warmer air. Darkness. A trace of
The same perfume that
Won't have washed out of your clean pillowcases when you get
  in your bed tonight.
The visitor slides one
Neatly shod foot forward.
He lets his focus shift from right to left.
  Look at him, the woman thinks: how he
  Forces his eyes to open wider and juts out his chin.
  Come see what I've prepared for us,
  Handsome stranger. I've got the whole scene set.
The space that the visitor's in
Assembles itself around him, piecemeal: first,
A gleam off the polished floorboards; next
The folds of the blacks stirring faintly here and there;
Chairs pushed back carelessly by absent spectators.
  He's snuffing at the dark with
  His muzzle in the air like an animal's.
  Keep moving, my
  Fine, distrustful gentleman. What kept you so long?
He takes another step closer.
The visitor looks solid to the woman, and taller than he is. His
Is the one definite shape among all those shadows.
  She thinks: He isn't going to help me.
  I have to go through with it, though, or I'm lost.
  This way. You're getting warmer.
Now the visitor makes out two paler web-like shapes, her hands
Disembodied in the blackness, bony fingers spread
(An image like an X-ray) with
The palms pressed to an invisible wall behind her.
Above them he sees a face with no features floating,
Holes where the eyes should be;
A rope of tiny pearls crossing a V-shaped patch of skin.
  At midnight, the woman thinks, the prince turns into a
  Rat, or the rat turns into a prince (shut up, shut up).
  You look at me that way and
  I don't want you to get any closer . . . .
The ball of the visitor's foot has

Touched down barely when,
Almost at his elbow, a pale disc surfaces like an inverted moon. He
Steps backwards. Brightness floods in his face,
Blinds him. He raises his hand, and
Out of the darkness between them there springs up, with an impeccable
Dazzle of white linen and coruscations of silver,
A small round table set for two—
A single long-stemmed rose (crimson, of course) in a narrow vase,
Crystal glasses,
The wine bottle, which he recognizes from the label,
Luxuriously nestled in a bed of ice . . . .
I'd like to be beautiful for
You this evening. I've got on
A touch of that pretty blusher, here and here.
I combed my hair finally. It's for
You that I'm wearing the elegant black velvet gown.
Holy shit, the visitor breathes, the candles and all.
The brightness is fading from the tablecloth.
Light them, she whispers. She's still
Flattened with her hands pressed to the blacks behind her.
And open the wine. The visitor
Grasps hold of one of the light little caneback chairs and swings it under him.
He plunks down his green silk cuffs on the snowy tablecloth.
(What game does she want me to play now, I wonder?)
You look fresh out of a bandbox, she says. She
Studies his expression but he's perfectly straightfaced once more,
Solemn even. Why am I so clumsy? she whispers. I feel like some
Crabby lunatic who's been let loose in your beautiful, well-
Regulated life. I'm sorry if I hurt you.
The matchbook turns,
Once to the left, once to the right, pinched between the visitor's
Thumb and his index finger. Silence.
He flips the cover up. Steam
Hisses through the radiator in the other room.
I was going to be your friend, wasn't I? You
Remember? Me
Of all people. He thinks to himself:
So now you want to get romantic. I can get
Romantic too. Just watch me.

I have something to tell you, the woman says. You're
Angry, I know. Please listen anyway.
He lights the candles with a steady hand
(Gray shadows spring up in his eye sockets, the flames
Flicker briefly in his pupils) but
Fumbles the corkscrew. The wine bottle
Skids sideways on the tablecloth. The corkscrew
Jabs in his finger. We'll save the apologies for later, he
Announces, with the bottle jammed between his knees.
One hour from now
I'm leaving for the city. She says:
Tomorrow, you said; you said tomorrow.
He thinks to himself: Was that a hit? Just
Look at this wounded little bird come fluttering down.
Now we'll play it my way. You rotter! she cries.
No, I can't believe you're going to walk out on this mess!
God help you, don't you want to give us a chance? You're going to
Ruin everything! You pack up your bags, sweetheart,
The visitor says. (A twist of his wrist, more
Vicious than it needs and with a sullen squeak
Out pops the cork from the bottle: I got it,
Bastard.) You're coming with me.
You hear me? he says. You're not
Listening. I said I'd like to have you ride back with me to the city.
She tugs at the skirt of her black velvet gown.
Ridiculous, she mutters at him. Why
Would I go to the city? Goddammit,
Don't you want to go with me? He skims
The rose, the crystal, and the silver ice-bucket with
A wave of his hand. Is this a game? he says. This
Set-up is yours, so you'd better not be holding out on me.
The woman glowers at the floor by the visitor's feet warily.
You're
Mad as hell at me. Whyever would you
Want me to go with you to the city? What
For? she asks. I need company.
He bends towards her with the wine bottle
Cradled in the crook of his arm. He sets it
Delicately on the tablecloth. Whatever it
Is with me tonight, I can't
Stand to go back to those two damn plants and a couple of
Six-week old beers in the refrigerator and a
Note from the Lend-a-Hand boy. You come with me.
She's lifted her eyes, not to his

Face, but to the motion of his adam's apple and
The glitter of the gold, half hidden by his collar.
You've had a few, she asks, haven't you? He
Stares ruminatively at the woman. Now
His fingertip is stroking up and down the petals of the rose. Well
You know what they say, he says.
Truth come out of the neck of a bottle. She
Flips her head from side to side.
She doesn't answer. The truth is:
Wouldn't you say this thing has got bigger than both of us? It's
Bigger than me, for sure, so
I plan to stop fighting it. The woman's eyes
Jerk level with the visitor's. She
Covers her mouth with her hand. Oh, you're not
Serious! she sputters at him through her fingers.
I'm supposed to believe that you . . .?
No! she says. You believe what you like but
You've got to come back home with me tonight. I get sick
Just thinking I'm not going to wake up in the morning with that
Brainy head of yours on my pillow. . . . Help, she
Murmurs. I can't handle this. Suddenly
He's turning sentimental. Something
Terrible must have got into you. . . .
I wasn't paying good enough attention and it's
Crept up on me, I
Guess, he says. What can it be? I
Miss the little irritations even, like
Having the books put back upside down, your
Bedtime snacks, the crumbs among the covers always, my
Goddam record that you scratched. I
Miss you. I can't explain it any better. Don't give me
A hard time, he says. You think it's
Easy for me to say these things to you, considering
What a rotten weekend this has been—up until now, of course?
I don't understand what you're telling me, she protests. . . .
  You do
So. What are you getting flustered about otherwise? You
Decide, he says. You give up this house, pack not more than
Two bags tonight, make all
Future complaints about me in writing and mail them to a fic-
  titious address. Then
The bastard of your dreams will carry you off in his little red
  rent-a-car and,
Angel, as you would say,

Make space in his closet for you. Don't
Do this to me, she entreats under her breath. What's
The matter with you? Are you pissed out of your mind? You're not
Asking me to move in with you? He
Frowns intently at the tablecloth with his cheek on his hand.
What do you want? he says softly. You want to
Cram every row you're ever going to have with me into just
One weekend? Sweetheart, I can't live at this
Pitch. I'm exhausted already . . . .
I told you, I'm sorry I upset you, she mutters. Oh
Heavens! you know what I have in this place, my
Friends, work, theater, the house, even the dog. Everything.
I know, he says, I'm very flattered.
How can I feel like this? she exclaims. I feel
Happy. The visitor fills up his glass in a hurry. The bottle
Slips from his grasp almost. Wine
Splashes on the tablecloth.
Who would have thought it? he murmurs.
This same fellow who was such a creep and a coward
Only a few hours back, who
She couldn't wait for him to
Crash in a ditch and be heaved through the windshield. Now
She wants to move in and cook his dinners for him. My, oh
My. This is some turnaround, I'd say.
The woman's standing at the table and she
Dubiously stares down in the visitor's face. She's
Half pulled out her chair. No,
She says. Just this once, don't make a joke of your feelings. Who's
Joking? he demands.
He grasps hold of the little table by its two sides as he leans over it. His
Grin spreads from ear to ear. I've got a
Great notion, he says. It must be five or six a.m. his time by now.
Let's call up your Dad.
I said, we'll call up your Daddy. Tell him
His little girl's about to be taken away out of this half-assed, middle-class poverty.
You don't like the idea? Dad's
A little old-fashioned maybe. Tell you what: You
Say to your Dad that I'll marry you in a couple of months,
Just as soon as my divorce is final. Yes.
You didn't know about that, did you? We

Decided to make everything legal at last, the old lady and I.
Well, why would I tell you?
She stands leaning on her pretty cane-seated chair with
Her hands jammed down on the back of it and
Her brows knitted.
My father, she murmurs. What makes you think
You could talk to him? You might as well be
A visitor from Mars for all you would have in common. His
Face swoops across the little table towards her.
The chain hanging from his neck swings with a
Chink against the side of the crystal vase with the rose in it:
Here, sir, he says. You, sir,
Mister Professor. Give me your
Lanky monster-daughter. What of it if
She's turned out to be something of a harpy and a scold? I
Guess I'm going to take her off your hands anyway. I've been
Shopping around for a real good bed of nails to get
Settled down on. . . . Sir, this is
It, I think. It's—she or nothing . . . !
She's turned away from the man. She's
Dragging on the caneback chair so its legs
Bump and scrape across the polished floor behind her. Now
  she's
Parked it squarely in the middle of the space.
She's kneeling on the seat of it. She
Touches her face to the velvety skirt of her gown.
You were fooling? the woman asks.
She thinks to herself: Is it
Me or is it him? Now what's his
Story, really? What if his brain's like a rat's (shut up, shut up)?
He remembers danger and pain in the cells of his skin but
Nothing connects with anything else, oh no. . . . I don't
Believe you! he says to her. He
Slaps against the table edge with the palm of his hand. I feed
  you this
Sentimental bullshit. . . . Good
God! he exclaims, and in two minutes flat you're
Lapping it up like a pussy at its saucer of milk—so I'm
Pining away for you in the city. Like
Hell, I am. All I have to do to get you down there is
Pick up the phone. Are you crazy? His lover
Presses her palms over her cheeks.
She whispers to the visitor as she peers up at him, sidelong:
I've got a joke for you too.

I wrote you a poem, she says, while you were gone.
He stares in the woman's face uncollectedly. He
Drops his hands in his lap. What the
Hell? he asks. What difference does it make?
You wouldn't want to live with me. Yes,
She cuts in on him. I wrote a poem for you but
It didn't come out right. I tore it into
Little pieces but it keeps going through my head this evening.
You want to hear it?
"You want to hear what I saw on 47th Street?
Lord, what a night to be out in. Going to get
A short in those bright lights . . . ."
Why don't you come down to the city for a couple of days
anyway?
"You want to hear what I saw . . .?"
A poem! he says. What poem? You and your
Damn poems. What is it? he demands of her.
A sonnet to my blue eyes? It's
A story, she says, about a
Rat who turns into a man or a man who turns into a rat.
"You want to hear what I saw on 47th Street?
Lord, what a night to be out in. . . . I'm
Chattering, soaked to the. . . ." Rats!
He exclaims. Now what's got into her? He
Dumps his elbow on the table and his chin on his hand.
So tell me your poem, he throws out at her. Begin! I'm listening.
She tips a little forward on
The seat of her caneback chair and repeats softly:
"You want to hear what I saw on 47th Street?
Lord, what a night to be out in. Going to get
A short in those bright lights. I'm
Chattering, soaked to the skin. Water's
Sloshing round my insoles.
The garbage is floating away. . . . Then, pow!" The woman
Throws up her arms suddenly and tosses off her hair from her
cheeks.
"With the crash of a trashcan lid,
A great gray rat, bigger than a baby,
Arcs up with a thrust of his strong gray thighs and
Smacks the sidewalk in mid-stride, streaking towards
Broadway.
Cold and wet don't bother him.
He goes so fast all you can see
Is the glint of his two canines and his eyes. Red neon

Flashes off his slick coat. He
Hits Broadway. Taxicab-for-hire screeches to the curb,
Its wipers going like crazy. Head-on leaps
The mad rat. He
Divebombs the passenger window, meets it with a
Sickening crack and—what do you know?
Vanishes totally." What
Is this? the visitor asks.
Listen, she says to him. Didn't you say you'd listen?
"Well, I'm here to tell you: Dead rat, stunned rat,
I'm shivering and dripping at the traffic light and
That rat was gone. But there's a fellow in the back of the cab
Now, and he leans forward. He peers out
At the bright lights and the rain with the ghost of a smile on
his face.
He looks like a guy who put his money in the right place.
The most beautiful man you ever saw. . . ."
Thinks the visitor: Shit, I'm a
Rat, is that it? This is what I get for
Sharing my cab with a half-drowned female admirer.
She says: You did a good job but—
But, she says, but, she goes on. . . . They've got a
Television in the place. Well, I'm telling myself
Trouble, trouble, I know it when I see it, and I'm
Watching them losing the ballgame out of the corner of my
eye. . . .
She says: "The rat is a prince! Yes, the Rat
Prince it was, ladies and gentlemen, who
Rescued me out of the cold and the rain, this
Brand-new man, lounging in the back of his cab with
No baggage in the trunk and not a care on his shoulders.
He'll never let me on the street again, he doesn't
Trust me with his secret." No, he doesn't
Trust me, she parenthesizes to the visitor.
"Now my darling is my jailer and tormentor, my
Entertainer. He's the joker in the pack. He's painted
Pictures of windows and doors for me on the walls of his room.
I've got
A view of the park, blue sky, a hallway full of sunlight, but I'm
Trapped in his pad like a rat. I can't get
In or out. There isn't any glass in his mirror.
All you can see in it is
A picture of a painted man smiling at you from a painted room.
I tried the drawers of his dresser. He's screwed these

Shiny brass knobs on them but they're just fake fronts,
None of them open. I pulled down the books from his shelves.
I threw them all over the floor because
The pages were blank. I tore up his mail—
Will you look at these letters that he's getting?
Secondhand envelopes, all of them, sealed and empty—
Don't leave me alone here! I'm going crazy in your
Funhouse. I'll dash out my brains on your
Nice white bathroom tiles, I
Mean it. . .!"

No, it's altogether too
Much, fumes the visitor, what you want from me. He
Nurses his glass against his green silk shirtfront.
What is it with the woman? I've got
The door half shut on her and she just stands there,
hanging on my belt.
She says she wants to watch me while I'm peeing.
I don't let her. I tell her she's really perverted. What! she
Says. How can you screw around the way you do and be
So prudish about that? I tell her it's quite different.
She says: Did you never used to let your wife watch you—
Or any of your other lovers? I don't answer her. Now
She unknots my tie. She's telling me she
Wishes she could have had a little brother who looked just
like me. . . .

She says, "I don't know what it is that he's looking for
Nights, when he's out on the town. I'm
Huddled in the dark on the Rat Prince's bathroom floor.
Whimpering and banging my head on the toilet seat, stupid
Maniac. . . . Well, here he comes, people.
Whoops!" she exclaims. "He
Flips open the big brass-studded doors and
In he marches. Ranks of glittery glasses
Twinkle in the gloom. Twelve princes
With their natty suits, silk shirts and
Eyes that flick from side to side
Spring up along the back of the bar in a dozen mirrors. He
Turns heads. He slaps his money on the counter.
Yes, all you folk, this really
Is the Rat Prince. But say hello to him. He won't
Bite or scratch. He's got
The rat by the tail and it's trapped,
It will never run loose again. . . . The
Pattern on his black-and-white bathmat is driving me crazy. . . ."

Who needs her? thinks the visitor.
I threw out all the notes that she'd written me. It's
The middle of the night and I'm
Crawling around on my hands and knees, surrounded by a
Litter of torn newspaper clippings, letters
Read and unread, receipted bills, photographs, old bank
statements.
At three in the morning, the whole damn lot's
Tossed or filed away neatly. My room's
Real shipshape. I
Fall into bed and I don't give a second thought to any of it. I
Sleep good. . . .

"At three in the morning," the woman says, "the Rat
Prince's key turns in the deadlock softly.
When he comes home at last,
I creep into his lap as gentle as a kitten. I
Push my face against his prickly cheek.
He smells of whiskey and good soap. He gives me
Tender kisses and I open my mouth for him. Sometimes,"
The woman says, "He crushes me up in his fierce embrace so
Tightly, as if he thought it was
Me who could finally make him a real human prince. But
Forget it. When I go to sleep in your arms,
Prince, I get nightmares.
I dream that you're a great gray rat
Who's bounding through the city sewers.
One butt of his skull and he
Sends the manhole cover flying. Now he's coming,
With his slick fur plastered to his skin, with
His wild red eyes and shit on his neat little paws.
He's going to burst straight through your bedroom window
glass—
Oh, where have you gone
Now, Mr. Nice Guy? What did you do?
Your claws are tangled in the tasselled coverlet and you've
sunk your
Two sharp canines deep in me."

They hear the dog bark twice. It
Scrapes with its nails at the hallway door,
Whines softly. Then it falls silent.
Impulsively, the woman drags in her chair so far she finds
Her knees colliding with the visitor's beneath the tablecloth.
Your

Old dad, he says finally.
He's filled up her glass and he's still
Sitting forward with his chin propped on his hand. He
Touches the ice-cold bottle to his cheek. Your
Wicked old dad. I can just picture it. Yes . . . .
He settles himself back deliberately in his little chair,
Muscle by muscle. Some
Mild old man, he resumes. Some
Maybe mildly eccentric professor who's still
Shuffling around with his bifocals and his butterfly net and Miss, his
Grown daughter here, is determined she's going to have a monster for her daddy.
The woman's face is buried in her forearm. She
Hasn't moved. She isn't listening perhaps.
He reaches out his hand with the bottle in it.
Till you started this trouble,
Did I ever once do you harm? he asks her.
At length she raises her head. Mussed
Strands of her hair fall over her face and she
Pushes them off brusquely. Believe me,
He says. He watches his glass turn
Pale gold to within a centimeter of its rim.
Life is too short for us to live up to your fantasies.
You can sit here like
The wicked princess in your fairytale castle which in
Reality is a junky, badly heated clapboard shack and is
Probably infested with termites and is
Going to fall in on your head some day soon, but
Me, I'm down there in the real world earning a fucking living.
I'm working my ass off while you sit around and
Spin out these horror stories about your dad and me. So don't tell me it's
Me who is frivolous. I know what's what at least.
The woman's eyes move over the visitor's face
Haltingly, like
A hand feeling for a switch in a dark room. Your
Faa-ther, he mocks her. I'm betting he's a
Harmless old gentleman in carpet slippers who can't make
Head or tail of you. I could be wrong but then
I figure you'll have given him as good as you got. You're
Nobody's victim. That
I do know for sure. He watches the
Lips of his lover part slightly. Words, it

Seems, form on them, but she doesn't say anything.
He gently grinds the bottle down among its ice cubes.
Baby, baby . . . he whispers. He bends over
His glass, twisting with his free hand at
The stem of the rose till it snaps. Its crimson head
Lolls over the neck of the vase. See? This is
You. Right? He throws it on the tablecloth.
The woman straightens in her chair. She
Continues staring in the visitor's face and is silent. But
What good is that now,
Angel . . .? (The words come out of her with a
Jolt. She seems to skip a breath or two. Her eyelids
Blink shut. They are folded and creased. They look
A heavy weight to him. . . . And darkness, he notices,
Is moving in behind her head and from the edges of the room.
The candles are burning lower now.)
It's all well and good, isn't it?
In your eightieth year,
Suddenly to seem like someone who must always have been
gentle. So
What? when you're a tired-out old man and you
Don't want to tramp over the dunes or the bush or
Set up your tent in the jungle anymore. When
You can't spell anymore or you
Write down a word and another one comes out.
You eat and drink but nothing has a taste anymore, and
You're scared to drive in the dark. When
Your whole life has to be
Planned around finding the next bathroom because
Your bladder doesn't work properly anymore. . . . Don't you
think that
Even you would be subdued? But
Nothing's going to change now, she exclaims.
Is it? my father and I
(What a pair), now we can sit and be
Sociably unsociable together in the same room, and it's
Comfortable to know next to nothing about one another. We'll
Never ask each other any questions. Questions
Are nothing but trouble. They make trouble. You
Know that. . . . Her eyes
Have fixed upon the visitor's and though
He freezes with his mouth clamped to the rim of his glass in
Mid-sip, his fingers continue
Working on the petals of the rose, obliviously

Massacring it till she shoves his hand aside.
The pathetic old bastard, he says. You should
Let him go. He's your father, that's
All. He's only your father. Yes,
He's only my father, she repeats. Her palm's
Lingered against the visitor's. Her fingertips, he sees, have
Settled on his wrist as if they're
Searching for the pulse perhaps, for
Where the blood is pumping. But
Imagine, she says,
Forty years of being married to a man who doesn't know
How to look at what he feels, let alone
Say what it is. See, my late mother, now
There was a gentle, obstinate woman who
I think never gave up the fight for him entirely, but
A gentle, gentle lady. And it was
A good marriage. Anybody would have told you that. So
I used to wonder to myself, how
Come she would end up, as she did, in
Such despair? I mean, she had me who would
Never shut up telling her what I felt. And then she had
Him. Forty years of
Struggling to keep your end up so as not to get
Bull-dozed. Forty years of sitting opposite a wall without
Footholds or cracks. Who
Is it inside there? Musn't she want to know
What keeps his heart ticking over for forty years? It's
Got to be more than just a fascination with bees . . . .
No, it doesn't have to be more. The visitor
Draws back his hand. He
Shifts his body sharply in the little chair. His eyes are
Brilliant now. They seem to glitter in the fading candlelight.
Why should it be more? Because you, sweetheart, you
Happen not to give a shit about bees, is that it?
But he doesn't know what he's doing, she says.
Darling, listen to this. She's
Thrust her elbow forward on the tabletop. Her
Knee is digging in the visitor's (she doesn't notice it).
The night that she died
They warned us we should come and sit with her.
He wouldn't go because he said she would
Never know anyway, and it would be
Painful and for nothing. Probably it was
Indecent, he felt, in some way to

Suffer more than was absolutely unavoidable. So
At midnight, I'm getting off the underground.
The payphone is there and I pass right by it,
Right at the foot of the station steps, and I say to myself: yes,
Call. Tell him, get in the car, this is
Idiotic. Drive me there. What are you doing,
Daddy, Daddy . . .?
Then I walked back to his house and slept.
Six o'clock in the morning, when the call comes and
There is no longer any such person, only
Possessions to be collected and a body to inspect,
Up we stumble out of our beds, a
Couple of pathetic freaks: him who didn't have
The wits to know what he needed and
Me who knew and didn't have the wits to ask.
Now I can't go on this way with you, she says. Not
Another day, another hour, another minute!

The flats of the visitor's hands are
Planted firmly on the tabletop. He's
Dead erect in his chair. The pressure on his knee has
Eased a little. Though his gaze is
Riveted upon the woman, the sound that he's listening to
Is from out in the yard: wind
Stirring, shaking the coating of ice on the sycamore twigs.
How did this happen? he says.
Last spring all I was looking for was
A warm body to hold. Now and then a good time.
And I land up with you. Oh,
Nobody knows what you want really, or why you're
Sitting here. What do you care anyway?
Go back to your little pad in the city.
Double-bolt the door and put the chain on it, she says.
Turn on your high-tech lamp. . . . It
Doesn't matter. Nothing ever matters to you, does it? or
You don't want me to find out that it matters to you.
Who knows which? There's
The glimmer of a smile on the visitor's face.
He pushes his glass to one side. He doesn't answer. You
Hold me off at arm's length, she says. I wish I knew
Why it is. I wonder what I did or if it's
Anyone who cares about you. I wonder if you get
Lonely. Sometimes I wanted to call you so much . . . .
All of these months . . . she persists.

Now tonight you tell me. . . . She
Stares at the gold band on his finger. That was,
What was it? eleven years, ten? out of your life.
Brushed under the rug, finished with. You
Don't feel a thing. You think I'm
Stupid, don't you? The base of the visitor's glass shifts
Another inch or two across the tablecloth. He gives
A barely perceptible shake of his head at the woman opposite.
Say something! she says. Talk to me!
He says to her: Is it
My past or yours? If you
Want to cry over it, go ahead.
I've got other things to do with my life.
Why do you carry that picture around with you? She
Tosses out the question at the visitor, then
She follows it up in the air with a look—as if it might
Detonate visibly. He hasn't moved. His
Bland expression hasn't altered.
Picture? he says to her. You're
The one who chooses, she says. You're the one who
Always has everything under control. That's
What you let me think. But I don't know anything anymore.
He asks her: What picture is that?
The woman with the wide-open eyes. Looks
Like a startled bird. Looks
Not at all like me, but
Who can tell really?
I don't remember that I ever showed you that. That's
My wife, he says. I know, she answers.
He stares back at her. Two
Faint red spots appear where the skin tightens on his cheek
  bones.
Wherever did you see that? he asks her.
She glances at his hand which rests,
Claw-like, with a fold of the tablecloth caught up in it. She
Shakes her head. Where? he asks.
Don't you know where you keep it? Say
Where, he says. Since you're so perfect. The one
Woman I can trust, isn't that it? and in
Such a hurry to pass judgment on
Me. What other way . . .? she begins. Where, damn you!
Where it is of course! Looking for some
Small clue, for a sign, anything. . . .
In your wallet, where it is.

In between the credit cards. When?
He ask her. Up in my room, when
You didn't leave, you wouldn't
Leave. What does it matter? So
Maybe I'll think you still care about her a little bit. Is that
Something to be ashamed of? I
Have nothing to be ashamed of, he says, and with his
Whole strength, he tugs
Upwards and sideways at the tablecloth. It
Billows up between them, and for an instant
Forks and knives, candleflames, ice cubes, crystal
Hang in the air, then
Slide together in a glittering stream. The wine bottle
Hits the floorboards with a dull crack and everything
Shoots sideways. Sprays of broken glass
Erupt from under one of the pewter candlesticks (she
Covers her face with her arms), the other
Crashes off the baseboard. The flames are exstinguished. She
Glimpses the chair opposite knocked on its back. Then
She rises to her feet in the pitch darkness, hears
Glass crunch under her slippers, feels her way forward. . . .

**ii.**

He's stomping all over the mattress. He bellows,
The keys! His shadow leaps up on the bedroom wall. He hollers,
Just get me the keys! (Like a rat in a trap.) He
Thumps with the flat of his hand on the ceiling.
Car keys! You've taken them, haven't you?
Where are the keys to the car!
Her print by Chagall with the scarlet cardinal's hat which
Hangs at the head of the bed is knocked quite crooked.
She thinks: He trashed my room.
All the crashing and banging, I
Came up the stairs with my heart in my mouth.
I'm off to the city. Best
Give me the car keys, he hisses.
She steps through a jumble of sweaters and underwear. The
Drawers of the dresser are all up-ended. One of his
Boots has been tossed in the sink. My
Photos, she says. As quick as a lizard he
Shifts his foot sideways and treads down her hand in the
coverlet.

Give me the keys or I'll rip 'em. He
Reaches for the photographs, he slaps them up against the
  ceiling.
Your precious old daddy! God help me,
I've taken on you and your daddy. Damn idiot, I'm
Showing you a good time, and what d'you want?
Fights, misery, misery, paranoid fantasies—
Give me the keys or I'll rip 'em! And under his thumb
She catches a glimpse of blue Brazilian sky, a
Thorntree upside down, a butterfly net.
She drags out her hand from under the sole of his shoe. You can
Rip them, she says. She's folded one arm
Around each of his legs. Now
She's gripping him tight by the back of the knees.
Goddammit, I've got to get back to the city!
Just give me the car keys! She
Presses her face to his thigh.
I love you, I love you, she says to him.
Jesus! he yells. (Torn scraps of the photographs
Float past her cheek like confetti.) Who are you
Kidding! And right by his heel
The woman in white who's torn in half at the waist
Looks out from one fragment serenely, a fair-haired zoology
  student,
She's got a new dress, her life is ahead of her.
Great! he exclaims. She loves me. What
Else do you want to know,
Lover? He's kneeling on the coverlet in front of her. He's got
Her skinny wrists squeezed up in one fist and he
Hauls her a little to and fro. C'mon, c'mon, baby!
You want to humiliate me some more?
What d'you want to know? Go ahead!
You want to ask me what I said to my gentle wife on
The night I walked out of there? You want me to tell you what
She said to me? You want to know if she
Cried? You want to know if
I cried? You want me to tell you if I fucked my gentle wife
  afterwards? Well, why
Should I have any privacy? I'd
Split open my own head, just like a watermelon, if I could,
For you, for you, because you love me! Right?
She says: You act like a man with no past. Some
Superman who can wake up with a clean slate each morning.
You don't have any secrets. You don't give a damn.

Everything's peachy! He asks, so
Why couldn't you leave it that way? He
Hikes her up against him. Because
You feel something about me, I don't know what. . . . Because
You'd just walk out of my life, not for
Any good reason, just on a whim. All I'd be then
Is a slight ache in the middle of the night, a
Toothache, an attack of gas . . . would you
Ever even know it if you missed me? Bullshit,
He says. I've got feeling like a toothache and I
Know it's you. From the very first day . . . you come on so
Sweet, make no trouble. No, you don't
Call me. Not you. I tell you it has to be
This way or that and you go along.
I'm not fooled though. I see you
Sitting tight like your daddy on his high lab stool, and I'm a
Slit frog, splayed on a slide so you can
Get in my guts, study me good.
Baby, I can't move hand or foot . . . I open my mouth and
I see you turning the words over in that busy little brain of yours,
Biting on them, chinking them to check if they ring
True. You watch me. Even when I kiss you you're
Fighting me to keep your eyes open as long as you can. You
Judge me, you second-guess me. Like some
Animal that never lets up has got in under the foundations
  and is
Burrowing away there. Why, half the time
I fuck you and you won't come with me—Stop that! she
Cries out. I've told you a million times—
You think I do it on purpose? I
Love you, you fool, I love you! What
Good does that do me? he asks. You can love
Shit. Just a half-educated, muddle-headed,
No-account bastard is all I am to you, who
It happens you want to fuck, who
You want to get dressed up for you (he
Tugs at the gold chain hanging from his neck) put
Pretty things on me, like a doll, your
Blond doll, your angel, angel. . . . Who are
You, he exclaims, tears springing in his eyes, to
Judge my life? He holds out his fist with
The snapped chain dangling from his knuckles. Things you do!
I'd be ashamed to have them pass through my head even. . . .
  Well,

It's not here nor there to me if you want to show me any respect. I
Know where I'm at, what I'm worth, and
Just what I can do. I always have, and I will. You can
Love me till you're blue in the face, nothing's going to change
that.
Forget it, forget it. I'm
Never going to cover myself in sackcloth and ashes for
You. You'll never see it.
Ah, she says,
So this is what you feel. . . .
The shadows of the overturned lamp
Fan out on the bedroom wall behind them.
She's bent over. Her unkempt hair
Laps on his sleeve as she
Stares down at his outstretched fist with the chain in it.
She raises a finger to touch it, and as if it was
Utterly strange really, as if it was something that was utterly
new, it
Bears in on her, with a jolt, how
The skin is drawn and wizened there between his knuckles, and
The puffiness where the vein traverses the back of his hand.
She kneels upright, and around his neck, beneath
The red welt where the chain jerked taut, she notes how
Two deep lines are scored already and the flesh is grainy.
You're obstinate, she says.
He stares back at her as she gazes at him full in his face. Now
All she can see
Is a vision of an old, old man, snow-white hair,
Folding his fragile bones into a taxicab, on
The corner of Broadway and 47th Street. He's
Broad-shouldered still, gives
A sharp look out of rheumy blue eyes at
The young fellow handing him in. . . .
He's wearing an expensive overcoat. He's got
Mud on his old-fashioned boots. . . . I
Find myself, I don't know how, holding him. His cheek
Jars on mine. The way he shudders, my
Arms feel like steel hoops around a barrel that might
Fly apart without this pressure. He says in my ear:
I can walk to the city.
Then I'm pushing my mouth over his and I fish for his
Blinking keys in my pocket, find his
Hand. I'm kissing him and I press the car keys into his
Open palm and fold his fingers around them, one by one. He's got

His eyes screwed shut. God, it
Jolts my spine—his
Fist with the keys in it jams in the small of my back. He's let
His tongue slip in my mouth and it's like
Flesh frozen to cold metal (don't tear it away). And look, I
Plunge free now, head over heels, somersaulting,
Trussed in the harness of his arms. . . . Oh, she thinks,
Wildly, with terror and exhileration,
I've been a sky diver falling, falling. I'm
Waiting for my parachute to open. But
Whether you stay or you go, nothing
Will ever be the same again!

The dog butts open the bedroom door with his head
And he walks in. It's the right room because
He picks up her familiar smell immediately, along with that
  other smell, but this odd
Clutter everywhere is not how it is as a rule. I
Stand pat, by the door where I am, and flick my tail.
Can this be packing or moving? Is it a disaster?
The dog catches a slight movement from the bed and he makes
  out
The head of the stranger. The stranger is lying with his
Head skewed round sideways on the woman's shoulder. His
Eyes are fixed straight on mine. Ah . . . ha . . . ha. . . the whole
World's gone downhill, it seems, since this rapacious fellow in
  the suit arrived.
The dog stretches his neck forward. He lets out
A small rolling growl from the back of his throat, not
Grandstanding. Just enough to let the woman get the point.

She draws down her arm that was left
Clasping the visitor's neck, languidly. She begs:
Sit, good dog, her cheek
Turning against the visitor's sharply turned cheek with an effort.
Please sit, good dog. I'll make it up to you tomorrow.
She thinks to herself: tomorrow. Whatever I
Did tonight, I can't deal with it until tomorrow.
Says the visitor: tomorrow. . . . He's
Subsided off her body on the coverlet, but he's watchful, one eye
(With his hand still thrust
Absently under the skirt of the black velvet gown) following the
  dog as it
Turns in intent circles, settling itself down
Finally, shifting its muzzle forward on the rug. It gives

A heavy sigh. He says: Tomorrow at noon
I have to walk in that door like
A man who knows he's the tops,
Well got-up, clean-shaven, bright as a button. . . . She
Half turns his way, her knee,
As his chin is lowered on her shoulder, nudges against his but
Randomly, he thinks, as if she were a young child sleeping. He's
got
An image of a big desktop now, neat as a pin, with
A green blotter on it and a phone that
Rings and rings and rings . . . there's
Nobody in, hold all the calls, he's
Gone, the fucker . . . thirty-seven years of him,
Face-down in the pillow . . . .
For some reason, he says—and he glares out at the wreck of her
room: scarves,
Pantihose, a raggedy nightgown with a lace trimming on it
Suspended from an upturned drawer of the dresser;
The roses he brought her are scattered on the carpet—
From the very first day, I wanted you to like me. That's
More absurd than it sounds. I never worry about that. Her
Hand, he feels, hovers up close by his ear,
Lingers a beat, and
Lapses on the coverlet. He says in a while:
It's cold in your room, and he starts
Heaving around until they haul and tug the heavy quilt from
under them.
Send that dog of yours downstairs, he adds. All I need
Is to be savaged by some hostile animal while I'm sleeping.
She feels past the visitor's face for
The switch of the capsized lamp. She
Touches her forehead to his shoulder.
Leave him be, she says.

Later that night, when it had got
Warm and comfortable under the heavy quilt, and
She'd felt in the visitor's hair and found
A piece of one of the torn photographs sticking to it, she had
said:
If I see you again some day . . . but she realized that
The man had long since dropped off with
The car-key ring still hooked over his finger, and his head in the
crook of his arm, so

She never finished whatever resolution she had meant to
announce, or
Whatever promise she'd intended to make him, which
Was probably just as well. In fact,
Even over the wake-up cup of coffee, very little more
Was said by either of them. Some
Current of milder air had swirled up from the Gulf overnight
And flakes of snow,
Just a few of them blowing and drifting at first, had
Begun to settle on the driveway. He agreed it would be
Smart to get on the road before
Too much more of the white stuff had come down. Doubtless
His mind was on his interview and both of them were
Numbed slightly, moving carefully like
People who have shut a body in the closet and
Are not yet ready to plan for its disposal. This
Was why it was early still, well before eight, when she
Leant her head against the window and
Stared over at the foot of the hickory tree where
The little red car had left its mark with
The trail of his bootprints leading up to it:
An oblong patch of gravel in the snow.
Thoughts began to tumble through her mind, as she stood there.
They turned over in
Slow motion, drifting, in
No special order. One,
More vivid than the rest, was a memory in full color.
It was a wooden fort for the tin soldiers. It was
Painted green with the battlements picked out in red.
The drawbridge worked. This makeshift toy,
Rough but serviceable, her
Entomologist father who was
No carpenter and not clever with his hands, had
Built for her during the worst of the war when
Toys were hard to get.
It wasn't really what she'd wanted.
Now she briefly imagined him, once the nine o'clock news was
over,
Getting down to it with a hammer in his hand,
Spreading out newspaper on the rug, growing
Tense and even more uncommunicative when the nails went in
crooked. . . .
As she stood by the window, she wondered to herself
If this should be enough, or not? Meanwhile

The snow came down more thickly.
The path to the summerhouse had vanished, and
The oblong of gravel in the driveway, the prints of the visitor's boots.
It was all whiteness,
Motion and silence like an ancient movie,
Flurries of white whirling past the tops of the sycamore trees.

The End

Mac Wellman

# *The Bad Infinity*

MAC WELLMAN is a poet and playwright living in New York. His recent productions include *Cleveland*, presented at BACA Downtown and directed by Anne Bogart; and *Dracula*, at River Arts Repertory, directed by Len Jenkin. His play *Harm's Way* is published by Broadway Play Publishing, and his *No Smoking Piece* and *The Porcupine Man* (with music by Michael S. Roth) appear in Broadway Play Publishing's *Short Pieces from the New Dramatists*.

Mr. Wellman edited *Theatre of Wonders*, published by Sun & Moon. His books of poems are *In Praise of Secrecy*, *Satires*, and *A Shelf in Woop's Clothing*, forthcoming from Sun & Moon. Sun & Moon also will publish *The Fortuneteller*, his first novel. He has been commissioned by NYSCA to write a new play for the Shaliko Company. He is a member of New Dramatists.

*The Bad Infinity* premiered at the Brass Tacks Theatre in Minneapolis on 3 May 1985 with Patty Lynch, Artistic Director. John Richardson directed the following cast:

| | |
|---|---|
| MEGAN | Anne Devitt |
| DEBORAH | Karen Esbjornson |
| JOHN SLEIGHT/SAM | James R. Stowell |
| RAMON | Howard Dallin |
| BLAISE, WAITER, BEAR | David Fenley |
| SENATOR ARMITRAGE, WAITER, DOG | R. Ponzio |
| LIZARD MAN, WAITER, CHEF | Tracy Anderson |
| PIANIST | Carl Jones |

Michael Sommers created the Set Design; Michael Murnane, the Lighting; and Patty Lynch and Susan Haas, the Costumes. Wayne Hendricks was the Stage Manager, and Lawrence Fried did the Sound Effects.

THE BAD INFINITY

follows *Energumen, Diseases of the Well-Dressed, The Professional Frenchman,* and *The Self-Begotten,* and concludes the gestural—highly elliptical—antic progress of these across the hollow land of modern Empty Time.

Most of the persons of the play have appeared in different guises earlier in the series. Nevertheless all are briefly described on the following page.

*The Bad Infinity* is dedicated to the proposition that the theatrical body and soul of the world is not to be found in propositions *per se,* but in the dialectic of language and gesture, parable and pratfall, dialogue and disorder.

*The Bad Infinity* is for Yolanda

The persons of the Play:

a Cat Burglar, the legendary Blaise?
Megan, an appearance variously modulated
Deborah, an apparent appearance, more Substantial than Apparitional—much to her chagrin
Dog, the victim of Chronic Depression
John Sleight, alias Sam, a Master of Many Identities
Ramon, an International Entrepreneur, and Real Man trapped among phantoms
Senator Armitrage, a person fallen from a great height, a political Humpty Dumpty
three Waiters, at the Alibi Club
a Chef, a Sensitive and Artistic Nature, in apparent exile
Sam, alias himself, a rank amateur of Many Identities
and a Man with Wings, a dead Santa, and an Animal of Unknown Species.

## Scene One

(*A lavish penthouse apartment somewhere in Northern Virginia. Fireplace. Door to bedroom. Door to hallway. A staircase leading to the roof garden. A large sofa with matching end tables. An upright piano. All these furnishings are of the most exquisite kind, arranged with a decorator's eye. An immense window, upstage, looks out on several other highrises. The* CAT-BURGLAR *enters in near darkness through an air-conditioning vent, which he knocks out. He is dressed in black from head to toe, and wears a mask and gloves. He looks around at various objects, including candlesticks, a stereo, some small bronzes and porcelains clustered on shelves, but seems pleased with nothing. This goes on for some time, but his search is in vain: There's simply nothing here worth the trouble. He looks in the liquor cabinet, and removes a bottle of bourbon. With bottle in hand he ambles over to the piano, and sits down. Drinks. Bangs out a few notes. Takes another drink, and begins to play a rag. Stops suddenly, as if listening for noise. Another drink. Now he launches into the main rag, playing with great enthusiasm. At times he vocalizes with the music. Suddenly he slams the piano top down, wipes his fingerprints, and bolts behind the sofa. Pause. He peers over the back of the sofa. Pause. Rushes over to the piano, grabs the bottle, rushes to the vent, and wiggles out. Pause. Blackout.*)

## Scene Two

(*The penthouse.* MEGAN *and* DEBORAH *talking in an animated fashion. Windows of other apartments are visible. A piece of twilit sky.*)

MEGAN: He's coming. Really, he's coming.

DEBORAH: Again?

MEGAN: No, silly, not *him*. Don.

DEBORAH: Don Who?

MEGAN: Anyhow, I think it's Don . . .
Ramon's friend. After all
with Sam gone we need
someone to cheer you up.

---

DEBORAH: I expect you've heard the good news.

MEGAN: Isn't it wonderful?

DEBORAH: An idea like that.
After all this time.
After all our doubts.

MEGAN: Oh, we shall all
have such a wonderful
time when it's begun.

DEBORAH: I'll say.
Can pack up my books and stuff it.

MEGAN: Pardon me, Debby.
(*She picks up the phone and rings. Pause.*)
Hello. Everything all right?

(DOG *barks. She goes to the window. The* DOG *appears in the window opposite, phone in hand, and waves.* MEG *waves back and hangs up.*)

MEGAN: Would you like a drink?

DEBORAH: Sure, a scotch would be nice.

MEGAN: A neighbor in the next building.
Going through a rough time. Family
trouble. A bit depressed. So I call
up every now and then.

(*Pours the drink and hands it to* DEB.)

DEBORAH: Aren't you sweet!

MEGAN: People have to help out.
It'll be different, soon.

DEBORAH: I expect we'll get used to the light.

MEGAN: When the statues come to life . . .

DEBORAH: When the statues come to life
you know what I'm going to do?

MEGAN: Throw away your glasses and buy a boutique . . .

DEBORAH: Throw away my law books is more like it.

MEGAN: What a waste that would be,
with your mind.

DEBORAH: Not really, Megan.

MEGAN: I've been grinning from ear to ear.
Inside. Since I've heard the news.
I've grown so fond of you, Deborah.
Do you know how the world was created?
Seriously, do you?

DEBORAH: Just like it is now, I would imagine.

MEGAN: No, it was created, according to
Egyptian myth, by an enormous
dung beetle. A scarab beetle.
Who went around rolling
and rolling this gigantic ball of shit,
until it got bigger and bigger and bigger.
Then it got quite out of hand. And so on.

(*While* MEG *talks* DEB *spies a pair of women's gloves, and picks them up. Pause.*)

DEBORAH: I didn't know you had invited her.

MEGAN: I didn't. She invited herself. Rude creature.

DEBORAH: In that case. (*Gets up to go.*)

MEGAN: No, please stay.

DEBORAH: You should know better than to pull
this on me. On a day like this.
With all our good fortune.
Where is she?

MEGAN: In the bedroom. Passed out. Really,
it wasn't my doing.
(*Musing*)
Times being what they are.

DEBORAH: Not to mention our exceeding good fortune.
(*Looks out the window*)
What are they doing down there?

MEGAN: Expect a little commotion
of some kind. A celebration,
perhaps in honor of the Coming.
The light is thrilling, isn't it?
After all these years, just
as I was beginning to doubt.

DEBORAH: I can't imagine you doubting, Megan.

MEGAN: Oh yes, I've had my moments.
Never talk much about them.
Don't see much point
in complaining.

DEBORAH: And now it's not necessary.

MEGAN: So now the future shall be just
like the past.
(*Musing*)
A happy throng of carefree
peasantry . . .
or something from a pageant.

DEBORAH: I hardly have the language
for what I feel. Not that I'm
worried, mind you.

MEGAN: You always were so gloomy, dear.

DEBORAH: But I promise to change.

MEGAN: I always change.
Change is my avocation.
That's why I'm so . . .

DEBORAH: Articulate? I understand.

(*They both look out the window. Pause.*)

MEGAN: Looks so real it almost looks fake.
A remarkable effect . . .

DEBORAH: Whatever are they doing down there?

MEGAN: Playing stickball with a human head, ah
here she comes. She's awake.
(*Tidies up.*)

DEBORAH: I promise to be good.

MEGAN: Oh, you have changed, Debby.

(*Both look expectantly to the bedroom door. A shadow appears. Pause. Blackout.*)

## Scene Three

(*The same.* JOHN SLEIGHT *has joined* DEBORAH *and* MEGAN. *They walk about casually drinking and smoking.*)

John: The big change came later when the banks
began to understand my work.
(*Pause*)
They found that by simply making
nothing happen they could advance
their own interests as well as mine.
All things come to those who wait.
Money is time, and empty time is
the most valuable because it
costs nothing, involves no risky
transactions with leftist regimes
or desperate small entrepreneurs.
It can all be done by computer tie-in.
If you plug into the system you survive.
If you don't, you don't.
(*Pause*)
It was this, in essence, I was trying
to tell Sam all along, but he was too
stubborn. Committed to an outworn
creed. A spiritual aborigine, so to speak.

Deborah: Must you mention his name?

Megan: I was just going to say the same thing.

(*Something strange happens.* Sleight *looks puzzled. They go back where they were at the beginning of the scene.*)

John: The big change came later when the banks
began to understand my work.
(*Pause*)
They found that by simply making
nothing happen they could advance
their own interests as well as mine.
All things come to those who wait.
Money is time, and empty time is
the most valuable because it
costs nothing, involves no risky
transactions with leftist regimes
or desperate small entrepreneurs.
It can all be done by computer tie-in.
If you plug into the system you survive.
If you don't, you don't.
(*Pause*)
It was this, in essence, I was trying
to tell Sam all along, but he was too
stubborn. Committed to an outworn
creed. A spiritual aborigine, so to speak.

MEGAN: Must you mention his name?

DEBORAH: I was just going to say the same thing.

JOHN: That was nearly perfect.

(*He looks at his watch and screams. He does a pratfall and lies motionless. A bluish fluid pours down one wall, changing its color. A red carpet rolls out from the bedroom.* GUZMAN *appears in the fireplace and enters.*)

MEGAN: Oh, Ramon, it's so good of you.

RAMON: Charmed. (*To* DEBORAH)

MEGAN: This is Deborah.

RAMON: I am delighted to make your acquaintance.

(*She spits in his face and sits with her back to the audience.*)

MEGAN: Ramon, this is John Sleight.

DEBORAH: (*Mimicking her.*) I'm not sure you've met. (*She giggles.*)

MEGAN: This is an exercise of Mr. Sleight's.
It's called "playing dead". Quite
good for body and soul, really.
May I get you a drink?

(SLEIGHT *remains motionless on the floor.*)

RAMON: Yes, Megan, I would like that.

MEGAN: John, won't you say hello to Mr. Guzman?

RAMON: Do not disturb him on my account.

MEGAN: We were just discussing the good news.

RAMON: You mean the
chiasmus in the time-fabric potentiated
by the isochronometric instigator?

DEBORAH: Of course, idiot.

RAMON: Where shall we be dining?

MEGAN: The club, of course.

RAMON: It might be fun to get out and go
to the theatre for a change.

(DEBORAH *tries to stifle wild laughter.*)

RAMON: Do something different.

(*Awkward pause.* SLEIGHT *is recovering.*)

RAMON: There're all these warm-hearted revivals
going on nowadays. Quite reassuring.

(DEBORAH *breaks up again.*)

RAMON: I am particularly fond of this play about
the mountain of styrofoam I am reading
about. This fantastic pile of ice and
stone and prehistoric merds is inhabited
by some people who are lost.
They discover meaning in their
lostness and are reminiscing
on how sweet life has been
when this monstrous avalanche
smash them to tiny fragments.
Quite moving theatre.

MEGAN: Not on an empty stomach, Ramon.

RAMON: Will Hilary be arriving soon?

SLEIGHT: Soon enough, Mr. Guzman. (*Getting up.*)

RAMON: Ah, you are recovered.

SLEIGHT: A taste of death is a fine tonic, sir.

RAMON: A medicine to be administered in small
doses, John.

MEGAN: Mr. Guzman is such a wit.
(*Pause*)
Can I get you something, John?
Debby, what about you?
Why don't you join us?

DEBORAH: Hilary won't be coming.

MEGAN: What a strange thing to say.
Of course she will.

DEBORAH: Beacuse she doesn't exist.

MEGAN: What nonsense, Ramon. Ignore her.

DEBORAH: Ignore me when I speak like that.

MEGAN: Would you like to see John's latest?

DEBORAH: Oh, I'd love to.

MEGAN: Not you, silly. I was asking Ramon.

(DEBORAH *knocks herself on the forehead in mock astonishment and collapses on the sofa and is motionless.*)

RAMON: No, Megan, I have no interest in such toys.

MEGAN: Then perhaps I shall go myself.

SLEIGHT: (*Pouring himself a drink.*)
I was just about to explain, Ramon
how the future can be controlled only
by changing it into the past.
Traditionally this has been
the function of life, but now
that mere life has become a
far too chancy enterprise
for those of us whose cat tracks
the pavement singing old Beatles'
dungbeetle. One requires a thorn.
I assure you, if you look out this
window you can hear shapes of your
eyesight drilling holes to China.
Rearing up dead heaps of dollar
bills. Banks going at it, bang, bang!
And cropped photos of famous
politicians turned into living turds.
My work is called 'The Bad Infinity'.

RAMON: It sounds fascinating.

(*Pause.* SLEIGHT *finishes his drink.*)

RAMON: You talk as if life were redundant.

SLEIGHT: When it works right, and the switches
mesh I can conjure up a whole fear
picture of picture's bungo. Some like a
boy and girl dreaming of a play upon
a bird's perch where they are dreaming
of a television set that can turn itself
off. All this reduced to a digital
diorama of a video game in which
the object of the game is to win points
by drinking blood. Or a theatre piece
based on a video game in which a

pair of TVs make love in the mind of a
young lady whose lives are recounted in a
miniseries as described in an unproduced
treatment recycled for TV by video people
for a talk show that is aired in the dark.
You get me? It's safe because it's blank.

RAMON: It sounds quite mad to me, but if you
can make money doing it, why not?
What do you think, Deborah?

DEBORAH: For blank read *dead.*

SLEIGHT: You haven't lost your harsh, judging side
have you?

DEBORAH: You see this lampshade? (*Holds it up.*)

RAMON: Whatever are you driving at?

DEBORAH: Why don't you wear it like a hat?

RAMON: A very good idea. (*He puts it on.*)

MEGAN: I'm going to see the 'Work'.
Then we'll go to the theatre.

SLEIGHT: Really, I think dinner would be
a more appropriate idea.

DEBORAH: If we don't go to the theatre I'll hang myself.

RAMON: Women, these Northern women.

DEBORAH: I'll hang myself from the rafters
And swing back and forth in the wind
like a big old beach towel, and the
rope will squeal like window hinges.
(*She demonstrates.*)
I'll hang till the birds pick me clean
and then I'll fly and fly and careen
over the city like a mad banshee and
I'll shriek till I deafen all the
fine people like you with your wars
and money and fine clothes and endless
boring technological bullcrap. I will.
(*She grabs a bottle, takes a terrific swig, and pours the rest in a flowerpot. She climbs on one of the end tables. She places the bottle on her head and begins a malefic jig.*)

A moment of pure jade.
Forbidden thrust of fire.
Glass between the sun and moon.
Death on a stick, life on the run.
America.
Ameria.
Meria.
Mericanica.
Mericanicamera.
Bodiless ordinaria.
(*She freezes.*)
Photograph the photograph of the moon.
(*Pause*)
A sea of perpendictables.
Perpendictable paperdolls.
(*Pause*)
See. Look, man. Open your head.
(*She gets no response and quiets.*)
It's so like something no one ever saw
before. It's like the sudden appearance
and disappearance of a leopard in a
snake's dream. It's like cooking up a
really spectacular meal of raw food
starting with garbage.
(*Pause*)
Oh, the energy that goes into a thing.
Horrid. Horrd. Horrd. Hord. Hord.
Hrd. Hrd. Hd. Hd. Hd. D. D. D. D.
(*Pause*)
Take off that lampshade, you fucking cliché.

(*He puts it back on the lamp.* DEBORAH *freezes as a Greek Nike.*)

SLEIGHT: Care for a refill, Ramon?

RAMON: In the jungle, Sam, we practiced the
most unspeakable atrocities on the
natives. We did this not out of guilt.
As you *Norteamericanos* do. Or to improve
ourselves and the world. Bah, you liberals!
No, we do this for the hell of it.
Yes, for the hell of it. To give us pleasure.
Your blood has become thin.
You are weak. Simple human joys
as, for instance, of torture and slaughter
and rapine no longer appeal to your
delicate appetites. *Amigo*, I pity you.

SLEIGHT: You underestimate me, Ramon.
"Feed the fires of paranoia" I always say.

MEGAN: A toast to Intertop.

RAMON: I rather toast the devil.

MEGAN: Poor sport.

SLEIGHT: By the way, how did you know I was Sam?

RAMON: It says so in the program.

SLEIGHT: YOU CAN GET OFF THE FUCKING TABLE NOW.

DEBORAH: I was wondering when you were going to
notice me.

(*She gets down. Blackout. Pause. Lights back up. The* WOMEN *prepare to go see the Work of* SLEIGHT'S.)

SLEIGHT: Actually, I'm the Pseudo-Sam. The
Real Sam ran off to live in the forest.

RAMON: How original.

DEBORAH: "How original".

(*She spits in his face on her way out.*)

*Blackout*

## Scene Four

(*Darkness. Voices of ROMEO and JULIET from* III,v. *After a time. Silence. Lights come up on two tape recorders on floor with speakers facing each other, maybe fifteen feet apart. Just behind are two chairs facing each other, with mirrors propped up in both. Otherwise the room is empty.* MEGAN *and* DEBORAH *admire from one side, where the former has her finger on the light switch. They are a little drunk by now and giggle a lot.*)

MEGAN: Quite remarkable, isn't it?

DEBORAH: A gas.

(*She burps. Pause.*)

MEGAN: Almost a perfect 'bad infinity'.

DEBORAH: Almost?

MEGAN: You can't really perceive the
total effect. You see? If you
stand here, for instance,
(*She stands in between the mirrors.*)
your own image
blocks out a small portion
of infinity. You are left
with a taint of finitude,
which, despite the claims
of proud Mister John Sleight,
occludes the unending
accordion effect. It only works
when no one's looking at it.

DEBORAH: That's pretty much as it should be.

MEGAN: "Should", Debby?

DEBORAH: Sorry.

MEGAN: The nicest thing about Shakespeare
is that his works are a club to beat
down our contemporaries. A cudgel.

DEBORAH: Never thought about it like that.

MEGAN: My innocence must be rubbing off
on you.
(*Scratches herself.*)
I like it here.

DEBORAH: Shall we rejoin the gentlemen?

MEGAN: It's wonderful,
just for a short time
not to see the sky
not to hope
or dream.
Or wish.
Or want.
Or know.
Or think.
Or feel anything. To be entirely
vacuous in the presence of the Master,
Shakespeare. To be empty and to allow
the pure water of his meaningless
old hat dead language to wash over
us and make us clean. I want so
to be clean.

DEBORAH: You sound like me.

MEGAN: Shall we go up?

(*Pause*)

DEBORAH: You sound like me.

MEGAN: Shall we go up?
I didn't use "should", you notice.

DEBORAH: It's going to be such an extravagently
wonderful evening.

(*They start out. Blackout.* DEBORAH *giggles in the dark.*)

## Scene Five

(*The Penthouse. The four seated randomly throughout the room. Motionless. Long pause.* RAMON *whistles a few bars of "Knick Knack, Paddy Whack, Give Your Dog a Bone". Pause.*)

DEBORAH: What do you suppose ever happened to Blaise?

(*All are shocked at the mere idea. The MEN hunker down in their seats.*)

SLEIGHT: What do you suppose ever happened to Sam?

(*Sky turns lilac; a* MAN *appears on the wall of the building opposite, scampering like a lizard; the* DOG *appears in the window, howling and whining; on the edge of the roof garden above him a* MAN *appears with a pair of wings, which he flaps gingerly; a crowd of people begin leaping from windows, and over the edge of the roof garden; the* MAN WITH WINGS *leaps, flapping furiously and falls; lastly the* DOG *flings himself out of the window; in each case the fall is followed, after a short interval, by a terrible thud. The sky changes to a deep purple. A score or so of plastic WallWalkers appear on the wall opposite, where the first* MAN *had been scampering. They creep down the wall in typical Wall-Walker fashion.* MEGAN *yawns.*)

DEBORAH: Shall we go?

(*They get up and prepare to go. Blackout.*)

## Scene Six

(*Before the Club. The four stand, with overcoats on and backs to the audience, looking at something in the sky. Ex-*SENATOR ARMITRAGE *appears, kneeling on a low dolly, with a handful of pencils he is selling to passers-by. A placard of some kind hangs around his neck. He addresses the audience as the others gaze off into the distance.*)

ARMITRAGE: Fine people, seekers, all of you,
lovers of truth, art, and journalism,
Tell me, truthfully, what you have found!
What knowledge? Lord knows! The madness
of pure lust and impure ways! Suppose
you all mean to go in there?
(*Points to the Club.*)
The old Club.
(*He cackles.*)
The Alibi Club it used to be called.
Go in at your own risk. Things
have changed. They serve
human flesh nowadays
and they're not real particular
where it comes from. Be warned.
I know: I too have flown.
I too have skimmed the cloudtops.
(*Becomes puzzled.*)
Senators and Congressmen and
Congresswomen. Gents.
Snake meat don't
taste good. It turns
the wheel. You wonder
why?
(*Musing*)
Simple pleasures and
no apology, simple
murders
the joy
blasted
or blasting through solid bedrock
to become a firefly.
Tipped over.
Like a foot scratching another foot.
Because our American appetite
the happy voice of all the
empty land, empty
heart, making it full. What
the gods were
meaningless
meaningless

(*He looks around furtively.*)
I am walking up a gradual in-
cline that becomes steep. I
am all wind and silence and . . .
(*Pause*)
Bright, healthy!
(*Pause*)
thunder and hats . . .
(*Pause*)
The whole hay-heap be damned!
Must go on. The bright doom . . .
(*Collecting himself.*)
I too have landed in the mire,
burnt out, a relic. A proud man
reduced to abject debasement . . .
Machinations of lawyers, the press.
Vile, unsubstantiated charges.
Totally unproven. All of 'em. I was
betrayed and a million billion
bumblebees are forever singing
in my dreams and daydreams.
(*He buzzes.*)
Buzzing me back to Mad Wolf. But
I'm a proud man, unbended. I work
for my daily blood, *bread*. I can
see the future better than any man,
having helped instigate it, by gosh.
And I'm telling you:
Don't go in this place.
It's not safe. It's crawling
with demons, devils, foreigners and
monstrosities. The Chef has quit.
He's fled to the forest.
He's fled to the forest to get away.
AND DON'T TOUCH THE FOOD, bah . . .
(*Scornfully*)
You're not listening.
(*Pause*)
You go in there and you'll pull the
trip wire on the most incredible
series of bad infinities known to
man.
(*Pause*)
THE HORIZONTAL AVALANCHE!

(*Pause*)
The Chef has quit, I tell you.
(*In despair*)
Oh my god.
(*Pause*)
What it does to you.

(*He rolls himself off.* DEBORAH *turns around.*)

DEBORAH: What did that man say?

MEGAN: Shall we go in?

*Blackout*

## Scene Seven

(*Total darkness. A squeaking sound, very quiet. Over this, a magisterial* VOICE.)

VOICE: Ladies and Gentlemen. The sound you hear
is the sound of a million billion
bats. These vicious, feral
little monsters are in flight.
Perpetual flight. In
a space which contains all
of you, and all the visible
and invisible matter, imaginable
or unimaginable. Known
or unknown. In the entire
universe. This space is
roughly ten centimeters
on a side and weighs
approximately ten and a half
sestillion solar masses.
You will observe that no light emanates from this
space.
(*Pause*)
Only the cries of a million billion bats.
(*Pause*)
Creatures that have been in flight
since the beginning of time and not one
full collision has been recorded.
(*Pause*)

Only the occasional brushing of a wing against
a furred ear, or a whisker against a claw.
(*Pause*)
A bat infinity.
(*Pause*)
Perhaps you can feel the occasional, slight,
barely perceptible brushing of their wings.

(*Silence*)

## Scene Eight

(*In the dining room of the Club. The four are preparing to order the main course.* DEBORAH *is lost in reverie, a fact noticed only by* SLEIGHT. *[The substance of her reverie constitutes the previous scene.]*)

SLEIGHT: Are you all right, Deb?

MEGAN: Waiter, the lumpfish roe is alive.

FIRST WAITER: Well, fuck my ass. I done beat on it till
I thought I killed it, but I guess I'll
just go and beat on it some more.

(FIRST WAITER *exits with dish.* SECOND WAITER *brings bottles of wine.* MEGAN *gets up.*)

MEGAN: We're going to see the pit.
Aren't we, Ramon?

(*He gets up.*)

RAMON: Quite, yes.

(*They go.*)

SECOND WAITER: French wine.

(*He goes. Pause.*)

SLEIGHT: There is a thing we aspire to, which
is being continually lost, because
we don't see we already possess it.
So when we lose it, we don't even
know we had it once: What is it?

DEBORAH: Cut the crap, Sam.

SLEIGHT: How did you recognize me?

DEBORAH: You don't look like him in the least.

SLEIGHT: Do you believe all this "statues-coming-to-life" bullcrap?

DEBORAH: Hell no. Intertop's bankrupt.

SLEIGHT: Bullshit.

DEBORAH: It's true. I can feel it.

SLEIGHT: You're psychic, I suppose.

DEBORAH: It's in the numbers. Actuarial tables.

SLEIGHT: I don't believe it. Look, Deb.

(*He reaches for her.*)

DEBORAH: Don't touch me.
(*Pause*)
I don't want to feel anything.
It's too painful. I don't want
to be loved. I want to be feared.
I want to destroy everything human
in me. I want to become a monument
to my own incredulity, and to the
vileness and stupidity of the world.
(*Pause*)
And if you
so much as lay a finger on me
I'll scream. So help me I will.

(*He does so.*)

DEBORAH: I've seen the world.
I know what it is.
I can't be fooled.

SLEIGHT: There's still a possibility.

DEBORAH: How do you mean?

SLEIGHT: Shush. They're coming back.

(MEGAN *and* RAMON *return.*)

RAMON: It is very interesting, Mister Sleight.
You see a big hole with flames
licking about in the bottom, and
thunders animating the surrounding
miasmus. Very extensive I assure

you. Large serpents are writhing in
and around large flowerpots and
on the parquet. The members of the
staff throw live animals which are
torn apart by the creatures of the bottom.
The wailing of the voices of the damned
is quite something to behold.

SLEIGHT: A remarkable feat of engineering.

RAMON: An amusing display, to say the least.

MEGAN: I thought Ramon might be intrigued by the
new installation.

SLEIGHT: Of course the illusion is quite
realistic.

DEBORAH: You know better than me
about illusions.

MEGAN: Shall we order. I'm famished.

(THIRD WAITER *rushes out of the kitchen with a knife in his back.* FIRST *and* SECOND *follow in hot pursuit. Despite them he makes it to the table.*)

THIRD WAITER: Don't eat . . . the blood . . . sausage.

(*Collapses and is dragged off by the* FIRST. SECOND WAITER *comes up to the table.*)

MEGAN: My word.

SECOND WAITER: Ignore this man. Is new on staff.
Have not learned how to behave.
Sorry.
(*He goes.*)

MEGAN: Don't you find the question of behavior quite
neglected, Ramon?

(*The latter becomes agitated.*)

RAMON: Ah, yes. But in my opinion the question
of behavior is reducible by a process of
covert inspissitude to the more profound
question of decorum which is itself a
third-dimensional graphic explosion of
the two-dimensional crystallization of
the essential problem which is the matter of

PENMANSHIP. As you know, elegant
handwriting has fallen into a state of
neglect and disrepair, like the nation's
bridges and highways and viaduct system.
This must be remedied by a strict return
(*Rapping his spoon against a glass.*)
to fundamentals, as for instance the famous
curve and the perfect line, straight line,
not to be confused with the waving,
wavering, twisted line, and the oblate,
hyper bolic curve, which is abominated
by the divinities and is, in fact, the
Work of the Devil.
(*Pause*)
"Demons inhabit the intersections of circles",
as the poet tells us.
(*Pause*)
But, *au fond*, what is required is
discipline.
(*Pause*)
Otherwise the handwriting becomes personalized,
unscrutable, inscrupulous, unreadable, inane,
Evil. And if the hand come to delight in
(*Portentous pause.*)
eccentricity for eccentricity's sake . . .
(*Another.*)
who knows where next it may find pleasure?
(*He relaxes.*)
I know my views are "old hat", so to say,
but they come from the heart.
(*He bows, banging his head on the table.*)

MEGAN: (*To* SECOND WAITER)
Sir, we shall order now.

(WAITER *bows, stalks off without taking their order.*)

MEGAN: What do you suppose is wrong with him?

SLEIGHT: Wedged head syndrom. Quite common.

(*Begins doing push-ups.* SECOND WAITER *reappears, very nonchalant.*)

MEGAN: *Pardonne,* sir. We wish to order.

SECOND WAITER: I have already taken order.

MEGAN: But that is quite impossible.

SECOND WAITER: No, is truth. *Le vrai semblance.*

(MEGAN *stands up enraged. She belts him.*)

MEGAN: My friends and I have not ordered
yet and I find this behavior on
your part extraordinarily quadruped.
Not to mention negroid and beyond
the pale.
Skid mump. Poleax the hyperborean
tomato plant chop us the telephone
cancer monster boredom and
wretching dry heaves with a needle stitching all their
hearts together on a clothesline
beneath the oilous ombulations
of the sea swollen beyond its
border to eat. Melted . . .

DEBORAH: The man is trying to speak
Megan. Two wrongs don't
make a right. Remember
the golden rule. For Christ's sake.

(SLEIGHT *gets up from the floor.*)

SLEIGHT: You're right Deborah.

SECOND WAITER: I am learning to take order by telepathic
mysterium.
It is an outcome of acupuncture for lower
back syndrome. I go to Wu Chen Few.
One needle go in wrong place. KABOOM.
I am a genius of TABLE WAITING.
(*Pause*)
I know WHAT YOU ALL WANT. IN THE DARK-
NESS OF YOUR ABYSSAL CRAVING. I give
you what you need instead.

SLEIGHT: My god, I believe the man.

RAMON: John, is true. I noticed before
his genius halo.

(*A weird light appears.*)

MEGAN: And what is it we need, my good man?

SECOND WAITER: French wine. Eggs up the stream.
Chicken smashed pot. Blight.
Roasted plate. Bowel of lamb.
Verbatim all around.

MEGAN: A genius!

SECOND WAITER: Of a minor sort.
(*He bows.*)
I go now.

## Scene Nine

(*The dining room. After dinner. At the next table a customer is slumped over his meal. The room is filled with smoke. The* SECOND WAITER *is going about his business. The* MEN *look stunned.*)

MEGAN: Bet you've never seen the Revolving Sky Room.

DEBORAH: Nope.

MEGAN: Would you like to?

DEBORAH: Not really. Might get seasick.

SECOND WAITER: Are we finished with dinner?

(*They nod. The* WAITER *snaps his fingers. All trays, plates, bottles, and covered dishes get up, hop on the floor and scurry off into the kitchen.*)

MEGAN: Ah, but the sky, with its infinite spaces, its
unimaginable prospects, beckons.

DEBORAH: Oh all right.

(*They go. Pause.*)

RAMON: Sam, do you remember
Havana?

(SLEIGHT *puts on sunglasses. Pause.*)

SLEIGHT: Never been to Havana.
(*Pause*)
And the name is John.

RAMON: Intractable son of a bitch,
aren't you?
(*Pause*)
So:

You don't remember the flamingo
garden at the Hotel Palacio?
(*Pause*)
How we saw Hemingway get drunk?
(*Pause*)
All those good time, laughter and
dancing and hopes, yes, *hopes*,
before we learned
what the world is
made of and what
must be done to
survive.

SLEIGHT: Escapes me totally, all of it.
Never seen you before in my life.

RAMON: I tried to have you killed,
don't you remember?

SLEIGHT: How interesting.

RAMON: Even that you don't recall.

SLEIGHT: It must have been someone else,
I'm afraid.

RAMON: No, it was you. Only your name was
Ralph Graytree.

SLEIGHT: Impossible.
(*Pause. Takes off sunglasses.*)

RAMON: What a magnificent liar you are.

SLEIGHT: Just an ordinary s.o.b. One of the guys.

RAMON: There are fractures in the Egg of Time
that lead us down winding corridors
of consciousness into realms covered
with sawdust and spiderwebs.
(*He stands up.*)
basements . . .
(*He sits down.*)
basements of intellect, vestigial hiding
places where lurk phantasmal creatures
whose understanding of the secret
laws governing the inner clockwork
of human destiny are non pareil.
(*Pause*)
You understand?

SLEIGHT: You're mad.

(RAMON *stands up and falls down. His shoelaces have been tied together.*)

RAMON: Your agents have tied my shoelaces
together.

SLEIGHT: My agents have tied your shoelaces
together.

RAMON: It's all the same.
(*Pause*)
Untie my shoelaces.

(*Pause.* SLEIGHT *unties* RAMON'S *shoelaces.*)

SLEIGHT: Just a practical joke.

RAMON: Odd sense of humor you have.
(*Recovering his dignity.*)
So: You will not admit
your true identity. You
will not take on your
true destiny and act like a man.

SLEIGHT: Absolutely not.
(*Pause*)
And besides you have it all wrong
as well you know. It was I
who tried to kill you.

RAMON: IT IS YOU.

(*He stands. Pause.* SLEIGHT *stands.*)

SLEIGHT: Never saw you before in my life.

RAMON: BUT IT IS YOU.
YOU SENT SARPICON.
WITH THE THROWING KNIVES.
At last . . .

(*They both sit.*)

SLEIGHT: The truth is, it doesn't matter.
The mask I wear is a true mask.
Underneath is another mask.
And underneath that one is
another and another and so on.
There's nothing else underneath.
Do you understand that?

RAMON: Ah, but why not be friends?
We have shared the most
intimate of secrets, the secret
of life and death. Sam . . .
(*Pause*)
Or whatever your name is . . .

SLEIGHT: It doesn't matter . . .

RAMON: We have both hired killers to
murder one another. What
stronger bond can there be?
We are lovers in an infinite *pas de deux*
of murder and . . .

SLEIGHT: It doesn't matter.
You damn fool.
Don't you see?

(RAMON *weeps.*)

SLEIGHT: Money. Money is the only thing
that's left. Money.
(*Pause*)
I'm not joking. The only thing.
Money is a god. The only god.
Don't waste my time
with this wretched disquisition
on murder and quilt. And the rest.
(*Pause*)
It all belongs with fascinations,
curses, the Mystery of Love, the
Romance of the Rose.
(*Pause*)
The old Egyptian soft-shoe . . .

RAMON: Fool.

SLEIGHT: Even Marxism is a dead mask.

RAMON: Intertop is finished.

SLEIGHT: What.

RAMON: House of card. The banks
have begun to collapse.
Mexico. Poland. Brazil.
The Congo. Et cetera. Et cetera.
You've climbed on the wagon

too late. It is you, Sam, isn't it?
All the portfolios have begun to
detumesce;
our friends in the stabilized regimes
can't even pay the interest
on the interest on the interest.
The Mexicans?
Couldn't meet the scheduled payment.
We are on the verge of a
bad infinity of bank collapses.
The Holy City of Byzantium
is an apparition built on the shifting
mists hovering over another yet more
apparitional chunk of mirage and chimaera
floating over the lake . . .
(*He gestures grandly.*)
of oblivion. Non-entity. Unreal.
A bad infinity of bank collapses
such as the world has never seen.
We are all going to be swept
down the mouth of hell.
You, me, along with the rest.
(*Pause*)

SLEIGHT: Aw, shit.
Just when I get ahead of the game.
Just when some things are beginning
to happen for me. They close the show.
All these years.
Face to the grindstone.
Hustling. Chiselling. Always
being undone by the remnant
of my good intentions. And now.
Finally. When I have at last
stamped down. Crushed. And murdered
all that's decent in me. Even my goddam
curiosity. The whole show shuts down. Self-
destructs. Shit. Weasel shit. Just my luck!
(*Pause*)
WHY SHOULD I BELIEVE YOU? WHY
YOU TRIED TO HAVE ME MURDERED.
I tried to have you murdered.
We don't even speak the same
ontological language.

(*Rising*)
Waiter, would you say this looks
like a human being?

SECOND WAITER: Looks like one. To be sure.

RAMON: What about him?
WHAT DOES HE LOOK LIKE?

SECOND WAITER: Unconvincing replica of a thing. Mannikin.

RAMON: You see. The disease is catching.
You must conceal your unreality.
Hope for good weather.
A house of cards is better than
no house at all. Only must tiptoe.
Whatever your name is, you.

SLEIGHT: Shut up. Leave me be. You, (*To* SECOND WAITER)
say something.

SECOND WAITER: Have confession to make. Food is done
with mirrors. Cork on string and
*papier mache*. Food color and bottled smell.
Chef have run off to the forest in pay dispute.

RAMON: Difficult to find good person for service
industry.

SECOND WAITER: Every one wants to be Computer Genius.
(*He shrugs.*)
Me, I can count to two.

SLEIGHT: That's all you need.

RAMON: Ah, the ladies return.

SLEIGHT: You have any real champagne
(*Pause*)
back there?

*Blackout*

## Scene Ten

(*The Rotating Sky Terrace.* MEGAN *and* DEBORAH *behold the Starry Night. The latter carries a bottle. Scene begins with a pause.*)

MEGAN: Everything will be revealed.

DEBORAH: Apparently.

(*Pause*)

MEGAN: I don't know.

(*She takes the bottle from* DEBORAH *and drinks. Then hands it back. Wipes her mouth. Pause.*)

MEGAN: Life has been good to me.

(*Pause*)

DEBORAH: To me also.
Except for the snare.
And braces, early on.
(*She takes a long slug.*)
Got what I wanted. Sort of. Puke.
(*Pause*)
They sky opens to you as you open
to it. What do you suppose
ever happened to Blaise? Megan?

MEGAN: Oh, he comes around every now and then.
He's a full-time burglar now. Enjoys
his work immensely. Far more happy
than he was at the Embassy. Not
every man can make his hobby his
life's work, and still make a living.
He comes around every now and then.
Looks around and messes things up a bit.
Rarely takes anything. It's the danger
he likes. The thrill. A man with purpose.
I like to see that. Even if in terms of
gestural language he's a bit deranged.

DEBORAH: But he is coming.

MEGAN: Never can be sure.

DEBORAH: Look at the sky. It grows and grows.
Seems like the more you look at it,
the more of it there is. I love the sky.
Because it's so vast and dead and empty.
(*Pause*)
There's a way out. I know there is.

MEGAN: There's something wrong with you.
(*Pause*)

Everything will STILL be revealed.
Despite the cynics.
The statues will come to life.
The wind will carry our messages
across the emptiness. Our mortgaged
fantasies will come to life. As
predicted. No error. Perfect
management. And optimum level of
profit realization according to a
norm established by reference to
the sine-wave function of Money,
Need, Chance, and the Entropic
Function of these. All this
is perfectly clear because there
is no possible error. Machines,
Deborah, are the true innocents of our time.

DEBORAH: Our witches?

MEGAN: You might say.

DEBORAH: So there is, in your view, no way out?

MEGAN: None I would want to risk.

(*Pause*)

DEBORAH: Don't you ever reach dead end?

MEGAN: The series is infinite.

(*Pause*)

DEBORAH: Don't you ever reach dead end?

MEGAN: The series is infinite.

(*A star falls, then another.*)

DEBORAH: Look.

(*More stars fall.*)

MEGAN: Perhaps we should rejoin the men.

DEBORAH: To save appearances?

MEGAN: What appearances?

(*They laugh. Go out. Stars fall. Blackout.*)

## Scene Eleven

(*After dinner at the Club. The four are drinking brandy, smoking and talking in an animated fashion. Everyone is a little drunk.*)

RAMON: A toast to Chaos!

MEGAN: I won't drink to that.

RAMON: To Divine Necessity then.

DEBORAH: I won't drink to that.
It's the same thing.

(*Pause.* RAMON *becomes a touch distracted.*)

RAMON: How can you not . . . a source
of inspiration . . .
life wells up . . . in the heavens.
Everything comes from chaos,
and to chaos it returns.
What you see when you look at
the heavens is God's eye.

SLEIGHT: It is what god sees I would say.

DEBORAH: God is blind.

MEGAN: Rubbish.

RAMON: God may play at dice, but he is
certainly able to read what he
throws.

SLEIGHT: Nonsense. If he were able to see
he would hardly have made such a
phenomenal spectacle.

RAMON: Anthropomorphist!

(*Pause*)

MEGAN: Let's talk about something else.

SLEIGHT: Such as.

DEBORAH: Money.

SLEIGHT: Very good. You see money is the paradox
because money is happiness, and yet.
Nothing destroys a society quicker
than large sums of money in the hands
of the unscrupulous, which is to say,
the happy.

MEGAN: I am on the side of the happy. Personally.

(*Pause*)

SLEIGHT: (*To* DEBORAH)
Lovely ring you have.

RAMON: Happiness is only a mask for the bourgeosie.

DEBORAH: It is, isn't it?

RAMON: Without his happiness the bourgeoisie do not exist.

DEBORAH: Star sapphire. Plutonium setting by Omensetter.

MEGAN: Something about the sky tonight, it reminds me.
(*Pause*)
Deeply, passionately, convincingly,
of all the things I've never done,
of all the feelings I've never felt,
of all the thoughts I've never thought.
But then the rewards of being an American
are very great, aren't they? Boxed in
is safer, in the long run. We wouldn't
want to run amok, would we?
It would be so easy.

(FIRST *and* SECOND WAITER *carry a dead* SANTA CLAUS *from the kitchen. Pause.*)

SLEIGHT: You are assuming that the sky is
what can be seen, but there is far,
far more, that cannot be seen and
that *far more* is what interests me.

MEGAN: If you got close enough to it, you could see it too.

SLEIGHT: I don't mean that.

DEBORAH: Then what do you mean?

MEGAN: Don't argue. Don't argue. Everything
will turn out fine. It always does.
Is that your ring on the floor, Deborah?

DEBORAH: I was just thinking of how, when I was a
little kid I used to lie on my back in the
soft grass and look up at the night sky,
the Milky Way, the planets, and all the
summer constellations, and it felt as if

I were adrift, or falling endlessly and forever, on and on. Somehow it was a very safe feeling. I discovered better things to do with my summer nights before long.

SLEIGHT: But that's the point: You assume the universe is coterminous with what you can see.

RAMON: Coterminous: quite a big word. John.

SLEIGHT: Means "has the same boundaries as".

DEBORAH: Where's my ring? Oh, dear. (*She looks around the table.*)

RAMON: The sure progress of modern science has eliminated all such phantasma as you talk of, John, besides. If we can't trust what we can see with our own eyes what can we trust? A banker cannot run a bank without money. It's absurd.

SLEIGHT: Unless it's Intertop.

MEGAN: What does he mean by that?

SLEIGHT: A bad joke. Sorry.

DEBORAH: Where the hell is my goddam ring?

(*She looks under the table.* MEGAN *helps her.*)

MEGAN: I'll help you look for it, dear. Under here? Ramon, please. Lift your boot.

RAMON: The sure progress of modern science have made all such speculations useless.

(*While the* MEN *argue the* WOMEN *search all over the floor for the fugitive ring, occasionally cursing.*)

SLEIGHT: I'm not so sure of that. Modern science and all we know is based on a set of assumptions, assumptions that are as problematic as those of . . . illusion itself, Did it ever occur to you that the process of perception is TWOFOLD. Not only do we look at the things of the world. They LOOK right back.

The world is different, depending
where you stand.
It's as simple as that.

RAMON: Now you are talking Relativism.
Which is cultural rottenness.

DEBORAH: (*To* RAMON)
Watch it! With the feet!

SLEIGHT: What are you doing down there?

DEBORAH: Looking for the god damn ring.

RAMON: Infinity is an idea without blemish.
Let's drink to that.

DEBORAH: I know it's down here.

SLEIGHT: Would you get up so I can finish
my goddam story?

MEGAN: We can hear you, believe me.

DEBORAH: Go on. Please. It's fascinating.

(*The* WOMEN *touch. Then embrace. Then kiss.*)

SLEIGHT: In order to perceive you become a NOTHING.
That way the images before you can
approach and occupy your space.
In order to be whole, one must be
empty. If the universe is truly a
universe, there must be more than
we can see, than we could ever see.

(WOMEN *resume the search for the ring.*)

If the world we know: with its wars
of mercenary faction, its Intertops and
Trilateral Commissions, its webs and
tracery of memory vaults and electronic
global political hijinks, is on the
verge of collapse.
And it must be because its ugly visage
fills every inch of the monitors of mind
and heart and imagination. Then I say
it must be a PHANTASM . . .

RAMON: You sound just like Sam. Ha!

SLEIGHT: An illusion.
A mere appearance . . .
I *do* sound a little like Sam.
(*Pause*)
. . . then the new world must be concealed underneath somehow, so close we can't perceive it, so near we could touch it, but we can't because we couldn't tell the new world if it came up and BIT US ON THE ASS.

RAMON: Very strange reasonings, Sam.

DEBORAH: Found it.

(*She gets up. Brushes herself off. So does* MEGAN.)

SLEIGHT: (*To* DEBORAH)
You don't understand?

MEGAN: What's there to understand?
(*She lights an exploding cigar. The cigar explodes.*)
And besides, it's about to happen.
The Great Apparition . . .
The pouring forth of light, from the divine beaker of infinitude.
The statues will come to life . . .

DEBORAH: And we will seem exactly as we are.
(*She laughs.*)

SLEIGHT: You're mad.

DEBORAH: I'm getting out of here.

(*She gets up.* SLEIGHT *tries to stop her. She pulls away from him.* RAMON *tries to restrain* SLEIGHT. *She stops a few paces away. Turns.*)

RAMON: Let her go, John.

DEBORAH: (*To* SLEIGHT)
I wouldn't fuck you
if you were dipped in light
and rolled in stardust . . .

(*She strides rapidly out.* MEGAN *weeps.*)

RAMON: Let her go, John. She doesn't belong with us.

*Blackout*

## Scene Twelve

(*In the forest.* SAM *and* THE CHEF *are fishing.* SAM *wears a dunce hat.* THE CHEF *wears a cook's hat, and carries a large drum strapped around his neck which he beats now and again with a soup spoon. The forest itself consists of a few potted palms, and the stream is a piece of cloth. The sky boils overhead.*)

CHEF: Do you hear drums, Sam?
I think I hear drums.

SAM: Nope.

CHEF: I must be imagining things.
Perhaps from a previous
existence in which I was scalped
or eaten by bears.

SAM: You know the story of Rip
Van Winkle? Well the true
story of Rip van Winkle
runs as follows: There's
this old fart who went
to sleep for twenty years
and woke up to find
everything THE SAME.
(*Pause*)
Except him. He was twenty
years older.
Was he ever surprised.
And horrified.
EXACTLY THE SAME.

(*Opens a small door in a nearby tree and pulls out a can of beer which he opens and drinks. Pause.* CHEF *looks skeptically at the stream. Gets up disgustedly.*)

CHEF: *Sacre bleu*! What one must do.
The President Reagan has even
poison the waters of these remote
purlieus so that are no fishes.

SAM: All you think about is food.

CHEF: At least we are FREE.
(*Walks around beating on his drum.*)

SAM: Stop that. It scares the fish.

CHEF: And the bears.
Have you thought about the bears?

SAM: Bears are extinct.

CHEF: Don't believe it. I have seen pairs
of fiendish eyes out there at night.
Bears' eyes.

SAM: We're safer here than back there.
(*Pause*)
Even if it is a shit hole.

CHEF: You are a pessimist.

SLEIGHT: I am a realist.

CHEF: It does not matter. The words.
I have decided I will not go back.
You may go back but I will not.
I will live among the natives and
eat nuts and berries. I will
become pure in mind and body.
(*Takes a deep breath. Exhales.*)

SAM: You're kidding yourself.

CHEF: How do you mean?

SAM: We're exiles, damn you, don't you see?
(*Crushes the beer can and tosses it away.*)
Slowly we'll degenerate. Become
Slovenly, misshapen, feral.
Crouched over in our weeds
and rags. Stinking from filth,
disease, and unimaginable lecheries.
We'll slowly become deranged. Mad.
Our resilience will go first, then
morale, then health, and finally
life. Bugs and vermin will feast on
our unremembered bones. A true pity.

CHEF: You have a black way of looking at
things, Sam.

SAM: I am a realist.

CHEF: I think you bear a deep grudge.

SAM: ME!? A DEEP GRUDGE!? Ha!

CHEF: A deep, festooning wound.

SAM: The word is festering. You ignorant Frog.
I do not.

CHEF: You may correct my words, but
still. I am right.

SAM: I left because it was futile to
oppose a world so involved in
madness, that it mirrors madness
in every pair of eyes I see. Every
pair. In every head. Business
men's. Artists' Pretty girls'. Even
the little kids' on their way to
school. Madness. Murder. Blood
lust to blow the world apart
and howl at the pieces while the
dead in their graves shall roast
in whirlwind fires of the holocaust
and rise, like mandrakes, shrieking.
I see it.
(*Knocks at the door of the tree. It opens.*)
Humanity disgusts me.
(*Takes out another beer. Opens it.*)
Fuck it all.
But I don't delude myself. Like you.

CHEF: I am an artist.
An artist he have an
an elevated view of things.
Otherwise he die. Like
a butterfly in the mud.

(*Pause*)

SAM: Only reason I'd go back
now is to raise hell.

CHEF: I would go back but
no one can tell me
how to cook. In my
own kitchen I am a god.
I do not do these
adulterations of the
cuisine which are
now required by the

bottom-line philosophy.
*La nouvelle cuisine*!
That disgust me.
I am an artist.

(*A phone rings. An* ANIMAL *walks up with the phone in its mouth. It looks expectantly at the* CHEF. *He takes the phone and listens.*)

SAM: Repetition upon repetition . . .
A nightmare.

CHEF: (*Into the phone.*)
HALLO! NO! *Absolute non.*
I am not a yo-yo. I have
come here to the wilderness
in order to communicate
with the vast celestial
stillnesses, not in order
to enhance my bargaining
position. I do not want
to be *Maitre D'* at the Savoy.
Tell Alphonse that. I am
a proud man. My sense
of honor forbid me to plan
these kind of calculation.
(*Pause*)
I know . . .
I know . . .
You have your thought police
in the wind, but this instant
they are telling mistruths.

(*Hangs up.* ANIMAL *carries away the phone.*)

SAM: You're an idealist, Pierre.

CHEF: What idiocy! They want an
artist but they pay for an un-
skilled hammerer of wood boards.
Impossible. In America
only lawyers make the money.
Artists is shit here.
(*Walks around beating on drums.*)

SAM: Art is meaningless without
a socialist state, Pierre.

CHEF: You and your socialist state.
I have seen your socialist.
In the true socialist state
the first one they put up to
the wall is you and me.
Bam. Bam. We are gone.
You think too much.
Big mistake if you ask me.
You should learn to make
a souffle.

(*Phone rings.* ANIMAL *returns.*)

CHEF: I am not here.

(SAM *takes the phone.*)

CHEF: I am indisposed.
(*Walks around beating on his drum.*)

SLEIGHT: He's indisposed. (*To phone. Pause.*)
It's the President.
He wants to ask
you a question.

(CHEF *turns his back and crosses his arms.*)

SAM: C'mon Pierre.
(*He waits.*)
He won't come, Mr. President.
He's making a souffle.
But if you give me your
number I'll have him
call you back. How's that?
(*Pause*)
Hung up.
The bastard.

(ANIMAL *takes phone away.*)

CHEF: You see! You are a grand
fool. You have your President
and you do not speak out
your objections to his policy.
Your wild anarchist shit.
Because you have watch
so much television your head
is rubberized. Like a football.
(*He laughs.*)

I am a man of principle.
Fucked up, it is true.
If I have an opportunity
to confront your friend Jacques
I tell him to his face: *Scum,*
*you are not an artist. You*
*are only a lawyer disguised*
*as an owner of a restaurant.*
*It is a repulsive spectacle*
*to work for such a man.*

(*Pause.* SAM *laughs and snaps his finger.*)

SAM: I've decided. (*He gets up.*)

CHEF: What are you doing?

SAM: Going back.

(*Pause*)

CHEF: Why. What for?
(*Laughs. Pounds his drum.*)
The hater of humanity is going back
to the city. Ho! Ho! A mystery!

(SAM *begins to collect his things which he stuffs into the duffle bag.*)

CHEF: They will not welcome you
with open arms. They will
say your hair is looking most
peculiar with vines and twigs.
They will say you are mad.
And they will be right.
I prefer exile.
Penury.
(*Pause*)
Troglodytes are free. You,
you cannot be serious.
How am I to maintain
my sanity in this howling
uncivilized place without a
friend to share the fire with?
Sam! Listen! You must not!

(SAM *finishes packing.*)

CHEF: Go on. I need no one.
(*Pause*)
Man is born free but everywhere
is in chains.
It is a loathsome prospect,
humanity.
One could do worse than stay.
(*Scornful*)
What will you find? Will you
find love in the city? Bah!
Love is for children.
For idiots.
A beautiful woman is a false
beautiful woman.

SAM: But she's still a beautiful woman.

CHEF: True.

SAM: I'm going now.

CHEF: Clown!
Compromisist!
Tool of the Bourgeoisie!
Fascist!
Pessimist!
Gourmand!

SAM: I've got to get out of this place. (*He goes out.*)

CHEF: So much for Intertop.
Alone with the fish.
And the sky.
(*Pause*)
And the bears.
(*He looks around.*)
I shall beat myself to death
with my own fist.
(*He batters himself. Then stops.*)
Pain is boring.
(*Pause*)
I shall dream and live out
my days as a dreamer.
(*He shuts his eyes.*)
And I shall forget.
And forget. And forget.
(*Pause. He opens his eyes. Pause. He recites.*)

O saisons, ô châteaux!
Quelle âme est sans defauts?

J'ai fait la magique étude
Du bonheur, qu'aucun n'élude.

Salut à lui, chaque fois
Que chante le coq gaulois.

Ah! je n'aurais plus d'envie:
Il s'est chargé de ma vie.

Ce charme a pris âme et corps
Et dispersé les efforts.

O saisons, ô châteaux!

L'Heure de sa fuite, hélas!
Sera L'Heure du trepás.

O saisons, ô châteaux!
(*Pause. He scratches his head.*)
"Feed the fires of paranoia",
he told me.
(*Pause*)
I shall keep off the bears
by making faces.

(*He makes faces. A giant scarab beetle rolls the sun across the sky. Slow blackout.*)

# Not an Essay

## Constance Congdon

**1.** I think there is too much concern about New Forms—writing is new because a living writer just wrote it. After that, the concern should be the quality of the experience that piece of new writing will create when it's produced. You can find lifeless writing anywhere—in the avant garde and in the mainstream (whatever those two terms may mean at any one time). And there are lifeless productions—of "old" and "new" plays. There is naturalism and then there is everything else, and the battleline seems to separate intellect and heart, naturalism falling into the "heart" category. A play, however, is a product of the spirit, and those other two forces, intellect and heart, are fuel and engine or engine and fuel, depending on the writer. Without the spirit, the thing will never fly, no matter how hot or fast it runs.

**2.** When I talk about spirit, I mean the source of the imagination.

**3.** Writing a play is such a long process. I write it and then it goes into rehearsal. I spend a lot of time revising it, working on it—it's got to be something that means something to me that all the trials of other people working on it and other people seeing it can only enrich.

**4.** The best territory for me, the most "fertile" area, is an area that calls up opposite or even warring responses from me. I think I look for some sort of truth when I write, rather than trying to manipulate material to speak whatever "truth" I come in the door with. Somehow writing becomes more of an act of faith than it normally would be because I'm taking the risk of finding things out that hurt me emotionally or make me question my basic assumptions. And the next thing I do is try to have fun with it all—think of things that are exciting for their own sake, things an audience would like to see.

**5.** I write for an audience—I always imagine an audience there, as palpable to me as what I'm putting on stage. I watch the audience when one of my plays is on stage, and I'm always amazed that they *are* there—in a theater—when we live in a movie and television culture—where movies and television supply us with our iconography, where movie and television watching are the primary suppliers of fictional experience. And I'm not even talking about content here—the *experience* of movie watching is so different than play watching. Movies are an almost private experience and, because they are frozen on film, we can get up and leave, talk out loud, eat, fall asleep, cry, laugh, applaud, and never have the least effect on what is happening on the screen—in this sense, movies are the perfect twentieth-century experience. Movies are maddeningly eternal—each frame will always be the same, forever. Sometimes I feel movies, passive and unchanging, are watching *us* as we change through the decades.

**6.** Plays, however, are public. And because they are created by actors living in the moment, everything an audience does has an effect—in fact, plays can't exist fully without that audience. Plays change in small ways nightly and in immense ways, production to production, age to age. They change with use because they aren't frozen. Plays are mortal.

## Some Notes on Theatre

### Len Jenkin

I always like the opening: the houselights fade, the room goes black, the voices around me quiet, the first lights come up in the shoe box, and the figures start to move.

Once that's over, for something to hold me, as author or audience, there needs to be a continuing sense of *wonder,* as powerful as that in fairy tales, moonlight, or dreams. This can be present in any sort of work for the stage—realistic to sublimely outrageous—and it's a quality that can't be fused into or onto something with clever staging or sideways performances. It's gotta be there, in the text and through and through.

The other thing that needs to be there for any genuine theatre to exist is what I call *heart.* This doesn't mean I want to look at people struggling bravely through their emotional problems. It means that the author is not primarily an entertainer; that he/she is a preacher, and a singer, and a human being. And that the deep twined nature of what binds us and what makes us free is going to be out there on the stage.

Actors, *good* actors, are braver than hell, and I have an enormous respect and admiration for them. Bad actors have no courage at all, and don't need it. It's easy for them.

What I try to make when I write or direct is the same as what I value when I'm looking at the stage as audience—and that's also the same as what I respond to when I see or feel it in the "actual" world: moments (and the roads toward and away from them) where the life within breaks through, where it signals out through language, object, gesture; where the bubble breaks, and all the cold air or all the heat within escapes with a whoosh, right at me. . . . this doesn't need to happen in a noisy way, though it can—it's also able to be silent and still.

A theatre, like an individual artist, needs to take its own road. It should just be there, doing what it does because of its nature, its community, and the artists it attracts. If the people like it, and get something from it, they'll be there too. If not, that theatre will change, or die—or have a huge subscription audience. . . .

The competition—movies and TV—labors under a huge disadvantage: It needs to make things that appeal to a huge segment of the population, 'cause its production costs are so pleasingly enormous. However, the movies and TV do one thing right: With the exception of a few revival houses in college towns, they don't show work by the dead to be seen by the living, and they don't try to be engaging classrooms, or an innovative sort of museum.

I'd love to see theatre energetically stomping around the U.S.A.—rent 7-11s, and put on plays by the highwayside (the plays already offered at the 7-11 are pretty good, and the lighting is amazing)—or tractor-trailers full of men in hats and beautiful women, pulling into town and setting up on the high-school football field. I'll be glad to be in the cab of the first truck in line—the one that says "ALIVE" in a bullet on its side.

## An Afterword

### Jeffrey M. Jones

This play is born of writer's block. In 1983, after a series of increasingly autobiographic plays, the constant sound of my own voice had become oppressive. I felt it was very important to introduce voices other than my own into my work, but could imagine no way to invent a character that was not my own voice, disguised. Invention itself became suspect; writing dialog impossible. In desperation—and, as I imagined, only as a way of keeping busy until inspiration returned—I started to see if I could construct "other" voices by manipulating the words of other writers. I would try any text that came to hand—literature, scripts, transcripts, periodicals, advertisements, instructions, private correspondence—choosing whatever passages caught my eye. My initial approach was to edit them down to find their essence, which had more to do with their intent or style than with their ostensible content. Out of these, I made primitive monologs or, by assigning texts to a number of voices, dialogs. As these odd little assemblages piled up, I began to juxtapose or intercut them into even larger structures, which in turn suggested contexts in which they could have "meaning." In a reverse process, I began to see how much original source material could be replaced or eliminated before sense was lost; and how interpolations having a structure themselves could be introduced. In aggregate, these rather arbitrary individual decisions began to take on recurring patterns. But only in the final stages—and therefore, in a very real sense, only incidentally—did it become possible to say what the play was about.

In fact, rather than speak of content, I feel it is more helpful to consider this work in the light of its structure, which consists of several distinct levels, all of which are fundamentally discontinuous. On the broadest level, two familiar and simple narratives —a soap opera romance and the conquest of Peru—are juxtaposed. Despite few apparent connections between the original sources—Prescott's *Conquest of Peru* and Robert's Harlequin romance, *Night of the Scorpion*—the juxtaposition makes these stories appear to comment on each other. The stories not only shape the play, but because a great deal of information can be left out of them before they lose their own structures, are themselves easily shaped. On another level the play consists of five discrete narrative scene-chains: "Prescott" telling the story of Pizarro and Atahuallpa; "Faithless" concerning the romantic triangle of Jason, Shannon, and Carol; "Romeo" concerning the romantic triangle of Jason, Shannon, and Cliff; "Campaign" concerning the enterprise for which Jason and Selden recruit Cliff; and "Toxin" being the scorpion/strychnine subplot. Again, each story can not only stand independent of the others, but itself consists of a sequence of discontinuous scenes. Finally, there are similar discontinuities on the levels of scene and sentence. Sometimes, an original coherence is disrupted by interpolations, ellipses, and substitutions; or, conversely, a series of unrelated elements may be juxtaposed to suggest coherence. In *Romeo 5,* for example, the highly recognizable situation of a man and woman in love is disrupted by shifts between three different versions of this event—a contemporary soap opera, *Romeo and Juliet,* and *The Importance of Being Earnest.* Though the sources are recognizable, the quotations are clearly compressed versions of the originals. In fact, even the most stylistically coherent passages in the text are highly edited versions of their originals and contain numerous breaks.

Given the way in which the play is constructed, I believe any directorial approach must do three things. It must encourage the actor to break the text down into the greatest number of components; to chose whatever interpretation the actor prefers for each component, based solely on the evidence of that component itself; and, finally, to assemble whatever subtext arises out of these individual interpretations by creating a context in which they seem plausible. In other words, the acting method replicates the writing method. The actors I worked with in New York—Karla Barker, Keith Druhl, Zivia Flomenhaft, Patrick O'Connell, Barbara Somerville, and William Duff-Griffin, later replaced by Zach Grenier—shared a focus on character (through line) which proved eminently workable. Even when reading the play around a table we quickly preferred character readings which did not try to mirror the shifts in writing style, but used a common voice for all. As we began to analyze the actions of the play, we found that most scenes could have several interpretations, and began to construct alternative scenarios. In doing so, I urged the cast to look for as many separate thoughts in a text as possible and in that way discover where the breaks fell. Setting this work aside, we next blocked the play very quickly in the *lingua franca* of film and television acting: entrance, exit, cross, and focus. Thus, quite early on we not only had a simple, flexible vocabulary for expressing action, but could move quickly through large portions of the play to see actions in the context of other actions. The next step was to set this work aside too, and begin again, interpreting each scene expressively according to the alternative scenarios we had invented. Actors were free to move in any way, and imagine that they had the resources of a film studio to invoke any locale or any prop that would support a choice. Only in the last ten days—in the theatre on the finished set—did we edit down all these choices into our finished play. Instead of basing these choices on overall narrative logic, however, we chose the interpretations the actors liked best. We found that virtually any choice became believable when an actor believed in it, and that believability gave the play coherence regardless of the narrative assumptions on which the action was founded.

No less important to the style of acting and of the whole production was the use of music. From the very beginning, I had read collaged texts against various kinds of taped music as a means of giving them emotional coloration, a kind of "sense". Many of the eventual speeches were derived from nondramatic texts, and therefore had an ineradicable "flatness" that made them difficult to act. But by using music rather than acting to provide the emotional response expected by an audience, I found I could support both the actor and the text, and the performances took on a distanced quality that was very pleasing. The shifts in background music provided additional, powerful structural clues for an audience, and some of the most powerful effects were the result of deliberately mismatching the tone of scene and score. In rehearsal, composer Daniel M. Schreier introduced me to techniques developed by Richard Foreman for creating a full-length, multichannel theatrical sound score. Because I feel such a score is so central to the correct presentation of this play, and because the techniques involved, though perhaps initially unfamiliar, are so simple, I wish to explain them here.

The central problem is easily stated: Unlike the simple sound cue, which switches from silence to sound to silence, the basic operation in a continuous sound score is a crossfade between one sound source and another. Since most cues are set to a point in the action—and because rate of action fluctuates between from performance to performance—continuous cues (not broken by silence) cannot be prerecorded onto a single tape. They must be executed by an operator at a mixing board and happen in real time. For similar reasons, it is disadvantageous to set a cue relative to a fixed point on another sound tape. The ideal piece of music, therefore, would contain relatively few structural features with regard to time. And because simpler melodic structures blend into musical backgrounds more smoothly than complex structures, the basic unit of the real-time score is a cassette on which a tape loop has been recorded over the full length of the cassette. Loops—which, of course, must first be made on a reel-to-reel machine*—can have a variety of lengths (as a practical matter, loops begin to lose their repetitive qualities at around 30 seconds), and depending on the nature of the source material and placement of the edits, can have a wide range of expressive qualities. But whether a simple repetitive chord change or a lengthy and apparently seamless melody, all tape loops function as a "piece" of music that can be faded in and out at will. Full scores consist of perhaps 20 to 60 "loop" cassettes (again, remember that the actual loop is recorded onto a standard cassette), with a minimum of two playback decks, although a third cassette deck and supplementary reel-to-reel obviously provide far greater flexibility in mixing. I believe anyone conducting even the simplest experiments with this technology will be impressed by the implications of sound scoring for any kind of theatre.

*Digital sampling equipment has developed since this writing to permit an alternative technology of even greater flexibility.

# The Politics of Despair

Tony Kushner

Five separate events, occurring consecutively over a short period of time, precipitated the writing of *A Bright Room Called Day*:

**1.** Carl Weber, the German director and translator with whom I had trained at New York University, and from whom I have learned much of what I know about theatre, was leaving New York to begin a teaching job at Stanford University in California. I felt abandoned, and I compensated for Carl's departure by acquiring a huge appetite for histories, novels, and plays about German refugees in the 1930s (I didn't unmask the source of this fixation till much later; I am slow about such things).

**2.** The theatre collective I had helped to found, and with which my best work had been done, fell apart, suffering an abrupt and anticlimatically silent demise after four years of noisy and frequently productive existence. That the group had disintegrated under the pressures of no money and everyone's insufficiently analyzed craziness seemed a bitter sign and ominous predictor of the likely fate of any future collective enterprise. The alternative, life in the mainstream commercial theatre, looked appropriately grim.

**3.** My best friend and frequent collaborator, Kimberly Flynn, was seriously injured in a cab accident; and

**4.** My great-aunt Florence, a remarkable, compassionate, loving and generous woman, died suddenly on the eve of

**5.** Ronald Reagan's re-election.

The winter of 1984–85 was a calamitous time. The desolate political sphere mirrored in an exact and ugly way an equally desolate personal sphere. With a grim relentlessness that now seems almost magical, every day brought news of some global failure, some intimate loss, some variety of triumphant evil. Everyone was affected, or at least appeared to be; and the literature about Germany I was voraciously consuming began to have a nasty taste of the prophetic. I read Brecht's description of his era, "When there was injustice only/ And no rebellion", and felt it to be frighteningly applicable to the present.

One day in December, nearing the end of this unhappy time, I was looking at an exhibition of DeMille memorabilia (Cecil B.'s and Agnes') at Lincoln Center. A videotape was on display, showing Agnes DeMille at work on a new dance for the Joffrey Ballet. I was standing at the opposite end of the room, far from the tape, but I could hear it, and I thought I heard Ms. DeMille tell her interviewer that the title of her new dance was "A Bright Room Called Day." This sounded like fun and solace so I went over to watch the videotape, only to discover that the title of the piece was actually "A Bridegroom Called Death." From a bright room called day to a bridegroom called death: the metamorphosis seemed emblematic of the times.

My mishearing stayed with me, and eventually it came to sound like the right/wrong title of a play I had decided to write, a play about Germans, refugee and otherwise, caught on the cusp of the historical catastrophe about to engulf them. A small circle of close friends would dissolve, suddenly and silently, in the malevolent atmosphere of the day. For my friend Kimberly I wrote the part of Rosa Malek; in her clarity, intelligence, courage, and commitment, Rosa much resembles Kim, and Rosa escapes from Berlin. I didn't realize it at the time, but in that flight is expressed my certainty that Kim will escape completely the injuries she sustained in the accident. I named the main character Agnes, out of gratitude for Ms. DeMille's transformed title. Now I can see that Agnes is Florence—not an exact portrait, but the profile is unmistakable: good, trusting, well-intended, regrettably näive. And Reagan's re-election: Then as now, I see in Reagan's career a kindred phenomenon to Hitler's accession to power.

I never indulged in fantasies of some archaic form of fascism goosestepping down the streets of America. Reagan and the forces gathered about him seemed to me, in the flush of their demoralizing victory in 1984, the advance guard of a new and more dangerous and destructive form of barbarism. Marcuse writes, in *Counterrevolution and Revolt,* "History does not repeat itself exactly, and a higher stage of capitalist development in the United States would call for a higher stage of fascism. This country possesses economic and technical resources for a totalitarian organization immeasurably greater than Hitler Germany ever had." He lists, among other factors inhibiting the growth of American fascism, the lack of "charismatic leaders", but the book was written in 1972. Since then, the sweaty Nixonian conservative has been replaced by something more marketable.

It is an accepted commonplace that the Left is overwhelmed by morbid paranoia and visions of the apocalypse when confronted with a determined, successful, reactionary movement. Now that the Iran-Contra scandal is jeopardizing Reagan's popularity, the fears of the early eighties seem excessive. It is doubtful that Reagan will launch an attack on the Soviet Union as, in the days of "Evil Empire" rhetoric, he seemed capable of doing. It is also doubtful (though far less certainly so) that the Right will achieve its ambition and engineer an invasion of Nicaragua —even the contras are in trouble, though it would be premature, to say the least, to assume that U.S. support for their criminal war will cease. It is conceivable that Reagan, or at least many of his underlings, will wind up in some sort of legal trouble. And in the slow-breaking light of this new day Reaganism seems an aberration and not the start of a downhill roll toward darkness.

Regardless of the outcome and the ultimate assessment of this administration, I believe that the transhistorical metaphor on which *Bright Room* is based remains essentially valid. Reaganism is an event in the unfolding of a counterrevolution set in motion by the great social upheaval of the sixties, and as such is similar to the counterrevolution that was a response to the German social revolution that began at the end of World War One and was crushed, for the most part, by 1923. The Republican Party is not the Nazi Party. It is, however, composed of people who, as the behavior of the goons and thugs of the NSC so richly demonstrates, understand nothing of due process, civil rights, international conduct, justice, or freedom, or democracy. It is the respectable front for an increasingly militant Right—a militancy they have borrowed, along with a new rhetorical style and a stance of embattled underdoggedness, from the struggles of the people they seek to oppress. In this they are very much like the Nazis, who selectively and cleverly appropriated socialist and communist imagery and language to broaden their appeal. The current, slightly tarnished figurehead of the New Right is precisely the kind of leader history coughs up at regular intervals: A demagogue who helps bring out the absolute worst in his electorate, who cynically panders to the middle-class willingness to sell dignity and decency for a spurious economic security and a completely unearned domestic tranquility.

The Republicans are opposed, in the central political arena, by a party of Democrats even less deserving of the word "Social" than were their Weimar counterparts. Like the German Social-Democrats, the American Democratic party is a huge and unfailingly disappointing machine that devours some of the best political energy of the day, claiming the reluctant allegiance of progressive people through its unassailable position as the lesser of two evils.

The Republican are not Nazis, and Reagan isn't Hitler, but isn't Reagan's appalling silence in the face of the AIDS crisis—he has expressed to date almost no concern or sympathy, and has only timorously increased research funding years too late, when it has become clear that AIDS might threaten "nonmarginal" (straight, male, white) people—isn't this indifference to life ultimately the heart of fascist brutality? And hasn't his administration been remarkable only in the extent of its indifference to human suffering and human needs? We aren't fascists, we don't live in a fascist state, but for the last eight years we have, as a nation, played with an option to move in that direction, and it remains to be seen if this dalliance is done.

*Bright Room* was written in the valley of the shadow of a great and widespread fear, in 1984, when the President seemed very strong and his opposition incapable of opposing him. A great deal has happened since then: Marcos ousted, an increased effort to end apartheid in South Africa, and Gay Rights Bill in New York City, the bombing of Tripoli, the Rejkavik summit disaster (the Reagan-Gorbachev talks), and the Supreme Court's homophobic ruling of the summer of 1986. Things could be better, much, much better, but they have recently been much worse. There is life in the polity, and if Reagan is sleeping easily these days it's a measure of senescence, not smug assuredness.

As times change the play has needed to be reworked, and this will doubtless continue to be necessary. It remains a question for me whether the play, which is supposed to be about morbidity and mysticism in the face of political evil, is actually to a certain extent a manifestation of the kind of reaction it seeks to describe. Flat, unconvincingly optimistic rhetoric is as inimical to good political theater as bourgeois despair (and I believe that there is such an animal, a middle-class predilection for the goose-pimpley, lump-in-your-throat thrill of nihilism from which I have certainly not been exempted). When I was writing *Bright Room* all optimism felt flat and unconvincing, and despair, regardless of its class affiliations, was the order of the day. I concentrated on the history of the last phase of the collapse of the Weimar Republic, rather than on the crimes of the Third Reich, intending to rescue the play from hopelessness by showing a period of choices, when things might have turned out very differently if only. . . . The play's story ends before the worst nightmare begins, but its ending looks to the camps, the bombings, and even to the Bomb. After one of its performances in April of 1985, a man in the audience asked me whether, if I saw our situation as being a retreading of the path followed by Germany in the thirties, I saw any hope or point in resisting. The play is a warning signal, not a prediction, but I often ask myself: Is it politically effective? Will it galvanize an audience to action or, less ambitiously, will it make an audience think, argue, examine the present through the example of the past? Or will it merely confirm and voice for them what they may already suspect: That something unstoppable and horrendous is right around the corner?

There's a great scene in Bergman's *The Seventh Seal* between Jons, the knight's sidekick and serving-man, and a mural painter in a country church:

> JONS: What is that supposed to represent?
> PAINTER: The Dance of Death.
> JONS: And that one is death?
> PAINTER: Yes, he dances off with all of them.
> JONS: Why do you paint such nonsense?
> PAINTER: I thought it would serve to remind the people that they must die.
> JONS: Well, it's not going to make them feel any happier.
> PAINTER: Why should one always make people happy? It might not be a bad idea to scare them a little once in a while.
> JONS: Then they'll close their eyes and refuse to look at your painting.
> PAINTER: Oh, they'll look. A skull is almost more interesting than a naked woman.
> JONS: If you scare them . . .
> PAINTER: They'll think.
> JONS: And if they think . . .
> PAINTER: They'll become still more scared.
> JONS: And then they'll run right into the arms of the priests.
> PAINTER: That's not my business.
> JONS: You're only painting your Dance of Death.
> PAINTER: I'm only painting things as they are. Everyone else can do as he likes.
> JONS: Just think how some people will curse you.
> PAINTER: Maybe. But then I'll paint something amusing for them to look at. I have to make a living—at least until the plague takes me.

This painter is not a responsible political artist. He is, however, political, as Jons points out, as we all are, whether or not we choose to be, till the plague takes us. Not everyone who refuses the designation "political artist" wants to send his or her audience into the arms of the priests, and many such people have created powerfully progressive political work. Conversely, it is not at all unusual for someone who embraces this designation to accomplish nothing finer than terrifying others, which is more likely to promote prayer than activism. There is always the balancing trick, difficult to manage, of portraying powerlessness and empowerment at the same time, of evoking Hell without its traditional concomitant, eternal damnation.

Because *Bright Room* grew out of a period of grief and mourning losses, I haven't found a way to make it more "positive" without being false to what's there, much of which I like. But grief and mourning don't lie beyond the reach of history. All during that benighted year during which the play was written I became less and less politically active—a process that had begun, actually, a year before. I was losing my connection with activism because of an indolence born out of . . . well, indolence, but also perhaps out of fear, out of a sense of being overwhelmed, as a character in the play says. I'm certain that my stagnation in the realm of active involvement has had a tidal effect on the way the world presents itself to me, changing the face of the enemy from something fearsome into something irresistable. It's not merely that you may not have a right to write about issues of active resistance when you aren't actively resisting; it's more important that a removal from the struggle distorts any analysis of the struggle—distance, in this instance, not equal clarity. A resurgence of activism has altered the shape and tenor of the play, and so did Oskar Eustis' suggestion to "complexify" the despair. Through further research I learned that 80,000 communists died in the camps. The loss of life, and the lost battle that loss implies, are well worth despairing over, but the fact of such extraordinary resistance carries its own weighty imperative. The history of the Weimar Republic is more than a story of ineffectual decency and ascendant evil, more than the story of its impressive refugees. It is also the story of a heroic resistance that sends, from the mass graves, a mandate to the present, which speaks against the dangerous illusion of the inevitable unsuccess of opposition to oppression.

When we conjur up the past we run the risk of reawakening old nightmares, of being overwhelmed with horror. Conjuring the future is even more treacherous, because to attempt to envision the future we must resort to what is known, to the past, and if the past *as* past is nearly unbearable, how much more unbearable to look ahead and see only old nightmares staring back at us. Then again, considering the dire present, imagining that we have any future at all has got to be accounted a cause for celebration.

Those who govern us, in whose hands power is most concentrated, have as their objective, if we can judge by their actions, to bring time to an end, to abolish past and future. That this is so, that these men are who they are, that we have permitted them access to power and may permit worse yet, is so fundamentally and inconceivably threatening that we reject immediate knowledge of it; for, in the grip of that knowledge, every human action, including the making of theater, would have to be directed toward the riddance of those men, their objectives, and the system that nurtures them. The brightest hope for the future would be any event, theatrical and otherwise, that presses this knowledge closer to home.

# The Hole in the Ozone

**Eric Overmyer**

Perhaps the imagination is on the verge
of recovering its rights.
Andre Breton (paraphrased by E.O.)

**1.**

The American theatre is a horror show, a triple-bill of B-movies flickering out of focus across a dilapidated drive-in movie screen. (Not to cast aspersions by comparison upon either drive-ins or B-movies, both of which consistently offer pleasures and provocations rarely encountered in the theatre. Joe Bob Briggs, drive-in movie critic of Grapevine, Texas, and one of the great post-modern stylists, says: Check it out.)

The dead hand of naturalism continues to flex its Zombie stranglehold upon American playwriting or, rather, American stages. The American naturalistic play lurches across the stages of America in all its numbing variety, presenting yet another American family in crisis, or illuminating the latest topical problem—abortion, Afghanistan, alcoholism, child abuse, bag ladies. These headline plays are really, and with any luck for their hopeful authors will become, Important TV Movies of the Week. (A literary manager friend of mine was recently asked by a producer who claimed to have "a hot new incest play" if the theatre she worked for would be interested in a co-production. "Have you done molestation?" he asked, in all seriousness.)

These "new" plays, which are produced precisely because they resemble old plays, and are thus recognizable to producers AS plays (producers being a dimmer form of humanity and often heard to utter when confronted with something ever-so-slightly off-center, "This isn't a play") are rooted in reductive, mechanistic psychology; have a linear and boringly predictable narrative; and are infested with characters who are the sum of their exposition and are described and circumscribed in terms of their jobs, family histories, ethnicity, age, sex, and current dilemma ("Why is this day different from all other days?" is the credo of naturalistic playwriting, along with "What's at stake?"). The characters of the American naturalistic play have pat and explicable motives, and are much less interesting than anyone knows in "real life". Ionesco: Americans have been ruined by realism; there is nothing "realistic" about reality.

With its penchant for melodrama and sentimental resolution (no ambiguous or open-ended or, God forbid, unhappy endings), the American naturalist play, which purports to be about "truth" and "life" and "reality", is in all ways the most artificial and unlife-like creature.

The perfect Zombie.

**2.**

These naturalistic plays derive from television most immediately, and more distantly from William Inge and Robert Anderson and Paddy Chayevsky, and more distantly still from Arthur Miller, and dimly indeed from Eugene O'Neill, a past that recedes and a future that grows ever more attenuated and feeble. They lack even the virtues of these writers' plays, their awkward energy and crude American "poetry". (Compare Williams and Miller—poor Williams, his unlucky fate to be lumped with Miller, and to be writing during the heyday of American naturalism and the Actors' Studio, naturalism's ally and proselytizer.)

As any playwright who has ever attempted to work in a non-naturalistic vein knows, the first thing most American actors will do when confronted with a non-naturalistic text is *naturalize* it. This usually consists of *relaxing* the language, adding *ums* and *ahs* and halts and pauses and stutters; restoring articles and conjuctions that the writer has deliberately pruned, running sentences together, ignoring carefully constructed rhythms, and generally rewriting so that the language feels more "natural" to the actor; seeking reductive psychological motivations and explanations for the play's actions; in sum, reducing the world of the play to one the actor feels "comfortable" with, a world that is "appropriate" for the actor's well-being and sense of self. This is the legacy of the Actor's Studio, and of film and television, and it has given most American actors not only inadequate technique, but a tragically small frame of reference. They are not comfortable with anything they have not heard or seen before—in this way, they are like producers. The actor is the most conservative force in the theatre, even more conservative than the producer, and the influence of the Actor's Studio *for naturalism* remains pervasive and insidious.

Naturalism is reflexive. It refers not to life, as it likes to think, but to other naturalistic plays, and to movies and television, and a style of behavior and a way of speaking that are far less interesting and strange and wonderful and poetic than the quotidian world. Naturalism proclaims its "reality" while avoiding the complexities and mysteries and riches of "real life".

**3.**

The American theatre, particularly Broadway and its putative alternative, the regional/resident theatre, is also the realm of the Ghoul. Revivals of Shakespeare, Shaw, Coward, and the "American classics"—witness the return to Broadway in recent seasons of *You Can't Take It With You* a few years ago, *Hay Fever*, and *Arsenic and Old Lace*. Museum theatre. Mummified productions.

The reanimation of dead tissue.

**4.**

Finally, the Vampire. The most pernicious of the three. After all, the Zombie of naturalism will fade eventually away—or not, but certainly if the theatre is to survive, it must; and the Ghoul of mediocrity will be forever with us. Bad theatre always predominates.

The Vampire is a debased demi-god, a creature who sucks the life out of another, and recasts that other in his own image. In this way, the Vampire has a hold and a claim on the future. Of course, the Vampire to which I refer, haunting the wings and rehearsal halls of the American theatre, is the post-modern director, sucking the life out of the living text, and making it his Minion.

This creature has nothing but contempt for the text and the writer, and in fact prefers to savage the work of dead playwrights—to these brave Indian fighters, the only good playwright is a dead one. I am not speaking here of the true investigative post-modern director, who illuminates, but of those ego-ridden monsters who travesty texts under the guise of reanimating and saving them.

There's little need to go on about the post-modern Vampire director. You all know the signs, the cheap tricks and arbitrary devices, the thoughtless juxtapositions, the panoply of post-modern cliches, the ravaged text.

**5.**

Kevin Kelly of *The Boston Globe* published an article entitled *Has Playwriting Reached A Hackneyed Dead End?* Although he didn't quite ever articulate his complaint, he was in fact voicing his frustration with the Zombie of Naturalism. This article was the latest in a long series that always asks the same question—Where are the new plays?—and, by extension, where are the new playwrights?

These articles are well-intentioned, but the critics, isolated and frustrated by the limits and low standards of performance—after all, they only know what they see, and if what they see is usually badly done, naturalistic or not, well, they have no way of knowing that the answer to the question is quite simple. It's another question. Hugh Kenner: Wrong questions, wrong answers.

*Where are the new plays and playwrights*? The only proper response is: *Where are the producers who will produce new plays*? By new, I mean *new*, not rehashed old plays. The answer to that question is: There are almost none. New plays are being written, but for how long, if they have almost no chance of being produced?

This state of affairs raises critical questions for the theatrical artist.

**6.**

Confronted on one side by the Zombie of naturalism and its partner, the Ghoul of museum theatre, and on the other by the Vampire of the post-modern director, what is the theatrical writer to do? Only what he or she has always done: Use the theatre for its theatricality, and abandon any notions of popularity. Niccola Chiaromonte: The theatre is for the few who love it. This is not an elitist position, merely a recognition and acceptance of the theatre's inherent marginality, a cultural position it shares with poetry. This acceptance helps clarify what the theatre can and should be, and avoids confusion with the electronic media, a confusion that can only prove fatal for the theatre—which is precisely why naturalism and behavioral acting are the theatre's deadliest enemies.

The resources of the theatre are many and few at the same time, and again the theatre finds itself allied with poetry: language, imagination, story-telling, myth, irony, image, performance. The theatrical writer who uses these resources places him/herself, no matter how avant-garde or radical his or her formal investigation may be, squarely in the great tradition of Shakespeare, Aeschalus, Lorca, Chekhov, Pirandello, de Ghelderode, Bulgakov, Gogol, Wedekind, Buchner, and every other *theatrical* writer, including, in this country, Williams, Shepard, and Len Jenkin.

So: I am for the theatre, and I am for the text. I am a radical classicist.

**7.**

We live in the post-modern era, by which is meant we live in an interregnum era, between wars, between styles, even between Ice Ages; an interglacial age of fear and trembling. The culture of Death holds sway over the planet at the same time a new consciousness stirs in opposition.

In the Hamptons, the affluent look up at the summer sky and see for the first time the Hole in the Ozone.

Kenneth Patchen: SLEEPERS AWAKE ON THE PRECIPICE.

After decades of denial, some of them are beginning to awake on the brink, while most of course continue to rush headlong over the edge in pursuit of money and death.

In a modern world where *everything* in the predominate Death Culture works to diminish love and the imagination, the theatre is a sanctuary, one of the last places one can work to reassert the imagination and recover its rights.

For those of us who have been working through the end of the world with pain and irony, to emerge not unscathed but still breathing, we can only say *So what?* and a well, then, *What Is to Be Done?*

The theatre needs to be reclaimed for the imagination; in other words, the theatre needs to be reclaimed for itself. There is no other task for the actor, designer, director, writer; for the *theatrical artist.*

# Afterthoughts on *In His 80th Year*

**Gillian Richards**

When I started writing again in 1979 after a twenty-year break, I was working as administrative director of the Iowa Theater Lab in Catskill, N.Y. For eight years I'd been living with, sometimes documenting, the Lab's obsessively intense explorations of what theatre is, or should be, what the relationship is of director to actor, actor to audience. So it happened naturally that when I finished my first twenty-minute, seven-page poem, it became a performance piece. First, I memorized the poem because I found I could put it over better if I didn't have to look at the page; then I "told" it to the actors in the upstairs rooms of our house, and later to slightly larger audiences in the Lab's performance space. I called it a dramatic-narrative poem. It was a "narrative" because the biggest breakthrough in this new writing cycle of my life came when I fell, almost accidentally, into writing "she" instead of "I." This led me into writing a third-person story about a character who was close to me but enough outside myself to leave room for some irony to get in. It allowed me to dump the confessional "I" that I'd come to detest in struggling with poems on and off during my fallow period. The new poem was "dramatic" because I never had intended it to lie on the page. It was written for my own voice and it wanted to reach out to/into the listeners, to get under their skin, unsettle them, draw them in—to do the same things that the Lab's work had always done for me.

My next piece, *Sex, Death and Ambition in NYC: Waiting for the Real Thing,* revolved around a trip we made to New York in 1980 with the Lab's vampire play, *Blood Addiction.* The poem was in ten scenes, beginning with a playful glimpse of the Lab actors killing off the vampire, and climaxing with an all-out sex-and-violence ballad—an eight-minute version of Oshima's *In the Realm of the Senses,* a film we all went to see during our run. In between, the poem passed through a wide range of rhythms and moods. It was easy to memorize and fun to do. The whole piece lasted a little over an hour which was just about the limit of my stamina and as much as the audience would want to take of one voice. I performed it, in whole or in part, in many different circumstances, formal and informal, from the Anspacher Theatre at the Public to Washington Square Park on a Saturday afternoon.

Though *NYC* was technically a step up from the previous poem, I had always suspected it was better in performance than on the page. I also tended to be suspicious of it as a crowd-pleaser and because it came relatively quickly and easily: There was very little gap between the way I imagined the poem in my head and the way it turned out. *In His 80th Year* was intended to be a solo performance piece like *NYC*, only more ambitious. I would try to create a sustained dramatic/narrative arc, starting the woman protagonist off in one place and, after much travail and probably a good many pages later, setting her down in another. I called it a "Poem in Two Acts" and assumed that it was likely to move a step closer to theatre than the other two pieces.

As it happened, the first thing that threw off my plans did also bring the poem closer to theatre. I was approaching the end of Act One and was finishing a long first-person monologue for the woman, when the man in the poem suddenly proposed to have a monologue of his own. Up to that point this man (the woman's lover) had been seen only through the woman's eyes or through the not-quite-impartial eye of the narrator. He was supposed to remain that way: viewed at one remove. In *NYC* voices other than my own had surfaced briefly, and of course in my far-back youth as a playwright in England I had written parts for men, but somehow the whole idea of a monologue for the man seemed a little audacious now. I resisted for a while, not sure if I could get inside this man's head or even if I wanted to. In the end I decided to give it a try, mainly because I liked the idea of his consciousness taking over from hers in mid-scene (the surprise this transition would be for the audience). After that, once the man had got his monologue and had his expensive boot in the door, he became a much more active participant in the poem than I'd planned. In the second act I found myself writing quite a lot of dialogue for the two characters (I even wrote a monologue for the woman's dog) and it seemed to me as if the poem was trying to break out of its narrative form and turn itself into a play.

While I was writing the second act, I had performed scenes from Act One on several different occasions. However, as I got to the end of Act Two, it was clear that the poem had become distinctly problematical as a solo performance piece. It had grown to nearly two hours in length, too long for one voice. It was harder for a listener to stay with it than with *NYC*; it was more introspective and ruminative; the images and rhythms were less aggressively theatrical. On a return visit to the Lab (by this time I had left the company and moved to New York), I tried performing the whole second act in the same projected, all-out style I'd used for *NYC*. This was not a success. No one could distinguish between the two voices in the dialogue, the progression of events became muddy, and the act dragged interminably. That fiasco confirmed my idea that the poem would have to become a piece for two performers, a man and a woman, who would take care of their own dialogue and interior thoughts and divide up the narrative between them. Sometimes I imagined a version where the two performers would stand reading at their individual lecterns and barely acknowledge one another's presence. There would be just enough complicity between them to give a frisson to the audience—a hint that before the end the formal setup could disintegrate and things go reeling out of control. But what tempted me more was a vision of a full-blown theatre piece where the performers would move around and there would be a set of some kind and lights and props and a director. Either way, I thought the key to performing the piece would be to use the ambiguity of the performers' roles as both actors and narrators, both inside the story and outside it. Since "story theatre" was a form I had always despised, I imagined this duality being used to unsettle the audience rather than to make them feel good. An element of danger would come from the fact that at any moment the "safe" impartial narrator could disappear and the character would take possession, inhabiting the same performer's body and looking out at the audience through the same eyes.

As it turned out, five years were to pass before I saw the piece on the stage. Immediately after I completed it, I spent some time working on it with another former member of the Lab's company. We tried working out how the lines might be divided up. We also tried moving around a bit, physicalizing what was going on in the poem. Frustratingly, everything felt awkward. Among other problems, I wanted the male performer to be actively involved from the beginning, but it nagged at me that perhaps he didn't really belong in the first three scenes, since I hadn't written them with a second performer in mind. After a few weeks, we abandoned these rather desultory experiments, and I started to work on a full-length play in prose.

When I came back to the poem in the spring of 1985, it was to include part of Act Two in a reading I was giving upstate for the Greene County Council on the Arts. On this occasion, I decided to avoid any attempt at "performing." I thought that if I didn't memorize the lines, I would have to cut out some of the histrionics (swaying around, hair getting in the eyes) and could concentrate more on taking my time with the transitions and making them clear. I would sit on a chair with the script and read, and try to let the characters take over my voice and eyes just enough so that the dialogue wouldn't be confusing. This low-key approach worked much better: The audience seemed able to follow what was going on and appeared held and involved.

After that reading, I thought about why the poem had seemed so recalcitrant when we worked on it two years before. I realized that back then I had probably been too close to the material to be satisfied with any version that involved letting other people into it. But I also concluded that the real problem to be overcome in staging the poem was that, unlike a play, it was almost obsessively complete in itself. In writing it, the challenge was to try and calibrate and make clear an action that was purely interior: a seismic shift in the inner world of the two characters. As a result, the poem was dense with detail. It was crammed full of gestures, physical sensations, sounds, glimpses of objects, and flashes of color, which aimed to reflect the exact state of play, both between the man and the woman and inside each of them. I connected this use of detail with my memories of the Lab's strongly film-influenced work where images would often surface from surrounding darkness in a pool of light, and where the audience was always so close to the actors they could catch even the smallest, most precise movement of an eye or hand. In my poem, it seemed to me that the density of the texture would always make it hard to open up the piece and bring in other elements of theatre.

In fact, when Anne Bogart staged the first production of *In His 80th Year* at BACA in November 1987, she tackled this problem head-on by devising a choreographic poem of her own for two actors. Her poem ran parallel with the verbal poem, sometimes veered close to it, but only very rarely coincided with it in a direct, literal way. Through this parallel structure, director, designers and performers were able to add a new (physical/theatrical) dimension to the poem without doubling up on work that was already being done by the words. The BACA production convinced me that, in spite of its obvious pitfalls and my many misgivings, the piece really had turned out to be "theatre"—at least on the essential, nonrealistic level where the theatre that matters to me happens. I'd like to think of the poem continuing to have a life as a piece to be read to oneself, or read aloud, but perhaps it will find a future life for itself in the theatre as well.

## Poetry and Theatre

**Mac Wellman**

I am always astounded to hear what people in the theatre regard as poetry. Most usually it is a fake fustian—baroque, contrived, pseudo-bard or pseudo-pop; or, at a more rarified level, it is the cloud of sentimentality that pervades certain kinds of American family plays. This kind of "poetry" is typified most by the character of Blanche in *A Streetcar Named Desire*: a vague, eerie, and supposedly "emotional" character, at base a tissue of clichés whose knock-offs have become legion in our drama. But clearly both these kinds of poetry are for people who have no inkling of what poetry is, and probably never will.

Once, some years ago, a director acquaintance confronted me and asked why I wrote plays in "blank" verse. I hemmed and hawed, and said something to the effect that it was *free* not *blank* verse, and that I did not suppose I was writing deathless poesy, but that this was simply a writer's tool, one of many. He looked at me somewhat askance so I knew I was in for a lecture. Attempting to pre-empt this I responded further that because I started writing as a poet, continued to do so, I had retained line-breaks as a way of sculpting the work, that this allowed me to analyze what I wrote and revise it as spoken language.

Whom was I kidding!? The note of defensiveness was unmistakable in my voice. In Shakespeare, the director retorted, Nobles spoke Blank Verse and the vulgar spoke prose. Therefore, by employing the device of line-breaks I was suggesting to script readers that my plays were about very special persons (Nobles) and not the ordinary American Joe. This stunned me since I had not known I was writing about Nobles. "Have you ever heard of William Carlos Williams?" He had never heard of Williams nor Olson nor Oppen, let alone any more recent poet. I was not trying to one-up the man, but merely to suggest that these people and their verse had nothing to do with Nobles and that they were very concerned, as I was and am, with the language and hence *drama* of the ordinary American Joe. Miscommunication darkened between us. But, I cried, it all makes sense if you read it out loud. "Read it out loud!?" he snapped back, "There is no literary manager in the country who has time to read a script out loud." I guess I could have remarked that soap-opera scripts often seem to have line-breaks in them, but was too abashed. It was obvious that the director regarded me as an imposter, a dilletante, a mere poet.

Well, what is, in our age, the connection between poetry and the theatre? Indeed, should there be one? After all, since Ibsen and O'Neill serious theatre has been pretty much a prosaic thing, a vehicle for dealing with serious issues, rigorous discourse of social conflict, journalism with wings. An occasional poet, like Brecht or Lorca, may show up, but that does not materially alter the nature of theatre. And contemporary poets are, in the public eye, a sad lot: blue-haired old ladies who write about God, burnt-out hippies with greasy locks, wacky professors who screw coeds on the side and resort to banal suicide after careers of confessional self-indulgence. As a result, since the Sixties, poetry has receded from public view as a serious art. The only interesting new school of poets, the language-centered variety, seem largely a group of critics who have energetically mobilized and moved on to a new agenda thereby. These are poets of ideas, possessed and dazzled, like theatre critics by the new terminology of French poststructuralism and semiology.

And in fact the most serious poetry of our time may well be criticism, prose for the sake of prose. For critics have discovered they don't need an occasion for their ruminations, that they too are interesting persons. Even in the realm of contemporary fiction one may detect the aggressive exuberance of the new theory. The most acclaimed of recent novelists, the late Calvino and Milan Kundera, for instance, are cryptocritics: their cool, glassy surfaces are mirrors of criticism; what fiction is reflected in these is so clearly a fiction of fictions that it functions critically as well, as an intellectual appeal to the facts (as established infallibly by journalism of the Left or Right).

This astonishing burst of critical activity might seem to be unrelated to the question of dramatic activity, poetically considered. But it is not. For, obsessed with an aggressive new hermeneutics, theatre critics are tired of new writing other than their own. Ideas embedded in language they ignore. And for the new theory it hardly matters whether the theatre in question is good or bad, the writing sophisticated or a nest of clichés. In fact, the more it is the latter, the more the writing is, as pure *ecriture*, revelatory about the culture in this era of authorless textuality. A dramatic text that demands to be read in a certain way, as it is, and contains, as it were, its own interpretation—even if a multiplex one—and determines somehow the issue of its own contexts is not likely to be examined very closely by the poststructuralist or semiotician. For these the most successful theatre of our time is the theatre of images, one capable of being subject to a manifold decoding, a spider-eyed interpretation. This theatre is reductive and defensive, one devoted to cutting its losses, avoiding risks, and maximizing the pristine totality of concept. And it is what is generally left out of the mix—a smart, self-aware, and sophisticated language—that I miss.

I also think there is a place for poetry of a different sort in the theatre, a theatre that has nothing to do with the "facts" of journalism or the ideas of the new theory. What I am talking about is a theatre of language not considered exclusively as a sign or symbol, but as a gesture and as an object. The presentness of language, the sea of it we swim in, is surely a reality of immense import for the theatre. I am talking about the sheer *thinginess* of language as an ontological substratum in all of our lives. I think there is more of a place for language in this sense, and well below the level of corn-ball meaningfulness (i.e., the banal) in our theatre than we have heretofor reckoned. By contrast, the theatre of visual images seems ultimately to become an insubstantial ambiguous thing, the chic plaything of the rich and powerful. It rises above the hubbub of human intercourse, carried by the quasi-hallucinatory fantasy of television and our cinema: light-filled, exhilarating, and full of unspeakable desires. Language as gesture runs deep below, and is like Holderlin's god in *Patmos*, both near and hard to grasp. The writers I care for most, whether playwrights, poets, and critics, are those who seek access to this realm of language; who find in it a weight and heft that embodies a drama dense with our past and future, as a people and as individuals, as builders and lovers, children and parents, all sharing a destiny in this world.

This article, in slightly different form, first appeared in *Theatre Times*, Volume 6, No. 5, June/July 1987.